The Gospel 'According to Homer and Virgil'

Supplements
to
Novum Testamentum

VOLUME 138

The Gospel 'According to Homer and Virgil'

Cento and Canon

By

Karl Olav Sandnes

BRILL

LEIDEN • BOSTON
2011

This book is printed on acid-free paper.

Library of Congress Cataloging-in-Publication Data

Sandnes, Karl Olav, 1954–
  The Gospel "according to Homer and Virgil" : cento and canon / by Karl Olav
Sandnes.
    p. cm. — (Supplements to Novum Testamentum ; v. 138)
    Includes bibliographical references (p.   ) and index.
    ISBN 978-90-04-18718-4 (hardback : alk. paper) 1. Religion and poetry.
2. Christian literature, Early—Classical influences. 3. Bible. N.T.—Criticism,
Textual. 4. Homer—Influence. 5. Virgil—Influence. 6. Classical
literature—Influence. 7. Centos. I. Title.

  PN1077.S195 2011
  809.1'9382—dc22

2010051436

ISSN 0167–9732
ISBN 978 90 04 18718 4

MIX
Paper from
responsible sources
FSC
www.fsc.org   FSC® C004472

PRINTED BY DRUKKERIJ WILCO B.V. - AMERSFOORT, THE NETHERLANDS

CONTENTS

ABBREVIATIONS

Abbreviations follow the standard of *The SBL Handbook of Style*, Hendrickson Publishers (1999).

Worth mentioning in particular are the following abbreviations:

ANF	Ante-Nicene Fathers
BAGD	Greek-English Lexicon of the New Testament and Other Christian Literature (Bauer etc.)
CCSL	Corpus Christianorum Series Latina
CSEL	Corpus Scriptorum Ecclesiastiscorum Latinorum
GCS	Die griechische christliche Schriftsteller der ersten [drei] Jahrhunderte
FC	Fontes Christiani
LCL	Loeb Classical Library, Harvard University Press
LSJ	Liddell, Henry George, Scott, Robert, Jones, Henry-Stuart. A Greek-English Lexicon. Oxford: Clarendon Press 1996
NPNP	Nicene and Post-Nicene Fathers
OLD	Glare, P.G.W., *Oxford Latin Dictionary*. Oxford: Clarendon Press, 1982
PG	Patrologia Graeca (J.-P. Migne)
PL	Patrologia Latina (J.-P. Migne)
SC	Sources Chrétiennes
s.v.	sub verbo

PREFACE

For some years I have occupied myself with the early Christians' relationship to the literary culture surrounding them. For obvious reasons, this led me to include the Homeric epics as well, resulting in the book *Challenged by Homer. School, Pagan Poets and Early Christianity*, published by T&T Clark 2009. In the summer of 2006 I attended the annual meeting of Societas Novi Testamenti Studiorum (SNTS) in Aberdeen, Scotland. There I had the pleasure of meeting Dennis R. MacDonald, the doyen of New Testament studies against a background of Homeric epics. I had by then published an article in Journal of Biblical Literature, in which I questioned his Homeric reading of Mark's Gospel. Professor MacDonald directed me to Eudocia's *Homerocentones*, claiming that they basically confirmed his position. I admitted my ignorance, saying that I had never heard of these texts. Obviously, I had some homework to do. What I now present in this book is my homework on the centos. I owe thanks to Professor MacDonald for having drawn my attention to this literature. Working with them has rendered me great pleasure. The ancient centos appeal to scholars with different competence, such as languages, ancient history, Homer and Virgil particularly, and early Christian theology. Given the nature of the centos, confining oneself within the limits of one's special competence is challenged. Addressing the centos as a theologian has, I think, in some respects, paid off.

Margaret M. Mitchell (Chicago) has shown a keen interest in the process of this work. I thank her for helpful comments and encouragement. She is also to be thanked, together with her co-editor David P. Moessner, for having accepted the manuscript for publication in their series *Novum Testamentum Supplementum*. A reader, whose identity is unknown to me, made a constructive report with many helpful comments on my work. Mattie Kuiper and the staff at Brill (Leiden) have patiently guided me in the process of finishing the manuscript.

I was twice given the opportunity to present parts of my manuscript in seminars, to the joint seminar of MF The Norwegian School of Theology (Oslo), Gothenburg University, Lund University and the School of Mission and Theology (Stavanger, Norway) and to the Norwegian New Testament Fellowship (NNTFF). I thank those present at these occasions for comments and reactions. Samuel Byrskog commented on a first draft of chapter 2, thus helping me along the road. Assistant Professor in Greek, my colleague Glenn Wehus, kindly assisted me when necessary.

Decisive in the preparation of this manuscript was the time I spent at Pontificium Institutum Biblicum, Rome, in the Spring 2009. The library there proved really helpful for the project, and the staff willingly assisted me whenever necessary. Likewise, the library staff at my own school, MF The Norwegian School of Theology, are to be thanked for their efforts in helping me and other scholars working here. My school granted me money to have my English proofread. Dr. David Pugh did this with much patience and diligence. To all these I owe thanks; they are not to be blamed for errors and shortcomings that might appear.

Karl Olav Sandnes

CHAPTER ONE

INTRODUCTION: THE CONTEXT OF THE STUDY

"If you can't beat them, join them." This slogan may well summarize what happened among some Christians in the 4th and 5th centuries with regard to the classical texts of the Graeco-Roman Empire and its culture. Some well-educated believers embarked on rewriting biblical narrative texts, and the stories about Jesus in particular, in venerable hexameter style, not only imitating the style of Homer and Virgil, but also borrowing their lines. Rewriting biblical texts in this manner produced what we might call *biblical epics*. They thus Christianized the classical legacy with which Christians had struggled for such a long time. By "classical legacy" I mean the literature that made up the cultural canon of the ancient Graeco-Roman culture.[1]

At the centre of that classical legacy stood literature, and especially the Homeric and Virgilian epics. Throughout the preceding centuries of the nascent Church, believers had struggled to cope with aspects of Graeco-Roman culture; this applied to festivals,[2] serving in the army,[3] education,[4] the theatre,[5] and the baths.[6] How to cope with the legacy

---

[1] Teresa Morgan, *Literate Education in the Hellenistic and Roman Worlds* (Cambridge: Cambridge University Press, 1998), 313 lists the most common authors used in ancient schools in material taken from Egypt: Homer, Euripides, Menander, Isocrates, and Diogenes; cf. pp. 71–72, 316. As for Latin texts, Virgil ranked highest. Hubert Cancik, "Standardization and Ranking of Texts in Greek and Roman Institutions," in *Homer, the Bible and Beyond. Literary and Religious Canons in the Ancient World*, ed. Margalit Finkelberg and Guy G. Stroumsa (Leiden, Boston: Brill, 2003) demonstrates that texts where ranked according to genre and guidelines. When Quintilian in his *Inst.* 10.1 addresses the question of what texts to read for students of rhetoric, he adopts the Greek language of contest in ranking literature: "he (i.e. Virgil) is second (after Homer) nearer, however, to the first than to the third" (*Inst.* 10.1.86 cf. 1.8.5–12). For the literary canon in Rome, see Amiel D. Vardi, "Canons of Literary Texts at Rome," in *Homer, the Bible and Beyond. Literary and Religious Canons in the Ancient World*, ed. Margalit Finkelberg and Guy G. Stroumsa (Leiden, Boston: Brill, 2003) and Chapter 2.3.2 of this study.

[2] Peter Guyot and Richard Klein, *Das frühe Christentum bis zum Ende der Verfolgungen. Eine Dokumentation* (Darmstadt: Wissenschaftliche Buchgesellschaft, 1997), 111–4.

[3] Guyot and Klein, *Das frühe Christentum*, 52–67.

[4] Guyot and Klein, *Das frühe Christentum*, 68–97.

[5] Guyot and Klein, *Das frühe Christentum*, 98–109.

[6] Guyot and Klein, *Das frühe Christentum*, 114–21.

found in the literature was, however, much more fundamental than the aforesaid challenges: "They could, more or less, do without participating in these institutions. But could they do without reading? This is precisely the implications of the challenge of Homer to the Christians."[7] Education and the classical literature became vehicles for ground-breaking hermeneutical discussions in the early church.[8] The reason is that classical literature was at the heart of ancient school-teaching and child-rearing.

Christians reacted differently to the challenge of having their children reared by Homer and Virgil and other classical texts. The question was whether classical poetry could offer anything other than idolatry, mythology, and immorality? The positions varied from blunt rejection to resigned acceptance and critical participation. This diverse situation continued even after the time of "the Constantinian *Wende*,"[9] as demonstrated in my recent book, *The Challenge of Homer. School, Poets and Early Christianity* (2009). Against this background it is worth noting that some Christians found Homer and Virgil useful when paraphrasing biblical texts. They found ways to present "Gospels according to Homer and Virgil."

Some New Testament scholars, particularly Dennis R. MacDonald, have argued that these later attempts, to which this book will turn, actually have their precedents in the New Testament itself, primarily in the Gospels and The Book of Acts. In fact, the authors of the 4th and 5th centuries placed themselves in a common tradition of Antiquity when they presented their Christian paraphrase of the classical texts or *vice versa*, a classical paraphrase of biblical texts. The Gospels, which are the particular focus of the present investigation, and the later biblical epics, may thus—to some extent at least—be considered analogous. MacDonald has suggested that this observation implies that the Gospels must be read as attempts to imitate the classical Greek tradition.

---

[7] Karl Olav Sandnes, *The Challenge of Homer, School, Pagan Poets and Early Christianity* (London, New York: T&T Clark International, 2009), 11.

[8] In my book *The Challenge of Homer*, 276–7, I draw the conclusion that the Homeric challenge triggered a most fundamental hermeneutical debate in the Christian church.

[9] See sourcebooks on the relevant period; e.g. Guyot and Klein, *Das frühe Christentum*; A.D. Lee, *Pagans and Christians in Late Antiquity. A Sourcebook* (London, New York: Routledge, 2000).

According to this view, the time is now ripe for looking beyond Form Criticism's model of pre-gospel traditions which are later incorporated into the narratives of the Gospels, and instead to focus on the implications of Mimesis Criticism. MacDonald argues that "before Mark...no one had heard of Jesus stilling the sea, manifesting his glory to three disciples, sending disciples to follow a water carrier, or agonizing all night about his death."[10] The implication is that these stories are not necessarily traditions, as form critics are keen on debating, but texts that originated from the process of imitating Homer. The bulk of the narratives found in the Gospel of Mark issued from the author's attempt to emulate classical Greek epic.

We may rightly call the "Homeric and Virgilian Gospels" of the 4th and 5th centuries a maximalist approach to the question of how Christians should relate to the pagan legacy handed down in the literature of the great poets. The primary focus of this book is to investigate those who really took a maximalist approach, namely the centonists who composed the so-called *centones*, a stitching-together of lines from the classical texts, which restricted the author from using any source other than the classical epics that inspired their paraphrases. In short, a *cento* is a pastiche of lines or quotes from a classical text.[11] They thus became Gospel-like Jesus stories, in the style of the venerated literature of Homer and Virgil, remaining entirely within their limits. The centonists imposed upon themselves the limitations set by what they found in these texts. The Christian *centones* of the 4th and 5th centuries were specific attempts at coming to terms with the foundational texts of the culture of Antiquity.

What is the nature of these *centones*? Why did some Christians combine Gospels and pagan legacy in this way? Against what background is this literature to be understood? What light might they shed on the canonical Gospels? These are questions to be addressed in the following. In order to answer these questions, the centos have to be put into a wider context, in both recent research and the ancient world.

---

[10] Dennis R. MacDonald, *The Homeric Epics and the Gospel of Mark* (New Haven CT, London: Yale University Press, 2000) 190. This is emphatically stated in his "My Turn. A Critique of Critics of 'Mimesis Criticism'," accessed May 2008, http:www.iac.cgu.edu where he seems to reject historical bedrock in the Gospels generally.

[11] More on centos in Chapter 4 of this study.

1.1 New Testament and Classical Literature

The attitudes of Christians towards Homer and Virgil varied from opposition (turning their back on this legacy, considering it disguised idolatry) to embracing it (considering this legacy as "propaideutic" and therefore as paving the way for higher knowledge provided by faith only).[12] At the centre of this debate in the early church naturally stood the texts in which citations from the classical legacy do appear in New Testament writings. Judged by direct quotations, the presence of classical literature is quite meagre in the New Testament. There are, for sure, three well-known examples, found in 1 Cor 15:33, a possible citation of a maxim from Menander or Euripides;[13] Acts 17:28 quoting from the introductory lines of Aratos' *Phaenomena*;[14] and Tit 1:12 from Epimenides the Cretan.[15] It is evident, however, that the influence of classical literature goes far beyond explicit quotations.[16] This is clearly suggested by two instances in the Book of Acts. Acts 26:14 is a possible *paraphrasis* of Euripides' Bacchae 795,[17] and some distinct Homeric

---

[12] A summary of this history with regard to Homer is found in Sandnes, *The Challenge of Homer*, 231–43.

[13] For a discussion, see Robert Renehan, "Classical Greek Quotation in the New Testament," in *The Heritage of the Early Church. Essays in Honor of Georges Vasilievich Florovsky*, ed. David Neiman and Margaret Schatkin (Roma: Pontificium Institutum Studiorum Orientalium, 1973), 29–34; Karl Olav Sandnes, *Belly and Body in the Pauline Epistles* (Cambridge: Cambridge University Press, 2002), 181–5; Ronald F. Hock, "Paul and Greco-Roman Education" in *Paul in the Greco-Roman World. A Handbook*, ed. J. Paul Sampley (Harrisburg, PA: Trinity Press International, 2003), 225; Beryl Rawson, *Children and Childhood in Roman Italy* (Oxford: Oxford University Press, 2003), 175.

[14] Renehan, "Classical Greek Quotation in the New Testament," 37–42.

[15] Renehan, "Classical Greek Quotation in the New Testament," 34–37; Sandnes, *Belly and Body in the Pauline Epistles*, 1, 36–37. As late as the end of 4th century, Jerome attests that Paul was accused by fellow Christians of having lapsed into idolatry, on the basis of his citation in Tit 1:12; see Sandnes, *The Challenge of Homer*, 205–8.

[16] As for Paul, Renehan, "Classical Greek Quotation in the New Testament," 27–28 considers 1 Cor 12:4–11 as remarkably similar to Homer's *Il.* 13.729–34, and he points out (pp. 24–26) that Euripides might have contributed to Paul's famous section in Rom. 7:14–25; thus also Sandnes, *The Challenge of Homer*, 53.

[17] W. Nestle, "Anklänge an Euripides in der Apostelgeschichte," *Philologus* 59 (1900) argued that the author of Acts was familiar with Euripides, and mentioned a number of parallels; e.g. Acts 5:39; 12:7; 19:35; 26:14; see also Renehan, "Classical Greek Quotation in the New Testament," 21–23. Nestle-Aland's 27th edition points out this link only with reference to Acts 26:14. Euripides was a favourite in the classical Greek canon; see Morgan, *Literate Education*, 322. For the indebtedness of Acts to Graeco-Roman discourse in general, see e.g. Eckhard Plümacher, *Lukas als hellenistischer*

phraseology in the sea voyage in Acts 27:41 (ἐπέκειλαν τὴν ναῦν).[18] Quotations and phraseology form only the wider background directing the readers towards a more sophisticated and creative interplay with the culture and its foundational texts and stories. A relevant example may here be Paul and Socrates in Acts 17. Vv.18–20 provide a paraphrase of the charges against Socrates, but the interplay between the two figures moves beyond this literary echo by including also the setting of the market, the activity of dialogue [διαλέγεσθαι] with the philosophers there, and the rhetoric of concealment [*insinuatio*].[19]

To judge the influence of Homer and Virgil from the quotations only would, therefore, be much too narrow, and would in fact be misleading (a minimalistic approach) as to how these texts formed the cultural foundation of society.[20] This opens the door to wider comparisons with the Homeric or Virgilian epics, or classical literature in general. Next to the Old Testament, these epics would be the most natural comparison, given their prominent role in the ancient world. It is Dennis R. MacDonald's most important contribution to have

---

Schriftsteller. Studien zur Apostelgescichte; "Die Missionsreden der Apostelgeschichte und Dionys von Halikarnass," *NTS* 39 (1993); "TERATEIA. Fiktion und Wunder in der hellenistisch-römischen Geschichtsschreibung und in der Apostelgeschichte," *ZNW* 89 (1998); and the collection of essays in *Contextualizing Acts. Lukan Narrative and Greco-Roman Discourse*, ed. Todd Penner and Caroline van der Stichele (Atlanta: Society of Biblical Literature, 2003).

[18] This is pointed out by F.F. Bruce, *Commentary on the Book of Acts* (Grand Rapids: Eerdmans Publishing Co., 1965), 498; Susan Marie Praeder, "Sea Voyages in Ancient Literature and the Theology of Luke-Acts," *CBQ* 46 (1984):701; Dennis R. MacDonald, "The Shipwrecks of Odysseus and Paul," *NTS* 45 (1999):95; Loveday Alexander, *Acts in its Ancient Literary Context. A Classicist Looks at the Acts of the Apostles* (London, New York: T&T Clark International, 2005), 175.

[19] See Karl Olav Sandnes, "Paul and Socrates: The Aim of Paul's Areopagos Speech," *JSNT* 50 (1993); O. Skarsaune, "Judaism and Hellenism in Justin Martyr, Elucidated from his Portrait of Socrates," in Geschichte—Tradition—Reflexion. Festschrift für Martin Hengel (Tübingen: Mohr Siebeck 1996), 589–91 and recently Dennis R. MacDonald, "A Categorization of Antetextuality in the Gospels and Acts: A Case for Luke's Imitation of Plato and Xenophon to Depict Paul as a Christian Socrates," in *The Intertextuality of the Epistles. Explorations of Theory and Practice*, ed. Thomas L. Brodie, Dennis R. MacDonald and Stanley E. Porter (Sheffield: Sheffield Phoenix Press, 2006), 215–25.

[20] As for Homer, see Sandnes, *The Challenge of Homer*, 40–58. As for Virgil, see Stefan Freund, *Vergil im frühen Christentum. Untersuchungen zu den Vergilzitaten bei Tertullian, Minucius Felix, Novatian, Cyprian und Arnobius* (Paderborn: Schöning, 2000), 14–19; Richard Lim, "Augustine, the Grammarians and the Cultural Authority of Vergil," in *Romane Memento. Vergil in the Fourth Century*, ed. Roger Rees (London: Gerald Duckworth, 2004); Scott McGill, *Virgil Recomposed. The Mythological and Secular Centos in Antiquity* (New York: Oxford University Press, 2005), 55–56.

disabused New Testament scholars of the misconception that authors
of the New Testament had no other texts than the Old Testament and
related Jewish literature in mind. It is against a narrow minimalistic approach that I will here look into those texts representing quite
the opposite view, the centos, and see what knowledge can be gained
from them with regard to the Gospel literature. Before proceeding to
this inquiry, let us consider the accessibility of Homer and Virgil in
Antiquity.

1.2   Homer and Virgil: Ubiquitous Poets

Homer and Virgil were the true companions of life in Antiquity, particularly for those who had received some education. Quintilian, the
rhetorician of the 1st century C.E., describes a practice when he says:

> It is therefore an admirable practice [*institutum est*], which now prevails,
> to begin by reading Homer and Virgil, although the intelligence needs to
> be further developed for the full appreciation of their merits: but there
> is plenty of time for that since the boy will read them more than once.
> In the meantime let his mind be lifted by the sublimity of heroic verse
> [*heroi carminis*], inspired by the greatness of its theme and imbued with
> the loftiest sentiments (*Inst.* 1.8.5).[21]

The teacher of rhetoric implies that the life of the student is enveloped
in Homer and Virgil. The two accordingly ranked highest in the literary
canon that he presents in *Inst.* 10.1 (see Chapter 2.3.2). This is stated
even more emphatically by Heraclitus, the Stoic philosopher from the
1st and 2nd centuries C.E.:

> From the very first age of life, the foolishness of infants just beginning to
> learn is nurtured on the teaching given in his [i.e. Homer] school. One
> might almost say that his poems are our baby clothes, and we nourish
> our minds by draughts of his milk. He stands at our side as we each grow
> up and shares our youth as we gradually come to manhood; when we
> are mature, his presence within us is at its prime; and even in old age,
> we never weary of him. When we stop, we thirst to begin him again.

---

[21] If no further notice is given, quotations are taken from LCL. This picture is
confirmed in Suetonius *Gramm.* 16.3. Virgil was celebrated as the Roman Homer,
Vergilius, alter Homerus apud nos, as Jerome puts it in his *Ep.* 121.10; see Karla
Pollmann, "The Transformation of the Epic Genre in Christian late Antiquity," in
Studia Patristica Vol 36 (Leuven: Peeters, 2001), 61–62.

In a word, the only end of Homer for human beings is the end of life (*Homeric Problems* 1.4–7).[22]

Augustine may serve as a spokesman for the role of Virgil in Roman education. He reports a thorough memorization of Virgil—ironically though—in *Civ.* 1.3:

> ...they paid a fee to be taught their works [i.e. *auctores sui*] and held the state to boot, as well as of marks of honour. Without question Virgil has—and they read him in their early years precisely in order, yes, in order that when their tender minds have been soaked in the great poet, surpassing all in fame, it may not be easy for him to vanish from their memory.

It is assumed in both texts that students revisited these great poets, and never left them behind.

The accessibility of Homer is the starting point for Dennis R. MacDonald, and I fully concur with his observations on this. As he rightly puts it, "Homer was a cultural inevitability".[23] In my study *The Challenge of Homer*, I summarized the position enjoyed by Homer's epics in four points: he was omniscient, inspired, formed the identity of a culture, and there was an obsession with interpreting and criticizing him.[24] The enormous efforts made to interpret the poets is the wider context of the present investigation (see Chapter 2). According to Cicero, the poets were considered *sancti* (*Arch.* 18);[25] this reference

---

[22] Quoted from Donald A. Russell and David Konstan, ed. and trans. *Heraclitus: Homeric Problems* (Atlanta: Society of Biblical Literature, 2005).

[23] MacDonald, *The Homeric Epics and the Gospel of Mark*, 8; Dennis R. MacDonald, *Does the New Testament Imitate Homer? Four Cases from the Acts of the Apostles* (New Haven and London: Yale University Press, 2003), 2–3. To exemplify this, I refer to the Roman historian Velleius Paterculus, who lived during the principates of Augustus and Tiberius, calling Homer the "greatest beyond compare, who by virtue of the magnitude of his work and the brilliance of his poetry alone deserves the name of poet" (*Hist.* 1.5.1).

[24] Sandnes, *The Challenge of Homer*, 40–58; as for canonicity see pp. 47–48 in particular. For the idea of a cultural or secular canon, see Robert Alter, *Canon and Creativity. Modern Writing and the Authority of Scripture* (New Haven and London: Yale University Press, 2000), 1–2, 171. For a nuanced presentation of Homer as analogous to the role played by the Hebrew Bible for the Jews, see Tessa Rajak, *Translation & Survival. The Greek Bible of the Ancient Jewish Diaspora* (Oxford: Oxford University Press, 2009), 239–40.

[25] The immediate context makes it clear that this refers to their divine inspiration. In Chapter 3 of Heliodorus' *Aethiopica* (*An Ethiopian Romance*), second or third century C.E. may be found a discussion of Homer's origin. He is said to have kept his true origin in Egypt a secret, in order to claim every country as his fatherland. A story of his mysterious birth is told here as well. He bore his name Homer, meaning

is supported by Ennius, and Homer is mentioned in particular. The popularity of Homer is, according to Cicero, attested by the rivalry among cities over to whom he rightly belongs. This competition is seen in Colophon, Chios, Salamis, Smyrna and many other places [*permulti alii*] (*Arch.* 19). Virgil represents a Roman memory of *the Iliad*; its Roman continuation, so to say. Aeneas' flight from Troy, which sets the scene for the *Aeneid*, is the narrative bridge between the epics of Homer and Virgil.[26]

Homer and Virgil were, of course, primarily available to those who could read them. But their presence and influence on daily life in Antiquity far exceeded their actual readership. Scott McGill refers to comic graffiti found in Pompeii, exemplifying Virgil's presence in everyday life.[27] Homer and Virgil were school-texts, presented piecemeal to the students in order to facilitate memorization. They thus became stories told and remembered; they were also performed orally by rhapsodes and they became a source of amusement (see Chapter 4). On the top of this, the ubiquity of these epics is also demonstrated by the fact that episodes from them were pictured in private homes as well as in public. Their stories were practically everywhere.

Their stories, or particularly some stories, were illustrated visually in both private and public spaces, in the form of frescoes, statues, sculptures etc. Text and picture were not so far apart as we might think. Lucian reminds us of this, as he has one of his figures say: "We have Homer, the best of all painters [τὸν ἄριστον τῶν γραφέων]" (*Imag.* 8). In presenting their story, poets took liberties with facts; hence it was common to compare poets and painters (Plutarch *Mor.* 16B–C).

In Trimalchio's dinner, recounted in Petronius' *Satyricon,* Homer's epics are present, visually as well as in words, and even in the entertainment of the guests. As the visitor entered the home of Trimalchio, he found the portico, hall and walls decorated (*Sat.* 28–29). Following immediately upon the picture of a dog painted with an inscription *Cave canem*, the visitor observes a number of *picturae* and utensils,

---

'the Thigh,' as a reminder of his parentage, a long strip of hair growing on one of his thighs. When his mother went to sleep in the temple, Hermes consorted with her, and she gave birth to Homer.

[26] This scene is a favourite among pictures found in Roman art; see David L. Balch, *Roman Domestic Art and Early House Churches* (Tübingen: Mohr Siebeck, 2008), 95–96; Richard Brilliant, *Visual Narratives. Storytelling in Etruscan and Roman Art* (Ithaca and London: Cornell University Press, 1984), 54–55.

[27] McGill, *Virgil Recomposed*, 55, 198 n. 14.

some with inscriptions. This is worth noting, because it implies that some of these pictures were seen also by outsiders (see below). He saw a picture showing a slave-market in Rome where Trimalchio himself, prominent in the picture, was being led by Mercury, his patron deity, to purchase slaves. The picture presented Trimalchio as a good steward [*dispensator*]. Next is mentioned a picture showing Mercury, the god of business, whisking Trimalchio to his official position [*in tribunal excelsum Mercurius rapiebat*]. Fortuna was also in this picture, with her abundance, and the three Fates [*Parcae*] spinning threads of gold. Then was seen a company of runners practising; a shrine with the *lares* (household gods);[28] a marble image of Venus and a golden box in which was laid Trimalchio's first beard. Among the *picturae* in the hall [*in medio*] was found the *Iliad* and the *Odyssey*, although their precise visual forms are not commented upon. In the dining room—and then the private zone—were found symbols as well as inscriptions affirming Trimalchio's position in Rome.

I have taken pains to list the most important visual items mentioned in this passage, because they provide a context for understanding the visual presence of Homer's epics. Together the decorations present 'trophies,' lauding Trimalchio as a citizen of Rome. They also demonstrate a common familiarity with Homer's epics, or at least with episodes from them. If Trimalchio, as an upstart freedman with no taste, had commissioned his house from an interior decorator who threw in Homeric scenes as a mass-produced cultural product, this is even better evidence of the universality of Homer than if somebody like Maecenas had specifically asked the interior decorator for them.

As pointed out by David L. Balch,[29] the architecture of a Roman villa welcomed uninvited guests into the *atrium* and peristyle. This is precisely where some of the pictures, including those of the *Iliad* and *Odyssey* seem to be located. The aim of these *picturae* was, as pointed out above, to present Trimalchio as a *public* person. It makes no sense, therefore, to imagine these as private and secluded from the public; they are there to be gazed upon also by the public.

Clement of Alexandria assumes that Homeric decorations were commonly found in private homes (*Protr.* 4/53P(GCS 12a.46/60.1–2):

---

[28] For the shrines of the household gods, see Balch, *Roman Domestic Art and Early House Churches*, 52–54.
[29] Balch, *Roman Domestic Art and Early House Churches*, 35–38.

"they [sc. οἱ πολλοί] have their homes decorated with pictures representing the unnatural lust of the daemons...they adorn their cham-
bers with painted tablets [πίνακες] hung on high like votive offerings,
regarding licentiousness as piety." The context leaves no doubt that this
includes Homeric scenes. Such scenes are found, Clement says, both in
homes and in public [πανδημεὶ]. Clement's purpose is to describe the
omnipresence of idolatry. This may well have lead him to exaggerate;
nonetheless, he seems to be fundamentally right: people familiarized
themselves with Homeric and Virgilian scenes not only through reading, but also by looking. A minor detail in Clement's text is worth
commenting upon. He speaks of the paintings with the Greek term
γράφειν. This corresponds to the terminology found in Lucian *Essays
on Portraiture* [Εἰκόνες].[30] David L. Balch has pointed out that when
in Gal. 3:21 Paul speaks of picturing [προεγράφη] Christ crucified, this
must be understood in the light of decorations found in homes and
villae particularly. He assumes his readers' familiarity with the practice
of painted walls. Furthermore, if our observations above on a connection between *picturae* and public identity are correct, then Paul is
here challenging Roman values of identity, and is probably more of a
sceptic than the Christian centonists we will meet later.

In *De Architectura* 7.5, Vitruvius (1st century B.C.E.) discusses wall
paintings [*picturae*]; in 7.5.2 he mentions that scenes were imitated,
whether tragic, comic or satyric in style. Thus the pictures clearly echo
literary genres, and demonstrate that literature inspired the practice
of wall paintings. Vitruvius goes on to say that statues, images of
gods or legends [*fabulae*] were pictured, *non minus troianas pugnas
seu Ulixis errationes* ("not least the Trojan battles or Ulysses' wander-
ings"). Vitruvius thereby points out the frequency with which scenes
from both the *Iliad* and the *Odyssey* were used in painting [*per topia*].
Vitruvius mentions long painted porticoes illustrated with scenes from
the *Iliad* or *Odyssey*. An example of this was discovered in 1848, on
the Via Graziosa in Rome. Seven panels are completely preserved; it is
likely that the group comprised between a minimum of 35 and a maxi-
mum of 100 paintings, representing detailed scenes from the entire

---

[30] For references see David L. Balch, "Paul's Portrait of Christ (Gal. 3.21) in Light
of Paintings and Sculptures of Suffering and Death in Pompeiian Roman Houses,"
in *Early Christian Families in Context. An Interdisciplinarian Dialogue*, ed. David L.
Balch and Carolyn Osiek (Grand Rapids: Wm. B. Eerdmans, 2003), 87.

Odyssey.[31] Visual presentations of Homeric scenes are also found as frescoes in homes, in public buildings and on urns.[32]

To borrow a phrase from Dennis R. MacDonald, narrative poetry, as we know it in Homer and Virgil in particular, was "the oxygen of Graeco-Roman culture."[33] The epics of Homer and Virgil were indeed ubiquitous. For proponents of Mimesis Criticism this fact is crucial to their argument that authors, in our case the Evangelists, could engage in intertextual play with these epics without finding it necessary to advertise the fact. Is this claim justified? The present investigation addresses this question. A somewhat broader presentation of what Mimesis Criticism really is about, however, must be provided first.

1.3   MARK'S GOSPEL

In *The Homeric Epics and the Gospel of Mark*, published in 2000, MacDonald introduced the method of "Mimesis Criticism."[34] MacDonald claims that this gospel is transvaluating the classical epics of Homer, the *Iliad* and the *Odyssey*: "...the key to Mark's composition has less to do with its genre than with its imitation of specific texts of a different genre."[35] MacDonald has accumulated a lot of material of interest for the question of how readers well-versed in the classical epics might have read this Gospel. His focus, therefore, shifts from the history, background and genre of Mark to its character of being literary fiction

---

[31] See Filippo Coarelli, "The Odyssey Frescoes of the Via Graziosa: A Proposed Context," *Papers Presented for the British School at Rome* 66 (1998).

[32] See Balch, *Roman Domestic Art and Early House Churches*, 98–99, 181 n. 45; Brilliant, *Visual Narratives. Storytelling in Etruscan and Roman Art*, 61–65. These date from pre-Augustan or perhaps Neronian times. Brilliant pp. 47–49 gives two examples of funerary urns from Etruscan times, both depicting Odysseus and the suitors. For frescoes from Pompeii, see *Pompeii: Pitture e Mosaici* Vol. 1, 202–222 (figs. 13–46), reproduced second-style (pre-Augustan) frescoes of the *Iliad*, ending with Aeneas' flight from Troy, and pp. 296–305 (figs. 20–43), reproduced fourth-style reliefs (perhaps Neronian) from the same house (Casa del Criptoportico e Casa del Sacello Iliaco) (I. 6,2.4) in Pompeii. I owe thanks to Prof. David L. Balch who kindly assisted me in finding these references.

[33] Dennis R. MacDonald, "Imitations of Greek Epic in the Gospels," in *The Historical Jesus in Context*, ed. Amy-Jill Levine, Dale C. Allison Jr. and John Dominic Crossan (Princeton and Oxford: Princeton University Press, 2006), 372.

[34] In this book MacDonald's previous observations presented in *Christianizing Homer. The Odyssey, Plato, and The Acts of Andrew* (New York, Oxford: Oxford University Press, 1994) and "The Shipwrecks of Odysseus and Paul" come to fruition.

[35] MacDonald, *The Homeric Epics and the Gospel of Mark*, 3.

aimed at transvaluating classical Graeco-Roman literature and mythology. Mark transvalues the Homeric stories by making Jesus "more virtuous and powerful than Odysseus and Hector."[36] Mark's Jesus story is
an anti-epic in which Jesus supersedes key characters in the *Iliad* and
Odyssey. Episodes are modelled after similar episodes in these epics;
Jesus calls fishermen to follow him, just like Athena summoned a crew
(*Od.* 2.383–7); the calming of the sea transformed the tale of Aeolus'
bag of winds (*Od.* 10.1–69); Jesus dies heroically like Hector, and his
death takes on several narrative elements found in the story about
Hector's death (*Il.* 22 and 24) etc. In Mark's Gospel Jesus is portrayed
in a way that makes him superior to both characters and episodes in
the Homeric epics. MacDonald labels this transformation "transvaluation" or "emulation." He defines transvaluation in the following way:
"transvaluing occurs when characters in the hypertext (viz. the derivative text) acquire roles and attributes derived from a system of values
not found in the hypotext (the targeted text):"[37] "Most notably, unlike
the *Iliad*, the earliest Gospel is indeed good news: Jesus, unlike Hector,
rises from his grave."[38] MacDonald claims that his reading of Mark's
Gospel has implications for gospel research; it is simply "enormous."[39]
The primary cultural context of the Gospel is Greek religious tradition,
not Judaism, although "Mark's Jewish concerns or the influence of the
Septuagint" are not to be denied.[40] The bulk of Mark's stories about Jesus
were created; i.e. they were derived from the author's artistic creativ-

---

[36] MacDonald, *The Homeric Epics and the Gospel of Mark*, 3.
[37] MacDonald, *Christianizing Homer*, 6; *The Homeric Epics and the Gospel of Mark*, 2.
[38] A helpful summary of MacDonald's reading of Mark's Gospel is found in his *Does the New Testament Imitate Homer?*, 171–72; quotation found on p. 172.
[39] MacDonald, *The Homeric Epics and the Gospel of Mark*, 189.
[40] MacDonald, *The Homeric Epics and the Gospel of Mark*, 189; thus also *Does the New Testament Imitate Homer?*, 4. To some extent this is lip-service. Judged by e.g. Gregory J. Riley, "Mimesis of Classical Ideals in the Second Christian Century," in *Mimesis and Intertextuality in Antiquity and Christianity*, ed. Dennis R. MacDonald (Harrisburg PA: Trinity Press International, 2001), 94–95, there is a tendency to neglect the Jewish background among advocates of Mimesis Criticism: "...we would go no farther in understanding its [i.e. the New Testament] basic message using Plato than we do using Moses and the Deuteronomists" (p. 95). The flaw in Riley's article is that he looks upon the Old Testament as static. But even Old Testament traditions developed and took on new dimensions, some of which make them an amalgamation of Jewish and Greek traditions. 4 Maccabees is an apt example; here the deuteronomistic tradition of the killing of the prophets is embedded in a Greek philosophical discourse on virtues; see Odil H. Steck, *Das Gewaltsame Geschick der Propheten. Untersuchungen zur Überlieferung des Geschichtsbildes im Alten Testament, Spätjudentum und Urchristentum* (Neukirchen: Neukirchener Verlag, 1967).

ity in reading the Homeric epics in the light of Christian faith. For Gospel research this implies "a reorientation from history or tradition to aesthetics".[41] Basically, Mark wrote not history but fiction, aimed at making a competition of myths, stories and symbols.

MacDonald has been subjected to criticism arguing that the relationship between Mark's Gospel and Homer is not in any way advertised.[42] But MacDonald imagines Mark saying to his critics: "What more do you want? These parallels are not hanging by a slim thread; they are bonded by mimetic Velcro."[43] This claim is substantiated by reference to the similarities between the deaths and burials of Jesus in the Gospel and Hector in *Il.* 22 and 24.[44] MacDonald lists the comparisons between Hector's and Jesus' heroic deaths[45] and also gives a list of the Homeric counterparts to minor characters in the two stories.

Hector finds himself alone with his enemy Achilles outside the walls of Troy. His troops have fled into the city. Likewise, Jesus is abandoned by his disciples in Gethsemane and denied by Peter. Achilles, so prominent in the story about Hector's death, is by MacDonald given two counterparts in Mark, both the Roman officer (see below) and Pilate who gave the body to Joseph of Arimathea. The latter echoes Priam in the *Iliad* whose request for the body of his son Hector is granted. Hector is abandoned by the gods; he expected Phoebus Apollo to stand by him. But Athena disguised herself as Hector's brother, Deiphobus, and then when Hector asked for his brother's help, he was nowhere to be found. Similarly, Jesus found himself abandoned by God (Mark 15:34). In *Il.* 22, emphasis is laid on Hector's flight from Achilles, before the inevitable fight. There is no real counterpart to this in Mark's passion story. In this case, MacDonald invokes Achilles' gloating over his enemy after having killed Hector, whom the Trojans considered divine (*Il.* 22.393–4),

---

[41] MacDonald, *The Homeric Epics and the Gospel of Mark*, 190.

[42] Margaret Mitchell, "Homer in the New Testament," *JR* 83 (2003); Karl Olav Sandnes, "Imitatio Homeri? An Appraisal of Dennis R. MacDonald's Mimesis Criticism," *JBL* 124 (2005).

[43] MacDonald, "My Turn," 15.

[44] MacDonald, *The Homeric Epics and the Gospel of Mark*, 135–68. In "My Turn" the comparison is carried out on pp.13–14. The Jesus-Hector comparison in the passion story is MacDonald's favourite example; see also his "Imitations of Greek Epic in the Gospels," in *The Historical Jesus in Context*, ed. Amy-Jill Levine, dale C. Allison Jr., John Dominic Crossan (Princeton and Oxford: Princeton University Press, 2006), 375–8.

[45] I doubt that most ancient readers familiar with the cheerful death of Socrates would consider Jesus to have died courageously, due to the anxiety ascribed to him in Gethsemane (Mark 14:32–42).

which then corresponds to Mark 15:37–9. MacDonald takes this to be the Roman officer gloating after the killing of Jesus. V.39 is then paraphrased ironically: "Yeah, right, this mortal was a son of god!"[46]

1.4   The Acts of the Apostles

Marianne Palmer Bonz, *The Past as Legacy. Luke-Acts and Ancient Epic* (2000) argues that Luke-Acts is an adaptation of the great fundamental epics of Gilgamesh, the Homeric epics, and Virgil's *Aeneid* in particular. Luke consciously imitates and transvalues these, and primarily the last, in order to provide a foundational story of Christian origins, a prose epic. Loveday Alexander has rightly drawn attention to the question of genre, and whether Luke-Acts can really be called analogous to the great epics of the ancient world.[47] This is not to deny that there are similarities between the *Aeneid* and Luke-Acts. The following structural similarities can be extracted from Bonz's presentation:

1) Virgil is writing at a turn of the tide, dramatic changes are taking place; success and challenges inspired his foundational epic. Likewise, Luke also creates his foundational epic in a time of success, but also in a time where the vision of the church is crumbling.[48]
2) Both epics are about the turning of the ages or the inauguration of a new epoch.
3) The Trojan War finds its fulfilment in the creation of a new group, the people of Rome. Similarly, the promises of Israel in the Old Testament are fulfilled in the new community of Christian believers.[49]
4) Both stories are marked by supernatural portents and prophecies.
5) Journeying occupies a central role in both stories.
6) Luke-Acts is a subversive story in which the Kingdom of God implies a reversal of the religious and political claims of *Imperium Romanum*.[50]

---

[46] MacDonald "My Turn," 14; see Chapter 1.5.1 of this study.

[47] Alexander, *Acts in its Ancient Literary Context*, 166–81.

[48] Marianne Palmer Bonz, *The Past as Legacy. Luke-Acts and Ancient Epic* (Minneapolis MN: Fortress Press, 2000), 26. The crisis is not resolved in Bonz's book and remains hanging in the air.

[49] Bonz, *The Past as Legacy*, 192–3. According to Bonz, the divine plot to form a new people "affords the most significant agreement between Virgil's presentation and Luke's" (p. 111).

[50] Bonz, *The Past as Legacy*, 181–3.

No doubt, there are overlapping themes between the two bodies of literature, and some of these overlappings imply confrontation with Roman ideology, but the genre question remains an obstacle to adding these observations up to the conclusions that the *Aeneid* formed the paradigm for the composition of Luke-Acts, and that the latter is a conscious transvaluation of the *Aeneid*.[51]

Bonz and MacDonald have worked independently, but they share a concern for reading New Testament texts in the light of the great stories of antiquity, thus exemplifying a need to construct an alternative to these foundational stories. I will restrict myself to commenting upon "the most significant example,"[52] namely Acts 10:1–11:18. MacDonald's interpretation of the Cornelius incident takes its point of departure in the role assigned to visions and omens in this text in comparison with *Il.* 2, which relates how Hera, Zeus' wife, sent a dream to Agamemnon, telling him that the Greek troops could now take the city (*Il.* 2.1–41). This dream deceived Agamemnon into launching a fresh attack on Troy. In the epic, this is the first battle-scene.[53] To the interpretation of this deceitful dream is later added an omen, which Odysseus brings to the minds of his fellow Greeks (*Il.* 2.301–20). In the sign there appeared a serpent approaching a nest with eight helpless chicks and their mother. The prophet Calchas interpreted this

---

[51] Chris Shea, "Imitating Imitation: Vergil, Homer and Acts 10:1–11:18" in *Ancient Fiction. The Matrix of Early Christianity and Jewish Narrative*, ed. Jo-Ann A. Brant, Charles W. Hedrick and Chris Shea (Atlanta: Society of Biblical Literature, 2005) follows in the footsteps of Bonz, arguing that Virgil works as a model for Acts, especially Acts 10:1–11:18. He identifies a comparable pattern in this passage and the *Aeneid* book 8. The comparison opens with the following observation: "The story starts with the captain of a troop of foreign invaders currently involved in hostilities that the reader knows will lead to a great war." This matches the description of Aeneas in *Aeneid* 8. This starting point does not find corroboration in the story of Acts itself; nothing in the story is indicative of an impending war. Consequently, Shea makes a reference to Acts being composed after C.E. 70; hence the original readers were familiar with the Jewish-Roman War. Failing to find support in the text itself, Shea turns to historical circumstances *external* to the story, and makes a literary reading dependent on facts not mentioned in the text. Furthermore, the context for Cornelius in Acts is not that of hostilities; on the contrary, Acts 10:2 makes him a friend of the Jews, even at the point of his being introduced. This is a reminder that models may be helpful guidelines, but more sensitivity towards the text to be interpreted is necessary.

[52] The central role assigned to this event in Luke's narrative is well pointed out by MacDonald, *Does the New Testament Imitate Homer?*, 19–20.

[53] This lying dream from Zeus is often mentioned by Homer's critics as indicating the immorality of Homeric gods; see MacDonald, *Does the New Testament Imitate Homer?*, 26–77. This dream appears often in Christian criticism of Homer; see Sandnes, *The Challenge of Homer*, 43.

allegorically as a symbol of nine years of war before victory would be won in the tenth. According to MacDonald, "Luke needed no history, legend, or source for the creation of Acts 10:1–11:18. All he needed was *Iliad* 2.1–335."[54] The stories found in *the Iliad* 1–2 were among the most popular parts of the Homeric epics in antiquity,[55] a fact which may suggest a reading along MacDonald's lines.

What Luke does in this narrative is to recast his model so that it "reveals a threefold emulation: the virtues of Cornelius exceed those of Agamemnon; and the result of the two visions was the removal of hostility between East and West, not deadly warfare".[56] Thus Cornelius' dream, in opposition to the dream that initiated the first battle-scene, appears as both true and peace-bringing. This conclusion is supported by a number of parallels, including the following:

- *Il.* 2 has a combined dream and portent, while Acts 10–11 has a similar combination of twin dreams, given to Cornelius and Peter, and the two work together in the story.
- Both stories are about interpreting bewildering divine signs.
- In both stories the visions are important to the narrative as a whole, and serve to inform the reader about the story.
- In both stories a dream is given to a high-ranking officer.[57]
- In both the omen and Peter's dream, animals are understood as representing human beings.[58]
- Agamemnon's dream is reported three times, as is the incident with Cornelius in Acts.
- The setting of both stories is an important seaport.
- Both stories are concerned with, albeit in quite different ways, the relationship between Europeans and barbarians, or West *versus* East.

---

[54] MacDonald, *Does the New Testament Imitate Homer?*, 22.

[55] Raffaella Cribiore, *Gymnastics of the Mind. Greek Education in Hellenistic and Roman Egypt* (Princeton, Oxford: Princeton University Press, 2001), 194–5.

[56] MacDonald, *Does the New Testament Imitate Homer?*, 64. At another place, he puts it like this: "The visions of Cornelius and Peter transvalue the primitive theology and ethnic strife of the epic. God does not lie, and Greeks and barbarians no longer need to fight" (p. 151).

[57] The sending of a divine messenger to a leader with commands to wage war, and notifying the reader of a deadly debacle, became a standard way in which the scene for important battles was set; see MacDonald, *Does the New Testament Imitate Homer?*, 40–41.

[58] This is certainly true, but the emphasis of the omen is on the number of animals involved; see *Il.* 2.328. This finds no correspondence in Acts 10–11.

This list of similarities is worth noting.[59] His interpretation makes perfect sense for readers well-versed in Homer, and in *Il.* 2 in particular. Readers with that competence might have found the Cornelius event a foundational story aimed at reworking the story about the archetypal war. However, I still think that MacDonald's interpretation is an attempt to reconstruct a reader rather than to provide textual interpretation; it is a reading for "the hermeneutical haves", as MacDonald appropriately calls them.[60]

1.5   MIMESIS CRITICISM: A LITERARY APPROACH?

It is the merit of Dennis R. MacDonald in particular to have accumulated a lot of material worth considering as relevant analogies to New Testament narrative passages. Mimesis Criticism has opened up a fascinating approach, enabling us to see how New Testament narrative texts communicated against the background of the foundational stories of the culture. Mimesis Criticism is a trueborn child of recent literary approaches to New Testament studies, and is itself a stimulus to engage with New Testament texts as literature. MacDonald rightly criticizes a minimalistic attitude to the influence of the classical legacy in New Testament texts.[61] In my view, the problem is that Mimesis Criticism acts similarly, i.e. minimalistically, when New Testament passages are compared with Homeric texts. The texts are compared as isolated units, meaning that plot, narrative structures and strategies are not sufficiently accounted for. When it comes to interpretation, MacDonald neglects the narrative setting and reads the story in Acts 10–11 as an episode isolated from its context in Luke-Acts. More attention should also, in my opinion, be given to the function of the elements being compared.[62]

---

[59] I find MacDonald's reading of Acts 10–11 more intriguing, consistent and relevant than his interpretation of Mark's Gospel. Nonetheless, I find the third point listed above problematic. Precisely the Lukan narrative as a whole militates against his reading (see 1.5.2 below).

[60] MacDonald, *Does the New Testament Imitate Homer?*, 150.

[61] See Chapter 1.1 above.

[62] In his "The Breasts of Hecuba and those of the Daughters of Jerusalem. Luke's Transvaluation of a Famous Iliadic Scene," in *Ancient Fiction. The Matrix of Early Christianity and Jewish Narrative*, ed. Jo-Ann A. Brant, Charles W. Hedrick and Chris Shea (Atlanta: Society of Biblical Literature, 2005); MacDonald argues that Luke 23:27–31 is patterned according to the Iliadic scene of Hecuba showing her breasts to Hector, her son, thus hoping to persuade him to take refuge inside the walls of Troy (*Il.* 22.79–87). MacDonald suggests that the Iliadic scene of Hecuba's breasts

The relationship between God and Zeus is not a prominent topic in the narrative, although it might have been so to some readers. Mimesis Criticism, as we have hitherto known it, is in danger of betraying the literary approach that gave birth to this fascinating approach. In my view, there is a tendency among scholars of the Mimesis School to be carried away by their intriguing observations; they tend to ignore the actual texts that their comparisons are aimed at illuminating. Let me elaborate on this.

1.5.1   *Mark 15:39*

The story of Jesus' death in Mark's Gospel and the story of Cornelius in Acts 10–11 are both seen against the background of Old Testament texts. The reader is alerted to read the abandonment of Jesus as a fulfilment of the Scriptures (Mark 14:27, 49–50). Jesus cites from Ps. 22:2 to express this abandonment. Although those who stood below the cross did not understand this adequately, the reader is guided to Scriptural expectations about Elijah to attain greater understanding (Mark 15:33–37). This is not to deny that Jesus is depicted in a situation reminiscent of Hector, who was also abandoned by his deities. The lament of Jesus echoes biblical traditions about righteous suffering; he is not deliberately deceived by deities, as is the case with Hector. It is worth noting that Peter, who plays such an important role in Mark's story, is not given any Homeric counterpart by MacDonald. While Priam's search for the

---

(*Il.* 22:79–87) forms the model for Jesus' dictum: "Blessed are the barren, and the wombs that never bore, and the breasts that never nursed" (Luke 23:29). He gives an extensive list of texts to demonstrate that Hecuba's breasts had become an imitated trope in antiquity; but he fails to notice that there is no functional equivalence between this Iliadic scene and Luke 23:27–31. Hecuba's naked breasts are signs of a mourning that is about to come upon her. She shows her son the breasts that suckled him, hoping thereby to make him avoid the battle with Achilles: "Hecuba's appeal to Hector in *Iliad* 22 generated a vibrant literary tradition about women exposing their breasts in appeals for pity before the deaths of their children" (MacDonald, "The Breasts of Hecuba," 250). The literary motif of the breasts does not, however, work in this way in Luke 23. The text is not connected with mourning, but is an apocalyptic motif blessing those who keep themselves prepared for the crisis to come. The whole point of Hecuba's breasts is that they have given suck; the whole point of the 'apocalyptic breasts' is that they do *not* give suck. In view of the impending crisis, family and childbirth are seen as distracting the mind. This logic is well presented in 1 Cor 7:8, 25–31. The fact that transvaluation might be involved should not dismiss from observing that function may vary in comparisons which at first might look similar. The question of difference in function between Hecuba's breasts and apocalyptic breast is not mentioned among MacDonald's criteria; see *Does the New Testament imitate Homer?*, 1–15.

body of Hector really enriches Homer's story, Pilate's granting of Jesus' body to Joseph has no similar narrative role.

In a narrative perspective, MacDonald's ironical reading of Mark 15:39 is dubious. The immediate context contrasts the officer's affirmation with the mocking by the high priests and scribes in Mark 15:29–32. This fits a narrative pattern observable in Mark's Gospel, whereby the Jews, and sometimes also the disciples, misunderstand, while Gentiles and demons speak the truth about Jesus (Mark 1:24; 5:7; 14:61; 15:2, 9, 12, 18, 26). Furthermore, if one accepts the reading of the Nestle-Aland 27th edition, the officer's exclamation corresponds with the first sentence of this gospel,[63] and forms a kind of an *inclusio* to the story: "The beginning of the good news of Jesus Christ, the Son of God."[64] Judged by the narrative context, the exclamation in v. 39 is a reaction to Jesus' death, not a gloating over the mischief Jesus had made, as MacDonald says.[65] The transvaluative perspective, which MacDonald emphasizes in his comparisons, of which the climax is Jesus being raised from his tomb, cannot make up for the differences between Mark's passion story and *Il.* 22 and 24. The differences are too many and too significant to confirm authorial imitation.

1.5.2   *Acts 10–11*

A similar neglect of the theological and literary context of the scenes is, in my view, observable in the interpretation of Acts 10–11 as well. The role of the Old Testament as the archetypal story is not fully accounted for. The focus of the narrative of Acts is to show that the events being related represent a continuation of Israel's heritage and history. The narrative is constantly being connected to the foundational story of Israel,

---

[63] It is here worth noting the observation made by Elizabeth Struthers Malbon, "Ending at the beginning. A Response," *Semeia* 52 (1991):177: "Beginnings establish intertextual contexts. Beginnings let hearers/readers know in the light of what other texts the gospels are to be interpreted." This volume of *Semeia* addresses the role of a text's beginning for the reading of the Gospels on a wider scale.

[64] Stephen H. Smith, *A Lion with Wings. A Narrative-Critical Approach to Mark's Gospel* (Sheffield: Sheffield Academic Press, 1996), 36, 76, 80 holds a commonly held opinion when he considers 15:39 as a statement by one of the reliable characters in the story, a testimony which, in fact, forms the climax of the story. For a recent discussion, but with the same conclusion, see Kelly R. Iverson, *Gentiles in the Gospel of Mark. 'Even Dogs under the Table Eat the Children's Crumbs'* (New York, London: T&T Clark International, 2007), 153–7.

[65] MacDonald, *The Homeric Epics and the Gospel of Mark*, 142–3. See also Chapter 6.5.1 of the present study.

the history of the God of the Patriarchs. This clearly emerges from the frequent appearances of "the God of our Fathers,"[66] bridging the foundational story of Israel and the stories told by Luke in Acts. The speeches of Stephen (Acts 7:2–53) and of Paul in Pisidian Antioch (13:16–47) recall the main points of this story. Paul defends himself by saying that his ministry represents a fulfilment of Israel's hope and expectations (Acts 26:2–6; 28:20). These texts, as well as many others, relate the events told in Acts to the foundational story of the Old Testament:

> What is culturally significant about Luke's work, then, is precisely the fact that the model he chooses as his 'classic' is not Homer or Vergil but the Greek Bible. Our growing awareness of the cultural dominance of the classical epics merely throws this choice into relief as a conscious decision to inhabit an alternative narrative world. Luke's work proclaims at every level that it belongs to a 'different story', to the narrative world of the Bible: people and places, style and language, allusion and quotation, narrative management, plot devices, symbolic repertoire, ideology and values all proclaim a distinctive cultural location within the Graeco-Roman World...[67]

At issue in Acts is how the events related are to be evaluated in relation to the Old Testament foundational story. The narrative told in Acts, therefore, primarily represents a reconfiguration of the Hebrew Bible.

This applies to Acts 10–11. Peter's reaction in Acts 10:47 [ὡς καὶ ἡμεῖς] brings to mind the Pentecost story in Acts 2; this is confirmed in 11:15–17, where this is stated explicitly (cf. 15:8). The Cornelius event is thus linked to the giving of the Holy Spirit in Acts 2, an incident which *expressis verbis* is seen as a fulfilment of OT prophecies (Acts 2:16–21). Furthermore, Acts 11:15–17 links the event to the words of the risen Christ in Acts 1:4b–5. The event is thus linked to John the Baptist as well as the outpouring of the Spirit; in other words a motif

---

[66] See e.g. Luke 20:37, Acts 3:13, 25; 5:30; 7:2–32; 13:12; 22:14; 24:14.

[67] Alexander, *Acts in its Ancient Literary Context*, 171. Similarly John B. Tyson, "From History to Rhetoric and Back: Assessing New Trends in Acts Studies" in *Contextualizing Acts. Narrative and Greco-Roman Discourse*, ed. Todd Penner and Caroline van der Stichele (Atlanta: Society of Biblical Literature, 2003), 38–39 who points out that the renewed interest in rhetorical criticism in Acts tends to neglect the Jewish context of this narrative: "The major characters in Acts are Jews; the message they preach is expressed as the fulfilment of the Hebrew scriptures; the origin of the movement is located at the heart of the Jewish nation; Jewish rituals continue among Christian converts; and so forth" (p. 38). Furthermore, he says that the author of Acts, "despite his Graeco-Roman training and his immersion in that literary world, has an interest—one may say an obsession—with things Jewish" (p. 39).

of fulfilment running through the entire double volume. In Acts 10:43, Peter summarizes the foundational story in one main point, namely that the prophets proclaimed that forgiveness of sins was to be given to those who believed in Jesus, which according to Acts 15:14–8 included Gentiles, of whom Cornelius is a representative. This recalls the risen Lord's scriptural interpretation in Luke 24, and v. 47 in particular. Acts 10–11 bring the insight that the God of the Fathers has now included Gentiles in the foundational story of Israel.[68]

The larger narrative of which Acts 10–11 is a part shows no interest in pointing out continuity or opposition to the archetypal story of the Trojan War, or of Virgil's *Aeneid*. What it does stress, however, is the continuity between Abraham and the church. This story of Israel includes oracles, dreams and portents, which sometimes bring to mind stories from the Graeco-Roman world as well. But seen from the perspective of the Lukan narrative in its whole, this is a random phenomenon compared to the Abraham and Israel story.[69] This is not to deny that echoes of other foundational stories may be heard as well, but the primary is clearly the legacy of the Jewish tradition. As for MacDonald's interpretation of Acts 10–11, it is certainly true that the lying dream became a topic in the *agôn* on how to interpret Homer in Antiquity. MacDonald assumes that this is the *topos* underlying the discourse of Acts 10–11, thus neglecting the role assigned to this event in the Lukan narrative itself. Against the background of the narrative plot to which Acts 10–11 belong, his interpretation appears minimalistic. The debate on how to interpret Homer is never flagged in Acts. MacDonald's interpretation makes theology proper,—namely which god to trust, Zeus or the God of the Fathers,—a matter of concern. It is therefore an important aspect of his interpretation that God never lies, as did Zeus in Agamemnon's dream. This is certainly within the framework of early Christian apologetics, but it does not

---

[68] This perspective has been pointed out by many recent interpreters of Acts, see e.g. Jacob Jervell, "The Future of the Past: Luke's Vision of Salvation History and its Bearing on his Writing of History," in *History, Literature, and Society in the Book of Acts*, ed. Ben Witherington III (Cambridge: Cambridge University Press, 1996), 109–10, 125; Robert C. Tannehill, "The Story of Israel within the Lukan Narrative," in *Jesus and the Heritage of Israel. Luke's Narrative Claim upon Israel's Legacy*, ed. David P. Moessner (Harrisburg PA: Trinity International Press, 1999).

[69] Thus also Nils A. Dahl, "The Story of Abraham in Luke-Acts," in *Studies in Luke-Acts. In Honor of Paul Schubert*, ed. Leander E. Keck and J. Louis Martyn (London: SPCK, 1968), 152.

follow naturally from the narrative setting of Acts 10–11. In my view, MacDonald rightly observes the role assigned to the Cornelius event in the Lukan narrative, but he uses this observation only to point out the significance of the event, not to interpret it according to the narrative structure of the Book of Acts.

1.6 SETTING OUT THE STRATEGY

In spite of my critical comments above, I am intrigued by the attempts presented by MacDonald and other scholars working in ways related to Mimesis Criticism, although they might not necessarily all label themselves advocates of a particular "Criticism." The praiseworthy ambition is to root New Testament texts, and narratives in particular, in the Graeco-Roman world, the classical epics of Homer and Virgil in particular. The project raises a number of questions, such as what is *mimesis*, and what does it take to speak of mimesis, intended and conscious? This field of research raises many questions, some of which are inherited from studies on how The New Testament depends upon Old Testament texts. The question of *mimesis* will be a companion throughout the present work, but nonetheless, this is subordinated to another major question, namely that of analogies. Are there contemporary analogies to the procedure adopted by advocates of Mimesis Criticism, and if so, what can be gleaned from them with regard to the question of *mimesis*? The alleged procedure of composing texts where Homer and Virgil were not only literary paradigms, but also the proper sources from which Gospel traditions were created, is worth looking into. According to MacDonald,[70] the Gospel writers found the requisite literary precedents in the classical literature, and wrote the Gospels thereon. Do we know of Christians who proceeded in similar ways to accommodate the Christian message about Jesus to the foundational literature of this time? In his *Christianizing Homer*, MacDonald mentions examples,[71] ranging from Christians who made use of Homeric motifs, such as e.g. the Sirens,[72] to the composition of Christian poems

---

[70] His work is about Mark's Gospel, but he sometimes makes references which include the Gospels in general; see MacDonald, *Does the New Testament Imitate Homer?*, 7–9; thus also in his "Imitations of Greek Epic in the Gospels."

[71] MacDonald, *Christianizing Homer*, 23–27; thus also "My Turn," 6–7.

[72] For the use of the Sirens, see Hugo Rahner, *Griechischen Mythen in christlicher Deutung* (Basel: Herder, 1984), 281–328; and Sandnes, *The Challenge of Homer*, 134–7.

in hexameter, and even to some who rewrote the Gospels in hexameter. This is where the primary aim of the present study enters in.

I think it is necessary to distinguish between how Christian authors in general made use of classical texts, motifs and scenes—and there is no doubt that this happened on a larger scale than New Testament scholars have hitherto recognized—and the genre of Gospels. The focus in this study will be on the Gospels. An investigation of Acts would lead us into the legendary developments found in the many Apostolic Acts. This is where recent Mimesis Criticism so to say originated.[73] However, it is not possible here to delve into this flowering tradition of the early church. I will restrict myself to the way in which stories about the life of Jesus were paraphrased, which practically means the canonical Gospels. This puts a limit on relevant analogies, and takes us to the 4th and 5th centuries C.E. A survey of the most relevant texts will be given later.

Emphasis will be given to two Christian centos, both truly representing a maximalist approach in their attitude to the classical texts of Homer and Virgil. These analogies are included among the analogies whose procedure MacDonald traces back to Mark.[74] In limiting myself to this literature, my critical perspective on Mimesis Criticism will necessarily be equally limited. The centos are suggested since they are unique as a point of comparison with the canonical Gospels. They tell stories from the life of Jesus which—most of them at least—are easily recognized from the canonical Gospels. They are written in the metre of the classical epics. Finally, the text or the wording is that of either Homer or Virgil. This is why it makes sense to speak of a maximalist approach here; they are truly maximalists.

The centos represented an extreme form of what ancient rhetoricians called *paraphrasis*. This was an educational form, a part of the theory of imitation where texts were embellished in various ways.[75] It pertained to the nature of a cento that there was no other alternative for the composition than to adopt what the imitatee actually said. Thus Homeric or Virgilian texts did indeed place constraints upon

---

[73] See *Semeia* 38 (1986) on *The Apocryphal Acts of the Apostles*, an issue where MacDonald was guest-editor, and his *Christianizing Homer*.

[74] MacDonald, *Christianizing Homer*, 24–25; "My Turn," 6, 22.

[75] See Michael Roberts, *Biblical Epic and Rhetorical Paraphrase in late Antiquity* (Liverpool: Francis Cairns, 1985), 5–60. We will return to this later; see Chapter 2 in this study.

the writing; this is therefore intertextuality in its extreme form. But precisely this makes it possible to imagine that stories with little or no foundation in the Biblical text could find their way into the cento. The centos were thus liable to create or embellish stories with no foundation in the canonical Gospels. Furthermore, their playful nature contributes considerably to the possibility that this happened. They are thus a yardstick by which we might gain some insight into whether it is reasonable to consider the Gospel writers to be as creative as MacDonald does. Do the centos offer supporting evidence that stories were made up by emulation? We will begin this discussion by looking into the extreme forms of this, thus hoping to clarify some of the issues involved.

In addition to discriminating between genres, it is also important to observe differences between *paraphrases* performed in Greek on the model of Homer and those performed in Latin, having Virgil as their model. This should be kept in mind, since my chronological procedure may confuse this important distinction. Although the centos are at the centre of this study, it is necessary also to delve somewhat into their predecessors, *paraphrasis* in classical style of the Gospels. We will, therefore, proceed from Latin-writing Juvencus, to the Greek-writing Apollinarius, senior and junior, and then reach the oldest Christian cento, the Virgilian Proba, and finally the Greek *Homerocentones*.

It is my conviction that two important factors, one literary and one historical, contributed massively to the practice of *paraphrasis* of Biblical literature in Early Christianity. As for the literary reason, the Scriptures, and in the present study the Gospels particularly, did not match the standard required of classical literature. There was clearly a sense of embarrassment over the Gospels among learned Christians. As for the historical reason, the famous decree of the Emperor Julian, promulgated in 362, to restrict Christian access to the classical legacy, and Homer in particular, caused a crisis, which in itself did not last long, but with long-tem effects on Biblical *paraphrasis*. These two aspects will be presented shortly, but will also accompany the investigation throughout as we come across them in the history of Biblical *paraphrasis*.

This book presents some texts which really were Homeric or Virgilic poem-narratives about Jesus, the so-called Christian *centones* of the 4th and 5th centuries. These were patchwork literature, stitching together lines from classical texts in a way that makes them Christian Gospels. The present study thus picks out one particular attempt at coping with the pagan legacy from a Christian perspective. The Homeric or Virgilic texts are, due to some modifications and re-organising of the lines, considered to be Christian; they are "Gospelled." Some Christians definitely did not turn their back on the classical epics, but instead Christianized them. This study will put the practice of composing Christian *centones* into its historical context, work out the nature of the *centones*, and see if they throw some light on the nature of the canonical gospels.

1.7   A Renewed Interest in Centos

We will later see (Chapter 4) that the composition of centos was viewed with scepticism, not to say aversion, by many contemporary Christians. Their negative sentiments have percolated into the way in which scholars came to perceive this literature. We will see later that the text edition of Eudocia's *Homerocentones* suffers from the editor getting bored with this kind of literature, declaring it to be *sterilis*.[76] This attitude to the centos has often been taken, to the loss of true scholarship. W. Kroll in 1913[77] called the work of Hosidius Geta (see later) a "Machwerk;" the literary level being described as "sehr niedrig."[78] According to Joseph Golega, the Homeric centos are "weder des Druckes noch des Lesens wert."[79] This genre has thus been considered to consist of eccentric pieces devoid of all literary merit and theological value. This is hardly a helpful path if one wants to grasp the phenomenon of the centos in a wider context. In their own terms, centos were a playful way of demonstrating familiarity with venerated ancient texts, and thus to appear civilized: "Être cultivé, lettré, c'etait, pour un homme de ce temps, être nourri de Cicéron et de Vergile, les posséder a fond, le tenir sans cesse présents à sa mémoire."[80] Zoja Pavlovskis says that the derivative nature

---

[76] See Chapter 6.1.2.

[77] "Hosidius," *Pauly-Wissowa RAC*, 2489–90.

[78] McGill, *Virgil Recomposed*, XVII gives other examples, and concludes that most negative reviews can be attributed to prejudice considering the cento genre as kind of theft, which is not appropriate for a true understanding of the phenomenon.

[79] Joseph Golega, *Der Homerische Psalter. Studien über die dem Apollinarios von Laodikea zugeschriebenen Psalmenpraphrase* (Ettal: Buch-Kunstverlag Ettal, 1960), 1.

[80] Henri-Irénée Marrou, *La Fin de la Culture Antique* (Paris: E. De Boccard, 1938), 498. Similarly Susan Ashbrook Harvey, "Women and Words: texts by and about Women," in *The Cambridge History of Early Christian Literature*, ed. Frances Young, Lewis Ayres, Andrew Louth (Cambridge. Cambridge University Press, 2004), 382–4.

of centos, be they Virgilian or Homeric, has led to lack of attention from scholars, but she points out emphatically that this does not necessarily reflect any lack of originality; on the contrary, the "act of composing a cento is strikingly original."[81] This is certainly a true judgement, and the present study will expand on that conclusion. Pavlovskis sets Virgil against Homer, saying that his texts lend themselves easier to cento composers: "Homeric verse simply will not lend itself to such purposes very well... With Virgil this is not so. Ever-receding meaning is hinted and elusive. Neither the poet nor the reader can ever unequivocally penetrate all the significance inherent in a described action or thought or event. Everything shifts and changes."[82] This is indeed an apt description of the dialogue with both the poet and the biblical text in which the reader is engaged by the centonist. The contrast urged here between Virgil and Homer, with regard to this hermeneutical game, will not be substantiated in my study.

The animus against centos represents a neglect of what we know about schools and rhetoric in the ancient world. The Christian centos represent a fascinating and idiosyncratic attempt to rewrite the Gospels; in spite of their dependence on a playful heritage, they should be seen as independent theological achievements; they are Gospel harmonies in Homeric or Virgilian vocabulary and style. Cento composition is the art of recycling classical texts, a game with words, language and meaning, out of which there comes into existence a new text, no less classical in its appearance, holding now a dual classical nature, epic and biblical simultaneously.

With the exception primarily of some Italian scholars,[83] research into Christian centos has suffered from this inherited bias. This applies particularly to Eudocia's *Homerocentones*.[84] A change is now about to occur, not only due to the suggestions made by Mimesis Criticism. The last ten years have seen a growing interest in this phenomenon in general, and in the biblical epic in particular. As for the *Homerocentones*,

---

[81] Zoja Pavlovskis, "Proba and the Semiotics of the Narrative Virgilian Cento," *Vergilius* 35 (1989): 70–71; (quotation on p. 71).

[82] Ibid., 74–5. Pavlovskis says that the Homeric cento (of Eudocia) is "bald and bare," holding "the Virgilian counterpart" to be much more interesting (p. 73).

[83] E.g. Filippo Ermini, *Il centone di Proba e la poesia centonaria latina* (Roma: Ermanno Loescher, 1909) and A.G. Amatucci, *Storia della letteratura latina* (Bari: G. Laterza, 1929).

[84] Rocco Schembra, *Homerocentones* (Turnhout & Leuven: Brepols Publishers & Leuven University Press, 2007), XII–IV lists the most important contributions.

three text editions have appeared since 1998.[85] Some recent publications are worth mentioning in particular. Scott McGill's *Virgil Recomposed. The Mythological and Secular Centos in Antiquity* (2005) presents the background against which all the centos are to be understood. The collection of articles published by J.H.D. Scourfield (ed.), *Texts and Culture in late Antiquity. Inheritance, Authority, and Change* (2007), includes works on Proba and Eudocia. Most recently Martin Bažil presented his *Centones Christiani. Métamorphoses d'une forme inter-textuelle dans la poési latine chrétienne de l'Antiquité tardive* (2009), a study on *Cento Probae* in particular. He investigates her cento, and some others as well, primarily as examples of intertextuality and liter-ary theory, in which hypertext (the cento) depends semantically on its hypotext. Bažil understands this genre as an example of *aemulatio*, but he does not address the ancient rhetorical background of cento composition. Compared to the present study, Bažil does not pay much attention to the theological outcome of this intersection of Virgil and the Bible. Hence, what I will call the *res* of Christian centos is less accentuated. Furthermore, the present investigation addresses the role of the centos among the Christians more generally, and addresses this with a view to Mimesis Criticism. This is beyond the scope of Bažil's study.

Brian Patrick Sowers submitted his work *Eudocia. The Making of a Homeric Christian* in 2008. His study is devoted to her cento and her narrative of Cyprian's conversion, of which the first in particu-lar concerns our study. Sowers points out that "Homer could be used or reused for numerous purposes."[86] Eudocia's work resulted in a "Homeric Jesus."[87] Sowers rightly points out that the cento retells a pre-existing story in a new way. His study concentrates on Patricius' preface, added by Eudocia to her cento, and the story of Jesus and the woman in John 4. He argues that the centonist constantly works with an eye on the canonical text; a thematic continuity between the two texts is, therefore, apparent. Within this pattern, however, there is considerable modification, and even fabrication. Eudocia felt free to

---

[85] See Chapter 6.1.2.
[86] Brian Patrick Sowers, *Eudocia. The Making of a Homeric Christian*. A Dissertation Submitted to the Division of Research and Advanced Studies of the University of Cincinnattiin the Department of Classics of the College of Arts and Sciences 2008, www.ohiolink.edu/etd/send-pdf.sgi/sowers, 73.
[87] Ibid., p. 93.

elaborate and modify, but she proceeded from the biblical text. Sower's study shares insight to be conveyed in the present study. He now views cento composition within a wider rhetorical perspective, and he does not include a dialogue with proponents of Mimesis Criticism. Dennis R. DacDonald is briefly referred to with approval, but Sowers seems less aware that some of his own conclusions actually run contrary to those of MacDonald, if seen in holistic terms.

The centos are almost non-existent in biblical studies. An exception is, of course, Dennis R. MacDonald, who, in my opinion, makes undue use of them; he uses them only in principle though. There is no real engagement with the centos. This book enters a dialogue with him on the centos' relevance to New Testament studies. Christian cento composition belongs much too far down the road to be directly helpful for New Testament studies. Nonetheless, these studies have much to gain from interacting with the centos, which represent much interesting pieces of evidence in *Wirkungsgeschichte*. Much information can be gleaned from them with regard to the literary and rhetorical context in which Christians came to form their literature, New Testament included.[88] If New Testament texts are to be studied against a wider cultural background, not restricting oneself to other biblical texts, it is not at all far-fetched to turn to the centos. They also witness to how some Christians coped with the classical canon, and entered the ancient discourse on how to give a true interpretation of the classical texts; *in casu* how they were to be interpreted from a Christian point of view. Finally, the Christian cento writing is not a mechanical, concordance-like, collection of lines suited to expressing and transmitting Christian faith. Studying them has convinced me that they are early and advanced examples of a theological endeavour that we today would label 'contextualization.'

---

[88] Some scholars have made use of the centos to explain how New Testament writers put together Old Testament lines; see Chapter 4. These citations are, however, not real analogies to narrative centos.

CHAPTER TWO

THE RHETORICAL CONTEXT OF BIBLICAL EPICS

Mimesis Criticism has opened up a fascinating approach, enabling us to see how biblical texts communicated against the background of the foundational stories of the culture. This takes us into the field of intertextuality. We have seen that Marianne Palmer Bonz argues that Luke-Acts was composed by analogy with Rome's foundational epic the Aeneid, thus telling a new foundational story of another group of people, the Christians. If Bonz' thesis is to be judged by Virgil being cited or alluded to in the biblical text, then we should note that no such external support appears to exist. Dennis R. MacDonald makes a similar claim with regard to Mark's Gospel. Homer is not quoted, but MacDonald has accumulated a lot of relevant material to suggest that literary models are found primarily in the Homeric epics. This is argued with reference to hidden or subtle emulation intended by the author, and perceived by the readers, due to the status Homer enjoyed in Antiquity.[1] As for Acts, MacDonald argues similarly; and now a minor philological link between the two bodies of texts does occur: ἐπέκειλαν τὴν ναῦν ("they ran the ship aground") (see Chapter 1). These observations raise the question of the nature of intertextuality, how texts intersect, and what it takes to claim *mimesis*. Some of the questions arising are the following:

– Authorial intent or reader-oriented?
– Borrowing, imitating or allusion? While the two first imply a desire to equal a source text, the latter indicates a more loose and playful relationship.
– Conscious or accidental?
– Mimesis of a text or a story? Due to the prominent role played by Homer in Antiquity, cultural echoes may be present without quotations or any other signs of textual presence.

---

[1] As for MacDonald's criteria see his *The Homeric Epics and the Gospel of Mark*, 8–9 and *Does the New Testament Imitate Homer?*, 2–6. I concur fully with MacDonald's point of departure, namely the availability of Homer; see Sandnes, *The Challenge of Homer*, 40–58; see also Chapter 1.2 of the present study.

These are some of the issues involved in the discussion initiated by Bonz and MacDonald; and they call for a more thorough investigation than I can provide here. The primary interest of the present investigation is devoted to two related questions. In the first place, to what extent is advertisement required in *mimesis*? Did *mimesis* take the form of a hidden and subtle intersection of texts, due to the fact that the classical legacy was so much in the air, for composer and reader of the Gospels alike? If so, what does this kind of *mimesis* imply for the interpretation? This is the question whether intertextuality must somehow be proved or not by philological criteria. MacDonald has named such an attitude "philological fundamentalism."[2] However, accusations of practising "philological fundamentalism" make no sense with regard to centos. Verbal links to the hypotext or source-text are their very nature (see Chapter 4). I get confused when MacDonald reproaches my approach in "Imitatio Homeri? An Appraisal of Dennis R. MacDonald's 'Mimesis Criticism'" for philological fundamentalism, and simultaneously points to the *Homerocentones* as analogous to the composition of Mark's Gospel. One of the two claims is certainly mistaken. The centonist has subjected herself to a constraint that may well be labelled "philological fundamentalism." In the second place, is *mimesis* a means whereby texts are invented as well? If this is so, the question of historical bedrock in the Gospel traditions is superseded by the question of their literary models. It will take the entire investigation to suggest an answer to these questions, and this chapter initiates this. These questions demand also a historical investigation of how the Gospels actually came to be paraphrased (see Chapters 5 and 6).

2.1   Paraphrasis: A Rhetorical Exercise

"Reading and performing exercises on poets and prose writers constituted by far the largest element of literate education." Thus Teresa Morgan describes the constant recycling of classical texts in ancient education.[3] Retellings and rewritings of the classical texts, in short, trafficking in

---

[2] MacDonald, "My Turn", 11–12. The term is taken from Stephen Hinds, *Allusion and Intertext. Dynamics of Appropriation in Roman Poetry* (Cambridge: Cambridge University Press, 1998), 17–21. However, Hinds does not address the centos.

[3] See Morgan, *Literate Education*, 90; thus also D.A. Russell, "De Imitatione," in *Creative Imitation and Latin Literature*, ed. David West and Tony Woodman (Cambridge: Cambridge University Press, 1979), 1.

these texts, were tools to familiarize students with the literature. These exercises also assumed a basic level of familiarity with the stories of this legacy. The 4th, and even more the 5th· centuries C.E. made a whole industry out of rewriting biblical texts in the light of the classical epics, Virgil in particular. The hexameter form was imitated, and thus biblical texts appeared as Virgilian or Homeric, but altered with regard to invention, the content or *res* ("die Sache"). This literature is a primary stock of analogies referred to by proponents of Mimesis Criticism.

The undertaking of composing "classical" biblical texts is, in fact, a legacy from exercises practised in the schools of rhetoric as so-called *progymnasmata*.[4] Aelius Theon includes *paraphrasis* among the rhetorical exercises, and defines it in the following way: "*Paraphrasis* consists of changing the form of expression while keeping the thoughts;" thus clearly making a distinction between wording or form and content or *res*. Cicero praises his friend, the poet Archias, for—without writing a single letter—being able to paraphrase quantities of excellent verse dealing with current topics (*Arch.* 18); in other words he knew large amounts of text by heart. Furthermore, this knowledge is perfected in his ability to paraphrase: "How often have I seen him, when recalled, repeat his original matter with an entire change of word and phrase! [*rem dicere commutatis verbis atque sententiis*]." The distinction between *res* and *verba* made here by Cicero as well as Theon is of immense importance for the present study.[5] Means of doing this were variation in syntax, additions, subtractions, substitutions, recasting an assertion as a question or a possibility, or combinations of these (Theon, *Progymnasmata* 108 cf. 62–64).[6]

---

[4] Pace Reinhart Herzog, *Die Bibelepik der Lateinischen Spätantike. Formgeschichte einer erbaulichen Gattung* (München: Fink, 1975), lxx–xxii, 60–68, 155–211 who derives the practice from the Fathers' citing of pagan poets, especially Virgil, for their own ends. He thus neglects the ancient rhetorical context of *paraphrasis*. Although the two cannot be entirely separated, emphasis is to be given to the latter. Christian paraphrasing of the Bible in epic genre follows literary ideals that can be traced to ancient rhetoric.

[5] In his letter on the disease of the soul, Seneca makes a distinction between *eloquentia* or *verba* and *res*. *Eloquentia* is not a end in itself, it is rather to serves *res* (*Ep.* 75.5). If eloquence fails to do this it is comparable to a physician offering a patient elegant discourse instead of treatment (6). A physician working in a pestilence cannot occupy himself with *verba*, but with *res*, which in this particular context means "what really matters."

[6] See George A. Kennedy, trans., *Progymnasmata. Greek Textbooks of Prose Composition and Rhetoric* (Atlanta: Society of Biblical Literature, 2003), 6–7, 70–71. Further evidence of *paraphrasis* is found in Roberts, *Biblical Epic and Rhetorical Paraphrase in Late Antiquity*, 5–60; Sandnes, "Imitatio Homeri?," 722–5.

Rhetorical education, as defined in handbooks of rhetoric[7] as well as in available exercises,[8] trained students in *inventio, dispositio elocutio*; in short the material or content, the organization and performance, be it oral or written.[9] The exercise of *paraphrasis* belonged primarily within the *elocutio* part and proceeded by changing elements, adding, subtracting or substituting. A typical exercise would be to take an oration of Lysias and to express the ideas in the style of Demosthenes, or even in Latin. *Paraphrasis* is, therefore, not primarily a matter of exegesis or extracting meaning from the text, but is a means by which to develop rhetorical skills or to make such skills known. From this follows that *paraphrasis* was done with an eye to gaining recognition as a virtuous speaker or writer, or to demonstrate erudition. An example is found in Seneca the Elder's *Suasoriae* 3.7, saying that Ovid imitated Virgil not to record him [*non subripiendi causa*],[10] but "meaning that his open borrowing [*palam mutuandi*] should be noticed [*agnosci*]." This is imitation, without concealment, done for the sake of being noticed. Generally speaking, the variations provided for by *paraphrasis* lie within the manner of expression, form and style. Quintilian states this very pointedly in *Inst.* 1.9.2–3:

> They should begin by analysing each verse, then give its meaning in different language, and finally proceed to freer paraphrase [*paraphrasis audacius vertere*] in which they will be permitted now to abridge [*breviare*], and now to embellish [*exornare*] the original, so far as this may be done without losing the poet's meaning [*poetae sensu*].

A concern for retaining the content in a way that makes it *recognizable* lies at the heart of this quotation. One is tempted to think that the rhetorical teacher has students in mind here, and that a stronger restraint on keeping the meaning of the original is laid upon them. But this ran counter to the comment Quintilian makes after this statement. "This is no easy task even for the expert instructor [*professoribus*], he says."

---

[7] See Kennedy, *Progymnasmata*.
[8] See Ronald F. Hock and Edward N. O'Neill, *The Chreia and Ancient Rhetoric. Classroom Exercises* (Atlanta: Society of Biblical Literature, 2002).
[9] For a recent presentation of *progymnasmata*, see Tor Vegge, *Paulus und das antike Schulwesen. Schule und Bildung bei Paulus* (Berlin, New York: Walter de Gruyter, 2006), 121–85.
[10] The LCL edition has "plagiarism" here, which I find too modern. Originality is not a primary concern in paraphrastic theory.

Michael Roberts brings his presentation of *paraphrasis* in rhetorical theory to the following conclusion:

> Paraphrastic theory emphasizes the importance of retaining the sense of the original; the theory of literary composition legitimizes the reworking of traditional material, but does not exclude the invention of a new subject matter. It is characteristic of the paraphrase to retain (in outline at least) the narrative sequence of the original and incorporate new material only when that material can be justified as stylistic elaboration and amplification.[11]

Two important observations are made here; first what seems to be a general rule of keeping the meaning of the original text clearly within sight, and then an option for *paraphrases,* which includes invention. The latter applies according to M. Roberts to "literary paraphrasis" which is to be distinguished from its "grammatical" counterpart.[12] The latter applies to minor modifications. Literary *paraphrasis* is of special interest, being necessarily more interpretative in nature, and also being more independent of the original. A number of observations serve to emphasize that *paraphrasis* was an accepted way not only of adding ornamentation to a text, but also of altering it and of making pure inventions. We need constantly to remind ourselves that Virgil's *Aeneid* reworked Homer in quite a thorough way. Out of this comes a story where there are many recognizable traits, but Aeneas was certainly transformed beyond the Homeric model. As we will see later (Chapter 4), *paraphrasis* in cento form approached the classical texts as "open" to yield fresh texts, and that the centonist, accordingly, as a reader of Virgil and Homer became, in fact, an author. This is precisely what Mimesis Criticism claims for Mark's Gospel. In my view, this theory applies primarily to the centos—and the Gospels are definitely not centos—if genre is taken account of in the comparison. Obviously, the Gospels are not formed out of lines and halflines from Homer, as are the Homeric centos. The only way to make sense of the centos vis-à-vis the composition of the Gospels is to assume that the obsession with Homer and simultaneously with the life of Jesus—as found in the Homeric centos—must have inspired a narrative epic of Jesus life, which in style, however, is not epic.[13]

---

[11] Roberts, *Biblical Epic and Rhetorical Paraphrase in Late Antiquity*, 35–36.
[12] Roberts, *Biblical Epic and Rhetorical Paraphrase in Late Antiquity*, 54–58.
[13] This is precisely what MacDonald does in his "My Turn," 16–22; see also Chapter 7.5 of the present study.

Paraphrasis also took the form of emulation or *zelos*, i.e. a competition or rivalry in surpassing the model: "But I would not have
paraphrase restrict itself to the bare interpretation of the original: its
duty is rather to rival and vie with the original in the expression of
the same thought [*circa eosdem sensus certamen atque aemulationem*]"
(Quintilian *Inst.* 10.5.5).[14] Although the precise context of Quintilian's
statement is about the literary style,[15] it seems right to assume that
literary *paraphrasis* when practised as *emulatio* justified *inventio*; particularly so in the centos.

What may possibly be an example of the playful way of going
about Homer is to be found in two of Dio Chryosostom's discourses
on Homer. According to *Or.* 11, the poet is a liar who turned falsehood into truth and deceived generations. The story told by Homer is
aimed at establishing the pride of the Greeks and amusing them. His
stories are compared to the intoxication of wine (41–43). Dio says
he learnt the alternative story, namely that Troy was not destroyed,
from an Egyptian priest who loved to poke fun at the Greeks (37).
Contrariwise, *Or.* 53 praises Homer for being the mouthpiece of the
gods. The two discourses can hardly be reconciled with regard to the
views they express about on Homer and Greek poetry. It is worth pondering if the contrasting picture is due to the playful way in which
Homer's texts and stories were handed down. Maybe this is an example
of the playful way in which people were acquainted with the Homeric
epics. Be this as it may; what is certain is that trifling with classical
texts and performing them in unexpected ways was a common way
of competing in literature, and also of amusing guests at a dinner
party. This is the context out of which the centos, the extreme form of
paraphrasis, seem to have developed, as we will see later (Chapter 4).
Paraphrasis in a playful form favours the option for invention pointed
out by Roberts above. That playfulness accompanied the practice
of paraphrase is demonstrated by Seneca the Elder's *Suasoria* 3.3–7;
4.4–5.[16] It here says about Fuscus that he tried to imitate [*voluit imi-
tari*] certain lines of Virgil, "but they were far from his point, and he

---

[14] Cf. Ps. Longinus, *On the Sublime* 13–14. Emulation is here defined as an attempt
to write in a way which makes the poets of former times present; Russell, "De
Imitatione," 9–14.

[15] See Sandnes, "Imitatio Homeri ?," 723–4.

[16] See Sandnes, "Imitatio Homeri?," 722–3 n.42 about public performances of this
practice. This is elaborated on in Chapter 4.

put them in almost against the interest of his theme [*valde autem longe petit et paene repugnante materia*];" a description pointing to Fuscus as a centonist making "stunt poems".[17] Fuscus used to take much from Virgil [*ex Virgilio multa trahere*] to make an impression on Maecenas. Seneca considers his attempt unsuccessful compared to the Virgilian lines themselves. This playful nature of *paraphrasis* is highly relevant when we will later approach the centos (Chapter 4).

The classroom exercises collected by Ronald F. Hock and Edward N. O'Neill are instructive with regard to the question of *inventio*, ornamenting the text to the extent that a new text appears. A short example is found in the *Progymnasmata* 3 of Nikephoros Basilakes. The *chreia* goes like this: "It's kindness that ever gives birth to kindness." The *paraphrasis* goes like this: "The result of doing good, he says, is receiving good. And all that a mother is to a child is kindness in return for kindness."[18] Here the *paraphrasis* is elaborating, expanding the *chreia*, and giving also an interpretation which is possibly within reach from the *chreia*, but which certainly takes it in a particular direction. This is a recurrent pattern in the examples provided. Such is also the case with a *chreia* found in Libanius' *Progymnasmata* 3:[19] "Diogenes, on seeing a youth misbehaving, struck his paedagogus, adding: 'Why do you teach such things'." The paraphrase goes like this:

> A Paedagogus was in the company of a boy, but the boy was not maintaining the proper decorum. To Diogenes his behaviour seemed to need correction. What, then, does he do? He ignores the young man and goes after the one in charge, inflicts many blows on his back, and adds to the blows the remark that such a man should certainly not be a teacher.

Again we see that the text to be paraphrased is "storied."[20] From this elaborating element implied in *paraphrasis*, one can imagine that a similar process went on in the formation process of the Gospels. To judge from this material, this seems to apply particularly to the contexts of sayings of Jesus.[21] The rhetoric framework in which biblical

---

[17] I borrow this term from Martha A. Malamud, *A Poetics of Transformation. Prudentius and Classical Mythology* (Ithaca and London: Cornell University Press, 1989), 35.

[18] Hock and O'Neill, *The Chreia and Ancient Rhetoric*, 295, 299.

[19] Hock and O'Neill, *The Chreia and Ancient Rhetoric*, 157, 159.

[20] For further examples, see Hock and O'Neill, *The Chreia and Ancient Rhetoric*, 140 and 143, 169 and 171, 189, 231, 249, 255.

[21] For *chreia* in the Gospels, see Samuel Byrskog, "The Early Church as a Narrative Fellowship. An Exploratory Study of the Performance of the *Chreia*," *Tidsskrift for*

paraphrasis is to be understood, therefore, includes the idea that biblical traditions were expanded on. Such are the rhetorical parameters
set for the following discussion of Homeric and Virgilian paraphrase
of the Gospels. Proponents of Mimesis Criticism argue that Homeric
paraphrasis of biblical texts penetrated deeply into the forming of the
body of the Gospels, even in creating texts whose proper source was,
in fact Homer. The argument is that the Gospel texts derived from
literary imitation rather than from tradition or source. This is a key
question to which the present study contributes. The question cannot
be resolved by reference to ancient rhetoric, but only by looking into
Christian practice of this legacy. But the question takes its start here:
To what extent did *paraphrasis* include creating texts *ex nihilo* without
any pre-existing source?

2.2   Mimesis and Emulatio

We have seen that the practice of paraphrase in ancient rhetoric also
included emulation, which could even involve expanding and also the
adding of new material to the model. Although this was primarily a
matter of style and eloquence, invention did occur, and it is important for the understanding of how Mimesis Criticism brings together
ancient rhetoric and the Gospels. The following will raise the question
of emulation when it takes the form of inventing material, and under
what circumstances this might occur.

In his treatise on *mimesis*, Dionysius of Halicarnassus defines the
difference between imitation and emulation. The definitions go like
this:[22] "*Mimesis* is the act of reproducing[23] the model by observance
of theoretical principles. Emulation is the activity of mind moved to
admiration of that which appears beautiful."[24] According to Dionysius,

---

Teologi og Kirke 78 (2002); Tobias Hägerland, *Jesus and the Forgiveness of Sins. An
Aspect of His Prophetic Mission* (University of Gothenburg, 2009), 23–26 argues that
progymnastic rhetoric, rather than prophecy (pace Rudolf Bultmann and Eugene M.
Boring) contributed to the expansion or growth of the Jesus tradition.

[22] This particular text is transmitted by Syrianus as Fragment 2; see Germaine
Aujac, *Denys D'Halicarnasse*, Opuscules Rhetorique Tome V (Paris: Les Belles Lettres,
1992), 27.

[23] The Greek ἐκμάσσω describes the work of an artist; see LSJ s.v.

[24] My translation with some help from Russell, "De Imitatione," 10 based on Aujac's
Greek text: Μίμησίς ἐστιν ἐνέργεια διὰ τῶν θεωρημάτων ἐκματτομένη τὸ παράδειγμα.
Ζῆλος δέ ἐστιν ἐνέργεια ψυχῆς πρὸς θαῦμα τοῦ δοκοῦντος εἶναι καλοῦ κινουμένη.

there is a difference between the observance of rules taught in rhetorical schools,[25] and emulation proceeding from admiration. The latter
allows for more freedom and creativity. In the *Epitome* of his writing
it is, however, clear that the emulation he has in mind is more or less
restricted to literary style. One ought to imitate the writings of past
ages, not only for the finding of subjects, but also for finding a style
learnt by those reading the ancients with love (9.1.1–2).

The *Epitome* gives two anecdotes to explain this. A farmer had a
body of not very pleasant appearance; he was simply ugly. He was
concerned that he would beget children, as ugly as himself. He therefore made a beautiful image of a child; with his wife he made a habit
of looking at it before having sex. After some time they had a child,
with an appearance like the one pictured.[26] Dionysius comments: "This
is also the way literature gives birth to *mimesis*…" (9.1.3). The second
anecdote brings out more clearly the element of ζῆλος. The much-
loved artist of Croton, Zeuxis, made a portrait of Helen in the nude.[27]
His fellow citizens brought him the most beautiful girls in town to
copy. Not so because they believed them to be especially beautiful. But
taken together; i.e. if Zeuxis copied the best from each girl individually, his picture would appear τέλειος (9.1.4). *Emulatio* is precisely the
result of combining the best from different authors into one. Mimesis
defined as amalgamation defines *zelos*, and the nature of this phenomenon makes it evident that defining or advertising sources becomes
impossible, not to say unwanted in an *emulatio*, as defined here by
Dionysius. This approach mentioned in the *epitome* is repeated when
he speaks about *mimesis* of the poets, of whom Homer is mentioned
first (9.2.1). Imitations of Homer do not proceed from various aspects
of his works, but from the totality [τὸ σύμπαν] which is then modified
[ἀλλάσσω] into a true and personal *mimesis*; the result of competing
with Homer:[28] "L'imitation ressemble donc au travail du mosaïste qui

---

[25] Aujac, *Denys D'Halicarnasse*, 147.

[26] For another example of gazing at a portrait during sex, and thus conceiving
a child with the appearance of the portrait, see Heliodorus' *Aethiopica* Chapter 4.
Persinna, the queen of Ethiopia, gave birth to Charicleia, the heroine of this literature, since she conceived while looking at the portrait of Andromeda. Charicelia was
thus born white, save for a small band of black around her arm; truly unusual for
an Ethiopian-born child. Her mother therefore feared accusations of adultery and
entrusted Charicleia to someone else.

[27] This is an example of the visual presence of Homeric scenes in antiquity; see
Chapter 1.2.

[28] Thus also in *Peri Miměseôs* 9.5.7.

ajuste des des cubes apparement disparates pour en faire, par juxtaposition des couleurs, une belle oeuvre d'art."[29] Thus ζῆλος is defined as an improvement thanks to its nature of being a mix of the best from various sources.

The story about the artist Zeuxis is found in Pliny the Elder as well (*Nat.* 35. 64–65). The context, though, is not literary imitation, but artists competing with each other. Pliny says that some of Zeuxis' contemporaries were his rivals [*aemuli*], one of whom engaged in a competition [*certamen*] with him. Zeuxis made a picture of grapes, so successfully that birds came and tried to eat them. His *aemulus*, Parrhasius, pictured a curtain, so realistically that Zeuxis requested it to be drawn aside and the picture displayed. He was deceived, and yielded up the prize [*palma*], saying: "I deceived the birds, Parrhasius deceived me" (66). The story clearly brings out the rivalry involved in *emulatio*, and also the futility of searching for the separate elements in which *mimesis* consists. Emulation in this text assumes presence and invisibility simultaneously. Cicero says that the composition of his *De inventione Rhetorica* took a form comparable to the story about Zeuxis and the girls (*Inv.* 2.1.1–5):

> In a similar fashion when the inclination arose in my mind to write a text-book of rhetoric [*ars dicendi*], I did not set before myself some one model [*non unum aliquod...exemplum*] which I thought necessary to reproduce in all details, of whatever sort they might be, but after collecting all the works on the subject I excerpted what seemed the most suitable precepts from each, and so culled the flower of many minds [*ex variis ingeniis excellentissima quaeque libavimus*]. For each of the writers who are worthy of fame and reputation seemed to say something better than anyone else, but not to attain pre-eminence in all points (4).

Like Dionysios, Cicero takes the story of the artist as a metaphor for literary imitation, thus implying that emulation does not proceed from *a single* source-text. According to Xenophon, Socrates addressed the topic of *mimesis* in similar terms (*Mem.* 3.10.1–3); again the scenario is that of an artist making a copy. When no perfect model [καλὰ εἴδη] is available, the artist proceeds by combining the most beautiful features of several models [ἐκ πολλῶν συνάγοντες τὰ ἐξ ἑκάστου κάλλιστα]; thus the work of art appears more beautiful than any models. The idea which comes out of this material is that *emulatio* in terms of literature

---

[29] Thus Aujac, *Denys D'Halicarnasse*, 153.

produces a new text. Since no perfect model is available, emulation does not proceed from a single source-text, but from a combination of texts. In fact, emulation does not only produce a text culled from various texts; it also proceeds from a combination of texts whereby the identification of where they are taken from, necessarily becomes impossible.

This brings to mind the role of the bees and honey in ancient rhetoric; explicitly so in Cicero's text quoted above. Honey is produced by bees collecting from various flowers. Seneca *Ep.* 84 is a text where the philosopher addresses the question of *paraphrasis* and *emulatio*,[30] and assumes a contemporary debate on the nature of emulation: "We should follow the example of the bees" (3). From various flowers they produce honey. Seneca considers this process a helpful analogy to how one should deal with literature. He describes this process in detail; the bottom line is that this process brings into being something new: "we should so blend those several flowers into one delicious compound that, even though it betrays its origin [*unde sumptum sit*], yet it nevertheless is clearly a different thing from that whence it came" (5).[31] There is thus an aspect of concealment involved in emulation; only what comes out of the imitation, so to speak its result, is exposed.

As I have previously pointed out with regard to this text, Seneca assumes that "a true copy [*imago vera*] stamps its own form upon all the features which it has drawn from what we may call the original [*quae ex quo velut exemplari traxit*]" (8). This metaphor for literate imitation is in itself pluriform; different aspects may be culled from it. The metaphor of bees and honey has two possible applications. Most obviously, Seneca emphasizes imitation as a moulding of traditions to form a new text. The "separate elements are united into one substance [*in unum diversa coalescunt*]" (4), an aspect which finds corroboration in the parallel analogy mentioned by Seneca, namely that of digesting food. How do you proceed to sort out the ingredients of the mix coming out of emulation? The answer is given; it is impossible, and the nature of *zelos* makes it a misunderstanding to attempt it. Nonetheless,

---

[30] See Sandnes, "Imitatio Homeri?," 725–8 cf. Ellen Finkelpearl, "Pagan Traditions of Intertextuality in the Roman World," in *Mimesis and Intertextuality in Antiquity and Christianity*, ed. Dennis R. MacDonald (Harrisburg PA: Trinity Press International, 2001), 83–84.

[31] Macrobius *Sat. Preface* 5–6 similarly speaks of imitating the bees: "...with the result that, even if the sources are evident [*ut etiam si quid apparuerit unde sumptum sit*], what we get in the end is still something clearly different from those known sources." The same ambiguity between sources and new text is thus expressed here.

Seneca assumes the presence of a source text [*unde sumptum sit*]. At
this point there is clearly a tension in his text. Finally, the metaphor of
the bees may also emphasize the critical and sifting process involved in
imitation. The metaphor of honey and bees was inherited from ancient
moral philosophy and became a stock image in Early Christian discourse on how to relate to pagan literature.[32] The process of selecting
the best and sifting between good and bad was a helpful way to express
a critical attitude. When applied to literature, the metaphor then points
towards some kind of acknowledgement of the texts involved; else a
sifting between good and bad is difficult. We thus see in Seneca's text a
duality with regard to intertextuality, precisely expressed in the metaphor of how bees produced honey: intertextuality either as concealed
or as advertised.

What Dionysius says in his treatise on *mimesis*, is throughout given
relevance to the question of style. The aim of emulation is to make sure
that the reading is well-received; hence it must be well ornamented
(9.5.7). Emulation is often sufficiently explained with reference to literary style aimed at demonstrating the erudition of the author,[33] embellishing the text, or facilitating the delivery and reception of it. In these
cases, emulation works well if subtle and concealed; in fact this is part
of the game of sharing texts in antiquity. We should not read intention
into all imitations, which, accordingly, is not the same phenomenon
in all occurrences. As pointed out by G.B. Conte, not all allusions or
intertextual links imply emulation.[34]

Furthermore, the above-mentioned texts tend to speak of emulation in terms of an ideal conceived in platonic terms. This is also how
Cicero tries to define the *summus orator* in De Or. 7–10; the ideal
clearly resembles Demosthenes, but it is more like a vision of the idea
of "eloquency;" in fact, Cicero refers to Plato's ideas.[35] When emu-

---

[32] Christian Gnilka, *ΧΡΗΣΙΣ. Die Methode der Kirchenväter im Umgang mit der
antiken Kultur I. Der Begriff des 'rechten Gebrauches'* (Basel, Stuttgart: Schwabe, 1984),
102–33; Sandnes, *The Challenge of Homer*, 130–1, 177–80, 241–2.

[33] See e.g. Seneca, *Apol.* 5–6 where Claudius the Emperor, after his assumption into
heaven, arrives at the abode of the gods. He hopes that citing some lines from Homer
will help him to enter; this demonstrates his erudition, his being *Graeculus*. When
he approaches the abode of the divine, he is asked who he is, with a quotation from
Homer (*Od.* 1.170). Claudius is, therefore, happy to find people trained in literature
there as well [*philologos homines*].

[34] Gian Biagio Conte, *The Rhetoric of Imitation. Genre and Poetic Memory in Virgil
and Other Latin Poets* (Ithaca and London: Cornell University Press, 1986), 36.

[35] *De Or.* 9 uses this analogy as well.

lation is explained in terms of how an artist collects the best from various models, and how bees make honey by sifting the best from various flowers, it makes less sense to identify one source text. This corresponds to the concealed imitation addressed by Seneca. However, when emulation amounts to a competition whose aim is to demonstrate some kind of superiority vis-à-vis a given text, things become somewhat different. Advertised intertextuality, as we saw in Seneca, then comes into play.

Transvaluation certainly adds dimensions to emulation, and must by necessity imply some kind of advertising.[36] The kind of emulation envisaged by Mimesis Criticism in Mark's Gospel has a view to more than the embellishment of the text; it includes collecting the best from various Homeric hypotexts. Transvaluation in the hermeneutical way in which MacDonald thinks of Mark's Gospel and Acts implies more than authors concerned about demonstrating their erudition by citing or alluding to Homeric lines or vocabulary. It is necessary to differentiate between various kinds of emulation, although they cannot be entirely separated. The more significance and transvaluation one attributes to intertextual links, the more difficult it becomes if these are subtle, and even hardly noticeable. The question is how slippery the emulations may be and still be given hermeneutical weight, or considered as guidelines to the *message* of the emulation. Emulation as *message*, and particularly so when competition is involved, is hardly accounted for in Dionysios' treatment of imitation.

2.3 Hermeneutical Emulation

Mimesis Criticism argues that emulation in the Gospels (and Acts) aims at interpreting, excelling, transforming and eventually replacing the model by embedding it into a new context. *Emulatio* then appears as a cultural struggle in which Christian texts become alternatives (*Ersatz*) to the dominant texts of the culture: "It requires us to refocus attention on these texts as products of a *Kulturkampf* far more extensive and focused than we have seen before."[37] When *mimesis* is pictured as a means within a "Kulturkampf," the nature of intertextuality must be

---

[36] See Sandnes "Imitatio Homeri?," 728–32; cf. Conte, *The Rhetoric of Imitation*, 76–77. In my view, this is not accounted for in MacDonald's model of imitation.

[37] MacDonald, *Does the New Testament Imitate Homer?*, 15.

affected. What does that perspective bring to the nature of emulation? Does the model of Dionysius apply to this? In my opinion the idea of "Kulturkampf"—which I think is well taken—involves that some kind of *message* evolves from the comparisons involved. How can a message come out of a concealed parallel? Who will then be the addressee of the message? Advocates of Mimesis Criticism have, in my view, not taken fully account of what it takes to add a "Kulturkampf" perspective to the rhetorical practice of emulation.[38] Dennis R. MacDonald deserves credit for having done so, but this perspective is hardly sufficiently addressed by reference to ancient sources defining emulation in terms of subtlety. It is here worth quoting John Pucci:

> A hidden allusion is no allusion at all. With regard to allusion's cover-sion, therefore, a distinction can be made between function and form. Allusion is not functionally covert, because it functions only after it is recognized. It appears hidden, obscure, unlike normal referential language. Only in terms of form, therefore, is allusion covert—that is, it is not necessarily easily, readily identifiable. But in terms of function, allusion advertises its "otherness", demands that a reader recognize it for what it is. In this regard, allusion is the boldest and most strikingly "overt part of a literary work, for the allusion does not seek, as plagiarized words do, to conceal its "otherness."[39]

The nascent church expressed its identity in various ways, Scriptural interpretation being one of them. Guy G. Stroumsa rightly says that early Christianity reached its major achievement in eventually becoming the dominant religion of the Roman Empire as a "textual community."[40] They engaged in Scriptural interpretation because they were not alone in claiming the Old Testament texts, and they interpreted them in ways which defined who they were vis-à-vis others. How did they go about doing this? All four versions of the story of Jesus are somehow related to the Old Testament, and the meaning and significance of his ministry is worked out through exegesis of texts drawn from there. This happened in no concealed ways; the relationship is attested on almost every page of the New Testament. It is to be expected that a similar attempt at a cultural struggle vis-à-vis the foundational pagan texts, would leave some

---

[38] See also Chapter 3.2.3 in the present study.

[39] John Pucci, *The Full-Knowing Reader. Allusion and the Power of the Reader in the Western Literary Tradition* (New Haven and London: Yale University Press, 1998), 39.

[40] Guy G. Stroumsa, "Early Christianity—A Religion of the Book?" in *Homer, the Bible, and Beyond. Literary and Religious Canons in the Ancient World,* ed. Margalit Finkelberg and Guy G. Stroumsa (Leiden, Boston: Brill, 2003), 153.

marks on the texts, even at its surface level. As for the centos their very nature is the interplay between two "texts," their mutuality, so to say (see Chapter 4). This interplay naturally depends on a dual nature of the cento. It is difficult to grasp how this genre can then be seen in terms of one text being the source for other "texts" involved. The argument betrays the nature of the centos. Cento composition is a particular kind of *paraphrasis*, an imaginative elaboration of a given text. Paraphrase implies that "elaboration is dependent on a canonical or received text from which it takes inspiration and/or narrative material."[41] The present study will demonstrate that this is indeed the case with the Virgilian and Homeric paraphrases of the Gosples found in the centos; they are inspired by the biblical text. The recasting of the epics is informed by the stories of Jesus. It is, therefore, difficult to understand why they can shed light on the question of how the Gospels came into being.

2.3.1   *Evaluative Comparison:* Synkrisis

The rhetorical device of σύγκρισις, evaluative comparison, was common in Antiquity. Comparative criticism was applied to decide on conflicting historical sources, types of conflicts in Greek tragedy, to compare persons—as in Plutarch's *Paralell Lives* where Greek and Roman *bioi* are juxtaposed—rural v. town life, seafaring v. farming etc.; all aimed at praising one and defaming the other. In his classical presentation of the phenomenon, Friedrich Focke speaks of "die agonale Charakter" of *synkrisis*.[42] Comparing things Roman and things Greek was a popular exercise.[43] Not all comparisons were critical though; the outcome of *synkrisis* was not always ranking, but also "classification according to characteristic of their style."[44] Although a competitive element is included, this is not to be overstated. If I am right in considering Christian cento composition a literary *synkrisis* where two canonical texts are invoked, the comparison aims at demonstrating some kind of harmony rather than the one outdoing the other. It is a matter of fact though, that the

---

[41] Scott Fitzgerald Johnson, *The Life and Miracles of Thekla. A Literary Study* (Cambridge, MA and London: Harvard University Press, 2006), 75.

[42] Friedrich Focke, "Synkrisis," *Hermes* 58 (1923): 338–9.

[43] Focke, "Synkrisis," 363–6.

[44] Amiel D. Vardi, "Diiudicatio Locorum: Gellius and the History of a Mode in Ancient Comparative Criticism," *Classical Quarterly* 46 (1996): 495. For examples, see Macrobius, *Sat.* 5.11–13 where there is a long comparison of Virgil and Homer: Sometimes Virgil improves on Homer; at other occasions he is inferior.

Christianizing of Virgil and Homer implied some kind of "conquest."
In order to understand this composition it is necessary to distinguish
between *res* and *verba*, content and style or wording.

Comparative criticism was part of the preparatory exercises [*progymnasmata*] of rhetorical training.[45] This exercise [*exercitio compara-
tionis*] is described by Quintilian in his *Inst.* 2.4.20–25, and he applies
it to the question of which men to praise and which to reprehend,
contemplating vices and virtues, comparing the merits of persons [*uter
melior eterve deterior*], and which is preferable, town or country life
[*ut rusticane vita an urbana potior*] etc. Such comparisons proceed
from *exempla* representing *multa cognitio rerum* (wide knowledge of
facts), says Quintilian. This is no less important for literary comparisons, and points to *mimesis* within a recognizable framework. It is difficult to see how evaluative comparisons can be performed if the things
being compared are concealed. The rhetorical teacher needed accepted
authors and texts; this is clearly witnessed in Quintilian's advice on
what texts should make up the curriculum in the studies of liberal arts.
According to *Inst.* 1.8.5, prominence is given to Homer and Virgil;[46]
such is a result of *synkrisis*. It was a matter of "what authors should be
read and what their special excellences may be [*qui sint legendi, quae
in auctore quoque praecipua*[47] *virtus*]" in order to become a perfect
orator: (*Inst.* 10.1.37). *Synkrisis* abounds in Hellenistic literary criticism, and is closely related to the practice of *imitatio* and *emulatio*.[48]

2.3.2   Ranking Texts (Canon)

The practise of comparing classical texts with the aim of ranking them
is attested in Dio Chrysostom *Or.* 18, 33, 52, 55.[49] Dio speaks as though
he is the spectator of a literary contest. The mechanisms through which
a text established itself as better than others are derived from the musi-

---

[45] Focke, "Synkrisis," 331; Kennedy, *Progymnasmata*, 52–55, 83–84, 113–4, 162–4,
212–3; ibid., *Greek Rhetoric under Christian Emperors*, (Princeton NJ: Princeton
University Press, 1983) 31, 64, 146, 227, 234–7. Vegge, *Paulus und das antike
Schulwesen*, 163–4.

[46] See Sandnes, *The Challenge of Homer*, 28–31.

[47] The adjective *praecipuus* is the opposite of *communis*, and thus refer to what
separates texts from each other; in such a comparison, contest is involved.

[48] Vardi, "Canons of Literary Texts at Rome," 135–6. *Inst.* 1.8.5 is quoted in
Chapter 1.2 of the present study.

[49] See also Athenaeus *Deipn.* 14.652c; Pliny *Ep.* 1.20.4; Horace *Ep.* 2.150–64.

cal and literary festivals and contests in ancient Athens,[50] and literary *synkrisis* borrowed the language of contest from there. From Cicero's *Brutus* we may observe how literary criticism was practised. Literature was presented, discussed and ranked; everything with a view to whom to imitate when.

Gellius in *Noctes Atticae* gives many examples of literary *synkrisis*.[51] *Noct. Att.* 10.3 compares speeches given by Roman orators and presents criteria by which evaluative criticism proceeds.[52] In 19.9, Gellius tells us about a literary contest between Roman and Greek literature at a dinner party. Here the literary contest is part of the entertainment and a musical contest as well (see Chapter 4).

From this it follows that *synkrisis* was the evaluative method forming the basis for canonical lists of authors in epic, poetry, history, oratory, comedy etc. Canonical lists are attested by Quintilian *Inst.* 10.1; he devotes this chapter to the question of which authors to imitate. A fixed canon did not exist, but there is considerable flexibility within a pattern of recurrence, as demonstrated by Teresa Morgan,[53] thus attesting a well-established hierarchy of authors. The *agon*-like nature of the comparisons is compelling; it is a matter of finding *optimi auctores*, the best authors. Terms such as *victoria, palma, inferior, fides, eminentissimi, laus, proximus esse, secundus esse, princeps, summa, minor esse, certamen, melior* abound, and witness to the competitive nature

---

[50] Cancik, "Standardization and Ranking of Texts in Greek and Roman Institutions," 117–26.

[51] See Vardi, "Diiudicatio Locorum."

[52] *Noct. Att.* 9.9 addresses Virgil's imitation of Homer in a way assuming that it is identifiable. *Noct. Att.* 15.24 renders Volcacius Sedigitus' canon (about 130 B.C.E.) of Roman comedies: *de comicis Latinis iudarit.* The literary contest is clear in lines likes this:
  - *quem ex omnibus praestare ceteris putet* ("which one he thinks surpasses all the rest")
  - *quemque in loco et honore ponat* ("what rank and honour he gives to each of them")
  - *palmam poetae comico cui deferant* ("to which poet they'd award the palm"). The decision is to give *palma* to Caecilus Statius, and then the rest are enumerated from *secundus* to *decimus*.

[53] Morgan, *Literate Education* speaks of a core and a periphery. This is demonstrated in her tables of schooltexts, see pp. 308–22. Although it is justified to compare the role played by some particular ancient authors to that of the Law among Jews and the Bibel among Christians, the literary canon in the Graeco-Roman World is certainly more open and less religious. It is utilitarian rather than aimed at drawing definite borderlines; see Tomas Hägg, "Canon Formation in Greek Literary Culture," in *Canon and Canonicity. The Formation and Use of Scripture*, ed. Einar Thomassen (Copenhagen: Museum Tusculanum Press, 2010).

of the comparison, ending up with a literary canon.[54] Quintilian structures his presentation by creating an *agon* between Greek and Roman
literature.[55] This "ethnicity" aspect causes a change in the function of
the canonical lists. They are no longer solely a tool by which orators
acquire the necessary skills of rhetoric or poetry, "but a body of texts
every educated should be familiar with, which is more or less what
we mean by 'literary canon' nowadays."[56] To Quintilian, Homer (*Inst.*
10.1.46–51) and Virgil (*Inst.* 10.1.85–86) ranked highest: "Virgil comes
second (to Homer), but is nearer first than third" (86 cf. 12.11.26).[57] It
seems that there developed lists that were remarkably similar when
it came to defining the canonical literature. In the lists drawn up by
Dio in his *Or.* 18,[58] within a text addressing training for public speaking, and Dionysios of Halicarnassus in his *Peri Mimêseôs*, one cannot
escape noting a striking resemblance to Quintilian's list.[59]

Synkrisis, leading to a ranking of texts according to a set of criteria, provides a highly relevant analogy to ecclesial practice of listing
texts reckoned as canonical. From a rhetorical perspective, the church
practised *synkrisis* when its texts were categorized, ranked and valued
in a comparison, and finally were honoured as belonging to the Holy
Scriptures. As pointed out by Daniel Sheerin, *synkrisis* is at home also

---

[54] In *Thuc.* 1–2, Dionysios Halicarnassus somehow summarizes his treatise *On Mimesis*, and now concentrates on Thucydides. He speaks of those authors setting the standards for the different genres: οἱ κανόνες (Usener-Radermacher 325.13 cf. 327.11).

[55] See Vardi, "Canons of Literary Texts at Rome," 146–9. There is also a comparison between authors of the same genre, as e.g. Sophocles and Euripides (*Inst.* 10.1.67).

[56] See Vardi, "Canons of Literary Texts at Rome," 149.

[57] Homer is among the poets as Rome is among cities, says Quintilian (*Inst.* 8.5.9).

[58] Cf. Dio *Or.* 36.33–35; in both texts the poets of old hold a special role. Supremacy and competition is clearly implied in words such as πρῶτος, μέσος, ὕστατος, οἱ ακροι, οἱ δευτεροι. Dio *Or.* 18.14 has ἄριστος ("the best") and λυσιτελέστατος ("the most profitable") cf. Lucian *Lex.* 22. In his *Letter to a Priest* 8Ep. 89b in Bidez), the Emperor Julian presents his ideal priest. One important aspect is what literature they are to read. Julian lists a "canon" of authors appropriate for them to study (300C–2D).

[59] For the lists see Vardi, "Canons of Literary Texts at Rome," 151–2; he does not mention Dio *Or.* 18 though. Vardi's findings justify the conclusion of Morgan, *Literate Education*, of a rather stable core with a flexible periphery, see e.g. pp. 71–73. In his *Commentaria Scholastica Rhetorica* 4 (p. 298.1–5) Ps-Dionysios says that rhetoricians should take their examples [τὰ παραδείγματα] from τὰ βυβλία (synonymous with τὰ βιβλία), which here includes Demosthenes, Thucydides, Xenophon, Plato, Euripides, the comedians, and Homer. This text witness to the idea of a fixed numbers of writers who together form a notion of "The Books"; thus bringing to mind the Bible.

in rhetorical criticism of biblical texts themselves.[60] When Patristic exegesis elucidates the comparisons made in the New Testament between:

- manna and John 6
- Christ and priesthood in Hebrews
- baptism and Red Sea (1 Cor 10)
- Jesus and Solomon (Matt 12:42)

there is an explicit awareness of practising *synkrisis*.[61] All these passages are what New Testament scholars traditionally label typological; i.e. texts, persons or events from the Old Testament are elucidated and being compared to their surpassing fulfilment in New Testament texts. The textbook example is, of course, Moses and Christ (2 Cor 3). G.A. Kennedy calls the comparison between the dispensations of Moses and Christ in 2 Cor 3:7–18 a *synkrisis*.[62] In doing so he is following in the footsteps of many patristic writers.

John Chrysostom witnesses to the fact that this evaluative criticism also was used in comparisons between the New Testament and the Hellenistic world as well; the Greek term σύγκρισις does not necessarily appear. *Hom. Matt* 10.4 compares John the Baptist to Greek Cynic philosophers. The comparison is introduced with a question: Ποῦ νῦν εἰσιν οἱ τῶν Ἑλλήνων φιλόσοφοι: "Where are now the philosophers of the Greeks"? There then follows a negative description of philosophers occupying themselves with riches, paving the way for a conclusion on the superiority of John: Ἀλλ᾽ οὐχ οὗτος τοιοῦτος ("But he was not like that") (PG 57.188).[63] *Hom. Matt* 33.5 compares the apostles to the philosophers and to the statesmen-generals Themistocles and Pericles. The comparison is introduced in this way: Ποῦ νῦν Πλάτων; Ποῦ Πυθαγόρας; Ποῦ τῶν Στοϊκῶν ὁ ὁρμαθος; ("Where now Plato? Where is now Pythagoras? Where is now the chain of Stoic philosophers?" (PG 57.392). As for Themistocles and Pericles, John Chrysostom turns to

---

[60] D. Sheerin, "Rhetorical and Hermeneutic Synkrisis in Patristic Typology in Patristic Typology" in *Nova & Vetera. Patristic Studies in Honor of Thomas Patrick Halton*, ed. John Petruccione (Washington D.C.: The Catholic University of America, 1998).

[61] For references see Sheerin, "Rhetorical and Hermeneutic Synkrisis," 25–31.

[62] George A. Kennedy, *New Testament Interpretation through Rhetorical Criticism*, 89.

[63] Later on (PG 57.189), other biblical figures are included as well.

a *synkrisis* of acts rather than texts and cultural legacy. The Athenians embarked on their ships to fight the Persians, thanks to the advice of their leaders. But this is "children's toys compared to the acts of the fishermen [Ἀλλὰ καὶ ταῦτα παίδων ἀθύρματα πρὸς τα τῶν ἁλιέων]" (PG 57.394). *Hom. 1 Cor* 4 on 1 Cor 1:18–20 is devoted to the topic God's words about the cross. This becomes, quite naturally, a point of departure for reflecting upon the nature of God's word: "For what sort of philosopher, which among those who studied logic, which of those knowing in Jewish matters, have saved us and made known the truth? Not one. This was entirely the work of the fishermen [ἀλλὰ τῶν ἁλιέων τὸ πᾶν γέγονε]" (4) (PG 61.32).[64] The point of comparison between the philosophers and the fishermen is here ἀλήθεια, which is independent of rhetorical style, demanded by the Greeks (PG 61.33). This example anticipates what will be addressed in Chapter 3 on the lack of culture, but presence of truth in the Gospels.[65] The Gospel— and here Chrysostom includes both message and literary style—has, in contrast to the Greek legacy, made it possible to find the highest good [τὸ κεφάλαιον τῶν ἀγαθῶν], a term drawn from classical Greek philosophy. In this text this brings Chrysostom close to the opponents of Clement of Alexandria, who claimed "faith alone" against Greek philosophy and literature:[66] νῦν δὲ οὐκέτι λογισμῶν, ἀλλὰ πίστεως δεῖ μόνης. In this way unlearned people have been turned into true philosophers (6) (PG 61.34). John Chrysostom then brings Socrates into this comparison (7). He was martyred as well, drinking the hemlock. Chrysostom argues that the martyrs of the Church deserve more attention than Socrates because they did not die out of force, but of their free will. *Hom. 1 Cor 4* has much in common with the presentation to be given in Chapter 3.1 of this study, on the development of arguments to adjudicate the literary and philosophical embarrassment on the parts of the Gospels. The paradox in short is thus: The cross persuaded through unlearned men [Ὁ δὲ σταυρὸς διὰ ἰδιωτῶν ἔπεισε] 69 (PG 61.33). Chrysostom makes clear that this was done within rhetorically given patterns, and the distinction between matter and style, *verba* and *res*, is a key to understanding this. The way he uses "truth"

---

[64] My own translation.
[65] As for John Chrysostom on the apostles as unlearned men, see Sandnes, *The Challenge of Homer*, 150–1.
[66] Sandnes, *The Challenge of Homer*, 125–6, 129–32.

in his *synkrisis* depends both on rhetorical criticism and a fundamental philosophical idea of the highest good.

Enter now epic paraphrases of biblical texts and Christian centos. The present investigation argues that these texts, which Mimesis Criticism considers analogous to the composition of Mark's Gospel, represent examples of *synkrisis* between two dominant canonical traditions, the classical epics and the Gospels. I think this should be a point of departure for a mimetic reading of this Gospel. The aim of evaluative comparisons is not necessarily to demonstrate that the one replaces the other, but rather that they both have a say. According to Christian opinion, standing on the shoulders of ancient rhetoric, the epics were classified as *eloquentia* or *verba* and the Gospels as *res* or *sensus*; when combined, the two held the role of *princeps* in literary contest—rhetorically speaking. This distinction is fundamental to rhetoric; this is seen in e.g. Ps. Longinus, *Subl.* 13.4, who distinguishes between δόγμα or ὕλη and φράσεις, and in Cicero, *Rep.* 4.8: "I admire the excellence, not only of the subject matter, but also of the style [*nec admiror rerum solum, sed verborum etiam elegantiam*]." This *synkrisis* then appears less triumphant than what we have seen with the examples from John Chrysostom. Seen in this light, the nature of emulation forming the backbone of biblical epics is to be considered. We have seen that *emulatio* is often involved with style, erudition, and embellishment. In such cases subtle and hidden emulation works well, and is, in fact, part of the literary game itself. When, however, emulation amounts to *synkrisis* of canonical texts, it takes on a hermeneutic dimension making subtlety difficult. In my view, it is the latter that applies to the question of "Christianizing Homer." For a literary 'contest' to be carried out, the participants in the *agon* must somehow be pronounced.

To substantiate this further in actual texts is now the task in front of us. A fundamental step in reading literary contests involving transvaluation is to recognize the body of texts involved. With Scott McGill, I find it helpful to distinguish between a macro and micro level of intertextuality.[67] The interpretive strategy is to preserve the memory of the classical text and to play with details within that parameter. The awareness of the classical text against which the paraphrasis takes place is, therefore, crucial. The allusiveness on the micro level can only

---

[67] McGill, *Virgil Recomposed*, 24–25.

work when this awareness is there. The recognition applies primarily to the macro level. Advertised intertextuality at this level paves the way for interpreting micro-texts accordingly, albeit that intertextuality is subtle and concealed. If, however, no sign of advertisement is found on the macro level, alleged intertextual links on the micro level should be approached with corresponding caution.

2.4 A Pioneer in Latin: C. Vettius Aquilinus Juvencus

2.4.1 *Juvencus who?*

The most important examples of hexameter versions of New Testament texts are Juvencus (see below); Sedulius' *Carmen Paschale*, based on the four Gospels (5th century); Nonnus of Panoplis, who wrote a paraphrasis of John's Gospel (5th century); and Arator, who paraphrased the Book of Acts (6th century).[68] Commodianus has often been mentioned as the first Latinist to write a biblical epic. He is mentioned in the *Decretum Gelasianum* among literature not recognized: *Opuscula Commodiani. Apocrypha.*[69] Contemporary scholarship dates him rather to the 5th than to the 3rd or 4th centuries.[70] Juvencus, with his *Evangeliorum Libri Quattuor,* is, therefore, the first Christian poet to present a *paraphrasis* of the Gospels.[71] This is very much a work of Constantine's time although the emperor is not mentioned explicitly before the epilogue. In addition to the text itself, these are the most important sources on Juvencus:

---

[68] For a presentation of these, see Roger P.H. Green, *Latin Epics of the New Testament. Juvencus, Sedulius, Arator* (Oxford: Oxford University Press, 2006). For Nonnus, who wrote in Greek, see Mary Whitby, "The Bible Hellenized. Nonnus' Paraphrase of St. John's Gospel," in *Texts and Culture in late Antiquity. Inheritance, Authority, and Change*, ed. J.H.D. Scourfield (Swansea: The Classical Press of Wales, 2007), 199–207.

[69] *Das Decretum Gelasianum de libris recipiendis et non recipiendis*, ed. Ernst von Dobschütz, (Leipzig: J.C. Hinrichs'sche Buchhandlung, 1912), Chapter 5. (315.8) p. 56.

[70] See L. Krestan, "Commodianus," *RAC* 3:248–52; Elizabeth A. Clark and Diane F. Hatch, *The Golden Bough, The Oaken Cross. The Virgilian Cento of Faltonia Betitia Proba* (Chico: Scholars Press, 1981), 1–2; cf. Green, *Latin Epics of the New Testament*, 2 n. 3.

[71] The text is available in PL 19.9–346 and Iohannis Hvemer, ed. *Gai Vetti Aqvilini Ivvenci Evangeliorum Libri Quatvor. CSEL 24* (Wien, Leipzig: F. Tempsky; G. Freytag, 1891).

Jerome *vir. ill.* 84
"Juvencus, a Spaniard of very noble family, and a priest, translating into hexameter verse almost word for word the four Gospels, published them in four volumes; also some other works in the same meter regarding the order of rites [*Iuvencus nobilissimi generis Hispanus, presbyter, quattuor evangelia hexametris versibus paene ad verbum transferens quattuor libros conposuit, et nonnulla eodem metro ad sacramentorum ordinem pertinentia. Floruit sub Constantino principe*]."[72]

Jerome *Chron.* 329
"Juvencus, a priest, Spaniard by nation, presented the Gospels in heroic verses (= hexameter) [*Iuvencus presbyter natione Hispanus evangelia heroicis versibus explicat*]."[73]

Jerome *Commentary on Matt 2:11* (SC 242)[74]
Matt 2:11 is about the wise men coming to Bethlehem, opening their presents [*thesaurae*] to the newborn child. Jerome interprets this verse by simply quoting Juvencus' *paraphrasis* of the text; Juvenvcus summarized Jerome's point nicely. The biblical text in its Latin version says: *et apertis thesauris suis obtulerunt ei munera aurum, thus et myrram* (Matt 2:11). Juvencus rendered this: *thus aurum murram regique Deoque Dona ferunt*; i.e. "the incense, the gold and the myrrh, these are their gift to the king, both man and God."[75] The biblical passage is thus read in the light of later christology. This is an observation of importance also for the centos to be examined later. Their interpretation of biblical passages reflects later Christian tradition and doctrine.[76]

---

[72] Translation from Thomas P. Halton, trans. *Saint Jerome On Illustrious Men.* FC (Washington DC: The Catholic University of America Press, 1999).

[73] My translation. For the Latin text, see Rudolf Helm, ed. *Die Chronik des Hieronymus. Eusebius Werke Siebenter Band: Hieronymi Chronikon.* GCS 47 (Berlin: Akademia Verlag, 1956), 232.

[74] For a French translation with Latin text, see Émile Bonnard, *Saint Jérôme Commentaire sur S. Matthieu Tome 1 (Livres 1–11)*, Paris: Cerf, 1977.

[75] Hvemer, *Ivvenci Evangeliorum Libri Quatvor*, p. 16 l.250–1. My translation.

[76] R.P.H. Green, "The *Evangeliorum Libri* of Juvencus: Exegesis by Stealth?" in *Poetry and Exegesis in Premodern Latin Christianity. The Encounter between Classical and Christian Strategies of Interpretation*, ed. Willemien Otten & Karla Pollmann (Leiden, Boston: Brill, 2007), 67 calls this "the oral element of Christianity".

Jerome *Ep.* 70.5

"Juvencus, priest at the time of Constantine presented the story of our Lord the Saviour in verses; but was not afraid to put the majesty of the Gospels under the rules of metre [*Iuvencus presbyter sub Constantino historiam domini salvatoris versibus explicavit nec pertimuit evangelii maiestatem sub metri leges mittere*]"[77] (PL 22.668).

In *Decretum Gelasianum* 250[78] Juvencus is mentioned alongside Orosius and Sedulius. The first is praised for his learned work *Historia adversos Paganos,* in which he gives a Christian perspective on Rome's history. Sedulius is praised for his *Opus Paschale* written in the style of heroic epics [*heroicis versibus*]: "Likewise, we do not despise, but admire the laborious work of Juvencus [*item Iuvenci nihilominus laboriosum opus non spernimus sed miramur*]."[79]

From these sources we gather that Juvencus was a Spanish priest who during the reign of Constantine composed his poem in a metric style characteristic of heroic epics. He imposes upon himself the constraints of metre, dactylic hexameter, but not in the way the later centonists did. While the latter were composed out of the classical epics *verbatim,* the paraphrase of Juvencus is less constrained. A consequence of this is that biblical names and places sometimes do occur here. Jerome says that he kept very close to the original [*paene ad verbum*], which literally means "almost word for word," but still there is a marked difference between Juvencus and the centos here.

As pointed out by Roger P.H. Green, Juvencus adds new material, often combined with adaptation, but he has no desire to invent stories. Compared to Sedulius and Arator of the 5th century, Juvencus is rather faithful to the stories found in the Gospels: "In general, Jerome's statement that he is pretty literal [*paene ad verbum*] is broadly acceptable."[80] In both *Ep.* 70.5 and *Decretum Gelasianum,* Juvencus' biblical epic is seen against a background of reluctance and even opposition. It says that he was not afraid of betraying the majesty of the Gospels, and his work was not despised. This is a reference, not to the literary quality of the Gospels (see Chapters 3.1, 3.2, 3.3, 3.4), but rather to the fact that

---

[77] My translation.
[78] *Decretum Gelasianum*, ed. Von Dobschütz, Chapter 4, p. 47.
[79] My translation.
[80] Green, *Latin Epics of the New Testament*, 374 cf. pp. 36–38, 43–44, 72.

the quality of the Gospels was judged as something idiosyncratic and not to be mixed up with pagan texts. These texts thereby give glimpses of a debate among Christians on how biblical epics were perceived.

In four books of dactylic hexameter, Juvencus presents the story of Jesus from the Gospels, following primarily Matthew, but including also some Johannine scenes, and childhood stories from Luke's Gospel.[81] Gospel narratives are recast in the prestigious style of Virgil. His work is not, however, a cento; he is not sewing together lines into a patch-work. His imitation is primarily that of style and the use of words and phrases from Virgil.[82] Imitating Virgil implies a universalizing of Jesus' story. It is a characteristic of the Virgilian epic, particularly the *Aeneid*, that the whole world is made the stage for the narrative of Aeneas' and Rome's destiny, and the use of this triumphalist epic underscores the universal horizons of Jesus' story.[83] By necessity this sometimes leads to what R. Herzog has called "Entjudaisierung,"[84] although R.P.H. Green is reluctant to use this term. He considers the playing down of Jewish names to be due primarily to metrical constraints.[85]

2.4.2   *Virgil Corrected or Elucidated?*

The question of why Juvencus wrote his poem, and why he did it in the Virgilian way, have been debated. This includes, of course, the question of the attitude he takes to Virgil: is he correcting Virgil or is he bring-ing out the deeper meaning of the poet? The preface and epilogue are key texts for this question. The 27-line preface is found in Huemer's edition,[86] before the story starts with King Herod of Judaea (l.1), while 4.802–12 form the epilogue.

The line of thought in the preface centres on glory. Everything in the world, including *aurea Roma*, is mortal and will pass away. In

---

[81] Mark's Gospel is very little used. For a list of the biblical scenes found in Juvencus' work, see Green, *Latin Epics of the New Testament*, 28–29. For a closer examination of how Juvencus organizes his poem according to the Gospels, see Ludwig Braun, Andreas Engel, "'Quellenwechsel' im Bibelepos des Iuvencus," *ZAC* 2 (1998).

[82] See Green, *Latin Epics of the New Testament*, 52.

[83] Pointed out by Green, *Latin Epics of the New Testament*, 103–4; see also Reinhart Herzog, *Restauration und Erneuerung die Lateinischen Literatur von 284 bis 374 n. Chr.* (München: C.H. Beck'sche Verlagbuchhandlung, 1989), 333.

[84] Herzog, *Die Bibelepik der Lateinischen Spätantike*, 111–5.

[85] Green, *Latin Epics of the New Testament*, 104–9, 375.

[86] CSEL 24, pp. 1–2; the preface is also found in Latin and with English translation in Green, *Latin Epics of the New Testament*, 15–16; as for the epilogue see pp. 3–4.

this world where death reigns, some, however, receive a special glory; among these are Virgil and the poets. The sweetness [*dulcedo Maronis*] of Virgil owed him this honour. The glory of the poets [*gloria vatum*] remains as long as God permits, which for Juvencus means till the end of time. The poets are called *vates*, with the dual meaning of both prophet and poet,[87] albeit that falsehood [*mendacia*] is attached to their poems.

Juvencus is himself writing on a greater theme; hence his poem will remain immortal. He seems to think that his poem will eventually save him from divine judgement: "For my song will be the life-giving feats of Christ, a divine gift to the peoples which is immune from the charge of falsehood [*nam mihi carmen erit Christi vitalia gesta, divinum populis falsi sine crimine donum*]" (l. 19–20). He firmly believes that the final devastating fire [*mundi incendia*] will destroy his *opus*, which eventually will also save himself from this fire [*me subtrahet igni*] (l. 21–22). The *mendacia* of pagan literature serves here not to put this literature down; it rather makes up an argument from the lesser to the larger, securing Juvencus the honour he deserves.[88] If poems in which *mendacia* is present has a lasting glory, how much more Juvencus' epic! His poem is thus explicitly presented as epic, but also, with regard to *res*, as sharply contrasted with traditional epic. The actions of Christ, which his poem is really about, are described as life-bringing; i.e. as bringing salvation to humankind.[89]

The preface ends with Juvencus inviting the Holy Spirit to inspire him to "utter things worthy of Christ [*ut Christo digna loquamur*]" (l. 27). He asks for the sweetness of Jordan [*dulcis Iordanis*] to overflow his mind and to inspire his song. Inspiration in terms of a flowing river is mentioned in l. 9 [*de fonte fluentes*], and now in terms of *rigare* (l. 26). Furthermore, the Latin text emphasises a connection between the sweetness of Maro and sweet river Jordan; Maro's text as well as his own poem are both inspired. A reference to Christian baptism is

---

[87] See OLD s.v.

[88] Thomas Gärtner, "Die Musen im Dienste Christi. Strategien der Rechtfertigung christlicher Dichtung in der Lateinischen Spätantike," *VC* 58 (2004): 431–4 demonstrates how Juvencus develops a Christian version, i.e. a spiritualized version of the topos of honour. In an argument *a minore ad majus*, Juvencus finds affirmation that his work and himself will find eternal protection.

[89] Michael Roberts, "Vergil and the Gospels: The Evangeliorum libri IV of Juvencus," in *Romane memento. Vergil in the Fourth Century*, ed. Roger Rees (London: Gerald Duckworth, 2004), 48.

possibly implied here.[90] However, as van der Nat points out, a baptismal reference is not sufficient to explain why Jordan here takes the place of the Muses.[91] The connecting link between the two includes the idea of inspiration as *flumen*.

At the heart of the preface is a comparison with a Virgilian text: The pagan poet includes among the inhabitants of the Elysian Fields *quique pii vates et Phoebo digna locuti* (*Aen.* 6.662); i.e. holy poets who had spoken worthily of Apollo. Juvencus himself appears in the preface as a holy poet, due both to his inspiration and to his writing on a theme greater than those of the pagan poets. There is also a contrast to Apollo here; he was the god of prophecy, and a god of music. Juvencus probably intended this to be noticed as well. Furthermore, he describes his poem as "speaking worthily of Christ" (l. 27), clearly echoing the Elysian poets. Finally, he expects for himself immortality, not in the Elysian Fields, but in the form of Christian salvation: "Sein Versschluss bildet eine typische Kontrastimitation."[92] This is a key term which will be presented more below.

The epilogue (4.802–12) links up with the preface in confirming the prayer for inspiration. Juvencus' *mens* is said to be inspired by the grace of Christ [*gratia Christi*], thus strengthening a baptismal echo. He was thus enabled to present the *lex* of divine glory in an embellished form [*ornamenta*]; i.e. in the human language of Virgil. *Lex* is synonymous with *vitalia gesta* in the preface, and is closely related to *lux* (light) and *pax* (peace) of Christ; both descriptive of the content of Christian faith. "Christ reigns forever" closes the poem, a statement that finds corroboration in Constantine's present rule. If the preface recalled the poets of the Elysian Fields according to Virgil, the epilogue echoes the ending of *Georgics* 4.559–66. Virgil there briefly sums up his topic and relates it to the warfare of Octavian. Juvencus similarly

---

[90] For the role of Jordan in baptismal theology, see E.C. Whitaker, *Documents of Baptismal Liturgy, Revised and Expanded by Maxwell E. Johnson* (Collegeville MI: Liturgical Press, 2003), 3; Maxwell E. Johnson, *The Rites of Christian Initiation. Their Evolution and Interpretation. Revised and Expanded Edition* (Collegeville MI: Liturgical Press, 2007), 57.

[91] P.G. van der Nat, "Die Prefatio der Evangelienparaphrase des Iuvencus," in *Romanitas et Christianitas. In Honour of Jan Henrik Waszink* (Amsterdam, London: North-Holland Publishing Company, 1973), 252–3.

[92] For this comparison see Van der Nat, "Die Prefatio der Evangelienparaphrase des Iuvencus," 253–4; Roberts, "Vergil and the Gospels," 48.

summarizes his work in the epilogue. The following observations can be juxtaposed:

Georgics' epilogue	The epilogue of Juvencus' *Evangeliorum Libri Quattuor*
Augustus	Constantine
Bellum	*Pax*
Viamque adfectat Olympo	*sacri sibi nominis horret imponi pondus*
(Augustus' achievements prepare his apotheosis)	(Constantine rejects the name of divinity)
jus dare	*lex*

Taken together, and particularly when Virgilian comparisons are advertised as is the case here, there is a strong case for saying that Constantine surpasses Augustus, and even so that he brings to completion peace, well-known from Augustan propaganda.[93] In this regard Juvencus' epilogue brings to mind the close of Eusebius' *Church History*, where Constantine's victory is seen as a renewal of the Roman Empire κατὰ τὸ παλαιὸν, according to the old style; i.e. united, peaceful, true piety and new prospects for human life (*Hist. eccl.* 10.9.6.7). The paraphrase of the Gospels is clearly Virgilian throughout the poem; this applies to metre, vocabulary and phrases, and still, the stories are easily recognized as taken from the Gospels; in the words of R.P.H. Green, what we have is "a new style, not a new storyline."[94] Furthermore, the emulation of Virgil is advertised in the preface as well as in the epilogue.

But how is this emulation to be understood; what are the implications? Due to many circumstances, such as reader competence, complexity in the links etc., it is a general fact that intertextual links may be difficult to identify, even more so to interpret. In Juvencus' *Evangeliorum Libri Quattuor* the intertextual links are clearly identifiable, but the interpretation remains a challenge. Do the intertextual links imply a hermeneutical aspect as well? The suggestions are

---

[93] For this interpretation, see Roberts, "Vergil and the Gospels," 48–49. For *pax* and Augustean 'theology,' see Gary Gilbert, "Roman Propaganda and Christian Identity in the Worldview of Luke-Acts," in *Contextualizing Acts. Lukan Narrative and Greco-Roman Discourse*, ed. Todd Penner and Caroline vander Stichele (Atlanta: Society of Biblical Literature, 2003). When Juvencus exploits imperial propaganda, he draws upon the idea that the Emperors were descending from Aeneas, the Trojan; see e.g. *Aen.* 1.283–96 about the Trojan Caesar and Seneca *Apol.* 5.5, where Claudius presents himself as a Trojan ['Ιλιόθεν].

[94] Green, *Latin Epics of the New Testament*, 132.

many, and they are not necessarily exclusive. The relationship may be pictured narrowly. Virgil is then to Juvencus a quarry or reservoir from where he finds "Einzelzüge,"[95] aimed primarily at embellishing or intensifying his poem.[96] Supportive evidence is found in 4.805 of the epilogue: The glory of divine *lex*, which in this context clearly refers to the life of Jesus, "can happily put on the worldly ornament of language [*ornamenta libens caperet terrestria linguae*]." *Lingua* here encapsulates Virgil's embellished language and style that now adorns the Gospel stories.

It is possible to think of Juvencus as critical of Virgil and Latin epics. The critique voiced in the preface, in short *mendacia*, adds to that view, and also the fact that Juvencus presents his own poem as a contrast, in terms both of content (falsehood vs. truth; warfare vs. peace), inspiration and lasting value and glory. In this perspective, the poem may be seen as replacement literature, as an attempt to sideline the *Aeneid* and other Virgilian texts. This view can, however, not do away with the fact that Juvencus deeply respects and values Virgil. We noticed that he speaks of the sweetness both of Maro and Jordan; in fact, the inspiration of Jordan finds in Virgil a better external appearance. The two are not exclusive. As pointed out by R.P.H. Green,[97] this confirms Juvencus' basic attitude to Virgil. There is no attempt to sideline him; rather to claim him for Juvencus' *res*.

Recent works on Juvencus emphasize that Juvencus' Virgilian emulation of the Gospels implies more than style and cosmetics.[98] The comparisons with the *Aeneid* and the *Georgics* made in preface and epilogue respectively (see above) add examples to this view. Not all intertextual links are equally meaningful; some are motivated by style, rhythm and language. But that fact is not a satisfactory description of the poem in general. In recasting the Gospels in the idiom of Virgilian epic, Juvencus seems also to claim that he brings Virgil's epics to some kind of fulfilment. His poem represents more than a bag or reservoir to embellish his poem, there is a hermeneutical concern at work as well. The relationship between Virgil and Juvencus' biblical poem is to

---

[95] Klaus Thraede, "Iuvencus," *RAC* 19:890.
[96] Herzog, *Die Bibelepik der Lateinischen Spätantike*, 93, 115 considers Juvencus as substituting Virgil. This necessarily leads to a narrow and more critical perspective.
[97] Green, *Latin Epics of the New Testament*, 22.
[98] See the discussion in Green, "The *Evangeliorum Libri* of Juvencus: Exegesis by Stealth?," 76–80.

be defined as being both a contrast and a high regard. Nowhere does he conceive of this relationship in terms of exploiting the "spoils of the Egyptians", a widely used biblical notion of a critical despoliation from the pagans of what is conformable to Christian faith.[99] That is an analogy of seizing or conquering. There is mutuality with regard to the two texts at work in Juvencus' poem; this makes it less appropriate to regard the "spoils of the Egyptians" as relevant. This paves the way for a more positive use of Virgil, even to the point of searching and finding events in Christ's life envisaged in the *Aeneid*. Fulfilment of prophecy is important in Juvencus' poem,[100] referring to what the Scriptures[101] say about the role of Jesus. The idea of fulfilment of prophecy finds corroboration in Virgil as well. In fact, Virgil provides Juvencus with appropriate terms for describing the order of ages or epochs.[102]

2.4.3   *Virgil Transvalued: Two Examples*

Klaus Thraede introduced the term "Kontrastimitation" to denote Juvencus' relationship to Virgil;[103] i.e. an imitation in which a contrast is also essential. By necessity, this implies a comparison in which the model is being surpassed. "Kontrastimitation" displays an ambivalent attitude to a source text, dependence and simultaneously, a bending of it. Thraede's term is more or less synonymous with Dennis R. MacDonald's "transvaluation", with inversion and reversal of values. In his words, transvaluation is "transformative artistry, and theological playfulness."[104] M.D. Usher speaks, with reference to Berthold Brecht, of "Verfremdung" in the centos. This is a heuristic device that aims at depriving "an event or character of any self-evident, familiar, or obvious quality, and to produce instead astonishment or curiosity about it in order to bring

---

[99] Pointed out also by Green, *Latin Epics of the New Testament*, 133–4. The notion is taken from an allegorical reading of Exod 3:21–22 and 12:35–36; see Sandnes, *The Challenge of Homer*, 144–7, 222–6. For a broader presentation of this motif, see Joel S. Allen, *The Despoliation of Egypt in Pre-Rabbinic, Rabbinic and Patristic Traditions* (Leiden: Brill, 2008).

[100] See e.g. 1.353, 1.405, 1.412, 4.530; see Green, *Latin Epics of the New Testament*, 70–71, 109–10.

[101] See e.g. 1.313, 1.412, where Isaiah appears.

[102] Green, *Latin Epics of the New Testament*, 70–71 refers to e.g. 4th *Ecloge* 5, *Aen.* 5.707; 9.107–8; 10.444 which are echoed in e.g. *Evangeliorum Libri Quattuor* 1.123, 1.308, 1.489, 2.173.

[103] Klaus Thraede, "Epos," *RAC* 5:1039.

[104] MacDonald, *Does the New Testament Imitate Homer?* 15; see also his *The Homeric Epics and the Gospel of Mark*, 2–3, 187–90.

about heightened understanding".[105] Juvencus demonstrates that this artistry—whether we call it "Kontrastimitation", "transvaluation", "transformation" or "Verfremdung"—works within a clearly advertised setting. The readers are invited to notify precisely how the Gospels imitate Virgil, be it in terms of embellishment, contrasts, fulfilment etc. This kind of transformative artistry becomes subtle and advanced only within a framework of recognized intertextuality. As Michael Roberts points out, Juvencus provides an *interpretatio Christiana* of Virgil's epic, but also an *interpretatio epica* of the Gospel.[106] This duality plays itself out in mutuality between the two texts, wherein one provides *verba*, and the other conveys *res*. In this mutuality, a constant element of "Verfremdung" is at work,—back and forth. Two examples now follow.

2.4.3.1 *The Storm*

An example of "Kontrastimitation" is found in the narrative of Jesus and the storm (2.25–40).[107] In great detail Juvencus' poem recalls the storm scene in *Aen.* 1.81–123, by which the Trojan fleet was scattered. Jesus blames his disciples: "Fear rushes into faithless minds,"[108] echoing *Aen.* 4.13. Here Dido praises Aeneas for his courage, while Juvencus has Jesus rebuking his disciples in similar vein. As pointed out by C. Ratkowitsch, Jesus is sleeping in the boat, as is Aeneas (*Aen.* 4.554–5). The panic-stricken disciples wake him up. Now Jesus acts differently from the Trojan hero. Jesus asleep in the raging storm is a sign of *fiducia* and not *timor*. Aeneas is awakened from his sleep by Mercurius who reproaches him for thus jeopardizing his given task:

> "Up ho' break off delay! A fickle and changeful thing is woman ever [Dido]." So he spoke and melted into the black night. Then indeed, Aeneas, scared by the sudden vision, tears himself from sleep and bestirs his comrades. "Make haste, my men, awake and man the benches! Unfurl the sails with speed" (*Aen.* 4.569–74).

Aeneas is frightened by his dream, and understands that his sleep was a temptation distracting him from the goal set for him, namely to keep

---

[105] M.D. Usher, *Homeric Stitchings. The Homeric Centos of the Empress Eudocia* (Lanham etc.: Rowman & Littlefield Publishers, 1998), 12–13.

[106] Roberts, "Vergil and the Gospels," 50.

[107] I am here dependent on C. Ratkowitsch, "Vergils Seesturm bei Juvencus und Sedilius," *JAC* 29 (1986) which also forms the basis of the presentation in Green, *Latin Epics of the New Testament*, 61–62.

[108] Translation from Green, *Latin Epics of the New Testament*, 61.

on sailing for Rome, his divinely given destiny (571–83). The reaction of
the disciples, "to what god is such power given?" (2.40) borrows words
from *Aen.* 9.97. Aeneas' mother prays for divine protection of the ships
Aeneas embarks upon. Jupiter then responds reluctantly to her prayer:
cui tanta deo permissa potestas? ("To what god is such power given?").
The reaction of the disciples is taken from Jupiter's admitting that the
request surpasses what it is permitted for gods to do. Contrariwise,
Jesus calms the raging sea and spreads quiet peace over the waters [*et
placidam sternit super aequora pacem*] (2.38). This is taken from *Aen.*
1.249 about Antenor, who founded Patavium, a peaceful dwelling for
his people, a model for what is to become Aeneas' Rome. In that city,
Caesar Augustus, of Trojan descent, will establish peace (*Aen.* 1.286–96).[109]
The significance of the storm on the Sea of Galilee is thus seen in the
light of imperial propaganda. Jesus surpasses Jupiter in calming the sea.
What Jupiter claimed impossible even for a deity, is performed by Jesus.
Furthermore, Jesus establishes peace like Augustus, the descendent of
Aeneas.[110] In the light of the epilogue (see above), this last aspect clearly
implies a "transvaluation" as well (see 2.4.2 and 2.3).

2.4.3.2   *The Baptism of Jesus*

The second example is the baptism of Jesus, found in Book 1.346–63.
Juvencus says that Jesus was determined to ask for the venerated water
of Jordan. John the Baptist, called *vates*, enters a dialogue with Jesus
that echoes the Matthean version quite closely. John's question out of
his reluctance is introduced: *et talia fatur* ("And he spoke thus") (1.348).
These words are taken from *Aen.* 3.485. At first sight, this appears as a
verbal link only, without any significance.[111] But this half-line—judged

---

[109] A text clearly echoing the propaganda of the 4th *Ecloge*.

[110] The raging sea and calming it was a topos in politico-religious rhetoric. In
Lucan's presentation of the *Civil War*, Caesar is rescued from a storm. The storm and
raging sea become symbols of the chaotic situation in the Empire (*Civ. Bell.* 1.73–80,
186–7, 288; 5.424, 504–7, 540, 630–7). In *4th Ecloge*, Virgil depicts the coming of
the Golden Age as a time when traders no longer cross the seas (*Ecl.* 4.38–39). He
here brings to mind Aratus' *Phaen.* 100–14 where the mythic past, a golden time for
humanity, is described as a time when there was no need to traverse the dangerous
sea. For further references, see Karl Olav Sandnes, "Markus—en allegorisk biografi?,"
Dansk Teologisk Tidsskrift 69 (2006): 290–5.

[111] We are reminded that textual links have a centrifugal impact on the reading.
Readers are driven to explore the wider context of the links. This is an important
factor in the biblical epics, and this is a factor which triggers layers of meaning in
them. For the centrifugal power of intertextuality, see Peter Phillips, "Biblical Study
and Intertextuality: Should the Work of Genette and Eco Broaden our Horizons?"

by itself not very meaningful—guides the reader to a Virgilian context of much interest. In calling John *vates* here, Juvencus echoes the wider context about Helenus' [*vates*] prophecy that strengthened Aeneas in his determination to reach *Italia*. There is, according to this prophecy, no rest for Aeneas before he has reached his destiny. The hub of the prophecy is that Aeneas must return to the ships and direct them towards the coast of Ausonia (*Italia*): "Make sail and seize it" (3.477). In other words, this is a passage in which Aeneas is reminded of his divinely assigned task. Juvencus was probably directed to this Virgilian context also by the fact that the prophet addresses Aeneas' father Anchises, saying to him: "You who are blessed by your son's piety [*o felix nati pietate*]" (3.480). This Virgilian background brings to mind the heavenly voice at Jesus' baptism, whereby a divine confirmation of his ministry and destiny is given. Jesus is confirmed in his mission.

In 1.354 it says that Jesus went through the water: *fluminis undas*, taken from *Aen.* 3.389 and the prophecy already mentioned. Helenus foretells the challenges that Aeneas will face, and gives him the sign by which he will know where to build the city of Rome. The sign is found "by the waters of a stream" [*fluminis undas*]; historically speaking the Tiber. The baptism is thus interpreted as the moment where Jesus will start "building his city." According to 1.357 the Spirit came down from high heaven [*descendit ab alto Spiritus*]. The words are taken from *Aen.* 8.423, and describe Ignipotens or Vulcanus descending from heaven. The background is that Venus, the mother of Aeneas, has turned to Vulcanus, the god of fire, and requested for his help. She prayed that he would provide for her son the weapons necessary to fulfil the task given to him. Vulcanus descends therefore, as into the workshop of a smith, and says: "Arms for a brave warrior must ye make [*arma acri facienda viro*]" (*Aen.* 8.440). In this light, Juvencus considers the baptism of Jesus also as an event whereby he is equipped for his ministry, very much in line with Luke 4:14 and Acts 10:38.

The baptism of Jesus is throughout this passage juxtaposed with the task given to Aeneas. Jesus resembles Aeneas. As he was given divine confirmation and protection, so the baptism of Jesus was a moment of assuring him of his ministry. Like Helenus' prophecy, the baptism at

---

in *The Intertextuality of the Epistles. Explorations of Theory and Practice*, ed. Thomas L. Broodie, Dennis R. MacDonald and Stanley E. Porter (Sheffield: Sheffield Phoenix Press, 2006), 39–41.

Jordan is the divine confirmation that Jesus has embarked on a divine mission. Furthermore, just as Aeneas is provided with the arms necessary to carry out his commission, so Jesus is also equipped by baptism; obviously a reference to his being endowed with the Spirit. There is thus a lot of *mimesis* or imitation here, but the imitation is contrastive as well. The missions of the two heroes are indeed different. Jesus is not building a city; he is not preparing for warfare. Vulcanus did not come down to equip him, but *Spiritus* did in the form of a dove [*columba*]. Juvencus' Virgilian version of Jesus' baptism is, therefore, illuminating as to the composition of his poem in general.

Compared to the biblical texts, there is considerable expansion here. An obvious example is 1.359 where it says that the sacred wind came over the body of Jesus [*et sancto flatu corpus perfudit Iesu*] after the descent of the Spirit at his baptism. No such thing is found in the New Testament stories, but it does not take much imagination to understand the background of this. *Spiritus* and *flatus* are combined, especially in Latin texts about inspiration of poets,[112] and Greek πνεῦμα and πνεῖν (cf. John 3:8; 20:22) strengthened this combination. This is a possible hint that Juvencus was familiar with either the Greek text or traditions derived from it. The expansions and alterations are easily recognized as reworking of the biblical texts, as is the case in 1.349 *tune meis manibus dignaris mergier undis* ("and you deign to undergo immersion at my hands?"). As pointed out by R.P.H. Green, the contrast between *tu* and *me* is highlighted here, but this is an adaptation of Matt 3:14: "It could be argued that nothing is added to the sense, at least for a reader familiar with the original context; the expression is somewhat fuller, but would not strike a Roman reader as in any way exuberant.[113]

Juvencus' use of *mergere* is worth noting. This verb implies sinking or being plunged into deep water.[114] This is not the verb corresponding to what we find in the relevant biblical passages. It is probable that this term echoes Christian baptismal practice as Juvencus was familiar with it. Tertullian uses the same term for Christian baptism as an immersion in *Bapt.* 7.2[115] and *Cor.* 3.3.[116] This observation is important

---

[112] OLD s.v.; see e.g. Cicero *Arch.* 18 says that poets speak on the basis of inspiration: *quasi divino quodam spiritu inflari* ("as infused with some kind of divine spirit").
[113] Green, *Latin Epics of the Nestament*, 37.
[114] OLD s.v.
[115] *In aqua mergimur* ("we are immersed in water").
[116] *Ter mergitamur* ("we are three times immersed").

because it reminds us that Juvencus depends not only on texts, but also on how texts were perpetuated in liturgical practice and piety. His poem is thus informed by the stories of Jesus' life and Christian tradition as he knew it.

Both Michael Roberts and Roger P.H. Green point out that Lactantius' program for a new Christian literature paved the way for Juvencus' poem.[117] Lactantius was well aware that in order to appeal to cultivated citizens, rhetoric and style was crucial. It was possible to defend truth without eloquence, but more successfully, "truth can be defended, as many often have defended it, without eloquence, nevertheless it ought to be illuminated and indeed maintained with clarity and splendour of utterance, so that it floods into people's minds more forcefully, with the equipment of its own power and religion and its own brilliance of rhetoric" (*Inst.* 1.1.10).[118] The cultivated reading classes found the stylistic level of the Bible, including the Gospels, as hindrance to embracing the new faith with its literature. In this situation, Juvencus accommodated their taste and presented an improvement of the Gospel texts. The next chapter will substantiate this. However, the presentation of Juvencus has demonstrated that his biblical epic is not primarily a matter of embellishing the stories about the life of Jesus, but that he engages in a discourse where Virgil is imitated and contrasted, echoed and surpassed—all in order to emphasize that a Christian reading of this classical text is possible, not to say that such a reading brings out a full meaning of Virgil's epic, once its *mendacia* is left out. R.P.H. Green summarizes the task undertaken by Juvencus, the pioneer of epic paraphrase of the Bible in the following way. "It is a bold and groundbreaking act of cultural appropriation that sought to claim the power and attraction of epic for the lowly discourse of the Christian gospels."[119]

---

[117] Roberts, *Biblical Epic and the Rhetorical Paraphrase in Antiquity*, 67–69; Roberts, "Vergil and the Gospels," 47; Green, *Latin Epics and the New Testament*, 128–9. See Chapter 3.1.3 in this book.

[118] Quoted from Lactantius. *Divine Institutes*, trans. Anthony Bowen and Peter Garnsey (Liverpool: Liverpool University Press). The Latin text goes like this: ... *tamen claritate ac nitore sermonis inlustranda et quodammodo adserenda est, ut potentius in animos influat et ui sua instructa et luce orationis ornata*. It is worth noting that Lactantius considers rhetorical power and style as means to convey the power of truth itself, which to him is Christian doctrine and tradition.

[119] Green, "The *Evangeliorum Libri* of Juvencus: Exegesis by Stealth?," 65.

CHAPTER THREE

WHY IMITATE CLASSICAL TEXTS?

The previous chapter pointed out that Juvencus was a pioneer in para-phrasing the story of Jesus in classical epic style. We saw that *paraphrasis* was a rhetorical exercise of wide currency in antiquity, and that this rhetorical and educational means was taken up by a Christian élite, such as Juvencus and others in the 4th and 5th centuries C.E. *Paraphrasis* of biblical narratives was therefore—from a rhetorical and educational point of view—quite natural. But this practice was initiated not only to comply with common rhetorical ideas. Juvencus' biblical epic was caused partly by what was considered the crude style of the biblical Gospels: they did not meet the standard of the classical legacy. He, together with other Christians, felt that they could and should be improved upon. The present chapter will substantiate this embarrassment on behalf of the literary style of the Gospels. Furthermore, I will argue that shortly after Juvencus wrote his *Evangeliorum Libri Quattuor*, Emperor Julian the Apostate promulgated a law that came to have a profound effect on how some Christians considered their own literature vis-à-vis the classical legacy. There are, therefore, both literary and historical reasons for the refashioning the stories of Jesus in the epic form.

3.1   A Literary Reason: The Gospels' Lack of Culture

An important assumption of the present investigation is that many cultivated persons found the literary style of the Gospels crude, and Christians of the same milieu found no reason for pride in their own literature. The taste of erudite citizens did not find Christian literature attractive. This assumption finds corroboration also in e.g. Jerome *Ep.* 53 and 70, both devoted to the question of the Scriptures, Christian faith, encyclical studies and classical literature.[1]

---

[1] For a presentation of these epistles, see Sandnes, *The Challenge of Homer*, 200–5.

In *Ep.* 53.2 the question of the Scriptures' inspiration is introduced through the citation of 2 Cor 13:3: "Do you seek a proof that Christ is speaking in me?" Paul's words had persuasive power, thus confirming the presence of the Holy Spirit in his words, and in the instruction of his disciples Barnabas and Titus the common rule of *viva vox* was confirmed as well (PL 22.541).[2] It is, therefore, says Jerome, astonishing to find that Peter and Paul were unlearned men [*litteras non didicerint*] (*Ep.* 53.4 cf. Acts 4:13). What came to others through daily exercise and study was given them by the Holy Spirit. Hence, they are called θεοδίδακτοί, a term taken from 1 Thess 4:9. Jerome makes an argument of the fact that he considered the Gospels as simple texts. He assumes a tension that we will come to recognize as a key strategy as to how the simplicity of the Scriptures was coped with by erudite Christians: The unlearned apostles are seen as substantiating the divine inspiration of the texts. There is a mutual relationship between simplicity and inspiration, corresponding to human *v.* divine. Jerome, therefore, urges his addressee to meditate upon the Scriptures, and not to let "the simplicity of the scripture [*simplicitas*] or the crudity of its vocabulary [*vilitas verborum*] offend you" (*Ep.* 53.9).[3]

This topic is continued in *Ep.* 70, where Jerome lists a number of Christians who showed their erudition in Greek philosophy and literature (4–5). The style echoes his *De Viris Illustribus*, where he demonstrates that the history of the church includes people well equipped in the classical legacy. It is worth noting that this list is preceded by polemical passages directed against Julian the Emperor, thus bringing together the literal and the historical perspectives addressed in the present chapter. The list is closed with the mentioning of Juvencus who "set forth in verse the story of Jesus, and did not shrink from forcing into metre the majestic phrases of the Gospel [*historiam Domini Salvatoris versibus explicavit...sub metri leges mittere*]." It is worth noting that Jerome brings together a discussion of the appearance of Christian literature as crude in comparison to classical literature, with Juvencus' attempt to improve upon the simplicity of the Gospels; thus confirming what we saw above in Chapter 2. From this we may deduce three observations of relevance to our investigation. In the first

---

[2] On *viva vox*, see Richard Bauckham, *Jesus and the Eyewitnesses. The Gospels as Eyewitness Testimony* (Grand Rapids MI, Cambridge U.K.: Wm. B. Eerdmans Publishing Co., 2006), 21–22.

[3] Quotation from ANF where this is *Ep.* 53.10.

place, Jerome proceeds from the simplicity of the Scriptures; he makes
no real attempt to rectify this picture. Secondly, this fact forms, in
his opinion, a background against which Juvencus' attempt may be
understood. Finally, the critique and legislation of Julian is lurking
in the background here. All these observations have a bearing upon
the present investigation and are relevant to understanding the role of
fourth-century Gospel paraphrase vis-à-vis the study of the Gospels of
the first century C.E.

The New Testament itself for obvious reasons does not address the
issue at stake here, but there are texts and motifs in its midst which
became building-blocks for polemics directed against the Christian
faith in general and its literature in particular, complaining about its
simplicity and intellectual crudity. Some of these allegations can be
summarized in the following way:

- The apostles were fishermen and thereby rustics (Mark 1:17; Matt
  4:19; Luke 5:10).[4]
- The apostles were unlearned men [ἀγράμματοί] (Acts 4:13). This
  is confirmed by how Paul describes himself as untrained in public
  speaking [ἰδιώτης τῷ λόγῳ] (2 Cor 11:6).
- Paul is accordingly accused of being a babbler [σπερμολόγος] by those
  representing the classical legacy in Acts 17:18. Etymologically this
  term describes birds picking seeds from wherever they find them;
  implied is the random nature of his knowledge. The term may refer
  to gossip, which is obviously not the meaning in Acts 17. The context implies that Paul is pretending, mouthing philosophical jargon
  without much understanding; that is, engaging in flattery or bluffing
  without any foundation.[5]
- Biblical passages indicating that Christian faith is for the unlearned,
  such as Matt 11:25–27; 1 Cor 1–2.[6]

Critics took advantage of such texts, and threw them in the face of the
believers. But allegations of the simplicity of the Gospels echoed feel-
ings of uncertainty and perplexity on the part of Christian intellectuals

---

[4] The rhetorical effect of this fact has been pointed out by G.J.M. Bartelink, "Sermo
Piscatorius. Die Visserstaal van den Aposteln", *Studia Catholica* 35 (1960).
[5] See LSJ and BAGD s.v. In modern terminology, Paul might be accused of being
merely a Wikipedia surfer.
[6] See Sandnes, *The Challenge of Homer*, 152–7, 200–1.

themselves. The allegations cited here were truly their Achilles' heel. Such
Christian intellectuals were, therefore, keen on developing strategies to
deal with the issue. The following will argue that the criticism uttered by
outsiders actually mirrors a Christian embarrassment as to the Gospels,
especially so among the élite. This is important for understanding the
biblical *paraphrasis* that came to life in the 4th and 5th centuries.

The question of the literary quality of the Gospels is often found
embedded in larger debates on the trustworthiness of the Christian
faith in general. The issue of the Gospels was therefore subordinated to
either apotreptic or protreptic arguments on a wider scale. Accordingly,
the texts to be investigated do not always target the Gospels *per
se*, but include them in a wider context of refutation or defence of
Christianity. In the famous *Ep.* 22 about his vision, in which the conflict between the literary quality of the Christian texts and classical
legacy is encapsulated,[7] Jerome says that the prophets appeared to him
as *sermo incultus* when compared with Plautus (*Ep.* 22.30/PL 22.416).
It would be misleading to take this as a dictum applied solely to the
prophets. To Jerome, as to most contemporary Christians, the pro-
phetical books were Christian books precisely because they witnessed
to Jesus. Keeping the prophets and the Gospels together therefore followed from his fundamental theological conviction about the fulfilment of prophecies. From this it follows that this text has a bearing
also on how Jerome viewed the Gospels as literary products.

John Granger Cook has elaborated how pagans conceived of the
Gospels and the traditions found in them.[8] In the material presented
by him it is possible to distinguish between the following types of
criticism:

- Historical arguments: the historicity and accuracy of the Gospels are
  questioned. These stories are fictitious, not true history. The stories
  are invented by unreliable witnesses; some events display sorcery.
- There are contradictions and inconsistencies between the Old and
  New Testament, and even within the Gospels themselves.

---

[7] See Sandnes, *The Challenge of Homer*, 196–9.
[8] See his "Some Hellenistic Responses to the Gospels and Gospel Tradition", *ZNW*
84 (1993) and "The Protreptic Power of Early Christian Language from John to
Augustine", *VC* 48 (1994); both articles are now embedded in his *The Interpretation
of the New Testament in Graeco-Roman Paganism* (Peabody MA: Hendrickson
Publishers, 2002).

- Philosophical implications found in the Gospels are questionable. This applies particularly to the claim of Jesus' divinity and to his resurrection.
- Morality: Christianity implies overturning the *mores parentum*, ancestral mores. Traditional life and values are jeopardized.
- Social status: The apostles were men of no education, and, accordingly, they attracted simpletons.

All these points have a bearing upon the Gospels. This is especially clear from how the rhetorical *topos* of consequence is applied. When combined with allegations that Christians were simple people, slaves, women and children, the rusticity of the apostles becomes an argument of persuasive force: by necessity simpletons attract similar people, and text produced in this environment is consequently not to praised. A Christian author named Eusebius[9] responded to Hierocles, a leading figure among the critics at the time of Diocletian. In his *Treatise* 2, Eusebius quotes Hierocles saying that "the tales of Jesus have been vamped up [κεκομπάκασιν] by Peter and Paul and a few others of the kind—men who were liars and devoid of education (ἀπαίδευτοι) and wizards."[10] The rhetorical force of this statement is quite clear: The Gospels mirror the people who wrote them and proclaimed their story. Apostles and their texts correlate in literary and rhetorical standards. The Greek κομπάζω certainly has an ironical ring, for the word means renowned or boasting; when unlearned men speak highly of the Gospels, what more is then to be expected than simple texts?! Hierocles contrasts this with the story of the *Life of Apollonius of Tyana*, composed by Philostratus, a man of highest παίδευσις, and handed down by reliable witnesses. Criticism of the apostles here clearly spills over into criticism of the Gospels themselves and *vice versa*. Although the literary style of the Gospels in comparison with classical literature does not play a prominent role in the criticism summarized above, the following will demonstrate that this is implied. We now turn to some specific texts to substantiate the claims to be made in this chapter.

---

[9] T. Hägg, "Hierocles the Lover of Truth and Eusebius the Sophist", *SO* 67 (1992) has thrown serious doubts on the traditional identification with Eusebius the Historian.

[10] For this *Treatise*, see F.C. Coneybeare ed. and trans., *Philostratus. The Life of Apollonius of Tyana. The Epistles of Apollonius and the Treatise of Eusebius*, LCL (Cambridge MA, London: Harvard University Press, 1969), 488–605. The actual text is found on pp. 488–9. In C.P. Jones' new edition (LCL 2005), the *Treatise* is left out.

3.1.1 *Origen* Contra Celsum

In his refutation of Celsus, Origen enters a discussion on the nature of
Christian faith, whether it is barbarian or not (*Cels.* 1.2). This immediately leads to the question how someone trained in Greek doctrines and
learning would judge the Christian gospel [ὁ λόγος]. Origen answers
with reference to rhetorical proofs [ἀπόδειξις]:[11] Truth is appreciated
by practice as well, which corresponds to what Origen finds in 1 Cor
2:4, the demonstration of Spirit and power. This is the only proof by
which Christian faith can be truly appreciated. The question of Greek
learning is thus introduced as a perspective from which Origen views
the Gospels.[12] His text reflects the fact that the social status of Christians
was seen as revelatory of the nature of their texts. Literature, literary
refinement and style were important factors in how people were viewed
socially, culturally and intellectually in antiquity. This is demonstrated
in Aulus Gellius *Noct. Att.* 9.9. A Spaniard is here considered both
barbarus and *agrestis* ("barbaric and rustic") since he did not comply
with the literary style of those Greeks who were present, although he
was a learned person. This attitude affected the Christians powerfully;
thanks to their own Gospels.

The question of lack of classical style and legacy in Christian proclamation, to which the Gospels certainly belong, is elaborated upon
in *Cels.* 6.1–7. Celsus compared texts from the Scriptures with Plato,
reaching the conclusion that the ideas are much better expressed
among the Greeks. From *Cels.* 7.59, we know that such comparisons
were among the methods applied by Celsus. To Celsus, the divinity of
Jesus was a claim designed to hide the fact that Christian literature was
indeed crude (*Cels.* 6.1). Clearly Plato here stands for the Greek legacy
in general, of which Homer was a prominent part. It is not, therefore,
an accident that he is mentioned in *Cels.* 6.7. This is, of course, not to
deny that Origen knew perfectly well that Plato rejected Homer from
his ideal of juvenal education.[13] The simple style of the Christian texts
forms the starting point of the passage. *Cels.* 6.2 states explicitly that
the dispute is about the mean style of the Scriptures, since this is exactly

---

[11] This is also the term used also by Paul in 1 Cor 2:4.

[12] Similarly in *Cels.* 1.18, although there he speaks about the laws of Moses. But
clearly Jesus is implied as well. For Moses was far superior to the poets and philosophers of the Greeks, and Jesus superseded Moses. Here also the proof lies in the
persuasive effect that the words have upon the listeners (the rhetorical argument of
consequence).

[13] *Cels.* 4.36; 7.54 cf. *Resp.* 379 C-D.

what Celsus and others hold against the Christian literature [περὶ τῆς κατηγορουμένης ὑπὸ Κέλσου καὶ ἑτέρων ἐν λέξεσιν εὐτελείας τῶν γραφῶν]. The Greek εὐτέλεια means shabby, mean or cheap.[14]

Cels. 6.1 states briefly and pointedly what will later be elaborated on. Origen takes advantage of Celsus' frequently reiterated view of the Christians as simpletons[15] by moulding this into the rhetorical proof of consequence.[16] With words of a seemingly shabby style [ἀπορρήτως εἰρημένα], the prophets as well as Jesus—thus confirming that the Gospels are implied in this discussion—were able to make a difference in the life of common people. The shabby Gospels brought improvement of the lives of ordinary people. Plato and his companions benefit a minority only, the intellectual few. Origen cites as proof texts 1 Cor 1:27–29 and 1 Cor 2:4–5:[17]

> And notice that, though what Plato said was true, it did not help his readers towards a pure religion at all, nor even Plato himself, in spite of the fact that he taught profound philosophy about the highest good. But the mean style of the divine scriptures [ἡ δὲ τῶν θείων γραμμάτων εὐτελὴς λέξις] has made honest readers inspired by it (*Cels.* 6.5).[18]

As did Jerome, Origen also takes advantage of the crudity of the Gospels. The Achilles' heel is turned into an argument.

3.1.2 *Origen* De Principiis

This major work is reckoned as the first attempt at putting together "A Christian Theology, although the genre is very much that of a traditional philosophical handbook."[19] Some passages are preserved in Greek through Origen's *Philocalia*; the whole work has come down to

---

[14] See LSJ s.v.

[15] See Cook, *New Testament in Graeco-Roman Paganism*, 82–88; Sandnes, *The Challenge of Homer*, 149–52.

[16] Cf. Cook, "The Protreptic Power of Early Christian Language from John to Augustine", 111–3. This argument is described by Aristotle in e.g. *Rhet.* 1.6.7; 1.23.14; arguments from the best consequence or benefit are persuasive. Paul makes use of a related kind of argument in his Galatian dispute as to the question of embracing Jewish ritual laws (Gal 3:1–5). He argues from the effects that their faith, prior to this demand, had on their lives.

[17] For the role of these texts in Celsus' polemics, see Sandnes, *The Challenge of Homer*, 152–7.

[18] Quoted from Henry Chadwick, trans., *Origen. Contra Celsum*, (Cambridge: Cambridge University Press, 1965). The same chain of arguments is found in *Cels.* 7.58–61.

[19] See e.g. Herwig Görgemanns und Heinrich Karpp, ed., *Vier Bücher von den Prinzipien* (Darmstadt: Wissenschaftliche Buchgesellschaft, 1976), 9–19.

us in Rufinus' Latin translation.[20] Book 4.1.1–27 deals extensively with
the divine inspiration of the Scriptures: *ostendere quod ipsae scripturae
divinae sint, id est dei spiritu inspiratae* (293.19–20).[21] This is the theological context of statements about Christian literature and proclamation
works. Clearly these statements are embedded in a rhetorical or rational
argument as well [ἀποδείξεως λογικῆς] (293.13). The argument is built
on the contrast between the human and the divine. This contrast runs
throughout the whole discussion, and the argument revolves around
their mutual relationship. This contrast forms a unified argument for
the divine nature of the Scripture.

The human side of this reciprocity consists primarily of three
related arguments. The first is the low status of most Christians, witnessed to in the Old Testament, which says that God will speak to a
foolish people (Deut 32:21),[22] and in the New Testament itself (1 Cor
1:26–28). The second is the fact that the apostles and their followers were unlearned men. The Greek text of *Philocalia* mentions only
the scarcity of teachers; they were not many relative to the enormous
growth of Christianity. Rufinus, however, gives more information and
reads: *vel satis idonei sunt vel satis plures* ("they [= *doctores*] were neither clever nor many") (295.17).

Thirdly, the crude style of the Christian scriptures themselves bears
witness to their human side. The vulgar, unpolished and unattractive
style of biblical texts is emphasized when Origen speaks of the splendour veiled in shabby and contemptible phraseology [ἐν εὐτελεῖ καὶ
εὐκαταφρονήτῳ λέξει ἀποκειμένη] (4.1.7/304.3). Rufinus reads: "the
treasure of divine wisdom hidden in vulgar and unpolished vessels of
words" [*in vilioribus et incomptis verborum vasculis divinae sapien-
tiae thesaurus absconditur*] (304.18–19), echoing even more clearly the
Pauline motif of treasures hidden in earthen vessels (2 Cor 4:7–12).

The divine side of the Christian texts, however, can be seen as
Origen's interpretation of Paul's words in 1 Cor 2:5 about the persuasive force, not of his words, but of the demonstration of Spirit and
power. Origen's argument is threefold. In the first place, signs and

---

[20] Lothar Lies, *Origenes' 'Peri Archon.' Eine undogmatische Dogmatik* (Darmstadt: Wissenschaftliche Buchgesellschaft, 1992), 25–26.

[21] I am using the textual edition of Görgemanns and Karpp.

[22] The LXX text has: ἐπ' ἔθνει ἀσυνέτῳ. Origen mentions that Paul cites this text in Rom 10:19, but not with the Christian application that Origen gives it here. Origen's argument is clearly rhetorical since he later says that both wise and foolish have embraced the Christian faith.

wonders testified to the truth of Christian faith (4.1.5). Origen here says that the "words of the apostles" testified in this way. The Greek text has the plural οἱ λογοί followed by the plural genitive αὐτῶν (301.7), while Rufinus' Latin has the singular *verbum* without any genitive. Rufinus seems to have turned Origen's use of Acts 2:43; 5:12 (cf Heb 2:4) about God testifying to the words of the apostles through miracles by their hands, into a statement about God's Word or Scripture in general. The argument from divine power echoes ancient thinking on diviners whose inspiration might be considered a proof. Origen, in fact, draws attention to this similarity himself in 3.3.3, saying that it is a common belief among the Greeks that even poets were filled with a kind of madness: *artem poêticam sine insania non posse constare* ("poetry could not exist without madness") (259.10–11).[23] Thus Origen thought that his argument based on 1 Cor 2:5 was not entirely out of touch with principles commonly agreed upon.

The second argument is the fulfilment of prophecy (4.1.2–3). Although true and inspired, the words of Moses were not proved to be so before the coming of Christ (4.1.6). We are thus reminded of the close connection between the Old Testament and the Gospels running through this discussion.[24] Finally, the acceptance and growth of Christianity is seen as indicative of the inspiration of their Scriptures (4.1.2; 4.1.5). This argument works in tandem only with the arguments of the human side. It is precisely because of the weaknesses pointed out above that the growth can be taken to be a sign of inspiration. This dual aspect Origen holds together with the help of a Pauline text, namely 2 Cor 4:7 about the treasure hidden in earthen vessels (4.1.7). Origen finds this to be an accurate description of the Biblical texts themselves, naturally including the Gospels. To this Pauline text he adds another metaphor from the Apostle, that of the veil (2 Cor 3) (4.1.6), but the meaning of this text is altered. The veil is no longer a reference to the Jews and the Mosaic Law, but to the literary style of the Scriptures, thus emphasizing this as the proper starting point of the whole discussion.[25]

---

[23] References in Görgemanns und Karpp, ed., *Vier Bücher von den Prinzipien*, 593 n. 13. This is pointed out also by Cook, "The Protreptic Power of Early Christian Language from John to Augustine", 121–3. This picture of the poets corresponds with the dual use of *vates*, noticed in Juvencus' preface (see Chapter 2).

[24] Pointed out also by Lies, *Peri Archon*, 31–32.

[25] See Henri Crouzel et Manlio Simonetti, ed. and trans., *Origène Traité des Principes Tome IV* (Paris: Cerf, 1980), 101–2.

This brings a duality into the Scriptures, a duality paving the way for the idea of God's pedagogy, whereby the Scriptures might be read both literary and allegorically, according to the intellectual level of the readers themselves. According to *De Principiis* 4.2.4 (312.1–314.5), Origen says that the sacred text is tripartite, composed of body, soul and mind, like the human body. He develops this idea from Prov 22:20LXX, where the reader is urged to listen carefully to the words of wise men. Their words are to be written three times on the tablets of the heart. "Three times" [τρισσῶς/*tripliciter*] is not found in the Hebrew text. From this, Origen deduces a principle of reading Scriptures in a threefold way. The literal meaning, labelled σάρξ τῆς γραφῆς, is for the building up of the simple-minded [ὁ ἁπλούστερος/*simpliciores*]. Thus every individual can understand divine Scripture at the level that suits him. From 4.1.9 this idea dominates the picture.[26] For Origen, the intent of the sacred text did not lay in the literary level, or in its words. Frances M. Young puts this aptly, saying that "consistency lay not in the text and its wording, but in the deeper spiritual realities to which the text referred."[27] This attitude naturally paved the way for a text not as given, but "open" to fresh and new meanings. Although cento composition is not in sight here, the very attitude taken to the texts by Origen opens up for ways to bend them.

3.1.3   *Lactantius'* The Divine Institutes

L. Caecilus Firmianus Lactantius is thought to have lived about 250–325 C.E.[28] In his *Inst.* 1.5.2 Lactantius says that the poets and philosophers are used against the Christians: *contra nos uti solent.*[29] This is precisely the reason that the argument must proceed "from them"; not because they have the truth, but they have the power to persuade. In *Inst.* 3.1.11–12, he reasons differently, stating that rhetoric must be seen as an attempt to conceal false wisdom in fine words, and applies this directly to the relationship between human and divine words. Rhetoric and discussion [*argumentari*] are not God's business; God is supreme, and He alone

---

[26] Lies, *Peri Archon*, 36–44.

[27] Frances M. Young, *Biblical Exegesis and the Formation of Christian Culture* (Peabody, MA: Hendrickson Publishers, 2002), 184.

[28] See Bowen and Garnsey, trans., Lactantius. *Divine Institutes*, 1–6.

[29] The Latin text is from Samuel Brandt, ed., *L. Caeli Lactanti, Divinae Institutiones et Epitome Divinarum Institutionum.* CSEL (Prague, Vindobonae, Lipsiae: F. Tempsky, G. Freytag, 1890). A text is also available in SC; see bibliography.

has the right to pronounce [*pronuntiare*]. This view paves the way for separating the Biblical texts from the Graeco-Roman literary legacy. This calls for a discussion, especially since in the preface of this writing (1.1.10) Lactantius made rhetoric and style a means whereby the power of Christian faith becomes persuasive. To this discussion Lactantius turns more fully in Book 5.1, where he summarizes how the Scriptures were estimated by erudite outsiders.[30]

The style of the Scriptures separates them from that of poets and philosophers. The latter spoke and wrote in order to delight their audience with polished and eloquent words, and this included the danger of being ensnared: "Philosophy, oratory and poetry are all pernicious for the ease with which they ensnare incautious souls in beguiling prose and the nice modulations of poetical flow [*quod incautos animos facile inretrire possunt suavitate sermonis et carminum dulci modulatione currentium*]" (5.1.10). Erudite people valued the Scriptures by looking at their embellishment [*ornatus*], or lack thereof, not by the truth to be found in them. It is evident that the nature of this argument is indeed rhetorical, inasmuch as it implies the classical idea of eloquence and *res*, which to Lactantius is conceived in terms of *veritas*. The erudite despised the Scriptures as being written in a common and simple style of speech, composed for the common people, the *plebs*:

> This is the principal reason why holy scripture lacks the trust of the wise, both scholars [*apud sapientes et doctos*] and princes of this world: its prophets have spoken to suit ordinary folk, in plain and ordinary language [*communi ac simplici sermone ut ad populum sunt locuti*]; they thus earn the contempt of people who will not read or hear anything not polished and eloquent [*nisi expolitum ac disertum*]. Nothing sticks in such people's minds unless it soothes their ears with its smoothness, and anything seeming coarse they think is stuff of old women, stupid and vulgar. Anything rough on the ears they assume is untrue, and nothing is credible unless it provides aesthetic pleasure; they weigh by garb and not by truth [*nemo rem veritate ponderat, sed ornatu*]. Hence their disbelief in God's word, because it wears no make up... (*Inst.* 5.1.15–18).

The Biblical texts had not been given any colour or beauty. Lactantius says this with reference to Lucretius, who addresses his own writings as being touched with the Muses' delicious honey [*quasi musaeo dulci*

---

[30] See also *Inst.* 5.3.1–3.

contingere melle] (*De Rerum Natura* 1.921–50).[31] The Muses add honey
to the wormwood [*absinthium*] of his writing, just like children are
deluded by the physicians' adding of honey to their bitter drugs. Such
is not the case with the Biblical texts; they are indeed *absinthium*, but
with no honey added to them. They were, according to Lactantius' text
given above, humble [*sordida*], and therefore considered old-womanish
[*anilia*],[32] foolish [*inepta*] and vulgar [*vulgaria*]. In his use of Lucretius,
Lactantius draws on the rhetorical distinction between *res* or *sensus* and
eloquentia, which will become important as we proceed.

We saw above that in his criticism of the Scriptures Celsus proceeded
from how the apostles appeared as unlearned men. A similar line of
thought can be traced in Lactantius' presentation of the erudite critics
as well; some of their sentiments echo Celsus' critique.[33] Their contempt
is not only directed against the Scriptures, but includes the instructors
in Christian faith as well, who were themselves not educated men or
only slightly so [*rudes aut certe parum docti*] (5.1.18). Worth noting
is that Lactantius introduces his presentation on the humble appearance of the Scriptures by saying: "Most people waver, especially those
of any attainment in literature [*maxime qui litterarum*]" (*Inst.* 5.1.9).
Anthony Bowen and Peter Garnsey rightly comment that this is a hint
that Lactantius is targeting not only erudite pagans, but also Christians
who were having doubts about their Scriptures, because of their inferiority as literature.[34]

Inst. 5.2.12–17 mentions Hierocles and his anti-Christian writing "The Lover of Truth" (*Philaletheis*), aimed at deconstructing
the Gospels. For our topic it is significant that Lactantius brings
into his discussion the point made by Hierocles that Peter and Paul
both were *rudes* ("untrained") *and indocti* ("unlearned"), even *pis-
catores* ("fishermen").[35] There is then a chain of intimate correspondence between the apostles—Christian Scriptures and contemporary
Christian instructors; they all fail to stand the test of classical legacy

---

[31] See Pierre Monat, ed. and trans., *Lactance. Institutions Divines. Livre V Tome II*
(Paris: Cerf, 1973), 28–29.

[32] Clearly in a contemptuous sense; see OLD s.v.; for the proverbial nature of this
indictment, see Monat, ed. and trans., *Lactance. Institutions Divines. Livre V Tome
II*, 27–28, 42.

[33] Sandnes, *The Challenge of Homer*, 149–58.

[34] Bowen and Garnsey, trans., *Lactantius. Divine Institutes*, 282.

[35] This hardly applies to Paul, but in polemics 'anything goes'. Lactantius himself
conducts harsh polemics against Hierocles in *Inst.* 5.3.

and erudition. John G. Cook has given a fine presentation of Hierocles'
criticism of the Gospels,[36] but he pays no attention to one piece of
information rendered by Lactantius: This critic, who was also an insti-
gator of persecutions of the Christians, was once a Christian himself.[37]
His betrayal of his Christian faith made it impossible even for someone like Demosthenes—the best advocate possible—to defend him
from the charge of *inpietas*. He became a *proditor* of the religion "that
inspired him, traitor to faith whose name he adopted, and traitor to
the sacred mysteries he accepted" (*Inst.* 5.2.15). The text is probably
formed in accordance with baptismal traditions as well as those of the
Holy Communion. It is difficult to know the veracity of this piece of
information; to my knowledge it is not known from any other source.
Furthermore, Lactantius himself presents another possible explanation:
Nisi forte casu ("if not, for another reason") introduces another possibility; that the Christian texts came into his hands by mere chance.
The latter is probably the more likely. However, it is worth pondering
upon the fact that Lactantius considers it a possibility that someone
might, in fact, turn from being a Christian to become a persecutor; i.e.
a reverse Paul. If Lactantius considers this possibility with Hierocles,
what would then likely be the reason for his abandonment of faith? In
the possibility set up here, we might have an example of someone who
was so embarrassed by the mean Gospels that he apostatised. I emphasize that this is a theoretical construct, not necessarily biographically
correct. Nonetheless, this construct is present in Lactantius' text, and
draws out the serious implications the "rude" Gospels might have had
for Christians trained in the literary legacy.

The Divine Institutes leaves us with a picture of an ambivalent
Lactantius. He knows that the persuasiveness of Christian faith
and Scriptures rely on style and rhetoric. In *Inst.* 3.1.2 he says that
he wished [*vellem*] that the Scriptures met these requirements, but
God wanted it [*deus voluit*] differently: "truth is to be more glorious by being plain and unadorned, for it is well enough equipped as
it is, and addition of extraneous ornament only masks and corrupts

---

[36] Cook, *The New Testament in Greco-Roman Paganism*, 250–76. See also Wolfgang
Speyer "Hierokles I", *RAC* 15:103–9.
[37] Neither does Monat, ed. and trans., *Lactance. Institutions Divines, Livre V Tome
II* pay much attention to this, but he notes briefly that "C'est peut-être un renégat—
dans ce cas, il est impardonnable—ou peut-être les a-t-il [i.e. les saints Ecritures] con-
nues par hazard, et dans ce cas il est bien téméraire de se hazarder à les commenter",
which is pretty much what Lactantius says himself (p. 44).

it..." (3).[38] *Eloquentia* and *veritas* follow separate rules, says Lactantius. The idea of a divine pedagogy found in Origen above, is not spelled out here, but this seems to be the theological notion able to cope with Lactantius' ambivalence here. *Inst.* 6.21.4–6 comes very close to doing this. Songs and well-polished speeches lead people's mind astray, he says: "Hence the reduced faith of educated people who have come to worship God through the teaching of someone comparatively uneducated" (4). But this is part of God's plan [*providentia*] "to make things plain deliberately, so that this universal message would be universally understood [*ut omnes intellegerent quae ipse omnibus loquebatur*]" (6). Lactantius thus turns the crudity of the Gospels, in terms of *verba*, into proof of their inspired *res* or *sensus*.

3.1.4   Augustine

In Book 3 of his *Confessions*, Augustine tells us about his life as a student at Carthage. At an early age he was taught rhetoric, *libri eloquentiae* (3.4.7). He adds a personal and retrospective note, namely that this served his private delight in vanity. This is a remark which becomes important in Augustine's dealings with the literary style of the Bible. However, Cicero's *Hortensius*[39]—which he considered the peak of *eloquentia*—made a deep impression on him, not primarily for its *eloquentia*, but for what [*quod*] was stated so well. This, it should be noted carefully, equals the distinction between style and *res*. The *res* of the Christian texts is the divinity of Christ, given in e.g. Col 2:8–9 (*Conf.* 3.4.8). The fact that Christ's name failed to appear in *Hortensius* put a strain on his enthusiasm: "Any book which lacked this name, however well written or polished or true [*quamvis litteratum, et expolitum et veridicum*] could not entirely grip me."[40]

When Augustine then took up the studies of the Scriptures, from which he expected so much, he was disappointed: "And this is what met me: something neither open to the proud nor laid bare to mere children; a text lowly to the beginner [*incessu humilem*], but on further reading, of mountainous difficulty and enveloped in mysteries"

---

[38] The Latin text goes like this: *ut simplex et nuda veritas esset luculentior, quia satis ornata per se est ideoque ornamentis extrinsecus additis fucata corrumpitur.*

[39] Now lost; some parts have survived as citations, many in Augustine's texts.

[40] Quotation from Henry Chadwick, trans., *Saint Augustine. Confessions* (Oxford, New York: Oxford University Press, 1991).

(*Conf.* 3.5.9). In short, compared to Cicero they were *indigna*, unworthy. Enters now the *vanitas* which was introduced above; Augustine did not find the *modus* of the Bible satisfying to what, looking back, he called his puffed-up pride [*tumor meus*].[41] The mean style of the Bible did not nourish the prideful ambitions of the Carthaginian student. But he describes how he came to realize that he hated to be *parvulus*, a little one; instead he had seen himself as a "bigshot" [*turgidus*].[42] For this reason he failed to understand that the Scriptures were composed in a way that made it possible for beginners to mature.

In his argument there is thus an element of divine pedagogy about levels to be unfolded in the Scriptures. There is certainly also a Pauline legacy here, about the danger of boasting.[43] The idea of a divine pedagogy is found also in *Conf.* 6.5.8. What first appeared to him as offensive absurdities [*absurditatem, quae me in illis litteris solebat offendere*], he came, with renewed reading, to understand as profound secrets, hidden in plain sight, concealed in a style of speaking which is very humble [*verbis apertissimis et humilio genere loquendi*], but precisely for this reason addressing those who are not light of heart [*non sunt leves corde*]. Augustine's argument is predominantly theologically, not to say christologically, motivated. The absurdities in Christian literature, Augustine initially found offensive, but they were revealing as to the *res*.

The christological emphasis, *res* itself, brings to mind his presentation of Platonist writings in *Conf.* 7.7–10. We touched above upon the relationship between eloquence and *res* in Lactantius; this is a stock rhetorical idea. This Augustinian passage certainly converges in many ways on the passage presented above. At the centre stands venerable pagan literature *v.* the Bible, and the pride of learned men. The pride is described as *cum superbe*,[44] *tumor meus*, *inflata facies*,[45] and *turgidus*. The reading of Biblical passages on humility paved the way to a new understanding. A key point in his argument is the well-known contrastive reading of Platonist literature and the Prologue of John's Gospel.

---

[41] In this context, *tumor* owes much to the Pauline idea of carnal flesh; see Jeffrey T. Schnapp, "Reading Lessons. Augustine, Proba, and the Christian *Detournement* of Antiquity", *Stanford Literary Review* 9 (1992): 101–2.

[42] This Latin term has the notion of something swollen up; see OLD s.v.

[43] See 1 Cor 1:31; 2 Cor 10:17. For the role of pride and ambition with regard to Augustine's attitude towards learning, see Sandnes, *The Challenge of Homer*, 217.

[44] "With arrogance" or "arrogantly."

[45] A swollen face that prevented the eyes from seeing properly.

The two bodies of literature indeed correspond in many ways,[46] but the key point of the prologue fails to appear in any pagan literature: That the Logos came to his own, was not received, and that the Logos gave them the power to become sons of God by believing in his name "I did not read there" (*Conf.* 7.9.13). That Logos was born not of flesh but of God and dwelt among men, "I did not read there" (*Conf.* 7.9.14). That Logos took upon himself the form of a servant and emptied himself, appeared in the likeness of men and was obedient to the death of the cross,[47] "that these books do not have"[48] (*Conf.* 7.9.14). Hence "those who, like actors, wear the high boots of a supposedly more sublime teaching [*doctrinae sublimioris elati*] do not hear him who says 'Learn of me, that I am meek and humble in heart, and you shall find rest for your souls' (Matt 11:29)" (*Conf.* 7.9.14). This passage clearly speaks of the quality of the Scriptures as defined primarily by Christology, what they have to say about Christ.

Augustine reasons, like other intellectual believers, within the parameters set by ancient rhetoric, those of the relationship between eloquence and content. In his *Orator*, Cicero represents the perfect speaker. At the end of this work, he summarizes it all as the relationship between style, rhythm and content. "…to speak with well-knit rhythm without ideas [*sine sententiis*] is folly, to present ideas without order and rhythm in the language is to be speechless [*sententiose autem sine verborum et ordine et modo infantia*]." True eloquence [*eloquens vero*] is to excel in all matters [*omnibus rebus*]; this also brings not only admiration and applause, but a true hearing (*Orat.* 236). Most Christians found a way out of this challenge by making a theological point out of the lack of balance between the two in the Gospels, while some others, like the centonists, did their best to present the stories of Jesus within *both* parameters set by Cicero in this passage.

Augustine adhered, more or less, to the theological construction. This finds corroboration in his *Doctrina Christiana* as well; particularly so in the section on the inspiration and *eloquentia* of the Scriptures (4.25–60). His presentation here can be summarized briefly in his own

---

[46] This fact Augustine explains with the help of the *topos* 'the spoil of the Egyptians' (Exod 3:22; 11:2) (*Conf.* 7.9.15) which allegorically justified the use of pagan traditions in a Christian setting; see Sandnes, *The Challenge of Homer*, 222–6 with further references.

[47] The prologue of John is here combined with Phil 2:6–11.

[48] …*non habent illi libri*. Augustine continues his comparison; enters now Rom 8:32 (that God had his Son die for the wicked).

words in *Doctr. chr.* 4.26: "It is appropriate to them [i.e. the spokes-men of God], and the humbler it seems, the more thoroughly it tran-scends that of others, not in grandiloquence but in substance [*non ventosiate sed soliditate*]."[49]

In his *First Catechetical Instruction*, Augustine gives advice to Deogratias, an instructor himself, on how to cope with the boredom involved in instructing the catechumens (*Cathec.* 1). Two chapters are devoted to the question of instructing students who are educated in literature and rhetoric (chaps. 8–9). One of the issues being addressed here is what to these students will appear as the weakness [*infirmitas*] of Scripture (*Cathec.* 8.12.3). Augustine's *Sermo* 87.12 summarizes the argument presented here:

> That's why the Lord to help us make light of the friendship of powerful people for our very salvation, didn't want to choose senators first, but fishermen [*Noluit (sc. Deus) prius eligere senators, sed piscatores*]. What wonderful skilful mercy…If he choose an orator first, the orator would say, 'I was chosen for my eloquence'… 'Give me first,' he says, 'this fisherman. Come here ye poor man, follow me. You have nothing, you know nothing, follow me. Common, uneducated poor man [*idiota pau-per*], follow, me…(now Augustine is quoting from 1 Cor 1:27–28).' To conclude, the words of these fishermen are still read, the necks of orators are brought low [*Denique leguntur verba piscatorum et colla subduntur oratorum*].[50]

The crudity of the Gospels, their lack of eloquence, becomes part of a theological argument. The crude nature of these texts makes theological reasoning necessary, out of which comes a sense of pride. Developing some strategies was therefore vital to educated Christians, like Augustine himself. One of these was to highlight the divine inspiration by down-playing the human efforts in the Scriptures: ἀγράμματοι served to prove θεοδίδακτοί. Taken to the extreme, this theology of divine inspiration in contradistinction to any human achievement, would lead to theories of "holy illiteracy" and "sinful eloquence."[51]

---

[49] Translation from Roger P.H. Green, ed. and trans., *Augustine. De Doctrina Christiana* (Oxford: Clarendon Press, 1995). For a discussion on style and content in Augustine, see Peter Gemeinhardt, *Das lateinische Christentum und die pagane Bildung* (Tübingen: Mohr Siebeck, 2007), 337–49.

[50] Quoted from Edmond Hill, trans., *Sermons III (51–94)* (Brooklyn, New York: New City Press, 1991). The Latin text is from PL 38.537.

[51] See Robert A. Kaster, *Guardians of Language. The Grammarian and Society in Late Antiquity* (Berkeley, CA: University of California Press, 1983), 79–80.

Summing up, we may say that the texts we have presented demonstrate a mixed situation: in the midst of embarrassment on the part of
the Gospels, we observe a sense of pride as well. They turn a drawback
into an advantage: the lack of classical style and legacy in the Gospels
are given both a theological and pedagogical solution: divine inspiration and mean style serve the purpose of winning over common
people.[52] For the present investigation it is important to note that this
situation must have tempted some to try to make a symbiosis of the
two legacies. W. Evenepoel observes that towards the 4th century the
literary value of biblical texts are gradually being pointed out.[53] Jerome,
a man of many ambiguities,[54] says that David is "our Simonides,[55] and
Pindar, Alcaios,[56] our Flaccus (= Horace), Catullus and Serenus,[57] all in
one" (*Ep.* 53.7/PL 22.547). This certainly contradicts what Jerome says
elsewhere, but this tension in fact characterizes the situation precisely.
Also Augustine illustrates rhetorical style with biblical examples. This
double background, embarrassment but also a sense of growing pride,
is the background against which we must understand the attempts
of the 4th century to rewrite the story of Jesus in classical idioms.
Although those who did try to build literary bridges between the two
bodies of literature were by no means like Tertullian,[58] they may well
have said the same as he said in his *De Testimoni Animae* 1: "Far less
do people assent to our writings, to which no one comes for guidance
unless he is already a Christian [*nemo venit nisi iam Christianus*]."[59]
Tertullian says this in a passage contrasting Scripture with the writings

---

[52] When addressing the contrast between the beauty of Greek literature and the
simple style of the books of the Christians, Origen says that the latter are "cooked
for the multitude" (*Cels.* 7.59); see Theo Kobusch, "Philosophische Streitsachen. Zur
Auseinandersetzung zwischen christlicher und griechischer Philosophie," in *Kaiser
Julian 'Apostata' und die philosophische Reaktion gegen das Christentum*, ed. Christian
Schäfer (Berlin: Walter de Gruyter, 2008), 30–32.
[53] W. Evenepoel, "The Place of Poetry in Latin Christianity", in *Early Christian
Poetry. A Collection of Essays*, ed. J. Den Boeft and A. Hilhorst (Leiden: Brill, 1993),
40 with further references.
[54] See Sandnes, *The Challenge of Homer*, 201–5.
[55] Greek poet of the 6/5th century B.C.E, see *Der Neue Pauly* 11:574–6.
[56] Mythical figure; *Der Neue Pauly* 1:493–6.
[57] Sometimes between 3rd/4th century B.C.E.; wrote medical works in hexameter,
may be this is what caught Jerome's address, *Der Neue Pauly* 11:451–2.
[58] His highly ambivalent attitude to the classical legacy is well-known; see Sandnes,
The Challenge of Homer, 111–23.
[59] Quoted from ANF; for the Latin text see R. Willems, ed. *De Testimonio Animae*
(CCSL 1; Turnholt: Brepols, 1955), 175.30–31.

of the poets and philosophers. He thus points up the isolated status of Christian literature compared to the ancient literary legacy.

It is important to notice that some of our sources belong to the period when epic gospels and Christian *centones* came to life. A complex picture emerges. The Scriptures of the Christians were not a match for the classics stylistically. The Gospels were of a mean style compared to the classical legacy, but it was precisely this fact that permitted the claim that they were inspired. From this we learn that the picture given here is theologically motivated. It would be misleading, however, to take this picture as being all there is to be said about the Gospels from a literary point of view. The relevance of Hellenistic rhetorical traditions to the reading of the Gospels has been amply demonstrated by recent research.[60] The theological argument we have seen owes equally much to current rhetorical patterns. Rhetoric as self-display, admiration and sophistry is denounced, but not the patterns of persuasion. The efficacy of Christian texts was not primarily due to their pleasing the audience, but their moving people to live a new life. The flexible literary canon in antiquity allowed for a core and periphery; it was not a matter of Homer or nothing. Not all literature was ἄριστος, but still worth reading. The Christians knew that their writings were not up to the classical standards, but they still knew how to play the game. It seems well-founded, however, to claim the Scriptures were often perceived as crude by outsiders, and even among cultivated Christians. For the present investigation it is important that this paves the way for understanding why biblical epic paraphrases and *centones* came to life. From the perspective of the "best authors" in antiquity, the Gospels could certainly be improved upon.

Mimesis Criticism argues that precisely these texts, which came into being to improve upon the simplicity of the gospels by proving them adjustable to the venerated classical style and texts, help us understand how the Gospels were composed. If the argument of this chapter is adequate, it casts doubt on the role assigned to the biblical paraphrases and centos by Mimesis Criticism. If there is some truth in claiming that the epic Gospels written in classical style were attempts at improving upon the reputation of the canonical Gospels, it is hard to understand

---

[60] The relevance of Hellenistic rhetorical tradition to the Gospels has been demonstrated by Burton L. Mack and Vernon K. Robbins, *Patterns of Persuasion in the Gospels* (Sonoma, CA: Polebridge Press, 1989).

how precisely these compositions may serve as models for how the
canonical Gospels came into being. It is rather the other way around;
the epic Gospels have the canonical Gospels as their point of departure. This will be substantiated further in the following chapters.

3.2   A Historical Reason: Julian—Emperor and Apostate (361–3 C.E.)

Encyclical education remained more or less the same throughout antiquity, primarily thanks to the role given to the literature and the epic poets
in particular.[61] In principle, therefore, this whole period provides texts
making an equal claim to be analogous to paraphrases of the classical
texts. This being said, the distance between the 4th/5th and 1st centuries
C.E. cannot be ignored. Firstly, because from Christian sources we glean
the fact that the debate and use of Homer and classical texts matured
over the centuries. In principle, therefore, it is difficult to explain the
Gospels with the help of texts of much later date. Secondly, Julian the
Emperor, the so-called Apostate, made an impact that considerably
affects our investigation. This impact far exceeds the brief duration
of his reign. It deeply affects our question: how are we to evaluate the
analogies from the 4th and 5th centuries with regard to their relevance
for the canonical Gospels? Among the analogies considered here, only
one is prior to Julian, albeit barely, namely Juvencus. In seeking an
answer to that question, I think chronology matters.

Julian was Emperor at the time of transition from paganism to
Christianity in the Roman Empire. He was raised a Christian, but was
instructed in Greek literature as well. The pagan authors made a lasting impression on Julian. When he seized power, he announced his
conversion to the ancestral traditions and gods. He later describes his
decision in a letter to his philosophy teacher: "The gods command me
to restore their worship in its outmost purity, and I obey them, yes, and
with a good will" (415D).[62] The Christian tradition therefore branded
him 'the Apostate.'[63] He saw himself as "an apologist and apostolic

---

[61] Sandnes, *The Challenge of Homer*, 16–18, 28–31.
[62] J. Bidez, ed., *L'Empereur Julien* (Paris: Les Belles Lettres, 1924) has this as text nr.
26 (*Ep.* 38); in Loeb's edition it is *Ep.* 8.
[63] For further references see Sandnes, *The Challenge of Homer*, 160–1 with notes.

father of Hellenism."[64] The Greek traditions making up the classical *paideia* he considered a unifying force for the empire, a function that also implied a revival of ancient religious practices. He targeted in particular Christians claiming a right to the Greek intellectual traditions preserved in *paideia*. Greek *paideia* could not, according to Julian, be separated from its religious basis and tradition. To get at the root of the problem, namely that Christians took advantage of the Greek intellectual legacy, Julian imposed restrictions on Christian access to school and education, and thus also to the Greek literary legacy.

3.2.1 *Restricted Access to the Classical Literature: Julian's Decree on Teaching*

The Emperor issued a law on teachers, known as the decree of 17th June 362, *Codex Theodosianus* 13.3.5.[65] In short, the law says that teachers [*magistri* or *doctores*] should excel in *mores*, and that restrictions are therefore imposed on those acting as teachers. The text is in itself not very informative; in fact, the Christians are not mentioned at all. The legal text stipulates only that teachers must excel in moral standards. As a legal text, it must therefore be interpreted within a wider context and practice.[66] The main questions involved are the following: 1) Does the decree target Christians? 2) Why does the decree focus on *mores*? 3) The decree itself imposes limitations on the activity of teaching or instructing [*docere*], while Christian sources (see below) say that it implied learning [*discere*], that is, the activity of students as well. So the question is: did the decree affect teachers only, or also children of Christian parents? Intertwined with all these questions is the issue of reconstructing historical realities. Most scholars would read this decree in the light of other Julian texts, particularly his incomplete Epistle on

---

[64] Polymnia Athanassiadi, *Julian. An Intellectual Biography* (London and New York: Routledge, 1992), 128.

[65] A translation of the decree is provided by Cook, *The Interpretation of the New Testament in Greco-Roman Paganism*, 319. For the Latin text, see text nr. 61 in Bidez, ed., *L'Empereur Julie*n, 72; a French translation is given there as well. See also Sandnes, *The Challenge of Homer*, 161.

[66] Against scholars holding the view that Julian's decree was an expression of long-standing ideals in Roman society, Gemeinhardt, *Das lateinische Christentum und die pagane Bildung*, 351–9 argues that it really was "einer Art heidnischen katechumenatunterricht" (359).

true *paideia* found in 422a–b.[67] With regard to school, teachers, and students, the legislation left many questions open for those who were to administer it, and this letter can be seen as his attempt at addressing some of the issues involved in the legal text. The epistle and the legal text are united in a common emphasis on *mores*:

> Therefore, when a man thinks one thing and teaches his pupils another, in my opinion, he fails to educate exactly in proportion as he fails to be an honest man. And if the divergence between a man's convictions and his utterances is merely in trivial matters, that can be tolerated some-how, though it is wrong. But if in matters of the greatest importance, a man has certain opinions and teaches the contrary, what is that but the conduct of hucksters, and not honest but thoroughly dissolute men in that they praise most highly the things they believe to be most worthless, thus cheating and enticing by their praises those to whom they desire to transfer their worthless wares. Now all who profess to teach anything whatever ought to be men of upright character, and ought not to har-bour in their souls opinions irreconcilable with what they publicly pro-fess; and, above all, I believe it is necessary that those who associate with the young and teach them rhetoric should be of that upright character, for they expound the writings of the ancients, whether they be rhetori-cians or grammarians, and still more if they are sophists. For these claim to teach, in addition to other things, not only use of words, but morals also, and they assert that political philosophy is their peculiar field....
>
> What! Was it not the gods who revealed all their learning to Homer, Hesiod, Demosthenes, Herodotus, Thucydides, Isocrates and Lysias? Did not these men think that they were consecrated, some to Hermes, others to the Muses? I think it is absurd that men who expound the works of these writers should dishonour the gods whom they used to honour.

The emphasis in the legal text on the morals of teachers is here clarified; it applies to those who make a living out of teaching texts which they elsewhere criticize. This ambivalence is addressed as intolerable. Thus the legislation is aimed at keeping closely together traditional piety, classical texts and *paideia*, and this naturally made Christian teachers,

---

[67] In Bidez, ed. *L'Empereur Julien Ep.* 42; in LCL *Ep.* 36. Bidez's presentation (pp.72–75) demonstrates that he takes the decree to issue measures explained in this letter; thus also Richard Klein, "Kaiser Julian's Rhetoren- und Unterrichtsgesetz", *RQ* 76 (1981): 75 and Klaus Rosen, *Julian. Kaiser, Gott und Christenhasser*, (Stuttgart: J.G. Cotta'sche Buchhandlung, 2006), 271–2. Thomas M. Banchich, "Julian's School Laws: Cod. Theod. 13.3.5 and Ep. 42", *The Ancient World* 24 (1993) suggests that tradi-tion has confused the decree with a law issued some months later; for comments see Sandnes, *The Challenge of Homer*, 162–3.

if not a specific target, affected by it; and the Emperor was, no doubt, in accordance, with this effect:

> Julian's concern was with Christians who claimed Greek education and cultural heritage as part of the Christian worldview. In his view, these Christians 'secularized' pagan literature by replacing Homer with the Bible while still making use of his texts. He feared a potential for conquering Greek culture from within.[68]

Somewhat ironically, therefore, the Emperor tells Christian teachers to "betake themselves to the churches of the Galileans to expound Matthew and Luke" (423D). Julian urges a contrast between Homer and Hesiod on the one hand, and the two Gospels on the other hand; this is clear from the fact that with both types of literature he speaks about expounding, using the same Greek verb for both groups of texts [ἐξηγεῖσθαι]. Schools & classical texts are here set against church & gospels; 'institutions' and texts are intimately connected, and the texts are not expected to cross their institutional boundaries. Julian's mindset here recalls some of the strongest Christian opponents of participation in encyclical studies, arguing that Greek *paideia* and religion could not be separated.[69] Familiarity with Homer, Hesiod, Demosthenes, Herodotus, Thucydides, Isocrates and Lysias was now to be abandoned by those who did not adhere to these texts more or less in full. Julian made an attempt to deprive the Christians of the common intellectual inheritance.[70] This is exactly the separation that made some Christians panic at the Emperor's decree.[71]

Judged by the bottom line of the Emperor's aim, namely to restore the old order of society, it does not follow immediately that the decree should be limited to Christian *teachers*. The passing on of Greek *paideia* to the Christians was not much affected by targeting teachers only; the effect of that must have been limited. Nonetheless, children

---

[68] Sandnes, *The Challenge of Homer*, 165–6; quotation on p. 172. One can easily imagine from this how the Emperor would look upon Christian *Homerocentones* or *Virgilocentones*. They would have represented his nightmare.

[69] Sandnes, *The Challenge of Homer*, 170–2.

[70] Frances M. Young, *Biblical Exegesis and the Formation of Christian Culture* (Peabody, MA: Hendrickson Publishers, 2002), 69–75.

[71] Gemeinhardt, *Das lateinische Christentum und die pagane Bildung*, 361–7 makes the point that the Christian reaction surpassed what is stated by the Law itself, and even more its episodic nature. It is worth reminding oneself that history is not to be understood in terms of facts, aims and purposes alone, but also by the viewpoints of those involved on both sides (see below).

are left unmentioned, in the decree as well as in the epistle. As for Julian's moral argument against the Christian faith, the teachers were highly important since they, so to say, personified the immorality of the Christians. Criticizing Homer and the classical literature for their inherent idolatry and simultaneously making a living out of precisely these texts, is what made the Emperor so indignant.[72] The epistle states explicitly that youths who want to attend schools are *not* excluded (424a). This is motivated by their ignorance, which can only be put right through participation. Julian, therefore, compares instruction given at schools with medical cures; it is precisely by allowing Christian youths to school that they may be cured of their insanity:

> Though indeed it might be proper to cure [ἰᾶσθαι] these, even against their will, as one cures all the insane [φρενιτίζοντες], except that we concede indulgence to all for this sort of disease [νόσος]. For we ought, I think, to teach, but not to punish, the demented [ἀνόητοι] (424b).

This description of *paideia* is traditional. In his *Lex.* 20–22, Lucian of Samosata likewise describes *paideia* as a cure [φάρμακον] helping Lexiphnes to recover from his sickness. After putting his fingers down his throat, and thus getting rid of his malady (i.e. his lack of literary training), he issues a prescription as a diet to follow after his catharsis— namely what authors to read and imitate.[73]

The Emperor seems to have had a somewhat naïve belief that, if only Christian youths could be exposed to liberal studies, the power of Christian persuasion would evaporate, simply through learning. Julian viewed the Christian faith as a disease[74] whose only cure—but an effective one—was *paideia*.[75] If the restrictions were applied also to children

---

[72] The emperor here makes the same allegations against Christian teachers as those directed against the profession of teachers in general in Antiquity, namely their pecuniary greed; see Sandnes, *The Challenge of Homer*, 26–27, 165–6.

[73] The analogy of a physician curing patients is found in Dio *Or.* 18.7–8 as well, in a context addressing what authors to read. I owe these references to Professor Peter van Möllendorf, Giessen, who in June 2010 gave a lecture on "Canon as *pharmakôn*" at a conference, held by Aarhus University in Ebeltoft, Dänemark.

[74] Thus also 401c (Bidez *Ep.* 27; LCL *Ep.* 58) and 454b (Bidez textnr. 89 *Ep.* 63; LCL *Ep.* 20). Unfortunately, the latter text is incomplete. The argument runs from a friendly presentation of the Jews towards a critical note. Enter then the Galileans; clearly Julian has prepared the way for a polemical statement. But the only thing left here in the fragment about the impious sect of the Galileans is that they are compared to a disease [νόσημα].

[75] In 295d–96b (Bidez text nr. 89b), Julian speaks about the cleansing power of encyclical studies and their illuminating power as well.

of Christian parents, Christianity would never be cured, and would therefore remain a treat to the ancestral mores. The very argument of the letter assumes their presence as part of a strategy to recover from the 'disease.' It seems, therefore, natural, to infer from this argument that the emperor wanted only Christian teachers to be targeted.[76] From this follows then, that the decree is about teaching and not learning. The Christian sources, however, distort this picture.

3.2.2 *Words from those affected*

Judging by what we have seen so far, Julian's decree therefore seems to have taken the view that children of Christian parents are welcome in the schools, by analogy with a patient in a hospital: the very purpose of a hospital is to welcome patients, not to exclude them. Thus his logic assumes the presence of children from Christian homes. Their presence is required for the cure to work according to his plans. Christian contemporary sources, however, give a more complex picture. It is, of course, to the detriment of the Emperor that the history has mostly been written by those affected by his law. These sources are not, however, without historical value; and certainly not in the present study where how Christians acted upon the decree is of primary importance. In principle, it is possible that the Christians acted upon a misunderstanding, but that by no means affects *how* they acted. What, then, can be inferred from the Christian sources then?

According to Socrates *Hist. eccl.* 3.12.7, the law forbade Christians to participate in Greek education [νόμῳ ἐκέλευε Χριστιανοὺς <Ἑλληνικῆς > παιδεύσεως μὴ μετέχειν]; this was to keep them away from improving upon their language and intellectual skills, enabling them to challenge the Greek intellectual tradition. Socrates here claims to be quoting Julian [φησίν]. According to *Hist. eccl.* 3.16.1, the Emperor's decree forbade participation: τοὺς Χριστιανοὺς Ἑλληνικῆς παιδείας μετέχειν ἐκώλυεν. The latter is repeated in 3.16.19: The Emperor did not allow Christians to receive Greek instruction [παιδεύεσθαι].[77] This is motivated by an insight, shared by Apollinarius as well, namely that

---

[76] For Christians who actually did give up teaching, see Bidez, ed., *L'Empereur Julien*, 45; Sandnes, *The Challenge of Homer*, 163.

[77] In NPNF, this is rendered "Greek literature" which certainly holds a key position here, but the Greek has a wider reference.

Greek *paideia* provided the Christians with weapons [ὅπλα] to use against the pagans.

According to Sozomen *Hist. eccl.* 5.18.1,[78] Julian did not allow children of Christian parents to be instructed in the Greek poets and writers [οὐ μὴν οὐδὲ τοὺς αὐτῶν παῖδας ξυνεχώρει ἐκδιδάσκεσθαι τοὺς παρ᾽ Ἕλλησι ποιητὰς καὶ συγγραφέας οὐδε τοῖς τούτων διδασκάλοις φοιτᾶν]. His reason for excluding Christians from the knowledge of the Greek literature was that they through such studies would acquire rhetorical skills and persuasive power.

According to Rufinus *Hist. eccl.* 10.33, he forbade Christians access to the study of pagan authors, decreeing "that elementary schools should be open only to those who worshipped the gods and goddesses [*studia auctorum gentilium Christianos adire prohibens ludos litterarum illis solis, qui deos deasque venerarentur*]."[79]

According to Theodoret *Hist. eccl.* 3.8.1–2,[80] he did not let the children of the Galileans [τῶν Γαλιλαίων τοὺς παῖδας] have any share in the words of the poets, rhetors or philosophers. Theodoret quotes Julian saying [φησί] that this is because the Christians in this way will arm themselves with the weapons of the Greek themselves.

In a context listing the various persecutions Christians had suffered from the beginning, Augustine asks rhetorically: "Did not he persecute the church who forbade the Christians to teach and learn liberal letters [*liberales litteras docere ac discere*] (*Civ.* 18.52)?" *Liberales litterae* refers to encyclical studies with emphasis on the role played by classical literature.

According to Zonaras 13.12,[81] Julian hindered the Christians from participating in Greek learning, to make sure they could not arm themselves by this knowledge: κωλύειν αὐτοὺς μαθημάτων μετέχειν Ἑλληνικῶν, μὴ δεῖν λέγων μύθους αὐτὰ ὀνομάζοντάς τε καὶ διαβάλλοντας τῆς ἐξ αὐτῶν ὠφελείας ἀπολαύειν καὶ δι᾽ αὐτῶν ὁπλίζεσθαι κατ᾽ αὐτῶν.

---

[78] Joseph Bidez, Günther Christian Hansen, *Sozomenus Kirchengeschichte*. GCS (Berlin: Akademie Verlag, 1960), 222.2–4, 8–10.

[79] My own translation; for the Latin text see Eduard Schwartz, Theodor Mommsen, ed. *Eusebius Werke Zweiter Band. Die Kirchengeschichte. Die Lateinische Übersetzung des Rufinus* (Leipzig: J.C. Hinrichs'sche Buchhandlung, 1908), 994.25–26.

[80] Leon Parmentier, Günther Christian Hansen, *Theodoret Kirchengeschichte*. GCS (Berlin: Akademie Verlag, 1998), 185.9–15.

[81] Ludovicus Dindorfius, *Iohannis Zonarare Epitome Historiarum* (Lipsiae: B.G. Teubneri, 1870), 211.14–24.

Taken together, these texts paint an unanimous picture, which truly differs from other relevant sources (see above). Julian's law aimed at keeping Christian *children and young people* away from being instructed in the Greek intellectual, rhetorical, and literary traditions. He feared that by participating they armed themselves to challenge this legacy and culture. Julian's decree is even listed among previous acts of persecution. At this point, however, there are a number of balancing voices worth listening to. Rufinus 10.33 says that Julian did not proceed by force, cruelty, and torture, but by giving rewards, honours, flattery and persuasion. Sozomen is also close to put together a summary of the Emperor's somewhat ambiguous attitude, in saying that he took measures to abolish Christianity and at the same time did not appear as a tyrant. Ammianus Marcellinus, a contemporary of Julian, serving in his army and not a Christian himself, says in his *Rerum Gestarum* 22.10.7: "But this one thing was inhumane, and ought to be buried in eternal silence, namely that he forbade teachers of rhetoric and literature to practise their profession if they were followers of the Christian religion [*illud autem erat inclemens, obruendum perenni silentio, quod arcebat docere magistros rhetoricos et grammaticos ritus christiani cultores*]."[82] Marcellinus makes two points of relevance here. Firstly, he considers the enactment of this law an unfortunate decision, and not in keeping with Julian's general manner of ruling. Secondly, he presents this as a law about *docere*, not *discere*.[83] The Christian Paulus Orosius (early 5th century) adds to this picture by saying that Julian attacked the Christians by cunning rather than by force [*arte potius quam potestate*] (*Hist.* 7.30.2). But in a public edict he ordered that "no Christian should be professor for the teaching of liberal studies [*ne quis Christianus docendorum liberalium studiorum professor esset*]"(3). The two last-mentioned texts complicate the picture given by the Christian sources.

There is one important factor, though, which throws doubt on a sharp distinction between *docere* and *discere*, and thus also the distinction between teachers and students as those targeted by the Emperor's law. The Christian authors almost unanimously take the law as having consequences also for children, and accordingly for learning as well

---

[82] For a comment see J. den Boeft, J.W. Drijvers, den Hengst, D., H.C. Teitler, *Philological and Historical Commentary on Ammianus Marcellinus XXII* (Groningen: Egbert Forsten, 1995), 194–5.

[83] Thus also in his *Res Gestae* 25.4.20.

as for teaching.[84] We could dismiss this as a biased view, if it were not for one observation that appears more than once. They claim to quote the Emperor's motivation for the legislation, namely to keep the Christians away from the encyclical studies that provided them with the necessary intellectual weapons. The facts that this is repeatedly presented as coming from the Emperor himself, and that it appears in several sources, constitutes a claim to veracity. If Christian acquisition of "weapons" was what Julian was trying to prevent, it made no sense for him to promulgate a rule targeting only the teachers. The policy of curing a patient is indeed redundant, not to say contrary, to this reasoning. The cure provided by *paideia* is, of course, also the armament provided by it, but while cure implies a strategy making *paideia* available, the second suggests a strategy of keeping it closed to everyone who might become "the enemy." We are thus left with a complex picture; the sources leave us in doubt on how precisely to understand the historical aim and context of the legislation. The law is explicitly said to be administered by local authorities, which, of course, complicates the picture further. If the Emperor had a double agenda, both to get rid of Christianity but also not to appear as a tyrant, this implies a situation where he might well have addressed the issue differently on different occasions, and left to local administrations to put things into practice. This law might therefore have been interpreted differently by the different local administrators, a fact which then contributed to the somewhat ambiguous picture rendered by the sources.

The Emperor's visit to Antioch in 362 is an example of the philosophically-minded man turning ugly when his mission there failed, due to what he considered to be Christian opposition: "Nun nahm seine Werbung für das Neuheidentum Züge der Unterdrückung des Christentums an. Unter seinem Onkel sowie weiteren Helfern (Felix, Sallustius, und Helpidius) kam es zu Verfolgungen verdächtiger Christen und Konfiskationen christlichen Eigentums."[85] The measures

---

[84] This interpretation finds some support in the fact that Libanius, the contemporary pagan teacher of rhetoric, considered Julian's Law as relevant to both teaching and learning, and hence was concerned about losing students; see Gemeinhardt, *Das lateinische Christentum und die pagane Bildung*, 360.

[85] Markus Janka,"*Quae philosophia fuit, satura facta est*. Julians 'Misopogon' zwischen Gattungskonvention und Sitz im Leben," in *Kaiser Julian 'Apostata' und die philosophische Reaktion gegen das Christentum*, ed. Christian Schäfer (Berlin: Walter de Gruyter, 2008), 180–5; quotation on p. 184.

some Christians took against the Emperor's Law must be understood against such a background.

However, for our purposes the pressing issue is not the reconstruction of this history, but rather what *came out of* the history. In this perspective, the Christian texts are naturally the most relevant, since they are written by the ones affected by the decree. We must remember that the voice of the victims is the better source for understanding how those affected understood the situation. Historical reconstructions may well question the validity of their reactions, but cannot deny that their agenda was determined by the way they perceived the situation. And it is precisely this agenda which is of relevance to the evaluation of the Christian reactions set in motion by Julian's decree. Be they wrong or right, the Christians took the decree as an attempt to cut them off from the ancient *paideia* which provided them with intellectual integrity, opportunities and social standing:

> Erschrocken beobachteten viele Christen der Oberschicht, wie Julian die Brücke einriss, die sie, oft zunächst zögernd und mit schlechtem Gewissen, für sich und ihre Kinder zwischen Glauben und heidnischer Literatur geschlagen hatten.[86]

As Gregory of Nazianzus put it, Julian was depriving the Christians of λογοί.[87] Roger P.H. Green, writes about the panic which this law caused among the Christians:

> …what seems to us an illuminating but eccentric blip on the screen of fourth-century history must have seemed to them a wicked attempt to put the clock back and perhaps the prelude to a lifetime persecution.[88]

Necessary precautions were now urgent. This is a plausible historical context for the material to be presented in the chapters to come.

3.2.3   Synkrisis *and Transvaluation in Julian's Argument*

In his Epistle on true *paideia* (see above) where the Emperor clarified issues pertaining to his legislation, his argument proceeds according to rhetorical standards. He is clearly familiar with common rhetorical

---

[86] Rosen, *Julian*, 273.
[87] For a presentation of Gregory's argument in his *Discourse* 4.4–6 and 100–9, see Sandnes, *The Challenge of Homer*, 168–9.
[88] Roger P.H. Green, "Proba's Cento: Its Date, Purpose, and Reception", *Classical Quarterly* 45 (1995): 560.

techniques. Two points are easily observable. Julian's main point, the argument from morals, the harmony between words and life, is a so-called proof from *ethos*. Aristotle describes the ethos of a speaker as the most important rhetorical proof [κυριωτάτην ἔχει πίστιν τὸ ἦθος] (*Rhet.* 1.2.4 cf. 1.9.1). The Epistle argues that *paideia* serves as a therapy for those infected by Christian teaching; this is an argument according to the rhetorical topos of consequence.[89] This kind of argument is strengthened in Julian's *Contra Galilaeos* 229C–230A where he presents his proof [τεκμήριον]:

> Choose out children from among you all and train and educate them in your scriptures, and if when they come to manhood they prove to have nobler qualities than slaves, then you may believe that I am talking nonsense and suffering from spleen. You are so misguided and foolish that you regard those chronicles of yours as divinely inspired, though by their help no man could ever become wiser or braver or better than he was before; while, on the other hand, writings by whose aid men can acquire courage, wisdom and justice you ascribe to Satan and to those who serve Satan.

Scholarly literature on Julian's school legislation have failed to notice a third rhetorical aspect involved here, namely literary *synkrisis* (see Chapter 2 above). In the Epistle, the two bodies of literature, pagan classics and the Gospels, are juxtaposed in a way which corresponds to this particular rhetorical exercise. This comparative evaluation where the superiority of Hellenic literature and culture is argued in terms of therapeutic language and morals is further developed in *Contra Galilaeos*; here the *refutatio* of Christian literature is argued with the aid of literary *synkrisis*.[90] Throughout this text Julian compares three cultures and the texts forming their identity, Greek, Jewish and Christian: Moses *v.* Solon and Plato; the Decalogue *v.* Greek laws, philosophy and *paideia*; Phineas *v.* the *clementia* of Greek tradition; Isa 11 *v.* *Od.* 11.316.[91] The *synkrisis* is nicely summed up in e.g. 221E–4E. Throughout this comparison, Julian leaves no doubt about his rankings. It is worth considering *Contra Galilaeos* 224C–E in the light of this. In the midst of his evaluative

---

[89] See Cook, *The Interpretation of the New Testament*, 316–8; Sandnes, *The Challenge of Homer*, 169–70.

[90] George A. Kennedy, *Greek Rhetoric under Christian Emperors* (Princeton NJ: Princeton University Press, 1983), 31 mentions Julian's use of *synkrisis*, but not on the topic addressed now.

[91] For the interpretation of this Homeric text, see R. Joseph Hoffmann, *Julian's Against the Galileans* (New York: Prometheus Books, 2004), 104 n. 313.

comparison whereby Greek superiority is demonstrated, Julian mentions as Solomon "the wisest man [ὁ σοφώτατος];" nevertheless Julian considers Solomon inferior to his Greek counterpart, such as Isocrates with his proverbs. Solomon is introduced in this way only to prepare the transvaluation Julian is here aiming at. The wisest man according to biblical tradition "worshipped our gods", says Julian (224D), claiming the support of 1 Kgs 11:4. Solomon's idolatry is here seen as worship of Greek deities. The transvaluation is this: Thanks to his wisdom, attested in the Scriptures themselves, Solomon worshipped the Homeric deities![92] Julian thus provides an example not only of literary *synkrisis*, but also of "Kulturkampf"; a hermeneutical claim of superiority is involved. The Biblical testimony on Solomon has not been fully appreciated by either Jews nor Christian; if the text is taken into full account, this testimony surpasses their reading, and instead embraces Julian's point. This is an analogy to what Mimesis Criticism claims for Mark and Homer. One difference is, however, to be noted; Julian engages with texts by mentioning them, paraphrasing them or even quoting them. His *synkrisis* and transvaluation is openly accessed by his readers.

Julian's decree marked a watershed in the history of how Christians related to the Greek intellectual and literary legacy. The simple fact that Juvencus presented his paraphrase during Constantine's reign implies that the biblical epic tradition that developed in the 4th and 5th centuries was not unthinkable without Julian. That is to say, the new climate of the 4th century paved the way for a new literature,[93] even without Julian. On the other hand, the fact that most of the attempts to write biblical epics postdate Julian suggests that his role is not to be disregarded.[94] Scott McGill is reluctant to give Julian such an

---

[92] There is no doubt that this argument made an impression on Christian opponents; see William J. Malley, *Hellenism and Christianity. The Conflict Between Hellenic and Christian Wisdom in the Contra Galileos of Julian the Apostate and the Contra Julianum of St. Cyril of Alexandria* (Roma: Universita Gregoriana Editrice, 1978), 338–40. The fact that Solomon was deceived by his wives into doing so, serves in Julian's argument only to show that even the wisest man of the Bible was led astray by women, which proved his inferiority to his Greek counterparts.

[93] The formative role of the new climate is pointed out also by Van der Nat, "Die Prefatio der Evangelienparaphrase des Iuvencus", 249.

[94] Thus R.A. Markus, "Paganism, Christianity and the Latin Classics in the Fourth Century", in *Latin Literature of the Fourth Century*, ed. J.W. Binns (London and Boston: Routledge & Kegan Paul, 1974), 2, 7; Alan Cameron, "The Empress and Poet. Paganism and Politics at the Court of Theodosius II", *Yale Classical Studies* 27 (1982): 282–3; Green, "Proba's Cento", 554–8; Whitby, "The Bible Hellenized", 197–8. She points out that the exercise of *paraphrasis* has fundamental links with education. Some

important role.[95] He points to the fact that his law was short-lived, and that a connection between the centos and Julian's decree is remote. I consider instead that the decree is one out of many factors leading to a new kind of Christian literature. This event is, in my view, certainly significant enough to question Christian post-Julian texts as being proper models for the composition of the Gospels. The decree of Julian is a turning-point, placing a heavy burden of proof on the part of those who make post-Julian texts paradigms for understanding the composition of the canonical Gospels. With regard to Gregory of Nazianus, Susanna Elm says that he, due to Julian's school legislation, "embarked upon a writing campaign which incorporated Scripture into Greek learning to the most comprehensive degree possible, with fundamental consequences for Byzantine thought."[96]

Commenting upon Julian's legislation on the Christians and the poets, Dennis R. MacDonald says: "Had there been only a few Christian Homeric scholars, Julian hardly would have bothered to legislate against them... The problem was not that Christians knew no Homer but that they knew him too well—on their own ethical terms."[97] This is, of course, entirely correct, but is not relevant to understanding the nature of the Gospels. MacDonald's interpretation of the situation is that Julian shut the Christians out from access to Homer's texts, urging them to turn to their own "Homeric" texts. This appears unlikely to me, since the driving force of the Emperor's legislation was to cut Christians off from use of the pagan legacy in general. Given the thesis proposed by Mimesis Criticism that the Gospels in general, and Mark in particular, were soaked in Homer, it is difficult to understand why the Emperor then directed the Christians to read the Gospels instead of Homer, thus trying to keep them away from Homeric and classical influences. Did it escape the attention of the Emperor that the Gospels to which he wanted to restrict the Christians were themselves soaked in Homeric culture? And if Christians such as Apollinarius (see 3.3

---

centos are also attested as school texts; see M.D. Usher, "Prolegomenon to the Homeric Centos", *American Journal of Philology* 118 (1997): 314. The connection between biblical epics and Julian's edict has been questioned by G. Agosti, "L'Epica Biblica nella tarda antichità greca: autori e lettori nel IV e V secolo", in *La Scrittura infinita: Bibbia e poesia in età medievale e umanistica* (Florence: Sismel, 2001), 68–70.

[95] McGill, *Virgil Recomposed*, 160 n. 53.

[96] Susanna Elm, "Hellenism and Historiography. Gregory of Nazianzus and Julian in Dialogue", *Journal of Medieval and early Modern Studies* 33 (2003): 504.

[97] MacDonald, *Christianizing Homer*, 21.

below) already knew the Gospels as biblical *paraphrasis* of Homer, why bother to compose an *Ersatz* literature if this was already in their midst, in the very Gospels themselves? The latter question anticipates the next section of this chapter. We turn now to the two Apollinarii, whose paraphrases the ancient sources see in tandem with how Julian's law is presented in Christian sources.

3.3   Pioneers in Greek: Apollinarius, Father and Son, of Laodicea (4th century)

According to Jerome *Vir. ill.* 104, Apollinarius was son of a presbyter also named Apollinarius.[98] In his youth he "devoted himself chiefly to the study of *grammatici*". Thomas P. Halton's translation[99] renders this as 'grammar,' which I find too narrow. This translation may cause misunderstandings, particularly among modern readers. *Grammatici* includes the knowledge of classical literature in particular.[100] Jerome mentions that he wrote innumerable volumes on the Scriptures. In addition he wrote 30 volumes *Against Porphyry*,[101] which were particularly appreciated.[102] It is probable that this work demonstrated erudition and familiarity with the pagan legacy. Jerome restricts himself to mentioning these works of Apollinarius. This might be due to the fact that Apollinarius has gone down in history as a heresiarch, thanks to the christological disputes of his town.[103] Jerome's presentation of him may also be seen as being precisely in accordance with the preface of his *De Viris Illustribus*. There he summarizes the hub of the criticism against the Christians,

---

[98] See also Philostorgios' *Church History* GCS 230.23–24 (Anhang). Kaster, *Guardians of Language*, 242–3 mentions Apollinarius the Elder in his prosopography of ancient grammarians.

[99] Halton, trans., *Saint Jerome On Illustrious Men*, 138.

[100] Sandnes, *The Challenge of Homer*, 26–28; OLD s.v.

[101] The text is now lost; some few fragments are found in Jerome, see Hans Lietzmann, *Apollinaris von Laodicea und seine Schule* (Hildesheim, New York: Georg Olms Verlag, 1979 = Tübingen: J.C.B. Mohr (Paul Siebeck), 1904), 150, 265–7. The genre must have been what we are familiar with from a host of other polemical texts in early Christianity and antiquity in general, the so-called *adversus*, *contra* or *refutatio* kind of literature.

[102] This work is mentioned quite often and must have been impressive; see e.g. Jerome, *Praef. In Danielem Prophetam* (CCSL 75A.771–772.10–11); *Ep.* 48.13 (PL 22.502); 70.3 (PL 22.666); 84.2 (PL 22.743) [*fortissimi libri*]; Philostorgios *Church History* 8.14 (GCS 115.7–9).

[103] For his christological and anthropolognal ideas, see Ekkehard Mühlenberg, *Apollinaris von Laodicea* (Göttingen: Vandenhoeck & Ruprecht, 1969).

as made by Celsus, Porphyry and Julian—"the rabid dogs barking [*rabidae canes*]"—in the following way: "no philosophers, no orators, no men of learning [*nulli philosophi et eloquentes, nulli doctores*]"; in short, this adds up to a criticism of the lack of learning, tradition and culture, as stated in e.g. Acts 4:13 itself. *De Viris Illustribus* presents a number of persons whom Jerome considers learned in Greek and thus able to refute this kind of criticism. His aim is, therefore, limited to refuting *noster fides* as *rustica* and *simplex*.[104] This is the wider context of Apollinarius' relevance for the present study. Furthermore, the case of Apollinarius witnesses to the role assigned to Julian's decree in the preceding chapter.

3.3.1 *Socrates' Church History: Gospels as Platonic Dialogues*

Nothing is left of the texts addressed above; the works of the Apollinarii were partly extinguished, due to what was considered false teaching. An important source for the two Apollinarii with regard to the topic of the present investigation is Socrates' *Hist. eccl.* 2.46, in which the two are introduced, and 3.16, in which their reaction to Julian's decree (362) is given.[105] Socrates explains that they slid into false doctrine (known as Apollinarianism) because of a controversy over their spending a lot of time with a Greek sophist Epiphanius, with whom they were close friends. From our perspective the heart of this conflict seems very typical of the two, both being well-educated, the father a γραμματικὸς and the son a rhetor (*Hist. eccl.* 2.46.1–8). According to 3.16, their background in the Greek legacy came to serve the church in a special way at the time of Julian the Emperor. After the decree of Julian, which imposed restrictions on Christian participation in Greek παιδεία, their training rendered them useful (χρειώδεις) to the Christians:

> The former who traded as a grammarian composed a grammar [γραμματικὴν Χριστιανικῷ τύπῳ συνέταττε] according to the Christian faith. He also translated [μετέβαλεν] in metric style the Books of Moses; what is said about the heroes and all of the Old Testament he put together in the genre of history [ἐν ἱστορίας τυπῳ]. And he did some according to dactylic measure, some dramatically according to the measure of tragedy [τῷ τῆς τραγῳδίας], and he made use of all rhythmic metres, so that no form of Greek language remained unfamiliar to the Christians [ὅπως

---

[104] The style of the work is inspired by e.g. Suetonius' work *De Grammaticis et Rhetoribus* which gives short biographies of famous teachers in Rome.
[105] For this decree, see Chapter 3.2.1 in this study.

ἂν μηδεὶς τρόπος τῆς Ἑλληνικῆς γλώττης τοῖς Χριστιανοῖς ἀνήκοος ᾖ]. The younger Apollinarius, who was trained in speaking eloquently, expounded the Gospels and the apostolic teaching in the form of dialogues [τὰ εὐαγγέλια καὶ τὰ ἀποστολικὰ δόγματα ἐν τύπῳ διαλόγων ἐξέθετο], as did Plato with the Greeks. Thus they found themselves useful (χρειώδεις) for the Christians. They overcame [ἐνίκησαν] the claptrap of the Emperor through their own efforts (*Hist. eccl.* 3.16.1–6).[106]

The following observations have a bearing on our investigation. The background against which the attempt to rewrite the Scriptures in classical style is to be understood is here clearly the situation created by Julian's law aimed at restricting the access of Christians to the classical legacy taught in schools. This created a crisis with regard to the instruction of the young, in which the classical texts made up the core curriculum; these passed on the knowledge necessary to have a say in society. This pedagogical aspect was clearly a concern for the two Apollinarii. The very purpose of their efforts was to keep the Christians on good terms with the Greek language as transmitted through the classical texts. The text is revealing as to their concern with different literary genres, styles and measures. They sought variety for pedagogical reasons. Texts from the Bible now serve as textbooks, as did normally Homer, Euripides, Virgil etc. in encyclical studies, but the form is taken from the legacy of the Greek texts. This method implies a negotiation with style and *res*.

Socrates' presentation assumes that the aim of the two Apollinarii was to substitute the role played by Greek literature in the training of the young. Genre, style and measures juxtaposed the idea of cultural canons in the ancient world.[107] Their concern with literary genres is worth noting, since this is indeed relevant for our topic. As for the Old Testament, it is natural to assume that the Homeric style is included, but this is not so for the New Testament. The younger Apollinarius presented the Gospels and Apostolic letters[108] in accordance with Platonic dialogues, not in Homeric metre. Jesus is then presented as a Socratic teacher surrounded by his students. The so-called diatribe style found in some letters lent themselves easily to a comparison with Plato's dialogues. Since this is the first known example of an attempt to rewrite the Gospels in Greek—and within a context very much concerned

---

[106] My own translation with some aid from NPNF.
[107] See Chapter 2 in this study.
[108] The Greek δόγματα refers to tenet, belief or system, which makes it appropriate to think here of the letters rather than the Acts of the Apostles.

with genre—this might cast some doubt on claims that Christians evidently did emulate Homer in the Gospels. For natural reasons the stories of the Old Testament were much easier to fit into a Homeric style.[109] The so-called "grammar"[110] composed by Apollinarius the Elder may have been a presentation of Greek literature viewed from a Christian perspective.[111] There is a tendency in Socrates' presentation to minimize the role of the two Apollinarii. His praise appears somewhat reluctant,[112] and he emphasizes that their efforts to deal with the law were overtaken by Divine Providence, that is, the sudden death of Julian. It is also a sign of divine providence, he says, that the works of the two Apollinarii are more or less erased from memory, as though they never existed.[113] Moreover, Socrates points out that the power to fight adversaries with skilled reason was not taught the Church by the Apollinarii (*Hist. eccl.* 3.16.18). It goes back to the Apostle Paul himself who cited from Greek classical texts (3.16.21–27), which brings us back to where our investigation started (Chapter 1.1).

The presentation of the two Apollinarii in Socrates' *Hist. eccl.* 3.16 is found within a more general discussion on Greek *paideia*. This is only loosely connected to the two figures from Laodicea. Socrates holds a common viewpoint in saying that Greek knowledge is necessary to defend faith with the weapons of the Greek themselves. Furthermore, he urges a distinction between good and bad in the classical legacy. This brings to mind well-established *topoi* such as the making of honey

---

[109] *Didascalia* 2 attests to this, by exemplifying how Old Testament texts are presented as replacing the genres found in pagan literature, from which the Christians are urged to keep away, see Sandnes, *The Challenge of Homer*, 103–4. Obviously, the two Apollinarii would strongly disagree with the assumptions of *Didascalia*'s advice, namely to keep away from it, but they concurred with regard to Homer and the Old Testament as somehow corresponding.

[110] Thus in NPNF.

[111] Franz Passow, *Handwörterbuch der Griechischen Sprache* (Leipzig: Fr. Chr. Wilh. Vogel, 1841), s.v. (p. 571) says that ἡ γραμματική is "die Geschicklichkeit Schriftwerke zu erklären"; thus making "grammar" a much too narrow translation; *pace* Paul Speck, "Sokrates Scholastikos über die beiden Apolinarioi", *Philologus* 141 (1997): 364 who thinks that he made a textbook on grammar with examples taken from the Bible.

[112] Whitby, "The Bible Hellenized", 197 says that Socrates "condemns" the activity of the Apollinarii. I regard this as an exaggeration.

[113] Speck, "Sokrates Scholastikos," suggests that the relevant works of the two Apollinarii are legends.

by the bees[114] and the spoil of the Egyptians;[115] in short the criterion
of usefulness (*usus* or χρήσιμον).[116] With reference to a seemingly lack
of coherence in *Hist. eccl.* 3.16, some scholars question the reliability of
the source.[117] If I am correct in pointing out that Apollinarius the Elder
composed a book which included how Christians could cope with Greek
literature, and the *topoi* presented just above, then the discussion on
Greek *paideia* and the attempt made by the two Laodiceans are not
entirely unrelated. They represented a continuation of a discourse that
can be traced far back in the history of the church, but since Julian
has created a new situation, what they did was still something new.
As for the Gospels, the Platonic dialogues were the analogy closest
at hand.

3.3.2   Sozomen's Church History (5th century): The Gospels not mentioned

The relevant passages in Sozomen's *Hist. eccl.* are 5.18 and 6.25. The latter text says that Apollinarius the Elder was a well-known γραμματικὸς
(6.25.10/GCS 271.20). Their friendship with Epiphanius, a Greek sophist, and their devotion to Greek pagan hymns, caused a conflict with
the bishop. It further says that Apollinarius wrote Christian poems in
metre for daily use among the believers (6.25.5/GCS 270.26–271.4). The
passage of special interest for us is found in 5.18.3–4/GCS 222.10–21.
Sozomen says that well-educated Christians like Apollinarius senior and
junior and the Cappadocians caused the anger of the Emperor, since
they through their learning in literature and rhetoric were prepared
to respond to the situation. This text has a direct reference to Julian's
decree, clearly stated in the introductory ἡνίκα ("for that reason"),
connecting the Apollinarii directly to what Sozomen has just told us
about Julian's decree:

> Apollinarius, therefore [ἡνίκα], employed his great learning and inge-
> nuity in the production of a heroic epic [ἐν ἔπεσιν ἡρῴοις] on the

---

[114] Gnilka, *ΧΡΗΣΙΣ*, 102–33; Sandnes, *The Challenge of Homer*, 130–1, 177–80, 241–2.

[115] Allen, *The Despoliation of Egypt*; Sandnes, *The Challenge of Homer*, 144–5, 222–6.

[116] See Gnilka, *ΧΡΗΣΙΣ* for a thorough presentation of this; cf. Sandnes, *The Challenge of Homer*, e.g. pp. 129–32.

[117] See P. Périchon et P. Maraval, ed. and trans., *Socrate de Constantinople Histoire Ecclesiastique. Livres II–III* (Paris: Cerf, 2005), 310–1 n. 1.

antiquities of the Hebrews [τὴν Ἑβραϊκὴν ἀρχαιολογίαν] to the reign of
Saul, as a substitute for the poem of Homer [ἀντὶ μὲν τῆς Ὁμήρου]. He
divided his work into twenty-four parts, to each of which he appended
the name of one of the letters of the Greek alphabet, according to their
number and order. He also wrote comedies in imitation of Menander,
tragedies resembling those of Euripides, and odes on the model of
Pindar. In short, taking themes of the so-called encyclical knowledge
from the Scriptures, he produced within a short time, a set of works
which in manner, expression, character and arrangement [ἰσαρίθμους
καὶ ἰσοδυνάμους πραγματείας ἤθει τε καὶ φράσει καὶ χαρακτῆρι καὶ
οἰκονομίᾳ ὁμοίας τοῖς παρ' Ἕλλησιν] are well approved as similar to the
Greek literatures and which were equal in number and force.[118]

The purpose of Apollinarius' effort was to put right what Julian's decree
damaged for the Christians and their offspring. Children of Christian
parents found themselves cut off from the legacy upon which erudition and education was formed, and thus found that their position in
society was jeopardized. This is the background that Sozomen gives in
the preceding lines, by pointing out how restrictions were imposed on
Christians' access to rights and offices in society.[119] In the words of Roger
P. H. Green, the Apollinarii created an alternative literature, "a complete
rival literature, classical in form but Christian in content."[120]

   This gives the whole project of Apollinarius a pedagogical aim; it
was designed to replace the textbooks of encyclical studies—i.e. the
classical literature—with Christian texts rewritten. This clearly refers
to the Old Testament described here according to its historical books.
They correspond to the drama of Homer, the heroic epics on warfare,
kings, love, obstacles to be overcome etc. Apollinarius did this in a
way that facilitates the learning of the passages. There can be no doubt
that the heroic epic referred to here is actually Homer's writings, due
to its role in encyclical studies. What is the precise aim of his *mimesis*[121] of comedies in the manner of Menander, tragedies after Euripides
and odes modelled on Pindar? From the Holy Scriptures he collected

---

[118] Quoted from NPNF with some alterations. A German translation is available in
Sozomenus. *Historia Ecclesiastica. Kirchengeschichte*, ed. and trans. Günther Christian
Hansen (Turnhout: Brepols, 2004).
[119] As for the historical reliability in such a picture, see Chapter 3.2.1 and 3.2.2.
[120] Roger P.H. Green, "Proba's Cento," 557.
[121] Apollinarius also wrote a book called Ὑπὲρ ἀληθείας (*For the sake of truth*) to
which Julian the Emperor gave the following response modelled after Caesar's proverbial report: ἀνέγνων, ἔγνων, κατέγνων ("I have read, I have understood, and I have
condemned") (*Hist.eccl.* 5.18.7/GCS 223.6–7).

themes able to substitute for the literature taught in encyclical studies; hence the different types of literature mentioned. This is most likely a reference to other parts of the Old Testament where corresponding genres are found. The mention of Homer, Euripides, Menander and Pindar echoes the core texts in ancient education and culture, and also reflects the discussion of a literary canon, as we saw in Quintilian and Dionysios of Halicarnassos. This is important, since it shed light on the aim of the two Apollinarii;[122] their literary work aimed at substituting a literary canon. For the topic of the present investigation it is worth noting that the Gospels are left unmentioned.

According to the early 12th century's chronicler Zonaras' *Epitome Historion* 13.12,[123] Julian raged [ἐξεμάνη] against the Christians, even to the point of shutting them out from Greek learning [μαθημάτων Ἑλληνικῶν]: He said that it was not possible simultaneously to call this learning myths and also to enjoy the benefits from them, and also to arm oneself [ὁπλίζεσθαι] against them. When Christian children were excluded from pursuing the poets, therefore, it is said that Apollinarius was moved to make a paraphrase [παράφρασις] of the psalms. Gregory, cognominated by Zonaras "the great in theology", is said to be moved to compose epics with the purpose that the young [οἱ νέοι], when they learn them instead of [ἀντὶ] the learning of the Greek, become Greek [ἐξελληνίζωνται] in language, and that they are taught metre as well (Zonaras 13.12/211.15–24).

The historical accuracy of this source may well be questioned. The paraphrase of the psalms is here wrongly attributed to Apollinarius. This is the work of someone else, Nonnus of Panoplis has been suggested.[124] Nonetheless, this source seems to pass on traditions relevant to the present investigation, and which concurs with older sources. In the first place, Zonaras introduces Apollinarius with reference to Julian's ban on Christian participation in Greek education. In the second place, he labels Apollinarius' work by the rhetorical term

---

[122] See Morgan, *Literate Education*, 313; Dionysios of Halicarnassus on *Mimesis*; Quintillian *Inst.* 1.8.5–12. In *Inst.* 8.6.71, Quintilian calls Pindar *princeps Lyricorum* ("the prince of lyrics"); similarly in *Inst.* 10.1.61. This brings to mind the literary competition against which the idea of a "canon" evolved. Further references in Chapter 2.3.1 and 2.3.2 of this study.

[123] Dindorfius, *Iohannis Zonarae Epitome Historiarum*, 211.14–24.

[124] The edition of these psalms is Arthur Ludwich, ed., *Apolinarii Metaphrasis Psalmorum* (Leipzig: Teubner, 1912); see also Ekkehard Mühlenberg, "Apollinarius", *TRE* 3:367.

παράφρασις (see Chapter 2 of this study). Although this rhetorical term is missing in the available sources on Apollinarius, senior and junior, this is, in fact, what he did. It is, therefore, not by accident that Zonaras 13.12./211.20 actually summarizes his work in this term. To be precise, it refers here to the psalms in particular. In the third place, he says his attempt, albeit that he wrongly speaks of the psalms here, was to make sure that Christian children were given a truly Greek education.

The sources give an unanimous picture of a son and his father extraordinarily well equipped for the task of rewriting the Scriptures in a classical fashion. The major work *Against Porphyry* is to be separated from their rewriting of the Scriptures, but certainly the two projects both drew heavily on their familiarity with the classical texts of the pagan legacy.

As far as we know, the two Apollinarii were the first to present *paraphrasis* of Biblical literature in Greek. They did so in a crisis (Julian's decree) where there was, in their view, an urgent need for providing Christian teachers with a textbook which also introduced the students to the literature taught in encyclical studies, particularly Homer and the literary canons of the ancient world. Their deliberate response to this crisis was, according to Frances M. Young, to produce "substitute literature."[125] They included Old Testament texts, but *not* the Gospels. As for the latter, they were paraphrased in the style of Platonic dialogues. Sozomen does not even mention the Gospels in his presentation of the Apollinarian project. Zonaras' *Epitome*, the 12th-century dictionary or encyclopaedia of nobilities of any kind in the ancient world, includes a passage on Apollinarius of Laodicea in Syria.[126] His Greek training (with Libanios) is pointed out, and his literary achievements are summarized in this way: "He wrote thirty books against Porphyry, and the entire Scripture of the Hebrews in the style of heroic epics. He wrote letters and many other commentaries (ὑπομνήματα)[127] to the Scriptures."[128] There is no mention of Gospel *paraphrasis*. His rewriting of the Gospels did not make much impression on posterity, and it was Platonic rather than Homeric.

---

[125] Young, *Biblical Exegesis and the Formation of Christian Culture*, 72.
[126] Suidae *Lexicon*, 615–6.
[127] For the translation of this term, see LSJ. The Latin text has *commentarios*.
[128] My translation.

This means that the first attempt to paraphrase the Gospel literature in Greek is Eudocia's *Homerocentones*, which we will come to later. That takes us into the beginning of the fifth century, and it was an inheritance taken over from Latin, i.e. from Juvencus and Proba in particular. Homeric imitation of the Gospels is, therefore, a phenomenon later than and subordinated to its Latin counterparts, and the first to do this in Greek did *not* include the Gospels in their Homeric *paraphrasis* of biblical texts.

CHAPTER FOUR

WHAT IS A CENTO?

Centos are poems made up entirely of verses lifted, verbatim or with only slight modification, from Virgil, if they are Virgilian centos, or from the *Iliad* and *Odyssey*, if Homeric centos.[1] A cento is thus a poem or a poetic sequence made up of *recognizable* lines from one or more existing poems, usually highly valued literature. The literary name for this genre is taken from Latin *cento*, meaning a patchwork garment.[2] The genre is an extreme form of paraphrase whereby the composition brings forth a new story consisting of familiar building-blocks. We have seen that Juvencus' paraphrase included many Virgilian lines; centonists take such paraphrase to an extreme. They are thus limited by what they find in Virgil or Homer. As for biblical centos, this naturally puts a constraint upon the use of biblical names, geography etc. Traditional citations are strung together to serve a new story. Centonists piece together verses to form a new, altered but still coherent text. The outcome is that the hypotext is being recast. Centos are therefore by their nature parasitic; the term is used here with no pejorative intention. Centonists are drawn

---

[1] This definition is taken from Usher, "Prolegomenon to the Homeric Centos", *American Journal of Philology* 118 (1997): 305. For an introduction to centos, see F. Kunzmann and C. Hoch, "Cento," *Historisches Wörterbuch der Rhetorik* 2:148–57 and Karla Pollmann, "Jesus Christus und Dionysios. Überlegungen zu dem Euripides-Cento *Christus Patiens*," *Jahrbuch der Österreichischen Byzantinistik* 47 (1997): 90–91. For a list of secular and mythological centos, see McGill, *Virgil Recomposed*, XIII, XV and for the Latin texts of these centos, see pp. 119–52.

[2] OLD s.v. The etymology of the term, however, is far from certain. It may be derived from Greek κέντρον, meaning a stick. This would make a cento something "der zerbrocken ist;" thus H. Frisk, *Griechisches Etymologisches Lexicon*, Vol. 1:820–1). See also LSJ s.v. Jeffrey T. Schnapp, "Reading Lessons. Augustine, Proba, and the Christian Détournement of Antiquity,"*Stanford Literary Review* 9 (1992): 100, says the use of this term for poems is derived from "a humble patchwork quilt of the sort that slaves or peasants might stitch together from rags". It is thus probably a metaphor drawn from the fabrication of textiles. Usher, *Homeric Stitchings*, makes a reference to Plautus *Epidicus* 455 as the first time (254–184 B.C.E.) *centones sarcire* is used metaphorically, with reference to speech [*praedicere*]. The context is here that of soldiers telling tales about the battles they have participated in. There is no intention here to describe speech as a collection of disparate scraps; it is here used in a negative way describing tales no one is eager to listen to; *eradicabam hominus auris* ("I uprooted men's ears") is indicative of the derogatory nature of the metaphor here.

to canonical authors. "To present a cento is always on one level to trade in cultural capital and to affirm one's highbrow credentials."[3] As we will see below, the practice of composing centos is attested among Christians in the 2nd century C.E., but the appearance is certainly not a Christian invention, and was in use much earlier.

Scott McGill has demonstrated that the practice of making narrative centos developed from "inchoate centos," namely isolated lines cited in a new situation. Seneca's *Apol.* 1.2 might serve as an example. This parody of Claudius' *apotheosis* is introduced by the claim that someone saw the dead Emperor walking *non passibus aequis* ("with stumbling steps"). This is taken from *Aen.* 2.274 about old Anchises following in the steps of his son while leaving burning Troy. Virgil is here used in a surprising and comic way; Seneca is poking fun at the Emperor's handicap[4] in a way that recalls the Augustean pride in Trojan descent,[5] truly an example of "Verfremdung." From this practice developed full-fledged centos. Thus the centonists did not stay outside the literary traditions of the ancient world; on the contrary, they stood on their shoulders and took the traditions some steps further. This perspective on the centos implies a critique of the commonly held negative evaluation of the genre (see Chapter 1.7).[6]

4.1 DECIMUS MAGNUS AUSONIUS ON CENTOS

The only ancient text to address the nature of cento-composing is Decimus Magnus Ausonius, himself a centonist. In the 4th century C.E., Ausonius[7] put together a Virgilian cento, the so-called *Cento Nuptialis*, about a wedding. The introductory preface addressed to the rhetor Axius

---

[3] McGill, *Virgil Recomposed*, XVI; cf. Karla Pollmann, "Sex and Salvation in the Vergilian Cento of the Fourth Century," *Romane memento. Vergil in the Fourth Century*, ed. Roger Rees (London: Duckworth, 2004), 79.

[4] This is referred to in *Apol.* 5.2 and Suetonius *Claud.* 21.6.

[5] McGill, *Virgil Recomposed*, XXII.

[6] Some Homeric centos are found in the so-called *Greek Anthology*, a collection of 3700 epigrams of different length. In W.R. Paton, ed. and trans., *The Greek Anthology in Five Volumes Vol. 1.* LCL (Cambridge MA and London: Harvard University Press and William Heinemann Ltd., 1980), 50–52 (text 119) is the preface to Eudocia's cento (see Chapter 6.1.2 in this study); 381 are 382 are two non-Christian centos included in this collection. Sowers, *Eudocia. The Making of a Homeric Christian*, 54–55 lists the centos that have survived.

[7] For his life and career, see J. Gruber, *Der Neue Pauly* 2:334–6; Roger P.H. Green, ed. *The Works of Ausonius, Edited with Introduction and Commentary* (Oxford:

Paulus,[8] and together with the closing lines, according to R.P.H. Green, *The Works of Ausonius*, p. 138.17–21 (LCL: 157–62), it forms an *inclusio* that is very instructive with regard to the nature of centos, what a cento is: *cento quid sit* (p. 133.24). Ausonius is the first to have formulated the "rules of the game", so to speak;[9] for composition of centos followed certain rules [*praecepta*] determining length and combination of lines and the rhythm and metre:

> so as to harmonize different meanings, to make pieces arbitrarily con-nected seem naturally related [*adoptiva quae sunt ut cognata videan-tur*], to let foreign elements [*aliena*] show no chink of light between, to prevent the far-fetched from proclaiming the force which united them, the closely packed from bulging unduly, the loosely knit from gaping (Prefatory address p. 134.44–46).

The prefatory address offers this definition of the phenomenon:

> So take this piece of work, continuous, though made of disjointed tags; one, though of various scraps, absurd, though of grave materials; mine, though the elements are of another's (p. 133.20–21).[10]

Ausonius here precisely defines the nature of cento composition; the dual structure revealing what a cento is, is very clear:

opusculum continuum ("a coherent piece of work")	*de inconexis* ("of dis-jointed tags")
unum ("one")	*de diversis* ("from various scraps")
ludicrum ("amusement ")	*de seriis* ("from things serious")
nostrum ("ours")[11]	*de alieno* ("from foreign")

From various scraps a unity is made, and from elements taken from another text, the text now becomes ours. One is reminded here of Jesus' words on new wine in old wineskins (Matt 9:17). Ausonius compares the composition of centos to a play [*ludicrum*] used by the Greeks in

---

Clarendon Press, 1991), XXIV–XXXII. The following owes much to McGill, *Virgil Recomposed*, 1–10.

[8] This has in the LCL edition of H.G. Evelyn White no numbering of lines. According to McGill, *Virgil Recomposed*, 1–2, this is l.38–40, and in Green, *The Works of Ausonius*, this is p. 132.1–134.50.

[9] What he did was, however, nothing entirely new; he put together what was already there in practice, as this chapter demonstrates.

[10] Quoted from LCL with some alterations.

[11] In the light of the immediate context, this plural has the primary meaning of "mine;" but the plural is a reminder that Ausonius considers his work to be according to standards already given.

which geometrically shaped pieces of bones [*ostomachia*] can be put together in numerous ways, thus forming

> a monstrous elephant, a brutal boar, a goose in flight, and a gladiator in armour, a huntsman crouching down, and a dog barking—even a tower and a tankard and numberless other things of this sort, whose variety depends upon the skill [*scientius*] of the player. But while the harmonious arrangement of the skilful is marvellous [*peritorum concinnatio miraculum est*], the jumble of the unskilled is grotesque [*ridiculum*] (p. 134.37–43).[12]

The point of this illustration is the dual nature of centos' manipulation of the given: on the one hand emphasizing the creativity of the game, and on the other hand emphasizing the limits involved. The *ostomachia* metaphor nicely brings out the interplay between *verba* and style, which is the given, and *res*, the organizing force and also that which in the end decides what comes out of the manipulation. In centos there is considerable, not to say complete, continuity with regard to *verba*, and discontinuity with regard to *sensus* or *res*, if compared to the source-text. And it is precisely in the interplay between these two that the meaning of a cento comes to life.

Ausonius put together his cento in the context of a literary contest or challenge presented to him. It was written at the command of the Emperor Valentinian, whose son Gratian Ausonius had tutored, "wishing to show by means of a competition [*contentio*] with me the great superiority of his production, he bade me compile a similar poem on the same subject [i.e *nuptia*]" (p. 133.12–13). The competitive context is seen also in the phrases *aemulus eminerem* ("If I rivalled and surpassed him") and *victor* (p. 133.16–17).[13] Ausonius was invited to participate in a duel, and certainly not an easy one, since it was with the Emperor himself. For the understanding of the nature of centos, this is important. Cento composition was, as this study will gradually unfold, an aristocratic phenomenon. It belonged to the leisure of intellectuals who entertained themselves playing with the literary legacy. In Ausonius' cento this calls for two observations. Terms related to play and amusement abound in the preface:

---

[12] For the educational toy that is Ausonius' illustration here, see Green, ed. *The Works of Ausonius*, 521.

[13] Cf. Chapter 2 in this study.

– Forms of *ludere* and *ludus* appear three times in the prefatory
address.
– The cento is in the preface and its closing called:
frivolum opusculum ("a trifling piece of work")
iocularis materia ("a humorous story")
ludicrum nostrum ("our trifling")[14]
ludus noster ("our play/game") (159)
noster iocus (157) ("our jesting or play")

Ausonius describes the cento-performance as "a task for memory
[*memoria*] only, which has to gather up scattered tags [*sparsa colligere*]
and fit these mangled scraps together into a whole [*integrare lacerate*],
and so is more likely to provoke your laughter [*ridere*] than your praise"
(Prefatory address p. 132.4–5). Ausonius thus presents his collocations
of lines as *ridiculum*:

> And if some people, draped in seriousness [*severitas vestita*] condemns
> aught in my playful piece [*in nostro ioco*], let them know that it is taken
> out of Virgil [*de Virgilo arcessitum*]. So anyone who disapproves of this
> play of mine [*cui hic ludus noster non placet*] should read it, or once he
> has read it, let him forget it, or if he has not fogotten it, let him pardon
> it. For, as a matter of fact, it is the story of a wedding [*fabula de nuptiis
> est*], and, like it or dislike it, the rites [*haec sacra*] are exactly as I have
> described (p. 139.17–21; LCL 157–62).[15]

Ausonius addresses the interplay between *res*, which is here wedding
and the sexual act, and the words taken from venerable Virgil. Precisely
this combination did upset some of his readers, some of whom found
his attempt must have been degrading to Virgil. In the lines preceding
the ones quoted above, Ausonius argues that themes that in themselves
might be inappropriate, were in fact addressed by Virgil himself. In the
prefatory address, however, Ausonius seems to agree with his sceptical audience: "For it is vexing to have Virgil's majestic verse degraded
with such a comic theme [*piget enim Vergiliani carminis dignitatem tam
ioculari dehonestasse materia*]. But what was I to do?" (p. 132.7–133.8).
There is a sense of rhetoric in the humble attitude taken by Ausonius
to his own cento, a so-called *captatio benevolentiae*; not surprising sine
he is duelling the Emperor himself. He even says that he composed the

---

[14] LCL renders *ludicrum* as "absurd", McGill, *Virgil Recomposed*, 166 n. 40 points
out that this is misleading. The term is derived from *ludus*.
[15] Quoted from LCL with some alterations.

cento hastily, in a single day and some hours of the night, probably an exaggeration. The playful nature of centos is, nonetheless affirmed in this text. It presents itself as "poetic ludism as a product of *otium*, or leisure."[16] Although some may find his attempt degrading to Virgil, Ausonius claims that his cento is after all *de Vergilio arcessitum* ("taken from Virgil") (158).

This leads to another important observation on centos, namely the advertised intertextuality. The interpretation of the individual intertextual links found in a cento and the level of intention in them is indeed a difficult matter, but Ausonius does not leave his audience in any doubt about his hypotext. In his own words, i.e. in non-Virgilic vocabulary, the prefatory address designates Virgil as the source-text, an attribution that can be substantiated by every reader familiar with Virgil. Only after the prefatory address does Ausonius proceed to the Virgilian lines. The playful element of the cento is definitely not that of being made to guess from what source the intertextual links are taken. That is a given; it is the topic from which the cento proceeds which starts the game. In the interplay between the two, "Verfremdung" takes place, and this cento becomes a playful text:

> If they are to appreciate the works fully, audiences need to be aware that the centos are Virgilian texts, created through a peculiar technique and displaying how writers handle that technique. Indeed, centos are fundamentally authorial demonstrations of skill in creating a new composition out of Virgil's verse units.[17]

This is also assumed in the closing line of the prefatory address. Ausonius invites his readers to judge his cento; if they find that he has not succeeded "this lump of verse may be 'returned to its proper treasury,' and the verse go back to the source from which they came [*ut cumulo carminis in fiscum suum redacto redeant versus unde venerunt*]" (p. 134.49–50). The prefatory address thus closes by advertising its epic source. Accordingly, within the playful manipulation of the source text there are also some strict limits, namely those of the verbal and metrical possibilities offered there. In spite of their playful nature, centos are nonetheless more confined in their art than other kinds of poetry. For

---

[16] McGill, *Virgil Recomposed*, 5. For the role of *otium* and literature, see also pp. 5–7. Reciting texts at dinners and drinking parties formed the ludic context of literary amusement and contests; see more below.

[17] McGill, *Virgil Recomposed*, 9.

example, this marks the difference between Juvencus and the centos. Juvencus does not impose upon himself the same restrictions as found in centos; hence the biblical references in his poem are, on the micro level, more easily recognizable than those in the centos to be treated in the proceeding chapters.

The genre demands memorization on a large scale. Scott McGill makes some considerations on how this might have happened: division of the texts into workable segments (verses, units or scenes) to be learnt by rote.[18] He seems to assume that the average Greek reader knew large sections of Homer's works, or even the entire poems, by heart. In my opinion, texts like Xenophon, *Symp.* 3.5, Dio Chrysostom, *Or.* 36.9 and Cicero, *Arch.* 18 should not be taken as evidence that people in general knew Homer by heart. The Borysthenic discourse of Dio praises the inhabitants of that city for having cultivated a special interest in Homer: "almost all at least know the *Iliad* by heart" (9).[19] In my view, the texts quoted in evidence of this describe exactly the aristocratic milieu in which centos were composed rather than giving a typical picture. It remains a fact however, that cento-composition as described here by Ausonius assumes familiarity with both sex and Virgil; it is this dual familiarity that makes the cento what it really is, namely a surprise at finding this topic clothed in epic style.

4.2   Playful texts

Ausonius demonstrated that centos were an upper-class amusement. In doing so, Ausonius places himself in a longstanding tradition of making ancient epics a means of amusement. Twisting and altering the venerable texts was important to this kind of entertainment. We

---

[18] McGill, *Virgil Recomposed*, 10–11.

[19] The epigraphical material does not support McGill on this. The investigations of Morgan, *Literate Education* and Cribiore, *Gymnastics of the Mind*, 194–7, 204–5 suggest a fragmentary knowledge of Homer among the average student; thus also Robert Lamberton, *Homer the Theologian. Neoplatonist Reading and the Growth of the Epic Tradition* (Berkeley, Los Angeles, London: University of California Press, 1989), 193. This finds corroboration in Aelius' *Varia Historia* 13.14: "Note that the ancients originally recited Homer's poems separately";. This means that the poems are divided into several parts to which particular names were given, Aelisu mentions some famous episodes from both the Iliad and the Odyssey. Aelius thus implies that there were Homer's epics were arranged primarily as episodes, not as one long story with a uniting plot.

will now elaborate on that. A cento of scattered Virgilian lines in the *Eclogues* and the *Aeneid* is found in Petronius' *Sat.* 132, in a way indicating the playful nature of this practice. Before looking at that text, let us work out the social context assumed for this cento. The *Satyricon* provides a context for this practice in Trimalchio's dinner: the food has been carried out, and the drinking-party proper is about to start. Then Trimalchio addresses his guests saying that it is time to give the fish something to swim in: *hoc vinum* (*Sat.* 39). To this belonged the entertainment, the so-called *post convivia* ('the after-dinners').[20] This included literature, music, dance, performances and sexual adventures. In the present context, the literature is of special interest. Trimalchio introduces the entertainment with the words *sic notus Vlixes*? ("is this the famous Odysseus?") from *Aen.* 2.44, adding "one must not forget one's culture [*philologia*] even at dinner." In Virgil this is Laocoön's question, warning the Trojans against the deceitful Greeks. No gifts of the Greeks, *in casu* the horse, are free from treachery! Trimalchio quotes this polemical saying about Odysseus in order to prepare the guests for the gastronomic surprises to come; truly an unexpected way to read Homer. The guests know Trimalchio better than to think that all he was offering was food on the table; there follows entertainment as well! It is necessary, even while drinking, to know one's *philologia*. This means literary study or in this particular context the classical literature.[21] This finds corroboration in *Sat.* 59, where Trimalchio stops a verbal fight that erupted between two of the guests by urging them to "start the fun [*hilares*] over again, and have a look at these reciters of Homer [*Homerotistes*]." Their performance, called a *fabula*, was a brief retelling of Homer's writings. *Fabula* is the term used by Ausonius as well to describe his amusing cento (see 4.1 above), thus demonstrating that he is picking up on a traditional genre.

Worth noticing is, however, that Trimalchio alters this story, or the hypotext, and presents a rewritten story. This is not a cento, but it demonstrates that the plot of the classical literature was a subject for play and entertainment. The twisting of the plot was a means of amusing

---

[20] See Karl Olav Sandnes, *Belly and Body in the Pauline Epistles* (Cambridge: Cambridge University Press, 2002), 79–93.

[21] *Philologia* in Latin may be used in a narrow sense, as does Seneca in his *Ep.* 108.23. He makes a contrast between *philosophia* and *philologia*, where the fist refers to the art of living, while the latter represents the perspective of minor details of less importance. This is not the meaning in the passage addressed now. It is more or less synonymous with *paideia*; see OLD s.v.

the guests. The plot, as reworked by Trimalchio, reaches its culmina-
tion in Ajax being wroth with Achilles who had been given Iphigenia,
Agamemnon's daughter, to wife.[22] At this signal the performers raise
a shout and a boiled calf with a warrior's helmet—here a symbol of
Achilles[23]—is presented to the guests. In this procession follows Ajax,
who attacks the calf, whereby the slaves have the slices apportioned
to the guests. Furthermore, according to *Sat.* 68 a slave enters and
declaims *canora voce* ("with a singing voice") from the opening line
of *Aen.* 5.1. This was clearly part of the party's amusement. The slave
recited in a shrill voice, put the wrong stresses on the words and mixed
up the verses. He combined Virgilian lines with old Latin comedy, so-
called Atellane verses. When the slave finished his performance, his
master made excuses for him, saying that he had not attended school
but had picked up his literature from street-performers.

It is now time to return to *Sat.* 132. Here Encolpius, the narrator,
reproaches his penis for not having performed when he was together
with his lover. The reaction of the penis in the love-scene is then
described by Petronius in a cento:

> *illa solo fixos oculos aversa tenebat* (= *Aen.* 6.469)
> *nec magis incepto vultum sermone movetur* (= *Aen.* 6.470)
> *quam lentae salices lassove papavera collo* (= modified *Ecl.* 3.83; 5.16 and
>   *Aen.* 9.436).

> it stayed there turned away with eyes fixed on the ground
> and at this unfinished speech its look were no more stirred
> than pliant willows are or poppies on their tired stalky necks.

The scene from which the two first lines are taken is when Dido realizes
that Aeneas is deceiving her and leaving Carthage for Italy. The first
gives her angry reaction, and the second says that now no words from
Aeneas were able to move her. She stood as "if she were set in hard flint
of Marpesian rock" (471). *Illa*, which refers to Dido in the *Aeneid*, now
appears in a new context, and describes Encolpius' penis. Indeed, it is
no surprise that Petronius did not include line 471 in his cento; that
would ruin his whole point, which was to depict a flaccid penis, unable

---

[22] See Michael Heseltine and E.H. Warmington, ed. and trans., *Petronius.* LCL
(Cambridge, MA and London: Harvard University Press and Wm. Heinemann, 1987),
128–9.
[23] The epithet "warrior of the waving crest [κορυθάϊκι πτολεμιστῇ]" (*Il.* 22.132) is
used for Achilles, but the related "warrior of the flashing helmet [κορυθαίολος]" is
also used for Hector (*Il.* 2.816).

to perform. As pointed out by Karla Pollmann, this identification is macabre and comic as well.[24] Dido, who is not moved by Aeneas' words, now lends her words to describing an impotent penis. The third line is taken from a description of Euryalus' death, which is compared to a flower withering when cut down. The lines from the *Ecloge* both speak of bending willows, which nicely fits Petronius' context. Petronius is playing with words and contexts, bending both of them. Dido and the penis have in common that they both failed to react as was expected of them. Petronius' sole point in the third line is the incapacity, not the lovely nature or inferiority of the drooping willows; here is incongruity in his use of Virgil. As for Euryalus' death as background for Encolpius' misperforming penis, there is, of course, an analogy. Petronius exploits the Virgilian context to give us a dramatic, vivid and comic picture of Encolpius' penis. From this example, Karla Pollmann formulates an important piece of insight for cento composition in general:

> On the one hand, the context of the original has to be neutralised to make the new meaning possible. At the same time, however, the old context has to stay in the readers' awareness in order to achieve its telling effect by way of contrasting transformation.[25]

It is precisely this interplay between the two texts which makes the new text a *bent* text, and therefore also able to surprise and amuse.[26]

A most interesting text is found in Lucian *Symp.* 17. At the climax of the carousal, when the guests have become drunk and the party is about to degenerate into chaos, Histiadus entertained the guests in "combining lines of Pindar and Hesiod and Anacreon in such a way as to make out of them a single poem and a very funny one [ἐξ ἁπάντων μίαν ᾠδὴν παγγέλοιον ἀποτελεῖσθαι]."[27] Three observations are worth making here. In the first place, the context is the 'after-dinner' described above. In the second place, Histiadus is called

---

[24] Pollmann, "Sex and Salvation in the Vergilian Cento of the Fourth Century", 83–84.

[25] Pollmann, "Sex and Salvation in the Vergilian Cento of the Fourth Century," 84. More on cento technique below.

[26] Among the pre-Christian *centones*, *De Panificio* ("On Breadmaking") tears down Virgil's text, particularly *Aen.* 6 on the punishments of Tartarus, and reconstructs a new text about breadmaking; see McGill, *Virgil Recomposed*, 57–64. This eleven-line cento is reproduced in Latin by McGill on p. 57. The initial lacuna leaves the question of a preface open, but a preface like the one we found in Ausonius is hardly to be expected.

[27] This formulation is very close to how Ausonius defines a cento; see above in 4.1.

ὁ γραμματικὸς, which means that he was an instructor in literature. This suggests that making a cento was an exercise associated with skill in the classical literature. It says that Histadius presented his cento as a recital: ἐρραψῴδει, thus suggesting that centos were performed according to the ancient rhapsodic tradition.[28] Thirdly, one gets the impression that this is a skill that took advantage of the moment and tried to clothe it in venerable words. It says that Histiadus included among his lines also some from *the Iliad*, which amused the audience particularly. He quoted *Il.* 4.447 in an abbreviated form ("They smote their shields together") and 450 ("Then lamentations rose, and vaunts of men"). The audience found both sentences to fit exactly the chaotic situation of the post-prandial atmosphere. Both lines are taken from the battle scene of *Il.* 4, but they are here used in an almost allegorical way. For what Histadius is describing is sexual carousal, as we know it from Ausonius' *Nuptial Cento*.

Plutarch *Mor.* 710A-3F (*Table Talk*) raises the question of proper entertainment as a dinner party. The discussion of literature appears to some to turn the symposion into a γραμμᾰτοδῐδασκᾰλεῖον, that is a school where literature is taught. The light-entertainment aspect is also seen in the fact that the participants preferred the comedies of Menander (712A-D).[29] This practice can be traced to the classical texts on *symposia*, such as Xenophon. There it is demonstrated that Homeric texts were part of the entertainment, and that details from Homeric passages were performed by the participants themselves. In *Symp.* 6.3, Xenophon compares the commonly used flute-girls to the recital of poetic verses as optional kinds of amusements; admittedly, also easily combined.[30]

These examples demonstrate how the texts of Homer were used for amusing guests. Twisting Homeric texts was part of the entertainment, and some parts of Homer were even performed by the so-called *Homeristai* or rhapsodists who knew these texts intimately enough to alter them.[31] This was a context from which developed the practice

---

[28] Usher, *Homeric Stitchings*, 19–31 has pointed out that rhapsodic performance in schools may be the seed-bed of cento composition.

[29] More examples are found in Athenaeus, *Deiphnosophistae*'s many texts related to the pleasures of eating and the partying accompanying the banquets.

[30] See also *Symp.* 3.5–6; 4.6–8. Juvenal, *Sat.* 11.162–81 has the singing of Virgil replace the dancing girl, due to lack of space where the party was being held.

[31] See LSJ s.v.; Ch. P. Jones, "Dinner Theater," in *Dining in a Classical Context*, ed. William J. Slater (Ann Arbor: The University of Michigan Press), 187–93.

of twisting pieces from the classical literature in unexpected ways. Intertextuality in all possible ways is the heart of the game. Naturally, this functions to amuse only if the passages in question were quite familiar also to the guests.

4.3   Hypotexts 'Open' to Yielding New Texts

We noted in Chapter 1.2 that Homer and Virgil were outstanding among the scultural canonical texts.[32] Curricula in education, epigraphical and literary evidence—all point to the fundamental role of these two epics in the ancient world.[33] It is, therefore, worth noting that the two most important Christian centos recast precisely these two representatives of Greek and Latin tradition. This observation by itself indicates that the centos were mediating between texts and culture, placing themselves within the foundational texts of the culture, but also bending them.

As we saw in Chapter 2, school exercises included paraphrases, which included alterations of well-known texts. Students were called to rewrite passages from the epics. Familiarized with such exercises, centonists were acculturated to recast both Homer and Virgil. Early on, students were taught that they 'could do things' with the classical texts. They were open to be recast, transformed, altered and reused for various purposes. Both Homer and Virgil could be "reworked to yield fresh texts."[34] School exercises inculcated this attitude towards the literary canons of the culture.

Two fundamental views commonly held on the classical epics furthered the idea that they were 'open texts.' In the first place, the great poets were often—due to their inspired nature—considered to transmit truth in a hidden way. For their texts to become useful, their true meaning had to be found by decoding them, which very often meant allegorical interpretation. Heraclitus the Grammarian's *Homeric Problems*, subtitled *Concerning Homer's allegorical interpretation of the gods*, is a good example:

---

[32] See also McGill, *Virgil Recomposed*, XV–XVI, 157 n. 27.

[33] As for their role among the Christians, see Sandnes, *The Challenge of Homer*; Freund; *Vergil im frühen Christentum*; Sabine MacCormack, *The Shadows of Poetry. Vergil in the Mind of Augustine* (Berkeley, CA: University of California Press, 1998). Especially on the role of *4th Ecloge*, see Stephen Benko, "Virgil's Fourth Eclogue in Christian Interpretation," *ANRW* II.1: 646–705.

[34] McGill, *Virgil Recomposed*, XVIII.

It is a weighty and damaging charge that heaven brings against Homer for his disrespect of the divine. If he meant nothing allegorically [εἰ μηδὲν ἠλληγόρησσεν], he was impious through and through, and sacrilegious fables, loaded with blasphemous folly, run riot through both epics. And so, if one were to believe that was all said in obedience to poetical traditions without any philosophical theory or underlying allegorical trope, Homer would be a Salomoneus or a Tantalus 'with tongue unchastened, a most disgraceful sickness' (*Homeric Problems* 1.1.3).[35]

This text clearly demonstrates that allegorical interpretation is a means to justify Homer against the alleged wrong notions he held.[36] Heraclitus considers the *Iliad* as "the poem of strife and war," while the *Odyssey* is the "poem of moral character." (60.2). In *Homeric Problems* 70, Heraclitus provides a survey of much of the *Odyssey*:

> Odysseus's wanderings as a whole, if carefully studied, will be found to be allegorical. Homer has produced in Odysseus a sort of instrument of every virtue, and has used him as the vehicle of his own philosophy, because he hated the vices which ravage human life…[now follows a broad sketch of Odyssean scenes]. These things are told as fables for the sake of the audience; but if one penetrates deeply into the wisdom which they represent allegorically, they will be found very useful to the initiated [τοῖς μεμυημένοις].[37]

In short, "the whole poem is full of allegory" (75.12). This enabled Heraclitus to extract science, knowledge about the nature and philosophy from Homer; Christian centonists extracted from the same texts the story of Jesus and salvation. Allegory paved the way for a variety of interpretations.

Secondly, the idea—so common in antiquity—that the poets were inspired, and therefore also omniscient,[38] also furthered the "open" nature of these texts. To Heraclitus, it is precisely the divine inspiration of Homer that also makes his works allegorical texts in need of

---

[35] Translation from Donald A. Russell and David Konstan, ed. and trans., *Homeric Problems* (Atlanta, GA: Society of Biblical Literature, 2005).

[36] See also *Homeric Problems* 6.1–2; 22.1; 76; 79; Sandnes, *The Challenge of Homer*, 49–58.

[37] Heraclitus' conclusion brings to mind how Christians coped with the literary style of the Gospels; to the initiated they revealed, in spite of their shabby style, divine mysteries (Chapter 3).

[38] With regard to Homer, see Sandnes, *The Challenge of Homer*, 44–47. Heraclitus' *Homeric Problems* 76.1 and 79.12–13 (conclusion) strongly promotes Homer as divinely inspired. The well-known practice of consulting Virgil's texts as an oracle [*sortes Virgilianae*], i.e. the employment of lots using texts from Virgil, and extracting from them the divine will, is worth mentioning here as well.

decoding; he thus calls Homer "the great hierophant of heaven and the gods" (*Homeric Problems* 76.1).[39] As Heraclitus says, Homer was a source from which knowledge on all matters could in principle be culled [ὥσπερ ἐκ πηγῆς τῶν Ὁμηρικῶν ἐπῶν] (*Homeric Problems* 18.1). This is important because it implies that the making of new texts, foreign to Homer's writings themselves, and to Virgil as well,[40] was consistent with how Homer was generally viewed in antiquity, albeit that idiosyncratic allegories were now offered. What to us appears therefore rather awkward, to the ancients was one particular way of expressing a commonly held view on Homer.

This naturally invited various methods and kinds of reading; they all accepted that the classical texts could be recast in various ways. Christian centonists took advantage of this notion and the school exercises. Homer and Virgil could be manipulated, and thus invited readers to become authors. The centonists exploited this opening. Although Dennis R. MacDonald has not worked out his Mimesis Criticism in this way, I think this must be the theory underpinning his idea of Homeric *mimesis* as making up new texts: As a reader of Homer, Mark becomes author of his Gospel. For the understanding of the Christian centos to be treated in the proceeding chapters, the "open" nature of the literary canon is crucial.

It must by now have become abundantly clear that centos by their very nature imply a lack of authorial respect.[41] Centos were liable to involve audience or reader in ways that have analogies in postmodern literary theory. In bringing together daily business and classical texts, as is the case with erotic centos or centos on breadmaking or dice, and even more so in Christian centos, where two bodies of classical texts merge, the centos leave their audience in a space of allusion. Joseph Pucci speaks of "the full-knowing reader," possessing a competence in both "texts" involved.[42] The powerful reader becomes the meaning-

---

[39] Cf. Ps. Longinus, *Subl.* 36.2.

[40] Similar claims were made for Virgil; see Pollmann, "The Transformation of the Epic Genre in Christian Late Antiquity," 63.

[41] Cf. the critique voiced by Irenaeus and Tertullian; see Chapters 4.5.2 and 4.5.3.

[42] Pucci, *The Full-knowing Reader*. I take Pucci's "full-knowing reader" to mean the same as what MacDonald, *Does the New Testament Imitate Homer?*, 150, calls "the hermeneutical haves". See also Pavlovskis, "Proba and the Semiotics of the Narrative Virgilian Cento," 76, saying that centos are only accessible to those "initiated, who will recognize implicit meanings that elude an outsider." This applies both ways, of course, to the hypotext as well as the hypertext.

making reader, making sense of the comparisons, dissonances, alterations, irony, surprises, contrasts etc. The audience is constantly invited
to resolve the interplay between the "texts" involved.[43] We will later
see, in Chapter 6.5, that in the presentation of the crucifixion, Eudocia
has a line from *Od.* 9.432 (l. 1866 = Scembra CP 1876) describing Jesus.
He is then presented in words about the best sheep in the flock of the
Cyclops, under which Odysseus could hide and eventually escape. It
takes a "full-knowing reader" to see this as a line informed by Christian
interpretation of Jesus' death which brings salvation. With reference
to Proba's cento, Zoja Pavlovskis says: "Remove the reader's familiarity with Virgil's poetry, and Proba's poem paradoxically loses all its
virtue…"[44] This applies, of course, also to the Christian centos, where
intimate knowledge of the Holy Scriptures and Christian tradition is
likewise assumed.

4.4 Cento Transformation

From Petronius' cento quoted above, we gained insight into the technique of cento composition, as well as its "deconstructional" nature.
Ausonius laid down rules for centonists, and demonstrated in practice
how they were to proceed. A cento consists of a macro and a micro-
level. The micro level is the many detailed intertextual links to be
observed. At this level numerous allusive links are made possible, a fact
which makes the question of authorial intention rather elusive.[45] The
macro-level informs the combination of lines occurring in the cento,
and the reasons behind the selections made throughout. At this level it
is decided if it is a cento about wedding and sex—thus Ausonius—or
about the story of Jesus—as with Proba and Eudocia. Karla Pollmann
distinguishes between different kinds of dependence between the hypotext and the new text coming into being through the cento technique,
and my presentation here owes much to her.[46]

---

[43] Ibid. p. 64–69 argues that this awareness of the reader's competence arose in late
antiquity and is witnessed in e.g. Macrobius *Saturnalia*'s many passages on Virgil's
borrowing from Homer.
[44] Pavlovskis, "Proba and the Semiotics of the Narrative Virgilian Cento," 76.
[45] See McGill, *Virgil Recomposed*, 25–30.
[46] Pollmann, "Sex and Salvation in the Vergilian *Cento* of the Fourth Century,"
86–87.

The surface level is episodic memory, recollection based on occurrence of key words.[47] Later in this investigation I address this in terms
of the centonist searching her "mental concordance." Implied here is
that the Virgilian or Homeric context of the lines may be more or less
ignored. For example, Pollmann mentions how Ausonius makes use of
Aen. 6.122 [*itque reditque* = "going back and forth"] in his cento l.126.
In Virgil this describes Pollux who "redeemed his brother by dying in
turn and so often *treads and retreads* the road of death"; accordingly
Macrobius (*Sat.* 4.5.2) says that Virgil took this as an argument that
misericordia should not be denied to Aeneas. In Ausonius' cento *itque
reditque* refers to the coital movements of the groom's penetrating the
bride. *Aen.* 4.690–1a about Dido's convulsion before falling dead, in
Ausonius (p. 138.122–3a) describes the bride while being penetrated.
We will see later (Chapter 5) that Proba (l. 618) describes Jesus at the
cross in words taken from *Aen.* 7.66: *pedibus per mutua nexis* ("one
foot fixed upon the other"). In Virgil this describes a swarm of bees
hanging with feet intertwined. Proba's text is here a Christianization
of Virgil, while Ausonius' is a sexualisation of the same text. To him
this line describes the intertwining of the couple during intercourse.[48]
These are examples where the Virgilian context seems to be of no help
in understanding the hypertext. The centonist is then guided primarily by the occurrence of key terms forming a bridge between the two
"texts" involved. Nonetheless, the centonist is always transforming
the hypotext by making it a building-block in a new text. This applies
when the original context is easily moved to the new one; often type-
scenes are involved, such as bridal scenes in Ausonius.[49]

In other instances, however, the centonist transposes the hypotext
by interacting with the context given by the hypotext. Despite the
Homeric or Virgilian straitjacket, the hypotext is considerably altered
and modified by transposing it into a new context, aimed at making
statements about e.g. Christian faith, whereby the source text is transformed.[50] This corresponds to Usher's "Verfremdung", MacDonald's
"transvaluation" and Thraedes's "Kontrastimitation." The author is

---

[47] See also McGill, *Virgil Recomposed*, 12.

[48] Pollmann, "Sex and Salvation in the Vergilian *Cento* of the Fourth Century," 92.

[49] For examples, see Pollmann, "Sex and Salvation in the Vergilian *Cento* of the
Fourth Century," 86.

[50] Pollmann, "Sex and Salvation in the Vergilian *Cento* of the Fourth Century," 92.
For degrees of transformation, culminating in transposition of the hypotext, see Gérard
Genette, *Palimpsestes. La Littérature au second degré* (Paris: Seuil: 1982), 14–47.

interacting with the hypotext at a deeper level. When Ausonius describes Encolpius' underperforming penis in language taken from Euryalus' death, it is worth considering the implications of this. In his *cento* p. 138.110a [*est in secessu*] ("in a secluded place"), Ausonius quotes from *Aen.* 1.159, a description of the beaches of Libya where Aeneas and his men found refuge from the storm: "disembarking with earnest longing for the land, the Trojans gain the welcome beach and stretch their brine-drenched limbs upon the shore" (*Aen.* 1.171–3). Ausonius makes this a description of the female genitals.[51] Obviously, the Virgilian wording that Ausonius here includes in his cento, receives meaning and significance from the Virgilian context: The safe haven has finally been reached! But Ausonius, without any outward indication of it, nonetheless, performs an idiosyncratic allegorical reading of Virgil here. In other genres, allegory of a given text is often introduced in either meta-sentences or formulations like τουτέστιν or the like.[52] The cento form does not allow such additions; the allegorical level, therefore, comes to existence in the interplay between the macro and micro level of the cento. Without the readers' knowledge of the hypotext, transformation does not occur. It works as interplay between two "canonical" texts which can only be understood with the allusions given by the hypotext's context in place.[53] It is here worth quoting Martha A. Malamud[54] on centos, and Ausonius in particular:

> For a cento, by its very nature, works on two levels, so that the reader cannot take it as a straightforward, self-enclosed narrative. The other text, the 'original' text, is always there; without it the cento would have no point. By the same token, the cento, by changing the context, and therefore the meaning of the Vergilian phrases, alters forever the reader's perception of the original Vergilian text. He cannot read the cento without recalling the original text, but after having read the cento, he

---

[51] Pollmann, "Sex and Salvation in the Vergilian *Cento* of the Fourth Century," 86–87.

[52] Sandnes, "Markus—en allegorisk biografi?," 279.

[53] Ilona Opelt, "Der zürnende Christus," *JAC* 7 (1964): 106–7 gives a precise description: "Der Centonendichter gebraucht einen fremden, von ihm als vorbildlich bewerteten Wortschatz. Trotz des Zwanges, trotz der selbst gewählten Beschränkungen auf eine fremde Palette, will er aber durchaus ein originales Werk schaffen. Er fügt vorgegebene kleinere Verseinheiten zu neuen Gebilden. Er ist also bereits im Kleinen durch Umdeutungen und neue Verknüpfungen schöpferisch, er ist, aber auch schöpferisch im Grossen wie jeder andere Dichter: nähmlich in der Komposition der Szene und in der Strukturierung des Gesamtwerkes."

[54] Martha A Malamud, *A Poetics of Transformation. Prudentius and Classical Mythology* (Ithaca and London: Cornell University Press, 1989), 37–38.

cannot read the original without finding the cento intruding. This leaves the reader caught between two texts, made fully aware of the unfixed nature of language, whose elements (in this case the metrical units) can be assembled and reassembled, at will or at random. But it also forces the reader to participate, for the cento's success as an amusement depends on the reader's knowledge of the Vergilian corpus and his perception of the incongruity between the language of the original text and the artificial plot contrived by Ausonius.

This is the light in which we have to evaluate Mimesis Criticism's claim that Mark's Gospel uses subtle emulation and that the *Homerocentones* simultaneously provide an analogy. Seen from the perspective of cento technique, these two claims are contradictory.

4.5   CENTOS AMONG CHRISTIANS

In Biblical scholarship, the cento literature has not received much attention, although the practice of centos among Christians is attested from the second century on. To judge from the examples, it seems that at this time centos were a means of putting together proof-texts, thus bringing to mind also scriptural exegesis of the New Testament. Elizabeth A. Clarke and Diane F. Hatch[55] rightly find it somewhat surprising that centos have attracted so little attention among New Testament scholars, since their intensive work on how the New Testament reworks and combines the Old Testament might be somehow related. David S. Wiesen suggests that Acts 1:20 and Rom 3:11–18 represent a cento format.[56] Luke 4:18–19 is worth mentioning as well; here Isa 61:1–2; 58:6 and Lev 25:10 together form a single Scriptural citation. I will however, emphasize that in spite of the cento-like format found here, they do not form narratives, as we know them from later Christian centos.

---

[55] Elizabeth A. Clarke and Diane F. Hatch, *The Golden Bough. The Oaken Cross. The Virgilian Cento of Faltonia Betitia Proba* (Chico: Scholars Press, 1981), 105.

[56] David S. Wiesen, "Virgil, Minucius Felix and the Bible," *Hermes* 99 (1971): 90. Some scholars introduce cento to explain the phenomenon of citations drawn from a mosaic of Old Testament texts; for references see Robert Simons, "The Magnificat: Cento, Psalm or Imitatio?," *TynBul* 60 (2009): 25–27. Simons himself says that Magnificat "falls short of the kind of formal structure that is required to claim that the Magnificat is a cento" (p. 27); *pace* Jospeh A. Fitzmyer and Raymond E. Brown. The formal structure is, according to Simons, Ausonius' rules for cento composition. Simons seems unaware that Eudocia did not comply strictly with these rules; see e.g. Chapter 6.2 of this study. Simons is, however, right in pointing out that Christian imitation of Old Testament ideas and models represent an example of rhetorical exercises, so-called *progymnasmata*. Thus Christian citations of the Old Testament and cento composition have common roots in ancient rhetoric; see Chapter 4.5.2 of this study.

Furthermore, the playful nature that is so characteristic of centos does not apply to how New Testament combines Old Testament citations. This is, of course, not to deny that "Verfremdung" is implied in New Testament Scriptural exegesis. The centos of special interest for the present study are those centonizing the life of Jesus, thus equalling the Gospels. This phenomenon is not witnessed before the late fourth century.

4.5.1 *Minucius Felix on the Creation*

The importance of Virgil for Christian apologetics is seen in e.g. Minucius Felix (early 3rd century C.E.). No pagan poet is more important to him.[57] It is therefore not surprising that he is the first Christian author to stitch together lines from Virgil in a manner that prepare the way for later Christian narrative centos. Minucius Felix does not leave his readers in any doubt about the author from whom his lines are taken. This is not due to ignorance on the part of his audience, but because it is precisely according to his purpose to interact in a Christian way with the Roman text *par excellence*.

The possibly first extant Christian cento is found in Minucius Felix *Oct.* 19.2, where he discusses, like Cicero's *De natura deorum*, the nature of gods and cosmology. He pieces together lines from the *Aeneid* and *Georgics*, and they are introduced in a way which establishes Virgil's and Homer's authority above other poets:[58]

> *Principio caelum ac terras* (a conflation of *Aen.* 6.724 and *Georg.* 4.222)
> *Spiritus intus alit et infusa mens agitat* (a combination of *Aen.* 6.726 and 727)
> *Inde hominum pedumque genus* (*Aen.* 1.743a)
> *Deum namque ire per omnes*
> *Terrasque tractusque maris caelumque profundum*
> *Unde hominum genus et peduces, unde imber et ignes* (*Georg.* 4.221–3 + *Aen.* 1.743b)

In the beginning Heaven and earth.
A spirit within nourishes and a mind infused stirs them.
From this arises the race of men and animal.
For God pervades all,
Both land and sea and heaven profound;
From which comes the race of men and animal, rain and fire.[59]

---

[57] Freund, *Vergil im frühen Christentum*, 108–67.
[58] See Freund, *Vergil im frühen Christentum*, 133–4.
[59] Slightly altered from the LCL edition.

The text starts with Anchises' speech in *Aen.* 6.724–51. Aeneas asks his father about the fate of the souls abiding in Hades by the river Lethe. Anchises presents the idea of the heavenly origin of souls, thereby expressing cosmology and theology. Stephan Freund calls this speech "der eschatologischen Offenbarungsrede der Anchises."[60] As pointed out by David S. Wiesen, Minucius is consciously replacing *Georg.* 4.224 with *Aen.* 1.743b: "The poet may now be understood to be saying, not that animals as well as men receive a portion of the divine at birth, but merely that God is the author of all nature;"[61] it is, therefore, not a lapse of memory. Run together, these Virgilian lines appear as analogous to Genesis, which Minucius thought was a proof that the two "canonical" texts may go together.[62] All the Virgilian texts used in some way deal with cosmology.

The text well illustrates Christian adoption of the method of cento composition. In the first place, the assumption is a detailed knowledge of and high respect for the classical legacy preserved in Homer[63] and Virgil. Secondly, the piecing together of Virgilian lines (micro level) is revealing as to the macro level of the cento, which here is Genesis or Christian cosmology. Finally, Christian doctrine may be expressed, and is liable to be expressed, in the form and words of the great authors of the pagan culture, if read correctly. The latter point implies that both are improved on through the cento.[64] As demonstrated by Barbara Aland, Minucius Felix's use of pagan literature demonstrates that he is addressing upper-class Romans.[65] Peter G. van der Nat has rightly pointed out that *Octavius* presents an ambivalent attitude to *eloquentia* and rhetorical style;[66] the obvious example being *Oct.* 16.6:

---

[60] Freund, *Vergil im frühen Christentum*, 134.
[61] Wiesen, "Virgil, Minucius Felix and the Bible," 87.
[62] Freund, *Vergil im frühen Christentum*, 136–9.
[63] *Oct.* 19.1 actually quotes from Homer as well.
[64] Freund, *Vergil im frühen Christentum*, 100 points to *Oct.* 7.5 where Caecilius present his reasons for keeping to the inherited *religio*. *Carmina poetarum* belong to the foundation for this religion. Freund comments: "…doch ist es für die Argumentationsstrategie des Apologeten bemerkenswert, dass tatsächlich die *auctoritas* der Dichter nicht gegen die Christen ins Feld geführt wird". As Freund points out, this is probably due more to the view of Christian apologetes themselves than to pagan opinion; see pp. 101–3.
[65] Barbara Aland, "Christentum, Bildung und Römische Oberschicht. Zum 'Octavianus' des Minucius Felix," in *Platonismus und Christentum. In Honour of H. Dörrie*, ed. Barbara Aland and Friedhelm Mann (Münster: Aschendorff, 1983), 11–30.
[66] P.G. van der Nat, "Zu den Voraussetzungen der christlichen Literatur: Die Zeugnisse von Minucius Felix und Laktanz," in *Christianism et Formes Litteraires de*

"Indeed, the more unskilled the utterance [*imperiotior sermo*], the clearer is the reasoning, for it relies not on tricks of eloquence, or graces of style [*pompa facunidae et gratiae*], but is sustained on its own merits by the rule of right [*recti regula*]." The latter is a reference to *veritas*.[67] The statement is responding to common accusations of ignorance and illiteracy on the part of the Christians and their literature. Minucius Felix adopted the cento form with Virgilian lines on account of their eloquence; as for *veritas* clothed in this style, the source was the Scriptures. This is precisely what characterizes also the Christian centos to be presented in Chapters 5 and 6 of this study. Cento composition, as it is presented here, was by some Christians considered to embody a potential danger when "in the wrong hands." To that we now turn.

4.5.2 *Tertullian: The "Deconstructional" Power of Centos*

In his *De Praescriptione Haereticorum*, Tertullian addresses the question of heresies on a general basis (*Praescr.* 44.13–14). It is, therefore, presented as an introductory essay to any doctrine speaking against true faith [*fides veritatis*] (44.12). Nonetheless, special attention is given to the Valentinians, Marcion and Apelles. Tertullian's arguments revolve around topics such as apostolic tradition and succession, origin *v.* posterity, faith *v.* curiosity, public preaching *v.* esoteric claims, Jerusalem *v.* Athens, catholicity *v.* individuality. Most important though, Tertullian holds it against the heretics that their teaching implies a rewriting of *regula fidei* ("rule of faith" = tradition) with the help of the Scriptures themselves. In short, they keep the words but alter the message. Tertullian presents the transmitted faith of the church in creed-like statements in Chapter 13: *haec regula a Christo…instituto* ("this rule established by Christ") (*Praescr.* 13.5 cf. 36.4–6). This is the faith that the heresies are now redefining, with the very help of the Scriptures themselves. In *Praescr.* 44.9–11 (cf. 30.15–16), Tertullian ironically presents Christ— speaking in the first person singular—as though he is regretting his teaching and now changing his *regula*. Christ admits that he was wrong [*erravi*] in his teaching. In Tertullian's well-known sarcastic style he conveys that the heresies are now finally amending Christ's teaching.

---

l'Antiquite Tardive en Occident, ed. Alan Cameron and Manfred Fuhrmann (Geneve: Fondation Hardt, 1977), 201–12.

[67] That term appears in *Oct.* 16. 6 as well; se also chaps. 14–15.

The means by which this happened was Scriptural exegesis. According to Tertullian, it is a matter of to whom the Scriptures rightly belong: *possessio scripturarum* ("ownership of the Scriptures") (15.4), *cuius sunt scripturae* ("whose are the Scriptures") (19.2), *nullum ius capiunt christianarum litterarum* ("they have no right to the Christian Scriptures") (37.3). Thereby Tertullian raises his main point, namely that the Scriptures are correctly interpreted within the framework of *regula fidei* only; judged solely from *verba*, the Scriptures are open to be bent.

The heresies fail to interpret the Scriptures correctly; on the contrary they alter *regula* by fitting the Scriptures into a different system. It is a matter not of details, nor of method, but of a false composition (17.3); in short an alternative *dispositio*. Thereby they keep the form, but change the *res*, all the time giving the impression of accordance and continuity. Chapters 38–39 are the hub of Tertullian's accusation against the heretics. Their corruption of the Scriptures consists primarily in altering the arrangement of the instruments of doctrine (= the New Testament writings) [*eos necessitas institit aliter disponendi instruments doctrinae*] (*Praescr.* 38.2). Marcion "used the knife" and excised from the Scriptures what he found inappropriate according to his teaching [*materia sua*] (38.8). Valentinus apparently made use of the entire Scripture [*integrum instrumentum*], but he took away more [*plus abstulit*] and added more [*plus adiecit*] by arranging everything into another *dispositio* (38.20). Clearly *dispositio* is a matter of concern here, which corresponds to the macro level of centos, the organizing substructure deciding what a cento is about.

The procedure of the heretics is described as an emulation of Scripture (*Praescr.* 38.6; 40.7). At this point an analogy [*exemplum*] is given; enters now cento composition. Such procedure is witnessed with regard to the classical literature of the culture: "You see today, that from Virgil a story of a wholly different character is composed; the content is arranged according to the verse, and the verse according to the content [*ex Virgilio fabulam in totum aliam componi, materia secundum versus et versibus secundum materiam concinnatis*]" (39.3).[68] This procedure is now exemplified. Tertullian describes cento composition according to its micro level = the verses are kept intact, and according to its macro level = an entirely new story is the result of an

---

[68] My own translation.

alternative *dispositio*; this in fact deconstructs the micro level while still keeping it intact outwardly. To Tertullian, a new doctrine is thereby disguised in the clothes of the Scriptures.

Tertullian mentions Hosidius Geta who rewrote *Medea* in 461 lines in hexameter, almost all taken from Virgil.[69] This is the first extant cento known. Geta's work must have been quite analogous to what the Christian centonists did to biblical texts. Worth noting is that this cento has a tragedy come out of Virgil's epics, which indicates that also the question of genre was negotiable. A second example given is that a relative of Tertullian himself turned *The Table of Cebes* into a cento of Virgilian verses: *ex eodem poëta intercetera stili sui otia Pinacem Cebetis explicuit* ("from the same poet he explained in some leisure productions of his pen, *The Table of Cebes*").[70] It is worth noting that Tertullian says that this work was a product of *otium*; which indicates that this is a ludic activity aimed at refreshing the mind.[71] Tertullian calls these texts *Homerocentones*; those who composed them "stitch together into one body a work of their own out of many scraps from here and there in the fashion of centos [*qui de carminibus Homeri propria opera more centonario ex multis hinc inde compositis in unum sarciunt corpus*] (39.5).[72] Centos are here defined in accordance with Ausonius' definition given above:

> *ex multis* ("from many")   *in unum corpus* ("into one body")
>   *propria opera* ("one's own work")

This is the *mos centonaris*, as Tertullian calls it. Tertullian thereby intends to have a well-known procedure on display; hence Tertullian speaks of *mos*, an established practice. The patchwork of lines taken from Virgil or from Homer does not create the story. There is a framework, an overarching and organizing plot into which the classical lines are fitted [*dispositio*]. Tertullian has in mind the custom of piecing together

---

[69] Fragments of this work is preserved in *Anthologia Latina* in the *Codici Salmasiani* 1761–79; see the Teubner text-edition of Fransiscus Buecheler and Alexander Riese, *Anthologia Latina Pars Prior. Carmina in Codicibus Scripta Fasc 1* (Leipzig: Teubner, 1894) and the new edition Hosidii *Getae Medea Cento Virgilianus*, ed. Rosa Lamacchia (Leipzig: Teubner Verlagsgesellschaft, 1981).

[70] This philosophical dialogue is attributed to Cebes, a friend of Socrates in Plato's dialogues, but it probably dates from 2nd century C.E. It pictures allegorically—hence it is called Pinax—human life; see von Arnim, "Kebes", *Pauly-Wissowa RCA*, 101–5.

[71] See McGill, *Virgil Recomposed*, 5–7.

[72] My translation with some help from ANF.

texts dislocated from their context and fitted into a new. Likewise—and this is what Tertulliam is aiming at—the heresies replace *regula* with another framework into which they fit lines from the Scripture. If *regula* is tampered with according to the procedure of *mos centonaris*, the Scriptures may be made to support a new faith. Tertulian knows the deconstructional power of cento composition. With regard to our topic, the following observations are relevant:

Tertullian knows the genre of *centones*, although nothing indicates that he is familiar with Christian *centones* as we know them from later time. He is making an analogy between this genre and the method of heresies, claiming that they are arranged to fool the unlearned. He is not claiming that the heresies actually composed *centones*. But this genre serves as a helpful example to point out the possibility of rearranging a given text, without necessarily tampering with the text itself, and still making an entire new story, simply in altering the *dispositio*: "Als Ergebnis seiner (i.e. Marcion) 'textkritischen' Methoden entsteht ein neuer Gesamttext, der unter dem Vorzeichen seiner Lehre steht."[73]

Biblical scholars might find that the approach of those composing centos brings to mind so-called testimonies or a collection of texts bound together around a certain theme or topic in order to add scriptural proof. Examples of this are e.g. 4QTest *florilegia*.[74] A marked difference is, however, that *florilegia* or anthologies are not storied; they are primarily textual collages. However, this distinction is blurred by Tertullian himself when in *Marc.* 4.13 he strings together a number of Old Testament passages as forming a prophetic basis for Luke's narrative about Jesus in Luke 6:12: "Now during those days he went out to the mountain to pray; and he spent the night in prayer to God. And when day came..." The background for this is Tertullian's refuta-

---

[73] Dietrich Schleyer, ed. and trans., *Tertullian. De Praescriptione Haereticorum* (Turnout: Brepols, 2002), 53.

[74] See Jürgen Paul Schwindt, "Florilegium", *Brill's New Pauly*, 5: 470–1. An extensive presentation of the phenomenon is given by Henry Chadwick, "Florilegium," *RAC* 7: 1131–60. He traces the *florilegium* method to ancient teaching where classical texts were learnt by rote (Plato, *Leg.* 810D-1A). Plato, however, discusses whether this applies to the whole works of the poets, or only to the *kefalaia*. Plato is renowned for his scepticism of the poets, Homer in particular; see Sandnes, *The Challenge of Homer*, 50–52; Russell and Konstan, *Heraclitus*, xix–xxi. Plato therefore suggests that discourse between philosophers would be better for instructing the young.

tion of Marcion, claiming that Jesus is also the Creator found in the Old Testament—all argued with reference to the Gospel of Luke, the only Gospel (with some alterations) accepted by Marcion. The piece of story told in Luke 6:12 is a fulfilment of Old Testament prophecies, whereby each verifies key elements of Luke 6:12:

Isa 40:9	"Get you up to a high mountain, O Zion, herald of good tidings, lift it up, do not fear; say to the cities of Judah, 'here is your God'."
Nah 1:15	"Look! On the mountains the feet of one who brings good tidings, who proclaims peace!"
Isa 52:6	"Therefore my people shall know my name; therefore in that day they shall know that it is I who speak; here am I."
Isa 52:7	"How beautiful upon the mountains are the feet of the messenger who announces peace, who brings good news, who announces salvation, who says to Zion, 'Your God reigns'."
Ps 22:2	"O my God, I cry by day, but you do not answer; and by night, but find no rest. Tertullian's Latin text here follows LXX: φωνῇ μου πρὸς κύριον ἐκέκραξα.
Ps 3:5	"I cry aloud to the Lord, and he answers me from his holy hill (mountain)"

Out of these biblical scraps, Tertullian presents Luke 6:12: "you have a representation of the *name*; you have the action of *the Evangelizer*; you have a *mountain* for the site; and the *night* as the time; and the sound of a *voice*; and the audience of the *Father*: you have (in short) the Christ of the prophecies".[75] In this rendering, Luke 6:12 appears as a story made up of the piecing together of these biblical passages. The common Christian paradigm of prophecy and fulfilment naturally makes Tertullian's procedure comparable to early Christian interpretation of Old Testament in general, but the literary style shows some similarities with the *mos centonaris*, as Tertullian calls it in *Praescr.* 39.5.

---

[75] I have put the key terms in italics; Father here comes from κύριος of course.

4.5.3   *Authorial Respect?*

In his polemic against the Valentinians, Irenaeus likewise applies the analogy of *Homerocentones* (*Haer.* 1.8–9). Irenaeus unmasks the dual nature of the heretics: on the one hand, their teaching [ὑπόθεσις/ *argumentum*] was not predicted by the prophets, not taught by the Lord, nor transmitted by the apostles. On the other hand, they claim the support of the Lord's parables, the sayings of the prophets and the words of the apostles. They are remote from the Scriptures and simultaneously clothed in the words of Scripture. This duality, according to Irenaeus, encapsulates the nature of the Valentinians, and the analogy of *Homerocentones* nicely fits this critique. In *Haer.* 1.8.1, Irenaeus summarizes his critique by saying that they alter the order and connection of the Scriptures [τὴν τάξιν καὶ τὸν εἱρμὸν τῶν γραφῶν ὑπερβαίνοντες/ *ordinem quidem et textum Scripturam supergredientes*]. The heretics are breaking the structure [λύοντες τὰ μέλη τῆς ἀληθείας/ *soluentes membra veritatis*], and making something entirely different out of it. Irenaeus' critique is entirely in accordance with Tertullian holding it against the heretics that they are tampering with *dispositio* of the Scriptures. The Valentinians are abusing [ἐπηρεάζοντες ταῖς γραφαῖς/ *calumniantes Scripturis/*] the Scriptures and supporting their own system with them [τὸ πλάσμα αὐτῶν ἐξ αὐτῶν συνιστάνειν/*finctionem suam ex eis constare*] (*Haer.* 1.9.1). Now enters the illustration of the image (mosaic) of a king:

> Their manner of acting is just as if one, when a beautiful image of a king has been constructed by some skilful artist out of precious stones, should then destroy [λύσας/ *soluens/*] the form of the human being, replacing the stones and changing and making them into the form of a dog or of a fox, and even that but poorly executed; and should then maintain and declare that *this* was the beautiful image of the king which the skilful artist constructed, pointing to the stones which had been admirably fitted together by the first artist to form the image of the king, but have been with bad effect transferred by the latter one to the shape of a dog, and by thus exhibiting the stones, should deceive the ignorant who had no conception what a king's form was like, and persuade them that that miserable likeness of the fox was, in fact, the beautiful image of the king. In like manner do these persons patch together old wives' fables[76] and then endeavour, by violently drawing away from their proper con-

---

[76] Cf. 1 Tim 4:7.

nection, words, expressions, and parables whenever found, to adapt the words of God to their baseless fictions (*Haer.* 1.8.1).[77]

This procedure is in *Haer.* 1.9.4 illustrated with the example of *Homerocentones*,[78] whereby what is κατὰ φύσιν/ *secundum naturam* is turned into what is παρὰ φύσιν/ *contra naturam*. Irenaeus is obviously familiar with the cento method, and characterizes it precisely by the duality of being both old and new, so that those ignorant of Homer are made to think that Homer actually composed them:

> they act like those who bring forward any kind of hypothesis they fancy, and then endeavour to support them out of the poems of Homer, so that the ignorant imagine that Homer actually composed the verses bearing upon that hypothesis, which has, in fact been newly constructed (*Haer.* 1.9.4).

Irenaeus quotes an example of citations taken from the *Iliad* and *Odyssey* to tell the story of Hercules' descent to Hades to free Pluto's dog. The cento given in Irenaeus' text recounts episodes from Homer, such as Aeolus sending the hero Odysseus away from the island (*Od.* 10.76) and Priam going to Achilles to beg for Hector's body (*Il.* 24).[79] The citations are, therefore, truly Homeric, thus aimed at deceiving the ignorant by being so well-ordered, but the Homer expert (ὁ ἔμπειρος τῆς Ὁμηρικῆς/*qui scit homerica*), able to restore the citations to their proper Homeric setting, cannot confirm the narrative. The point is that lines have been taken out of context and combined to make a story not found in Homer.

Jean Daniélou argues that this cento was used by Valentinian Gnosticism, with its allegorical interpretation of Homer, to prove that the mission of Christ was to be sent by the Father into the dominion of death.[80] That being so, one would expect Irenaeus to confront the cento more directly: "Irenaeus has little or no interest in the cento itself; he is only interested in it as an illustration, and a good one at that, of how completely ridiculous words can appear when one does

---

[77] Quoted from ANF.

[78] The text is also found in Epiphanius, *Pan.* 29.5–12/GCS 430.2–431.11.

[79] For a list of the Homeric lines put together, see Norbert Brox, ed. and trans., *Irenäeus von Lyon. Epideixis, Adversus Haereses. Darlegung der apostolischen Verkündigung, Gegen die Häresien I* (Freiburg etc.: Herder, 1993), 195.

[80] Jean Daniélou, *Gospel Message and Hellenistic Culture. A History of Early Christian Doctrine Before the Council of Nicea Vol. 2* (London, Philadelphia: Darton, Longman & Todd, and The Westminster Press, 1973), 85–89. For other scholars holding this position, see Whitby, "The Bible Hellenized," 198 n. 30.

not know their sense or intention."[81] Such is the case when biblical citations are not ordered according to ὁ κανών τῆς ἀληθείας/*regula veri-*
tatis, corresponding to Tertullian's *regula.* For the true believer "will
recognize the pieces of stone (mosaic); he will certainly not receive the
fox instead of the image of the king." He knows the true τάξις/*ordo*
of the words of Scripture. The cento itself, not being a direct reference to Valentinian teaching as J. Daniélou assumed, does nevertheless have a direct bearing on how Irenaeus imagines something new
coming out of the Scripture. This is clearly demonstrated by the way
his mosaic illustration and the cento cohere. Valentinians as well as
centoists make a game of Scrabble out of the texts at their disposal. In
Haer. 2.14.2, Irenaeus once again uses cento composition to illustrate
his critical stand vis-à-vis the Valentinians. He holds against them that
they are sewing together a motley garment out of a heap of miser-
able rags, thus furnishing themselves with a cloak which is really not
their own.[82] Stripped of the figurative speech, Irenaeus is accusing the
Valentinians for having kept style and vocabulary intact, but altered
the substance. The distinction between *verba* and *res* thus lies at the
heart of his critique.

In his *Ep.* 53.7 (PL 22.544–5), Jerome says that every believer interprets the Scriptures, for better or worse. The chatty old woman [*garrula anus*], the dotard [*delirus senex*] and the sophist of many words
[*sophista verbosus*] have in common that they practice the art of interpreting the Scriptures. But many teach before they have learnt [*docent,
antequam discant*]. Some have received encyclical training [*saeculares
litterae*] before turning to the Bible, like Jerome did himself. They form
their preaching in a style aimed at deceiving the ears of their audience. They combine passages in a way which neglects the intention of
those who spoke and wrote [*quid Prophetae, quid Apostoli senserint*].
They commit the worst of failures for a reader of the Bible, according
to Jerome, namely "to misrepresent a writer's views and to force the
Scriptures reluctantly to de their will [*depravare sententias, et ad vol-
untatem suam Scripturam trahere repugnantem*]." The critique levelled

---

[81] Robert L. Wilken, "The Homeric Cento in Irenaeus, *Adv. Haereses* 1.9.4," *VC* 21
(1967): 27. This does not mean, though, that Irenaeus himself composed the cento.
He introduces the cento itself in a way which makes that unlikely: "For example, one
has written…"

[82] *Quasi centonem ex multis et pessimis panniculis consarcientes, finctum superfi-
cium subtili eloquio sibi ipsi praeparaverunt.* This echoes Ausonius' definition of making one's own text out of scraps taken from elsewhere (Chapter 4.1).

by Tertullian, Irenaeus and Jerome proceeds from authorial respect, and an idea of an author's intent—a marked difference from the centonists. To make his point, Jerome now introduces in his argument the *Homerocentones* and *Virgiliocentones*. These are mentioned only in passing, but some observations of importance can be extracted from this short passage.

In the first place, Jerome, like Tertullian and Irenaeus, considers cento composition a way of altering the meaning of the Scriptures or the intention of biblical authors. The cento genre gave free hands to the centonist. In the second place, Christian centos are *puerilia*, and are to be compared to the plays presented by mountebanks [*circulatorum ludo similia*] (PL 22.545). Latin *circulator* was used for travelling entertainers. Seneca *Ben.* 6.11.2 is an apt example; combined here as well with *ludere*. This fits well with the context of amusement we have noted for many centos. However, *circulator* might take on a more sinister meaning, including deceiver, as seems to be the case here.[83] Thirdly, Jerome indirectly conveys that the technique of writing centos was something done by people of his own intellectual standing.

Fourthly, he says that Virgil was not a Christian, although some of his prophecies might be read in that way;[84] this usually applies to the Messianic nature of the 4th *Ecloge*, from which Jerome also cites here. This is a statement critical of Proba, the high-born Christian lady, who composed a Virgilian cento (see Chapter 5).[85] Jerome asks why Virgil is to be considered a Christian since he wrote the line *nova progenies*

---

[83] Thus in Quintillian *Inst.* 2.4.15, Tertullian *Apol.* 23.1; OLD s.v.

[84] Lactantius *Inst.* 1.5.11 gives a propaideutic-like view on Virgil and says that he was not far away from truth [*non longe afuit a veritate*]; see Harald Hagendahl, *Augustine and the Latin Classics.* Vol II (Stockholm: Almquist & Wiksell, 1967), 384–9; Harald Hagendahl, *Latin Fathers and the Classics. A Study on the Apologists, Jerome and Other Christian Writers* (Göteborg: Almquist & Wiksell, 1958), 189. Hagendahl seems to subscribe to some of Jerome's judgement in calling Proba's poem "preposterous" (p. 189).

[85] This is pointed out by Clark and Hatch, *The Golden Bough, The Oaken Cross*, 104–5 and Hagendahl, *Latin Fathers and the Classics*, 188–90. Both works point out, however, that Jerome's critique is surprising in the light of the fact that he himself, in *The Life of Paul the Eremit* 9 (*Vita S. Pauli Primi Eremitae*), quotes some of the same Virgilian lines (PL 23.25). Hagendahl refers to Jerome's *Ep.* 58.1 (PL 22.580) where he comments upon the death of Judas with quoting from *Aen.* 12.603: *Et nodum informis leti trabe nectit ab alta* ("And fastened with a knot he suffers a degrading death on a high wooden beam") (my translation). According to Hagendahl "it is rather amusing, in view of Jerome's disapproval of *Virgilocentones*, that the same line is applied to Judas' suicide in the *cento De ecclesia* v.73" (p.190). The text is found in CSEL 16. I. p.625.1.

(new offspring) in *4th Ecloge 7 (cf. Aen. 7.680)*, which is a key notion
in Proba's modelling Christ after Virgil's politico-religious ideas (e.g.
l. 34 in the cento).[86] There is sufficient evidence that Proba is being
targeted critically here. Jerome quotes from her poem:

- where it says regarding the crucifixion that "he stood affixed and
  there remained" [*perstabat fixusque manebat*] (Proba l. 624 which is
  taken from *Aen.* 2.650).
- Jerome cites Proba quoting *Aen.* 1.664 [*nate, mea vires, mea magna
  potentia solus*] (l. 403) as the heavenly voice speaking to Jesus at his
  baptism.[87]

This implies that *garrula anus* in *Ep.* 53.7 is not just any woman, but
Proba in particular; this is the common scholarly opinion.[88] Disagreement
arises, however, when it comes to the question why Jerome is critical of
Proba's cento. Some of the suggestions are:

- She taught before having learnt (see above), whence her bending of
  the biblical texts. Her l. 624, quoted by Jerome, speaks of crucifixion
  in a way that is not supported in the biblical narratives. This altering
  of the biblical text may represent flawed theology, as e.g. in Jesus'
  words on the cross about revenge (l.621–4), which militates against
  the biblical "Father, forgive them, for they know not what they do."
- Proba's non-ascetic interpretation of the Gospels did not satisfy
  Jerome's standards, as can be seen e.g. in his *Against Jovinianem*.[89]
- Applying a form that is essentially playful might have appeared as bad
  taste to Jerome. His description of the cento as *puerilia* and *vitiosis-
  simum docendi genus* ("the most depraved way of teaching") echoes
  the sentiments of more recent research as well (see 1.7).

---

[86] This will be developed in Chapter 5.
[87] "O Son, my strength, Alone my mighty power."
[88] Thus also Pavlovskis, "Proba and the Semiotics of the Narrative Virgilian Cento,"
78; Carl P.E. Springer, "Jerome and the *Cento* of Proba," *Studia Patristica* 27 (1993):
99–100; Scott McGill, "Virgil, Christianity, and the *Cento Probae*," in *Texts and
Culture in Late Antiquity. Inheritance, Authority, and Change*, ed. J.H.D. Scourfield
(Swansea: The Classical Press of Wales, 2007), 8–9.
[89] On Jerome's critique of Jovinian, see Sandnes, *Belly and Body in the Pauline
Epistles*, 238–41.

Carl P.E. Springer has discussed these alternatives, and suggested that Jerome's antagonistic attitude to Proba must be compared with his equally positive assessment of Juvencus' Virgilian *paraphrasis* of the Gospel.[90] He points out that some of the same criticism must also be levelled at Juvencus' Virgilian rewriting of the Gospels, albeit not that much. In principle, the suggestions given above seem not able to explain satisfactorily why Proba was singled out for special opprobrium. Springer argues convincingly that "Jerome's objections to Proba's poem were not based solely on theological and literary-critical grounds, but also on his conviction that it was shameful for Christian men to be taught by women."[91] This is actually stated in *Ep.* 53.7: "Others learn— what a shame!—from women" [*alii discunt—proh pudor!—a feminis*], may be influenced by biblical passages such as 1 Cor 14:33b-40 and 1 Tim 2:11–12. Once this was established, there were many other things to criticize as well, although they themselves hardly constituted sufficient ground for rejecting Proba's poem. As we will see later, Proba claimed for herself in the cento (l.12) the public role of prophet or inspired speaker [*vatis*]. This might have provoked Jerome. Zoja Pavlovskis makes a point worthy of consideration. She points to Jerome saying that his critique in *Ep.* 53.7, which is directed at Proba, is spoken *cum stomacho* (PL 22.545). However this is to be translated, it must express some kind of strong personal involvement on the part of Jerome; he is simply upset. Pavlovskis argues that the reason for this is that a synthesis between the two texts and the worlds involved was impossible for Jerome; they were in principle mutually exclusive: "Like Proba, he too combines them [i.e. the Christian and the Classical] but was tormented by guilt, as we can see in the famous story of his dream."[92] Pavlovskis argues psychologically that the "either-or" man Jerome must have found this unpleasant, precisely since it corresponded to his own struggle.[93]

A cento-like text is found in Augustine's *Civ.* 1.3. He launches criticism against the Roman gods, taking Virgil as his point of departure: "Without question Virgil has—and they read him in their early years

---

[90] Springer, "Jerome and the *Cento* of Proba," 102–5.
[91] Springer, "Jerome and the *Cento* of Proba," 104.
[92] Pavlovskis, "Proba and the Semiotics of the Narrative Virgilian Cento," 80.
[93] For this see Sandnes, *The Challenge of Homer*, 196–205. The torment Pavlovskis mentions is precisely what I meant when in that book I called Jerome an ascetic addicted to Greek learning. See Pollmann, "The Transformation of the Epic Genre in Christian Late Antiquity," 62 on how the classical texts "occupied" the mind of Christian intellectuals.

precisely in order, yes, in order that when their tender minds have been soaked in the great poet, surpassing all in fame, it may not be easy for him to vanish from their memory."[94] He then proceeds to quote Horace, and continues to quote passages scattered around the *Aeneid*. In between the lines of Virgil, Augustine adds his own comments. This is what makes the text appear as cento-like, bringing to mind the related genre of *florilegia* or anthologies. Augustine's text demonstrates that the cento approach puts Virgil entirely in his own hands: the Roman Virgil is turned against the gods in which *he* himself took pride.

We noted above that the classical literature was "open" to yielding new texts, turning the reader into an author. The examples taken primarily from Tertullian and Irenaeus demonstrate that with Christian centos a new situation emerges. When Ausonius recast Virgil into a poem about a wedding and sex, Virgil is the only canonical text involved. This changes dramatically when the centos involve *two* canonical texts; both hypotext and hypertext claim canonical status. Furthermore, the examples given above demonstrate that in Christian centos only the hypotext is an open text. The biblical text is—even in the centos—seen as a fulfilment which does not make it an equally open text. Nonetheless, it would be misleading to say that Homer or Virgil are here subordinated to the biblical text. This is definitely not the picture painted by the Christian centos. In a fascinating way, the centos confirm both texts as somehow canonical; one with regard to *verba* and style, the other with regard to structure, plot and *res* or *sensus*. This is a fundamental observation, albeit preliminary and therefore in need of substantiation. Ancient rhetoric distinguished between *verba* and *res* or *sensus*. The ideal of *paraphrasis* was to alter *verba* but keep *res*. With the centos this is turned upside down; the centonists keep the words but alter *res* dramatically. One reason why the practice of making Christian centos met with criticism is probably that the very nature of centos was a threat to this distinction, and if the Scriptures themselves were centonized like Homer and Virgil, anything at all might happen. This is the nub of the criticism voiced by Tertullian and Irenaeus; thus confirming that the presence of two canonical texts in the process of making centos represents a new situation.

---

[94] This is exactly what Plato says about the poets (*Leg.* 811A), Quintilian about Homer and Virgil (*Inst.* 1.1.19–20; 1.8.15) and Heraclitus, *Homeric Problems* 1.1–3, 76.3–5 about Homer—in all cases stated against the background of instructing the young.

Centos were valued differently in antiquity. It seems that, particularly among Christians, negative sentiments are found, probably due to the fact that this method of stitching texts together played into the hands of the person who made the arrangements. Cento was a method liable to break up contexts, belief systems, stories and established beliefs, and to clothe new ideas in a venerable form, style and language. This critical attitude is certainly well-taken, but it grew primarily out of theological concerns. This negative attitude is most strongly expressed in the so called *Decretum Gelasianum*, according to tradition issued by Gelasius I (492–496 C.E.), but probably somewhat later, declaring which were the canonical writings, and which were apocryphal. In Chapter 5 he lists the latter, among which is also found Proba: "The cento about Christ, put together in Virgilian verse (hexameter): Apocryphal [*Centonem de Christo virgilianis conpaginatum versibus. Apocryphum*] (285).[95] It seems natural to take this mention of Proba's cento as indicative of a certain popularity.

4.6   SUMMARY

We have seen how centos stitch together scraps from classical texts to create new texts. Centonists took advantage of Homer and Virgil as texts open to yield fresh texts and recast classical literature in a playful way. They represent a total or extreme kind of intertextuality restraining the literary activity of the centonists.

> In a *cento*, the author's ambition would be to recombine parts of verses from one author's works in order to create a new, unexpected sense, while at the same time moving (almost) exclusively within the metrical and lexical material of this author.[96]

The text comes into being through intertextuality on the micro level, but it is at the cento's macro level that the message of the text becomes visible; that is to say, in the organizing structure of the text. This playful literary art embraces limits not found in other literature. Although the phenomenon is most widely attested in late antiquity, it is firmly rooted in practices characteristic of antiquity in general. Christian centos are to be understood within these practices, but also representing a special

---

[95] See the text edition of Von Dobschütz, ed. *Decretum Gelasianum*, 52. He points out that it is somewhat strange that Eudocia's *Homerocentones* is left unmentioned, and also that Proba's work was quite popular among some Christians (pp. 299–300).

[96] Pollmann, "Sex and Salvation in the Vergilian *Cento* of the Fourth Century," 80.

case of the genre. The fact that *two* canonical texts are involved separates them from secular and pagan centos. The distinction between *verba* and *res* is helpful in understanding the manipulation of the classical texts by the centos in general, and by the Christian centos in particular.

Centos tended to represent transvaluations of the classical literature, and thus amount to a *synkrisis*, literary evaluations or contests; they are thus rightly seen as products of a "cultural struggle."[97] That does, however, not make them analogous to other ancient texts in which Homer or Virgil are emulated in a subtle way; they are much more specific. Subtle emulation is by no means characteristic of this genre. Scott McGill rightly says about Virgilian centos: "A fundamental step in reading the game of cento composition is to recognize that the cento has arisen out of Virgil's adapted language."[98] This is not to deny that the precise implications of the intertextual links on the micro level are difficult to define; they vary from simple references to verbal coincidence taken from the 'mind concordance' to hermeneutically significant and penetrating allegories or typologies. This practise of creating new poems by stringing together lines from the classical literature made it possible for Christian writers finally to cope with the pagan legacy in a way which overcame all dangers inherent in the texts of this legacy.

In my book *The Challenge of Homer*, I argued that Christians held different views on Homer and classical literature. The advocates of encyclical studies argued pro-paedeutically in accordance with the "spoil of the Egyptians," collecting the best like bees from the flowers (i.e. making right use of) and allegorical interpretations. The centos represent an idiosyncratic approach among those who did not wish to abandon the classical legacy. The pagan lines were now serving a new purpose, namely that of telling the story of Christ. The practice of composing centos was, of course, part and parcel of wider attempts at formulating the Christian faith in the forms and vocabulary of the celebrated past of the pagan society. Christian centos thus represent a dual attitude towards both the cultural canon and the Christian canon—both need to be refined, but in different ways. This will be substantiated in the chapters to come.

---

[97] MacDonald, *Does the New Testament Imitate Homer?*, 15.
[98] McGill, *Virgil Recomposed*, 24.

CHAPTER FIVE

FALTONIA BETITIA PROBA:
THE GOSPEL "ACCORDING TO VIRGIL"

As we now turn to the first example of a cento, we proceed chronologically. Hence, the first cento is Virgilian in nature. Our focus will be on what kind of biblical *paraphrasis* this is, what the cento form brings to the presentation of the biblical story, the story of Jesus in particular, and finally whether the centos bring forth interpretations, view points, dicta, texts or events unmentioned in the canonical Gospels. Thereby we are enabled to draw some conclusions as to how these texts came into being, and whether they in any way are analogies to the composition of the canonical Gospels.

5.1   A Lady and Her Cento

Tradition has associated Proba's cento with Faltonia Betitia Proba—the grandmother of Anicia Faltonia Proba, known to us from Augustine's letters—thus making the date of composition for her poem around 362.[1] Her poem is the earliest and best known of the Christian centos. It is the earliest complete and extant Christian work we can be sure was composed by a woman.[2] Proba is the only woman included in Isidore of Seville's *De Viris illustribus* 18.22, and she is mentioned in his *Etymologiarum* 1.39.26 as well; these texts date from the end of sixth century. They read as follow:

> Proba, wife of Adelphius the consul, the only woman placed among the men of the church; out of her concern for the praise of Christ, she composed a cento about Christ, put together of Virgilian lines. Her art we do not admire, but we praise her ingenuity. This piece of work is reckoned

---

[1] See the presentation and discussion in e.g. Clarke and Hatch, *The Golden Bough, The Oaken Cross*, 97–102; Springer, "Jerome and the *Cento* of Proba," 97–98; David Vincent Menconi, "The Christian Cento and the Evangelization of Classical Culture," *Logos* 7 (2004): 111–6; Green, "Proba's Cento;" McGill, "Virgil, Christianity, and the *Cento* Probae," 173–4.

[2] See Harvey, "Women and words: Texts by and about Women," 382–3.

among the apocryphal writings [*Proba, uxor Adelphii proconsulis, femina, idcirco inter viros ecclesiasticos posita sola pro eo quod in laude Christi versata est, componens centonem de Christo, Virgilianis coaptatum versuciliis. Cuius quidem non miramur, sed laudamus ingenium. Quod tamen opusculum inter apocryphas inseritur*].[3]

Proba, the wife of Adelphius, therefore, made abundantly a cento from Virgil on the creation of the world and the Gospels. The content is composed according to the verse, and with the verses organized according to the content [*Denique Proba, uxor Adelphi, centonem ex Vergilio de Fabrica mundi et Evangeliis plenissime expressit, materia conposita secundum versus, et versibus secundum materiam concinnatis*].[4]

The first text attests the ambivalent attitude towards Proba's work, while the second addresses the poem more precisely with regard to its content and principle of composition, namely an interplay between *versus* and *materia*, which corresponds to the rhetorical terms *verba* and *res/sensus* that the present study has unfolded as a key to understand cento composition. Proba's work is introduced ("therefore") with a reference (25) to how *grammatici* considered centos: scraps from here and there in the songs of Homer or Virgil are put together to form a single body, a work of its own character, according to *mos centonaris*, to serve its own content.[5] The reference to *grammatici* is worth noting since it suggests a didactic context for the poem.

Proba was a Roman lady of aristocratic background. Her family was among the highest-standing in the society of her time. Unlike many contemporary Christians she was not an advocate of celibacy and asceticism. She fitted herself comfortably into the traditional values of an aristocratic lady of the city.[6] Previous to her cento, Proba had

---

[3] My translation; for Latin text see PL 83.1093.

[4] My translation, for Latin text see PL 82.121.

[5] *Centones apud Grammaticos vocari solent, qui de carminibus Homeri seu Vergilii ad propria opera more centonario ex multis hinc inde conpositis in unum sarciunt corpus, ad facultatem cuiusque materiae*; this corresponds exactly to Ausonius' description of the nature of cento composition; see Chapter 4.1. The description of *mos centonaris* is a quote from Tertulian, *Praescr.* 39.5 verbatim.

[6] This is well argued by Clarke and Hatch, *The Golden Bough, The Oaken Cross*, 101–2, 109–21. They also point out some minor details in her text as revealing of her social status, such as having Jesus in the Sermon on the Mount (l. 477) speaking, in words taken from *Aen.* 6.609, about those who are sentenced to suffer in Tartarus for having treated their clients badly. See also Michele R. Salzman, *The Making of a Christian Aristocracy. Social and Religious Change in the Western Roman Empire* (Cambridge, MA: Harvard University Press, 2002), 163–4. For the role of Christianity among Rome's upper class in the 4th century, see also Gemeinhardt, *Das lateinische Christentum und die antike pagane Bildung*, 131–52. One is tempted to ask if this

composed an epic poem (now lost) on the civil war, probably the one between Constantinus II and Magnentius, to which she refers in her prologue to the cento. The two works are separated by a conversion that must have taken place sometime in the 350s. It is generally recognized that she composed her patchwork on Christ's work shortly after Julian's decree, a "law aimed a savage blow at an elite."[7] Proba's cento might, therefore, be taken as a response to Julian's decree and the implications thereof for the education of children from the Christian elite to which she belonged herself. In a time of crisis, Proba chooses a playful form for a very serious purpose. A.G. Amatucci suggested as early as in 1929 that Proba wrote the poem for the instruction of her own children.[8] The last two lines of the poem (l. 693–4) may be taken to support this view (see 5.2). An educational setting seems plausible, albeit that Amatucci's view stretches the text beyond what is directly stated.[9]

The cento is 694 lines,[10] preceded by a fifteen-line dedication. It is based mostly on the books of Genesis and Matthew's Gospel. Generally speaking, the patchwork nature of this work must have invited additions and revisions.[11] The poem itself has the following content:

---

increased Jerome's aversion to Proba (see Chapter 4.5.3). From his writings against Jovinian we know his *vestigia*; see Sandnes, *Belly and Body in the Pauline Epistles*, 238–41.

[7] See Green, "Proba's Cento," 554–60, an examination of the evidence. Clarke and Hatch, *The Golden Bough, The Oaken Cross*, 100; Jane Stevenson, *Women Latin Poets. Language, Gender, and Authority, from Antiquity to the Eighteenth Century* (Oxford: Oxford University Press, 2005), 67–68; Whitby, "The Bible Hellenized," 198, 217. McGill, "Virgil, Christianity, and Cento Probae," 186 n. 3, 187 n. 20 appears somewhat unclear on this. For a more critical stance to the common opinion, see Hagith Sivan, "Anician Women. The Cento of Proba, and Aristocratic Conversion in the Fourth Century," *VC* 47 (1993).

[8] A.G. Amatucci, *Storia della Letteratura Latina* (Bari: G. Laterza, 1929), 146–7.

[9] Clark and Hatch, *The Golden Bough. The Oaken Cross*, 100, mentions later educational use of the cento, with further references. This view find corroboration in Jerome's negative assessment of Proba's poem, which seems inter alia to be caused by the teaching [*docere*] of a woman (see 4.5.3 in the present study); this is pointed out by Usher, "Prolegomenon to the Homeric Centos," 318 as well.

[10] The Latin text is found in Carolus Schenkl, ed. *Poetae Christianae Minores Pars 1.* CSEL 16 (Mediolani, Vlricvs Hoeplivs, 1888). I have used Clarke and Hatch, *The Golden Bough. The Oaken Cross* where an English translation is also available. The references given to Virgil's writings are taken from Schenkl's edition. I use the translation of Clarke and Hatch. I owe thanks to Elizabeth Clarke for her help in finding out about the copyright. Through Stephanie Gray (AAR) I have been given permission to use the necessary portions of this book.

[11] See Sivan, "Anician Women," 140–50.

From The Old Testament

The Creation and Fall: This centres around the loss of the Golden Age
  (56–268)

Mankind outside Eden: The Iron Age begins, Justice withdraws from
  the earth (269–306)

The Flood (307–18)

A section sketching other Old Testament events (319–32)

A transitional section (l. 333–45) preparing for her "greater task" [*maius
  opus moveo*]

From The New Testament

The promised day arrives: "The Founder of a godly race" is born
  (346–9)

Birth-related stories: The Magi, Herod's Wrath and killing of the infants
  (350–79)

A Summary of the Ministry of "Source from Heaven:" The Golden Age
  Returned (380–7)

A Prophet by the Stream and Father Talking to His Son (Baptism)
  (388–414)

Confessional Digression: Proba's Faith (415–28)

The Serpent Tests the Man (429–55)

His Fame Spreads in the City (456–62)

"Eternal Power" speaks from a Mountain (Sermon on The Mount)
  (463–504)

A Rich Young Man (505–30)

Sailor's Fear and the King (*rex*) of the Waves (two biblical stories combined) (531–61)

Greeted by the Crowd while Sitting on an Ass (The Triumphal Entry)
  (562–5)

Caesar's coin in the Temple: He makes a Whip (The Cleansing of the
  Temple with the story of the coin joined to it) (566–79)

Tables in the Grass with Bread and Wine: A Lesson on *Ritus* (The Last
  Supper inspired by John 6) (580–92)

One of the *Comites* Rises against Him: The Impending Death (593–99)

Priests and People Murmur (600–6)

Bound to a Massive Oak: *Triste Ministerium* (607–37)

The Flight of His *Comites*: Where is now Our Lord and Master?
  (638–47)

The Third Day's Light: A Triumph with Spoils (648–62)

The Triumph Declared to His *Comites*: Peace (663–79)
The Work finished. He disappears riding on the Sky (Ascension) (680–8)

This "table of contents" is not given by Proba herself, but follows from the structure of her poem. I have made it with some aid from the edition of Clarke and Hatch, *The Golden Bough. The Oaken Cross*, but I have altered it particularly on one basic point. The headers made by them sound very much as if they are taken from the New Testament itself; I, however, have tried to keep more closely to Proba's own story. This means that the name of Christ does not appear; it is there only in Virgilian circumscriptions. Compared to the cento itself, the presentation given above wrongly gives the impression of a rather short Old Testament part; in fact, texts from the two bodies of literature are of equal length more or less.

Her cento is divided into two sections, one dealing with the Old Testament and the other with the Story of Jesus. The two are roughly symmetrical, and a clear break is marked between them: "each begins with an invocation and closes with a valediction."[12] A crescendo is marked between the two parts by Proba saying *maior opus moveo* ("a greater task I move to") (l. 334 see below). As pointed out by Jeffrey T. Schnapp, this structure betrays Proba's dependence on traditional Christian theology regarding the relationship between the two parts of the canon: "Proba's Christ-story 'completes' her truncated Old Testament narrative: it fulfills the promise of creation, reverses the effects of the fall from Eden, institutes the new and definitive covenant, provides a hermeneutical key."[13]

The backbone of her presentation of Jesus is easily recognized as following the basic pattern of the Synoptic tradition. Some traits of Gospel harmonies can be recognized as well. A consequence of the cento form is the absence of historical names, geography and mostly local *mores*; for obvious reasons temple, priests and *ritus* work well, however. In short, the specific historical framework of the story is not easily fitted into the cento. The disciples have become *comites*; the term

---

[12] Schnapp, "Reading Lessons," 110–2; quotation from p. 111.
[13] Schnapp, "Reading Lessons," 111. In short, this is the theological conviction of promise and fulfilment.

magi works well; fellow-Christians are *socii* (epilogue). The only exceptions are found before the cento form with its limitations is embarked upon, that is, in the dedication where *Christus* and *discipuli* appear, and in the preface l. 23, where the cento's topic is summarized as being about *munera Christi*. Latin *munus* describes a public duty or task, and is most appropriate to describe Roman piety. However, this word may also refer to kindness given by the grace of a person,[14] which makes it a useful term for Proba to describe Christ's ministry. These observations confirm how the cento form is working with a strong restraint imposed by the hypotext itself, but also the freedom of the macro level indicated in the preface and epilogue. Clearly, Proba's Virgilian Gospel needed some introductory comments that were not adequately expressed in purely Virgilian lines. This is seen in her proem as well as in the dedication added to her poem, most likely by someone else.

Karla Pollmann rightly points out that Proba's poem is about salvation.[15] *Salus* is mentioned at key points (l. 418, 472). Christ will rule; this Virgilian Caesar-like concept now applies to Christ, who rules in order to provide *auxilium* ("help") for humankind (l. 340). This is stated precisely in the cento's transition from Old Testament to the coming of Jesus. Salvation in Proba's cento, therefore, must be heard against a double background, the fall of humankind in Eden (Gen 3), and the loss of the Golden Age (Virgil).[16]

The Jewish setting of the story is, for obvious reasons, more or less replaced by a Roman context: "The Source from heaven" [*caelestis origo*][17] now walks right through the city [*per medias urbes*] (l.383); his fame reaches *urbes* (l. 456); he is concerned about the clients of his audience (l. 477); the Sea of Galilee is described as *mare* (l. 544).[18] Jesus lives in a world of ovations and triumphs (l. 659 and 666). L. 658 describes Easter Morning as a triumph: *spoliisque superbus* ("exalted

---

[14] See OLD s.v.

[15] Pollmann, "Sex and Salvation in the Vergilian *Cento* of the Fourth Century," 88–89.

[16] Virgil picks up the idea of the Golden Age from ancient myths. It was the imagined epoch in which humankind lived a life of ease, far from toil and sin, but which had been lost; see Hartwig Heckel, "Zeitalter," *Der Neue Pauly* 12.2: 706–9. The idea is given a classical presentation in Hesiod. *Op.* 109–26, Aratus *Phaen.* 100–14 and Ovid. *Metam.* 1.89–112. Virgil draws on this in his Augustan ideology; see also later in this chapter.

[17] Cf. l. 347 *divinae stirpis origo* ("founder of a godly race") and Chap. 5.4.

[18] This is not entirely unprecedented when compared to the Markan story itself, but it probably reflects a process of interpreting this event at work in Mark's Gospel itself; see Sandnes, "Markus—en allegorisk biografi?," 289.

by its spoils"). This is taken from *Aen.* 8.202 where Hercules rejoices in his capturing and slaying of the three-headed giant Geryon. Jesus resurrected is the proud Roman hero who has now conquered Death itself. All this reflects the life of Roman aristocracy rather than that of the Galilee where Jesus ministered.

The poem opens with a dedication written by someone else, and is therefore not really a part of the poem itself.[19] Lines 1–55 are Proba's own proem or preface to her poem. Much of the dedication and the preface are not in the cento form: "Proba presumably felt that she had some things to say which she could not express in Vergil's exact words."[20] From l. 56 on, starting with the Creation, she constructs her lines entirely from Virgil.

5.2   Dedication added to the Poem

Proba's own poem, which follows upon her proem, is preceded by a dedication added around 395, making up the first fifteen lines of the text.[21] The review of the biblical story in the dedication is very short indeed. Remarkable is the emphasis on creation, which corresponds to how the poem will later deal with the Old Testament. Remarkable is also the summary of Jesus' life, with an emphasis on stories associated with his birth, and some identifiable episodes, especially related to the sea. L. 10–11 are to be noted. Here the ministry of Jesus is summarized in a general and non-episodic way: "Here slavery's broken yoke, and life brought back by help of the one cross." Thus the author of the dedication summarizes the story as being about salvation. The review of the biblical story renews (= Virgil), "changed for the better with sacred meaning [*mutatum in melius diuino agnoscere sensu*]" (4). That is truly a precise definition of *emulatio*, involving imitation, amelioration as well as competition, and most important, altering *sensus*.[22] Proba clearly thinks Virgil is in need of being ameliorated, and this is precisely what her poem offers. Her own preface (l. 16–19) sheds light on this; she corrects Virgil according to common Christian belief. She says it is not

---

[19] Green, "Proba's Introduction to her *Cento*," 548.
[20] This important observation is made by Green, "Proba's Introduction to her *Cento*," 549.
[21] See McGill, "Virgil, Christianity, and the *Cento* Probae," 174.
[22] See Sandnes, "Imitatio Homeri?," 722–5.

her duty to make known broken vows, brawling deities and defeated *penates* (household gods), thus summarizing the Christian criticism levelled against the poets, namely the idolatry and poor morals found in their epics, whether Homer or Virgil. Her whole undertaking, however, implies that also the Bible needs amelioration with help from Maro.

The dedication mentions both the Emperor and the younger Arcadius. There are some uncertainties as to the precise identification of the two.[23] More important than the precise identity are, however, two other observations. In the first place, the dedication points to the upper level of society, both social and intellectual. The dedication speaks about the Emperor's house. Furthermore, the dedication looks beyond the present to posterity. The poem is handed down to Arcadius, who is expected to do the same to his offspring, thus initiating a tradition whereby Proba's poem will always be taught to children:

> Reread this poem, keep it safe through time,
> And hand it down to the younger Arcadius,
> Then to his own sons. May your august
> Posterity always receive this poem well
> And teach it always to their families [*doceatque suos*]
> (Dedication l. 13–15)

The poem is according to this a pedagogical tool whereby children were taught the Bible through the words of Virgil.[24] This is reiterated in the epilogue (l. 689–94) where a husband is addressed in the vocative [*o dulcis coniunx*]; Proba's husband, maybe.[25] The husband is addressed as being responsible for the instruction of the children in his house, thus keeping them in the faith: *maneant in religione nepotes*. This educational role of the poem finds substantiation in Proba's exhortations to more attentive listening to her poem, which closes the proem in l. 54–55.[26]

---

[23] See Sivan, "Anician Women," 140–50.

[24] Salzman, *The Making of A Christian Aristocracy*, 160, says that Proba's cento may have been composed for governesses, nurses or tutors who normally took care of childrearing and their instruction in aristocratic families.

[25] Thus Clark and Hatch, *The Golden Bough. The Oaken Cross*, 97–98, 193, 195. Her husband, who was not fond of her work, but testified that for her ingenuity she was the only woman placed among the men of the church. Clark and Hatch comment: "His estimate was correct: Proba is indeed the only female writer of early orthodox Christianity who has an entire work still extant" (p. 98).

[26] *Pace* Green, "Proba's Cento," 560 who limits the educational purpose to "the schoolroom"; parental instruction is in, my view, not to be excluded. This is, in fact, what is stated in the epilogue.

5.3   PROBA'S PROEM ABOUT PEACE (L. 1–55)

Upon the dedication follows the proem, which holds important keys
for reading the cento. The proem includes an expanded invocation.[27]
L. 1–8 are about an earlier poem composed by Proba,[28] a poem about
cruel wars and battles between relatives. The trophies captured were
not from enemies but from people of kin. These are memories of *mala*
("evil things"). Her poem was about the civil war within the imperial
family of Constantine. The present poem, however, is different, hence
it is called a sacred song [*sacrum Carmen*]. The contrast between the
two poems is summarized as *bellum* versus *pax*, which probably reflects
her conversion, since they summarize her previous and present poetic
activity in a contrastive way.[29] Her new religion was one of peace. As
pointed out by Martin Bažil, line l.1 ("From earliest times, leaders had
broken vows of peace") imitates Caesar's words when he crossed the
Rubicon: "Here I leave peace behind me and legality which has been
scorned already" (Lucan, *Civ.* 1.225).[30] Proba's previous poem is seen in
this light, the moment that plunged the Roman Empire into civil war.
That poem aligned itself with the history of the leaders, treacherous to
peace. The story she is now about to sing is, indeed, different. It equally
marks a moment of change in the history of the Empire, but now in
terms of *pax*. This brings to mind the epilogue of Juvencus where *pax*
summarizes what his poem is about. Proba, however, seems to have a
more nuanced view of *pax* and the Constantinian family.[31]

The message of the Sermon on the Mount is about *quies*, here used
synonymously with *pax*[32] (l. 474) (*Aen.* 3.495). This is what Aeneas is
longing for, as he is tired of his constant journeying. He praises those
who are not setting sail, but have found rest. Proba also includes a
line from *Aen.* 6.745 on the completion of the secular cycle. This is

---

[27] Thus also the text edition and translation of Clark and Hatch, *The Golden Bough.
The Oaken Cross.*

[28] Green, "Proba's Introduction to her *Cento*," 549–51 points out that her previous
poem on the war between Constantinus II and Magnentius was patterned according
to Lucan's *Pharsalia*, the history of the civil war between Caesar and Pompey.

[29] Her conversion took place sometimes in the 350s; see Clarke and Hatch, *The
Golden Bough. The Oaken Cross*, 97; Salzman, *The Making of A Christian Aristocracy*,
168. Gärtner, "Die Musen im Dienste Christi," 426 says that Proba's contrasting her
previous to her present literary work is to be called a biographical contrast *topos*.

[30] Martin Bažil, *Centones Christiani*, 121–2.

[31] See 2.4.2 in the present study.

[32] OLD s.v.

from Anchises' words in Hades to his visiting son. The Sermon on the Mount thus takes on the character of being instructions for the awaited time. When the resurrected Christ addresses his disciples [*comites*] he urges them to pray for peace and to keep it inviolate (l. 675–6).[33] The centrality of peace in the proem is thus confirmed in the poem. The cento she is about to perform marks a clear contrast to the recent imperial history, which she has previously addressed. From l. 9 the proem is an invocation that God will give her the necessary inspiration to do so:

> Now [*nunc*] God almighty, accept my sacred
> Song [*sacrum...carmen*], I pray; unloose the utterance [*ora resolue*]
> Of your eternal, sevenfold Spirit, and so
> Unlock the inmost sanctum of my heart
> That I may find all mysteries [*arcana...cuncta*] within
> My power to relate—I, Proba, prophetess [*vatis*] (l.9–12).[34]

This prayer for inspiration brings together traditional pagan and Christian motifs. The role of the introductory invocation echoes the role of the Muses. Poets were considered to be inspired by them, as was the case with Homer as well.[35] The sevenfold Spirit echoes the seven gifts of the Spirit in Isa 11:2.[36] *Ora resolue* is taken from *Aen.* 3.457 about the prophetess opening her lips to speak from the seat of the Sibyl.[37] Like Virgil's Sibyl, revealing mysteries [*arcana*] (*Aen.* 6.72), Proba is now about to reveal hidden mysteries. This Virgilian background leads Proba to make a series of negative statements: she does not seek the

---

[33] See Clarke and Hatch, *The Golden Bough. The Oaken Cross*, 123 for the role of peace in the poem.

[34] I am following Clarke and Hatch, *The Golden Bough. The Oaken Cross*'s translation with one important exception; I do not give names not found in the Latin text. When they have "Jesus" I avoid that in order to keep closer to this characteristic trait of the cento. For a fluent English translation it is impossible to stick exactly to the numbered lines of the Latin. I have tried to keep more closely to the Latin lines than do Clarke and Hatch. Some minor alterations in relation to their translation will therefore appear.

[35] Sandnes, *The Challenge of Homer*, 45–47; see also Dio Chrysostom *Or.* 36.33–35. Accordingly, poets were compared to prophets or seers [*vates*]. OLD s.v. gives two options for this noun, prophet or seer and a poet inspired by the Muses. Plato is compared to the poets, as they both were imbued with the divine fire of inspiration [*instinctis divino spiritu vatibus*], Quintillian *Inst.* 12.10.24 cf. Virgil *Ecl.* 9.33–34; Valerius Maximus, *Memorable Doings and Sayings* 8.8. Valerius calls Homer *ingenii caelestis vates* ("poet of celestial genius").

[36] Thus Clarke and Hatch, *The Golden Bough. The Oaken Cross*, 189 n. 4.

[37] A Virgilian expression for the opening of the lips to speak divinely inspired words (*Georg.* 4.452).

ambrosian drink,[38] nor does she speak from the holy mountain of the Muses (the Aionian peak), she trust neither in what rocks (the Sibyls) and laurel tripods (oracles) may say.[39] Instead she has been wettened by the Castalian font and drunk the offerings of the holy day. This is a surprising turn in the light of her many denials of Greek inspirational sources. But we may look at it in this way: She might have considered the Castalian font to be a symbol of inspiration cut off from its Delphic context; the well-known last utterance of the oracle, that the water of the Castalian font had been silenced,[40] may have contributed to this. Elizabeth A. Clarke and Diane F. Hatch take this as a reference to baptism,[41] which might find supportive evidence in Proba describing this as an imitation of the blessed [*beati*] (l. 20). From this follows then that l. 21 speaks about the Lord's Supper. While I tend to agree with the latter, I am sceptical about baptism here. The Castalian font of Delphi certainly had a cleansing role in the rite there, but it was preparatory for the oracles.[42] No such role of preparing for oracles is known with regard to baptism. The interpretation given by Roger P.H. Green is more attractive;[43] he takes the Castalian font as a reference to her putting the Biblical story into verse, an activity described as prophecy. She is imitating previous Christian writers [*beati*], among whom she also includes Old Testament writers.

L. 23 summarizes the overall theme of her cento briefly and aptly: "That Vergil put to verse Christ's sacred duties. Let me tell [*Vergilium cecinisse loquar pia munera Christi*]." Although this line, not surprisingly, has no exact correspondence in Virgil, it is clearly embedded in a Virgilian setting and style. When Proba says that she will now begin her song (l. 22), she does so in words taken from the opening

---

[38] Ambrosia or nectar is the food of the gods; see "Ambrosia" *Pauly-Wissowa* 1: 1809–11, see e.g. *Od.* 9.359.

[39] See Ps. Longinus, *On the Sublime* 13.2, for a combination of the tripod of the Pythian priestess and the poets.

[40] Ancient tradition says that Julian the Emperor made efforts to resuscitate the oracle cult of Delphi. According to Cedrenus (ca. 1050) the last prophetic revelation was given to Julian's envoy: "Tell the king, on earth has fallen the glorious dwelling. And the water-springs that spoke are quenched and dead. Not a cell is left for the god, no roof, no cover. In his hand the prophet laurel flowers no more;" see Wilmer Cave Wright, ed. and trans., *The Works of the Emperor Julian Vol. 3* (Cambridge MA and London: Harvard University Press, 1993), LVII.

[41] Clarke and Hatch, *The Golden Bough. The Oaken Cross*, 126–7, 189 n. 9.

[42] In "Kastalia," *Der Neue Pauly* 6.322–23 it is described as "Quelle der Inspiration;" see also Clement of Alexandria *Protr.* 2/10P (GCS 12a.10/11.1–2).

[43] Green, "Proba's Introduction to her *Cento*," 556.

of the *Georgics*: *hinc canere incipiam* (*Georg.* 1.5). The *Georgics* praise the *munera* of the deities providing corn richly (*Georg.* 1.7): *munera vestra cano* ("their work I praise") (*Georg.* 1.12). A strong Virgilian context, therefore, forms the background of how Proba presents her poem, which is transforming the opening of the *Georgics* into *munera Christi*, a song about Christ.

The work of Christ must be understood to include both the Old and New Testament, as the cento itself makes clear. This sentence about Christ's *munera* has, of course, no Virgilian counterpart. Needless to say this is of uttermost significance. For the making of a Christian Virgilian cento, it does not suffice to reorder the text and put the lines together in a particular form. A meta-perspective setting the schedule for the cento, needs to be stated; this corresponds to what we called macro level in Chapter 4. The proem provides the perspective; it is not sufficiently expressed in Virgilian terms, but quite traditional as being about the deeds of Christ.

Virgil is not alone in singing Christ's praise. The legendary poet Musaios,[44] who inspired the Muses, had sung [*cecinisse*] throughout the world about *quae sint, quae fuerint, quae ventura* (l. 37). This well-known tripartite prophetic formula ("what is, what was, and what is to come")[45] unites Moses and Virgil. Proba identifies Musaios with Moses of the Old Testament,[46] which is then—in addition to Christ in the proem—the only biblical name appearing throughout the cento. Both Virgil and Moses sang [*cecinisse*] prophetically about Christ. It is worth noting that Proba speaks of this in the past tense. This is relevant to the interpretation of Proba's use of Virgil (see 5.8.1).

To describe this as well as the creation of the universe is the task Proba has now taken upon herself (l. 46). Her former song about horses, arms and warfare makes no longer any sense; she has been

---

[44] See "Musaios," *Pauly-Wissowa* 16.757–67.

[45] See W.C. van Unnik, "A Formula Describing Prophecy;" *NTS* 9 (1962–3); Karl Olav Sandnes, *Paul—One of the Prophets? A Contribution to the Apostle's Self-understanding.* WUNT 2.43 (Tübingen. J.C.B. Mohr, 1991), 175.

[46] According to *Aen.* 6.669, Aeneas meets with the "best of the prophets" in Hades. To Proba this is Moses, not entirely unprecedented in the light of traditional Jewish and later Christian apologetic traditions about Moses vis-à-vis pagan prophets and scribes. Christian apologetics claimed Hellenic credentials for Moses; in fact the philosophers were "but Moses speaking Attic Greek," to allude to a famous saying of Numenius of Apamea, a contemporary of Justin (Clement *Strom.* 1.150.4); for this see, the study of Arthur Droge, *Homer or Moses? Early Christian Interpreters of the History of Culture* (Tübingen: J.C.B. Mohr (Paul Siebeck)).

given a greater task: *potior sententia* ("a better purpose") (l. 50). This corresponds to how Proba introduces the transition from the Old Testament to the New Testament in l. 333–4: *maius opus moveo*, thus equalling this transition with Aeneas' reaching his divine destiny, as he finally arrives at the mouth of the Tiber. This line is taken from the moment when Aeneas and his crew reached the shores of Ausonia. The actual line is found in Virgil's own presentation to Erato, one of the Muses, of the situation in Latium until Aeneas' arrival there, thus attesting to the role of this turning moment in his poem. The second half line of *Aen.* 7.44 [*maior rerum mihi nascitur ordo*] ("a greater order of the universe is born to me"), which describes the task facing Virgil, appears in l. 45 of the poem about Proba's task in composing the cento. This hardly implies that Proba saw herself as replacing Virgil, although she improves on him. It has been suggested that this 'greater task' marks the transition from history to panegyric.[47] I think this is a narrowing of the implications in *potior sententia*, and thus overlooking important aspects of the poem. In the first place, history and panegyric are intertwined throughout the entire poem. Secondly, the way the "greater task" is contrasted with Proba's previous story about warfare makes it natural to include a reference here to the content of the story now to be unfolded, namely peace contrasted with warfare.

Finally, the fact that *potior sententia* catches the decisive moment in the story of Aeneas is of uttermost importance here. When in Carthage, he fell in love with Dido who tried to keep him back from further travelling. He was tempted to give up his mission to build Rome for a woman's sake (*Aen.* 4.265–7). Aeneas is in much doubt on how to approach the matter and Dido herself. This uncertainty is replaced by his finding of *potior sententia*, a plan to prepare the fleet and set sail for Rome, leaving Dido behind without warning. In the destiny of Aeneas, the two words thus encapsulate the transition that led him on to fulfil his mission. Proba likewise considers the content of her poem to be epoch-making and laying the foundation for a new beginning.

From this follows naturally that the poem is about "*nova progenies* in whom every age believed" (l. 34). The last half line is taken

---

[47] See Clarke and Hatch, *The Golden Bough. The Oaken Cross*, 191 n. 33. Schnapp, "Reading Lessons," 112 points out that *Aen.* 7.43–44 comes around the middle of Virgil's work, thus corresponding to how Proba has organized her work.

from *Aen.* 7.680, about the common belief that Caeculus was son of Vulcanus, born of a virgin. Proba's view of Virgil as a prophet who with the help of Museaus had spoken about Christ here paves the way for Christianizing Virgil. The first part of this line is the very point where Virgil and Christian interpretations converge. We have previously seen that Jerome in this expression found a suitable way to describe Proba's cento, albeit a critically. The phrase *nova progenies* is taken from *Ecl.* 4.4–7, the very beginning of the Messianic-sounding work of Virgil:

> Now is come the last age [*aetas*] of the song of Cumae;
> the great line of the centuries begins anew [*saecolorum nascitur ordo*].[48]
> Now the Virgin returns, the reign of Saturn returns,
> now a new generation descends from heaven on high
> [*nova progenies caelo demittitur alto*].
> Only do thou, pure Lucina, smile on the birth of the child
> [*nascenti puero*],
> under whom the iron brood shall first cease,
> and a golden race [*genus aurea*] spring throughout the world!
> Thine own Apollo now is king![49]

This text demonstrates that *nova progenies* hits a nerve in the hopes of Virgil for the Augustan era, which Proba now transposes into a Christian world-view. The phrase *nova progenies* summarizes ideas looming large in the cento, providing the basic idea on which the whole cento is composed, combining Virgilian hope as well as christology.

The proem closes by admonishing mothers and men, young boys and girls to listen attentively to her words. This is done in lines taken from *Aen.* 5.71, 304 and *Georg.* 4.475–6, which possibly indicates that attentive listening is rewarding, since *Aen.* 5.304[50] is about Aeneas promising a prize to those who listen attentively: "Mothers and men, Youths and maids unwed, be silent, All, and turn attentive minds to me [*ore favete omnes laetasque advertite mentes*] (l. 54–55).

---

[48] See Proba's poem l. 45 on this.
[49] Quoted from LCL.
[50] This line introduces the Virgilian preface of Ausonius' cento as well (l. 1): *accipite haec animis laetasque advertite mentes*.

5.4 *Nova Progenies* (New Generation or Offspring)

This phrase in itself encapsulates new beginning and hope, as is clearly seen in Proba's l. 316, where Noah's family, rescued from the flood, represents the beginning of a new era: *genus nova*. But seen against its Virgilian background it is actually more specific, engaging Roman imperial history and symbolism at a very deep level. The idea of a lost Golden Age, the age of Saturn,[51] which is presently—in Virgil's opinion—under way with the Augustan era, nurtures the cento throughout. Within this world-view, put into verse by Virgil, Proba found prototypes for her epic hero, Jesus, and the story about his life:[52] "The mortal hero Aeneas is transformed into the resurrected Messiah who guarantees his followers the bliss of the future kingdom."[53] The idea of *genus nova* is to Proba rooted in the Bible as well; she presents Noah's rescue from the flood as the beginning of this new lineage (l. 316).

In l. 45 of her preface, Proba says that "a great ordering of the universe is born to me," a sentence which leads directly to the task now in front of her. The Latin of this sentence [*maior rerum mihi nascitur ordo*] is, as we have seen, taken from Virgil's *Aen.* 7.44 about his own task of narrating how Aeneas reached Rome. Virgil calls for Erato, the Muse of poetry to awake, since he is about to tell this great story. In *Aen.* 7.44 this leads to the sentence we have already seen, and which Proba has adopted for her poem: *maius opus moveo*. The story about the tide of events is about to be told. In accordance with this, echoes of *Ecl.* 4.5 on Saturn's Age appear as well. The lines immediately preceding l. 45 in the cento refer to the poetic description of fresh spring according to *Georg.* 2.334–43, making Virgil think of the days of the world's infancy. It is, therefore, quite natural that the traditions of The Golden Age come to life in Proba's Eden (l. 144–7), and that the Fall introduced the Virgilian age of iron with toil and hardships, a time without justice (l. 252–62, 296–306). But

---

[51] Cf. *Georg.* 1.118–46. For the idea of the Golden Age, see above and also Benko, "Virgil's Fourth Eclogue in Christian Interpretation," 692–4. According to Benko, it was the spirit of the Golden Age, attested by ancient writers, that "gave birth to the poem" (p. 694).

[52] Clark and Hatch, *The Golden Bough. The Oaken Cross* demonstrates this throughout, see e.g. pp. 3–5, 134–5, 168–81. The interpretation given of the Book of Acts by Bonz in her *The Past as Legacy. Luke-Acts and Ancient Epic* basically conforms to the same pattern of biblical interpretation; see Chapter 1.4 of this study.

[53] Clark and Hatch, *The Golden Bough. The Oaken Cross*, 5.

344	A man was coming to mankind and earth,	*Aen.* 7.69; 2.556
345	A man magnificent from heavenly seed,	*Aen.* 7.282
	Whose might would take possession of the world [*occupet orbem*].	*Aen.* 7.258
346	And now the promised day arrived, the day when first	*Aen.* 9.107
347	He showed his holy face, the founder of a godly race [*divinae stirpis origo*],	*Aen.* 8.591; 12.166
348	sent for dominion [*imperium*],[54] and virtue came in person	*Aen.* 6.812; 5.344
349	mixed with God: His cherished Father's image [*genitoris imago*] came upon him	*Aen.* 7.661; 2.560

This text on the birth of Jesus abounds with mythological aspect of Roman propaganda, thanks to its being a composite of Virgilian lines. Some of them are about the Trojan Aeneas, descendant of Priam, who were to rule the world. Aeneas is in *Aen.* 12.166 called *Romanae stirpis origo*, the origin of the Romans' race, while Christ here is the originator of the divine race. But even this can claim a Virgilian counterpart, since Aeneas in precisely this context is said to be armed by heaven (167).

5.4.1 Nova Progenies *and the Crucifixion of Christ*

There is no doubt that this affects the overall picture given of Jesus in the cento; Elizabeth A. Clarke and Diane F. Hatch rightly speak of Proba's understanding "of Christianity as a religion of 'law' rather than of 'gospel.'"[55] Nonetheless, this conclusion must be seen against the background of the entire cento. When Aeneas visited Hades, and accordingly jeopardized his divine destiny to rule the world, his return was safeguarded by a branch, the Golden Bough [*aureus rameus*]. It is easy, says the Sibyl to Aeneas, to descend into the place of Death (Avernus), but difficult to return. If he succeeds in finding the Golden Bough, he will be able to return, since this is a gift demanded by Proserpina (Persephone); else she will keep him there (*Aen.* 6.124–8). This bough thus becomes a symbol of life overcoming death, and a symbol of the rescue of Aeneas, to preserve him for his divinely given purpose. Thus this bough saved Roman rule from faltering. While in Hades, Aeneas was also prophetically shown the future Rome, with Caesar Augustus of

---

[54] The line starts with an Aeneas typology that ends in quoting a text about Numa, Rome's first king (*Aen.* 6.812).

[55] Clark and Hatch, *The Golden Bough. The Oaken Cross*, 128.

divine genus, who would again create the Golden Age in Latium amid the fields where Saturn once reigned (*Aen.* 6.793–4; cf. *4th Ecloge*). The Golden Bough kept this hope alive in Virgil's poem. This is the background against which Proba's text on the crucifixion is to be read:[56]

615	Laid hands upon the sacred symbol [*sacram effigem*]	*Aen.* 2.167
616	With bloody hands set up a massive oak,	*Aen.* 11.5
617	Its branches looped away all around, and bound him with great coils.	*Aen.* 6.217; 2.217
618	Then they stretched his hands, Made one foot fixed upon the other[57]	*Aen.* 6.314; 7.66
619	—a sad attendance [*triste ministerium*]—The leaders whom the rest, the young men, followed.	*Aen.* 6.223; 5.74
620	All dared commit a monstrous wrong, and what they dared to do, succeeded in [*ausi omnes immane nefas ausoque potiti*]	*Aen.* 6.624, 621

The cross is described as a tree bringing death, as did the two sea-serpents when Laocöon, the priest of Neptune, and his sons were strangled and killed at Troy for having opened the gates to the enemy (*Aen.* 2.212–24).[58] The personification is worth noting here. Jesus is killed by the cross itself, squeezing the life from him, by analogy with Laocöon. This gives Proba the opportunity to leave the soldiers, i.e. Romans, unmentioned here.[59] *Sacram effigem* comes from Virgil's description of a Trojan standard engraved with an image of Minerva. It probably refers to Christ's cross.[60]

Lines from *Aen.* 6.223 [*triste ministerium*] and 6.624 [*ausi omnes immane nefas ausoque potiti*] describe the sadness of Jesus' crucifixion; his enemies succeeded in a sacrilegious act. The first line is taken from the funeral scene par excellence in Virgil, that of Misenus. The "sad ministry" refers to the act of carrying the heavy bier of the dead

---

[56] Pointed out by Clark and Hatch, *The Golden Bough. The Oaken Cross*, 148–9.

[57] See Chapter 4.5.3, the Jerome part. The idea that Jesus was bound to the cross is not entirely without analogies in Christian literature; see Meliton of Sardes, *Pascha* 96, where the described as his being fixed [πέπηκται] and fastened [ἐπὶ ξύλου ἐστήρικται].

[58] For a visual presentation of this story, see Balch, *Roman Domestic Art and Early House Churches*, 93.

[59] Thus Menconi, "The Christian Cento and the Evangelization of Classical Culture," 118.

[60] Thus Clarke and Hatch, *The Golden Bough. The Oaken Cross*, 192 n. 54. Menconi, "The Christian Cento and the Evangelization of Classical Culture," 118 holds it to refer to Christ's body.

friend. The second line is taken from one of Proba's favourite scenes, Aeneas visiting Hades. Virgil presents "the sinners" found by Aeneas there; here are the notorious sinners according to ancient mythology and anonymous evildoers. Proba summarises their sins as follows: "All dared do monstrous things, and in their sins they succeeded." Thus both birth and crucifixion are for Proba to be interpreted with the aid of the Virgilian idea of a new beginning.

The liberty and life of The Golden Age returned was, both to Proba herself and according to the introductory dedication, thanks to "the help of the one cross." Thus the cross occupies a key role in Proba's concept of *nova progenies*, a fact seen in her interpretation of Jesus' death. In *Aen.* 5.815 she finds an apt description for the significance of his death: "For the sake of many shall one life be given [*unum pro multis*]" (l. 598 cf. 493). As a price for the safe journey of Aeneas and his crew, Neptune demands the death of his helmsman, Palinurus. While asleep he falls overboard. Stranded on the coast of Lucania, he is killed (*Aen.* 5.827–71 cf. 6.337–71), but his death secures Aeneas' safe journey towards Rome.[61]

The significance of Jesus' death in this cento is also conveyed through the signs taking place in nature immediately after his death (l. 625–37). Great events in history are recognized as such by Nature. Strange phenomena therefore accompany such events. As for Jesus, such events are described in Matt 27:45 and Luke 23:44–45. Proba finds these biblical apocalyptic traditions in the *Georgics*:[62]

627	godless Ages feared a never-ending night	
	[*aeternum…noctem*]	*Georg.* 1.468
632	Next, earth let out a groan and Ocean's plains	*Georg.* 1.469
633	gave their signs [*signa dabant*]:	*Georg.* 1.471
	Rivers halted, earth gaped wide	*Georg.* 1.479
637	Covered its (= the sun) glowing face in dim obscurity	*Georg.* 1.467[63]

All these lines are taken from the passage where Virgil describes how nature reacted to the death of Caesar. Since Proba's previous work on the war within the Constantinian dynasty was inspired by Lucan's *Civil War* that followed upon the assassination of Caesar, it is likely that she

---

[61] See Stephen J. Harrison, "Palinurus," *Oxford Classical Dictionary*, 1100.
[62] This is well pointed out by Bazil, *Centones Christiani*, 160–3.
[63] My own translation with some help from Clark and Hatch, *The Golden Bough. The Oaken Cross* and LCL.

is here consciously imitating. She was led to Virgil's description of the mourning nature by the biblical texts mentioned above. We see at work here both an analogical and a contrast imitation. As with the death of Caesar, Jesus' death likewise marked a dramatic shift in history; thus far an analogical imitation. But while the death of Caesar resulted in warfare, the death of Jesus introduced the peace that is an all-pervading theme of her poem. Here we see an analogical imitation of Virgil. As will become gradually clearer, there are a number of contrastive imitations as well. But these work within an idea of some fundamental analogies.

Furthermore, the new beginning has a personal aspect in her poem too. In her personal note—nearly a parenthesis in her narrative poem—about her own faith and salvation, Proba again uses the idea of the Golden Age. In her Christian faith she has embraced the age promised by Virgil. Proba makes her confession in a personal and devotional style (l. 415–28). This passage is emotional in its devotion to Christ, and adds balance to the picture she paints of Jesus as an imperial law-giver.[64] The style bears reminiscences of a conversion scene depicted in a traditional "before v. now" style. Her longing for Virgil's Golden Age has finally been answered in Christ. L. 417 is taken from Aeneas' words as he is about to leave Troy behind, his *patria antiqua*, and finds himself without hope, liberty and rescue [*spes, libertas, salus*] (*Aen.* 2.137).[65] Her longing includes a line taken from Tityrus' lament in *Ecl.* 1.44 "here he was the first to give my prayer an answer [*hic mihi responsum primus dedit ille petenti*];" he saw the smoke from the altar and took that as a divine response. With these words Proba says that she found an answer to her seeking. She says that she was then "sent back into my realm [*meque in mea regna remisit*]" (l. 421). The interpretation of this is less than certain. The words themselves are from a line in *Aen.* 2.543 in which Priam speaks thus of Achilles, who respectfully allowed him, his enemy, to return home safely with the body of his son Hector. In Proba's context, is it a reference to her life as a Christian, or is it an allusion to the tradition of the Golden Age? Eden, the original "native land", is regained by those who follow Jesus, *nova progenies*, who brings back the Golden Age. Cosmic and personal

---

[64] Thus also Clark and Hatch, *The Golden Bough. The Oaken Cross*, 134.
[65] *Libertas* and *salus* are taken from other passages respectively, and thus it is demonstrated how lines and words from various lines are being pieced together.

perspectives here merge. I hold the latter position, due to what the Creator says to men in Eden:[66]

141 This is your home, this your native land
[*patria*], A guaranteed repose [*requies*][67]
from honest toil.   *Aen.* 7.122; 3.393
142 On this I put no end, nor hour of destiny: *Aen.* 1.278
143 Dominion [*imperium*] without end I have
bestowed   *Aen.* 1.279; *Georg.* 4.208

5.5 The Baptism of Jesus "According to Virgil" (L. 388–414)

Proba's text is considerably longer and fuller than the New Testament texts on this event. It is remarkable how many basic biblical elements in the text of Virgil she has been able to identify. The text is preceded by a summary of Jesus' ministry, where Proba has a crowd of matrons say about him: "What vitality he has! What an impressive face and voice! Even his step as he walks!" (l. 386–7). This is taken from *Aen.* 5.648–9 when Iris, disguised as Beroë, set Aeneas' ships on fire. The way the Virgilian line works in Proba's poem makes the baptism a recognition scene bringing to mind a number of classical texts:[68] the true identity of Jesus is here being revealed.

Enters now John the Baptist [*vates*] by a chilly stream [*flumen*], saying: "The time has come. God behold! God in whom there lies out greatest faith in deed and word [*Tempus iat: deus ecce, deus cui maxima rerum verborumque fides*]" (l. 390–1). This is from *Aen.* 6.46, announcing that the Sibyl is about to make her prophetic utterance. The sentence echoes the notion of fulfilment found in the Gospels, see particularly Matt 3:15 [πληρῶσαι], and also the Johannine words of the Baptist in John 1:29 ("Behold, the Lamb of God"). In words taken from *Ecl.* 5.49 about Menalcus, who is happy to be second to Apollo, Proba brings out a key point in the biblical stories about the Baptist and Jesus' baptism, particularly found in his reluctance (Matt 3:14), since, as it says in *Ecl.* 5.64—not quoted here but clearly implied: *deus, deus, ille* ("God, God, is the one present"). John gladly accepts being

---

[66] I here follow Clark and Hatch, *The Golden Bough. The Oaken Cross*, 168–9.
[67] Cf. the topic of peace mentioned above in the discussion of the preface.
[68] For recognition scenes in ancient texts, see Kasper Bro Larsen, *Recognizing the Stranger. Recognition Scenes in the Gospel of John* (Leiden: Brill, 2008), 55–71.

second, praising Jesus as "Our hope and comfort [*spes et solacia nostri*]"; this is, according to *Aen.* 8.514, said about Pallas.

Jesus is now immersed [*mersare*] in the river. There is considerably more emphasis on the water in Proba's text than in the New Testament original: In l. 395–8 water is actually mentioned three times:

395–6	When the prophet[69] spoke, He received him	*Aen.* 2.790 etc.
	as he came to dip him in the wholesome	
	stream [*fluuio mersare salubri*],	*Aen.* 9.817
	and brought him out from gentle wave	
	[*ac mollibus extulit undis*].	
397	The waters proudly swirled [*exultanteque uada*],	
	and suddenly in urgent flight a dove winged	
	down,	*Aen.* 3.557; 5.213
398	and hovered above his head.	*Aen.* 4.702

L. 396 [*ac mollibus extulit undis*] is from *Aen.* 9.817 about Turnus' desperate leap into the river Tiber. Enters now the dove above his head: In urgent flight a dove winged down and hovered above his head [*commota columba…supra caput astitit*]" (l. 397–8) taken from *Aen.* 5.213. These are some examples where the Virgilian context of the actual line is of no significance. It is merely a matter of finding appropriate words. This observation, which applies frequently, is nevertheless important, because it is revealing as to the point of departure for Proba's cento. Proba starts with the biblical texts and Christian traditions and seeks to find appropriate words in Virgil. The second half-line appears theologically significant. It is taken from *Aen.* 4.702, a description of Iris, the divine messenger, as she proclaims news from heaven. Proba seems not to have been distracted by the fact that on this occasion Iris bore a message of death.

Elizabeth A. Clarke and Diane F. Hatch have rightly called attention to one important factor appearing now in Proba's cento. L. 400–1 about people streaming to the river—probably an altering of the many who were seeking John for baptism (Matt 3:5–6parr)—taken from Virgilian lines talking about Charon ferrying the dead across the river Styx.[70] This gives a rather pointed interpretation of the baptism of Jesus, a point hardly implied in the biblical texts themselves, and a

---

[69] *Vates* does not appear in this line, but picks up from l.388.
[70] Clarke and Hatch, *The Golden Bough. The Oaken Cross*, 146.

point requiring a wider perspective of baptismal theology as a transition from death into life.

The heavenly voice is in the second person singular, thus aligning itself with a Marcan tradition where the sonship is confirmed; but it also commissions him. The heavenly voice in the New Testament—in spite of textual variances—is rather short and pointed compared to Proba's longer version:

403	Called aloud his Son: 'O Son, my strength lone my mighty power	Aen. 1.644
404	and sweetest grace, Soon to requite your father in good measure,	Aen. 11.155; 10.505
405–6	From you is the beginning, and with you will be the end [a te principum, tibi desinet]. Listen, my Son [o mea progenies], I bear you witness: in whatsoever place the rising and setting sun	Ecl. 8.11; Aen. 11.559; Aen.7.97, 100
407	surveys the sea, Either side, from East to West—happy at your offsprings made complete,	Aen. 7.101
408	you shall behold all regions turned and ruled beneath your feet [omnia sub pedibus uertique uidebis].	Aen. 7.100, 101
409	Govern your subjects with authority [tu regere imperio populos], matrons and husbands both,	Aen. 6.851; 2.279
410	Their hearts forgotten how to love;	Aen. 1.722
411	Compassionate, with me, for sluggish men who do not know the way,	Georg. 1.41; Ecl. 8.24
412	go forth, and accustom Yourself to be called upon in prayer,'	Georg. 1.42
413	God said. He prepared to obey his mighty Father's	Aen. 4.238
414	Authority , pressing on with the task and the Kingdom To be [parere parabat imperio, ... regnisque futuris]	Aen. 4.239; 1.504

Thus goes Proba's lengthy version of the heavenly voice. The introductory lines are taken from Aen. 1.664; 11.155 and 10.507. While the first is addressed to Cupido, the god of erotic love (Amor), the other two to Pallas; in other words to pagan deities. This seems not to have bothered Proba; obviously, the wording had precedence over the context from which the wording was taken. L. 405 echoes Rev 1:18; 21:6; 22:13 (alpha and omega), but it is from Ecl. 8.11, where it summarizes an encomium

made to Pollio, Virgil's patron; he is praised from beginning till end
i.e. throughout. *Progenies* (l. 406) appears in the heavenly voice in the
vocative, thus echoing somewhat Ps 2:7. As we have seen above, this
term evokes Virgilian "Romeology". The commissioning aspect included
in the heavenly voice emphasizes power, rule and authority in terms
of *omnia sub pedibus* and *regere imperio populos*. Both phrases echo
Ps 110:1–2, a psalm easily linked up with Ps 2:7,[71] but which in the New
Testament primarily serves as a proof-text for the resurrection. In Proba's
poem these two biblical texts seem to converge in the heavenly voice.
But the lines are taken from *Aen.* 7.100–1 and 6.851, and Proba seems
much aware of their Virgilian context. This is hardly a "search and find"
operation in her mental concordance, since they fit in so nicely with her
adaptation of Virgilian "Romeology". The first reference is about king
Latinus ruling Latium and who was left without male descendants. By a
prophet he is told: "I see a stranger draw near…" (*Aen.* 7.69), which he
takes to mean that his daughter Lavinia is to marry a stranger. Troubled
by this, he consults the groves with a reputation for making known the
will of the gods (*Aen.* 7.81–91). He obtains the reply:

> Seek, not, O my son, to ally thy daughter in Latin wedlock, and put no
> faith in the bridal-chamber prepared. Strangers shall come, to thy sons,
> whose blood shall exalt our name to the stars, and the children of whose
> race shall behold, where the circling sun looks on either ocean, the whole
> world roll obedient beneath their feet (*Aen.* 7.96–101)

Having the story then change directly to Aeneas, Virgil leaves his
readers in no doubt about the precise meaning of the prophecy. The
prophecy is fulfilled in the story about Aeneas. The second Virgilian
line (l. 409) is from a similar, but more pronounced text praising
Rome: "You, Roman, be sure to rule the world (be these your arts),
to crown peace with justice, to spare the vanquished and to crush the
proud" (*Aen.* 6.851–3). The latter part is not cited by Proba, but show
similarities with her theology of justice being restored with peace (see
above).[72] All this naturally brings a strong element of ruling into the
act in which Jesus embarks upon his ministry. Proba's interpretation at
this particular point owes more to the Old Testament background and

---

[71] The biblical versions of the heavenly voice in the old Latin tradition, the Itala, are
not authoritative for the wording chosen by Proba; she sticks to her Virgil.

[72] Proba has *iustitia* in l.309 and 469, but *mores* (Virgil's term here) may well be used
synonymously as it refers to the establishment of law and tradition; se OLD s.v. *mos*.

the Virgilian vocabulary than to the ministry of Jesus as it is unfolded in the Gospels. She might be influenced by a certain Adam typology, since he is described likewise in 1.143.[73] Nonetheless, this picture of Jesus as embarking on a ruling ministry is balanced by the mentioning in l. 410–1 of those longing for rest and love, and who lack knowledge of *via*, taken from *Aen.* 1.722 about Dido whose heart longed for love, and from *Georg.* 1.41 about those ignorant of the way, that they will come to know the pity of Caesar.

L. 413 prepares for Proba's summary: Jesus is prepared to obey [*parere*] the *imperium*[74] of his Father and to press on with his work and future *regnum* (l. 414). These lines are taken from *Aen.* 4.239 and 1.504. The first is from Aeneas, who is about to be deflected from his destiny by falling in love with Dido. The gods intervene to make sure that he keeps sailing: *naviget*. That is the sum of his life, to reach Rome. Aeneas then prepares to obey this command of his heavenly father. The "new Aeneas" does likewise. The second half-line is about Dido performing her duties as queen of her kingdom.[75] Proba certainly bends the Virgilian *regnum futurum* here. The fact that Dido is reigning as queen of Carthage makes it necessary to render *futurum* as rising (thus LCL) or imminent. Proba is exploiting what she found as latencies in the Virgilian text, and finds here a term appropriate for the ministry at large which Jesus was given at his baptism.

---

[73] Thus Clarke and Hatch, *The Golden Bough. The Oaken Cross*, 164–5.

[74] As for *imperium*, see l. 348 on the birth of Jesus, there summarized as *missus in imperium*.

[75] Clarke and Hatch, *The Golden Bough. The Oaken Cross*, 126 make the observation that Jesus' baptism serves as a prelude to Proba's confession (see above). They take this to indicate her interest in Christian ritual and baptism in particular. It is hardly possible to reach a firm conclusion based on the scant evidence, but I think this suggestion is worth considering. Proba becomes personal and addresses her entering her native land, receiving salvation and being cleansed immediately after being told about Jesus' baptism. That Proba's "reaching the land" follows immediately upon the story of Christ's baptism, may also be seen in the light of liturgical practice witnessed in early Christian sources, that after baptism the baptizand immediately was given milk and honey, symbols of the Promised Land according to biblical tradition; for references see Chapter 6.4 of this study. It is likely that she here is here conveying a commonly-held baptismal theology, namely that the baptism of Jesus was considered the beginning of Christian baptism, and is therefore also the model upon which Christian baptism is patterned; see Hans Kvalbein, "The Baptism of Jesus as a Model for Christian Baptism. Can the Idea be Traced Back to the New Testament times?" *ST* 50 (1996). Schnapp, "Reading Lessons," 121 n. 36 has made a interesting suggestion. He argues that Proba's autobiographical excursus is linked to Jesus' baptism through a common denominator, namely parental instruction and obedience. This being so, the pedagogical nature of this work, stated explicitly at the end of the poem, is underscored.

5.6   THE TEMPTATION "ACCORDING TO VIRGIL"

This New Testament story (Matt 4:1–11parr) is found in l. 429–55. The Biblical story is marked by Old Testament citations. Jesus and the Devil engage in a "Streitgespräch" on biblical interpretation. It is, therefore, of interest to see how an author who has imposed upon herself the limitations given by Virgil tells this story.

The scene is introduced with reference to *Aen.* 7.375 in which a venomous snake appears. Proba introduces the Devil with a line taken from a longer scene (*Aen.* 7.340–405) about how Alecto, after being bitten by a snake, becomes frenzied and directs her anger against king Latinus. Proba keeps the implications of this metaphor throughout her version of the story. This is a recapitulation of motives from the same Virgilian scene found in the Fall story (Gen 3) (l. 177–99, 248–9). Furthermore, the Fall and temptation are also similar in the fact that the serpent opposes divinely decreed laws (l. 197. 438). Proba's version of the Temptation thus draws upon the Fall story: hence the Devil becomes a serpent. This clearly shows how she works, her somewhat unexpected version of the Fall is perfectly understandable within a wider biblical perspective. Another aspect worth noting is that Proba depicted the cross as a snake squeezing Jesus to death (Chapter 5.4.1). There is probably a connection here between Devil, snake and cross. This exemplifies how the cento form becomes such a fascinating phenomenon, where fixed meaning is difficult to affirm; one is rather thrown into a constant change penetrating into ever new layers of meaning.

Jesus walks through the grass when he finds the snake fiercely hissing, asking why Jesus trespasses on his borders (l. 432–4). This echoes Charon's query to Aeneas when he seeks to cross the border of the dead (*Aen.* 6.388–9). With Elizabeth A. Clarke and Diane F. Hatch, I find the echoing of Charon both here and in the baptism story to be examples of the Virgilian background expressing Christian theology in a creative way.[76] Proba here speaks from the perspective of early Christian baptismal theology as passing from death to life.[77] Clarke and Hatch read *tendentem adversum*, "stretching out for him" in l.433

---

[76] Clarke and Hatch, *The Golden Bough. The Oaken Cross*, 146.

[77] Such thinking on baptism can be traced to e.g. Rom 6. I think this applies also to the scene where the crucifixion is described as a stretching of his hands [*tendebantque manus*] (l.618), taken from *Aen.* 6.314. The death of Jesus is described as echoing the longing for reunion of those who have already crossed over the Styx.

as well in this light. This phrase is taken from the reunion scene in Hades between Aeneas and his father Anchises (*Aen.* 6.684). From among the dead, Anchises stretches out his hands to meet his son, the living man. The scene is moving, and rather distant from the inimical context that now sets the scene in the cento. This is an example where it is difficult to decide on the level of intertextuality, but it does make sense as a piece of baptismal theology.

Now follows a dialogue between the snake, uttering the words of Charon, and Jesus. A series of critical questions about Jesus' identity are presented: "Who are you by race?" (l. 437) and "who...bade you approach my home, to imbue men's ways [*mores*] with peace?" (l. 440).[78] The serpent accuses Jesus for bringing peace to the *mores* (see above). Proba has found lines enabling her to render one temptation from the New Testament stories, namely the Devil asking Jesus to jump from the top of the Temple [*domus alta*] (l. 443), a request expressed in terms of his trusting his Father who commissioned him. *Domus alta* is taken from *Aen.* 10.526 where Magus, within his fight with Aeneas, pleads for mercy and offers Aeneas his fine house he owns, and his silver and gold. Aeneas does not accept his offer, and kills him on the spot.

Jesus responds: "Smiling on it with heart serene he spoke, Not ignorant of prophets, fully aware Of the age about to come. 'Did you expect to trick me, treacherous snake'" (l.446–8). He is presented as confident, trusting fully in the prophecies, and his words to the snake are, in fact, combined with Dido's raging anger against Aeneas when she learnt that he was about to leave in secret (*Aen.* 4.305). There is hardly a real engagement in interpretation at this point in Proba's text. Jesus simply declares in Virgilian lines that the snake is doomed: "Submit yourself to God when you have hurled, face down, Your length of body on the ground" (l. 452). This line is taken from *Aen.* 5.467 where Aeneas urges angry Entellus to yield to the will of the gods, and to *Aen.* 11.87 about old Acoetes who falls to the ground. The snake recognizes Jesus himself[79] as *venerabile donum* ("the venerable Gift"), and presses cheek to ground and escapes by camouflaging itself with the shade. Proba possibly betrays her metaphorical language here; *frons*

---

[78] Slightly altered from Clarle and Hatch, *The Golden Bough. The Oaken Cross.*
[79] Thus also Clarke and Hatch, *The Golden Bough. The Oaken Cross*, 192.

would be a rather peculiar name for the head of a snake.[80] This is taken from *Aen.* 10.349 about Clausus who kills Dryops, causing him thus to fall dead on his forehead. Proba makes this event a fulfilment of the fall story; now the serpent is finally defeated.

5.7 The Sermon on the Mount "According to Virgil"

Proba recounts this important speech in the structure of Matthew's Gospel in l. 463–96, the end of which is somewhat uncertain though. Proba's version is more like a summary of Jesus' teaching than a rendering of this actual speech. In a text where distance between the cento and the biblical texts is the most apparent, there are still some similarities worth observing. The setting is *in montes* (cf. Matt 5:1). Furthermore, the Sermon on the Mount in Matthew's version brings to life a structure marked by "two ways",[81] and this structure is preserved by Proba. Jesus talks about life as a journey [*iter*] or a way [*via salutis*] (l. 472).[82] The expression *via prima salutis* ("salvation's chiefest path"), (l. 472) summarizing Proba's Sermon on the Mount, is taken from the words of the Cumae Sibyl in *Aen.* 6.96, assuring Aeneas that he will eventually reach his destiny in arriving in Italy, on the Lavinian shore. Thus this phrase captures the hub of Proba's poem: Jesus is *nova progenies* preparing the way of salvation. Parts of the text are organized according to a pattern of two kinds of conducts being contrasted,[83] which eventually brings two kinds of results:

---

[80] If used about animals, *frons* refers to the front of the head; see OLD s.v. and also F.P. Dutripon, Vulgatæ Editionis Bibliorum Sacrorum Concordantiae (Barri-ducis: Coelestini, 1874), s.v.

[81] In Matthew this sermon is enclosed by this pattern, namely in the Beatitudes (Matt 5:1–11) and the final parable of the fool and wise man (Matt 7:24–27); cf. Matt 7:13–14. Luke's version with the marked contrast between those blessed and those woed (Luke 6:20–26) added to this dual structure.

[82] This is a metaphor with currency in Graeco-Roman moral-philosophy as well as in Jewish and Christian paraenetical traditions. In classical Greek tradition this is associated with Hercules finding himself on the crossroad between virtue and vice; see Sandnes, *Belly and Body in the Pauline Epistles*, 44–45. In the Christian tradition, *Did.* 1.1 is a very good example: "There are two ways, one of Life and one of Death, and there is a great difference between the two ways."

[83] According to Bažil, *Centones Christiani*, 165 this is the protreptic and apotreptic parts of the sermon.

Intemerata fides ("faith unsullied")
Conscia recti ("a mind self-confident")

Sharing (with relatives)	Acquiring wealth and keeping it for one self [*solus*]
	Striking a parent
	Treating a client badly
Quies (Peace)	Death (impending judgement)

Striking a parent and the mentioning of clients are bold additions to the Sermon, as E.A. Clarke and D.F. Hatch put it.[84] The speech given "on the mountains" and this contrast pattern unite Proba's poem at this point with Matthew's Sermon; the rest, however, represents a deviation from what we know as the Sermon on the Mount. The instruction given by Jesus is summarized in the following way:

- *iura dabat legesque viris, secreta parentis* ("He gave religion and laws for men, and mysteries of the Father")[85] (l. 464), which is, in fact, a short description of Dido ruling as queen (*Aen.* 1.507). The last part is from *Aen.* 2.299, in which Anchises' house in Troy is described as hidden among trees. In Proba's text this rather trivial matter is transferred into a statement on the divine mysteries taught by Jesus, and imposed upon him by his heavenly Father. The link between the two texts is thus limited to the verbal level.
- *Spemque dedit dubiae menti* ("And he gave hope to irresolute minds") (l. 465). These are words of comfort to Dido as she struggles with herself over her infatuation with Aeneas (*Aen.* 4.55).
- *Curasque resolvit* ("and eased away their cares") (l. 465), taken from *Georg.* 1.302 in which Virgil describes the pleasure and rest of farmers during wintertime, when farming is impossible.

Proba's poem on this Sermon pictures Jesus very much as a powerful legislator; a picture that is somewhat modified by the two last points mentioned above. The caring aspect is included, and the half-line taken from the farmers' pleasures in winter becomes a short form of Christ's teaching on salvation, easily linked with *pax* elsewhere in her cento. In a presentation of Jesus' teaching and ministry these descriptions are

---

[84] Clarke and Hatch, *The Golden Bough. The Oaken Cross*, 119.
[85] Slightly altered from Clarke and Hatch, *The Golden Bough. The Oaken Cross. Ius* in plural may here also refer to jurisdiction at large; see OLD s.v.

weighty, but they seem rather accidentally drawn from Virgil. Justice and wealth are emphasized in Proba's text:

469	Be warned! Learn justice, succour the weary,	*Aen.* 6.620
470	each for his own sake; and, men, whatever	
	wealth exists For each of you, be glad,	*Aen.* 5.501, 100
471	and call upon Your common God.	*Aen.* 8.275

By means of these Virgilian lines the radical teaching of the Sermon on the Mount is softened, probably to adapt to the social context in which the poem was composed. The radicality of the biblical text is softened to address gratitude for riches and a sharing attitude, particularly towards relatives and clients [*sui/clienti*] (l. 477). Practicality, not radicality, has the upper hand here.[86] The rest of her rendering of this speech is more or less about Judgement Day as a motivation, not to say threat. Compared to the biblical Sermon, this is an invention. It follows from this that the section on Judgement Day [*dies flammarum*] (l. 497–504) following upon her version of the Sermon is in fact Proba's warning to her readers. This appears somewhat foreign, but is not entirely unprepared for in Jesus' closing words in Matt 7:27.

The patchwork nature of the cento allows for sudden shifts, and this happens also in her presentation of the Sermon on the Mount. There is a long section attacking sacrifices (l. 488–94). The only text in the Sermon on the Mount which could in any way be seen to offer some support for this is Matt 5:23–24. If this is the "source," Proba has altered it considerably from speaking about delay to abandonment. The nub of this criticism is that it is more helpful to believe [*credere*] than to slaughter animals. This echoes biblical teaching found in the Old Testament (Isa 44:9–20, Ps 51:18–19; Amos 5:21–26). As for Jesus' ministry, these cento lines represent a bringing-together of different ideas into an important Christian *theologumenon* about the end of sacrifices, and adding this to the Sermon in an awkward way. This becomes particularly clear when Proba explains Jesus' attack on sacrifices by saying: "One death, once for all, suffices" [*perisse semel satis est*] (l. 493).[87] Proba's cento moves rather freely between given texts and wider theological concerns, taken from the Christian tradition at large.

---

[86] Thus Clarke and Hatch, *The Golden Bough. The Oaken Cross*, 118–21.
[87] On this see Chapter 5.4.1 above.

5.7.1   *The Rich Young Man*

Upon the description of Judgement Day follows the story about the rich young man (Matt 19:16–30) (l. 505–30). The present tense "while warning" [*moneret*] in l. 505 connects the episode to the Sermon on the Mount. The text links up with Proba's rendering on riches in the Sermon on the Mount, and her softening of Jesus' teaching. Significant alterations now take place; the Gospel story is itself considerably bent. This is the only event from the actual ministry of Jesus described in the poem, in addition to the storm and Jesus walking on the sea; the latter two are united to form one story. The rich man is described in lines about the rich old Galaesus (*Aen.* 7.538–9) and the richness of life in the countryside that includes a lavish table (*Georg.* 4.133). The rich young man takes his refuge in Jesus: *ad te confugio et supplex tua numina posco* ("with you I take refuge, and suppliant, I invoke your divine favor") (l. 513). These are the words of Juno to Cupido (Love) (*Aen.* 1.666). With reference to Aeneas' request to see his father in Hades (*Aen.* 6.105), the young man requesting the grace of Christ claims that he has done everything, and now he asks: "what is now left [*quid denique restat*]?" (l. 515)—taken from Palinurus' prayer to the gods while drowning at sea (*Aen.* 6.365). There is a certain tension in Proba's version of this story. The rich man has performed everything, and yet still asks for salvation from his sins. Her version leaves this unaddressed. Furthermore, Jesus' response adds to the strangeness of her text:

520	'My friend, nothing you left undone [*nihil o tibi amice relictum*].	*Aen.* 6.509
521	This further I shall add to these behests, if your good will towards me is sure.	*Aen.* 7.548
522	Do learn, O lad, contempt for wealth, and also mold yourself as worthy	*Aen.* 12.435
523	even of God; and what Virtue is, and manliness, you will be capable of knowing.	*Aen.* 8.365; *Ecl.* 4.27
524	Hold the sufferer's hand and, brother, your brother do not forsake.	*Aen.* 6.370; 10.600
525	If eager he should be to bind himself in friendship, bind him willing.	*Aen.* 7.264; 5.712
526	Let chaste home preserve its sense and modesty. Come now,	*Georg.* 2.524; 3.42
527	Do not procrastinate, nor come resentful to a poor man's straits'.	*Georg.* 3.43; *Aen.* 8.365

Nihil...relictum is a slightly, but not less significant, alteration of the biblical text. The question of the rich man, according to Itala, *quid adhuc mihi deest?* becomes in Proba's text a statement of the fact given by Jesus, who in this passage is introduced as *hero*: *nihil relictum* ("nothing remains"). The contrast is, may be, most clearly seen if the Markan version is taken into account: *unum tibi deest* (Mark 10:21). The Virgilian line from where Jesus' *nihil* is taken is *Aen.* 6.509 where Aeneas meets with Deiphobus, son of Priam, in Hades, for whom he once held a funeral without having found the body. Deiophobus then says to Aeneas: "Nothing have you left undone!" It adds further to the strangeness of Proba's text that the rich man grows pale and backs off. The Virgilian lines with which her story is closed make perfect sense in the light of the biblical story, but not in the light of her own alterations. The young man's reaction is in accordance with the biblical text, but in the light of the way Proba has altered Jesus' response, his reaction is strange. What made sense as a reaction to what Jesus demanded of him in the Bible does not make equal sense when this demand is softened. Proba has not only altered the text beyond its biblical *Vorlage*, she has contradicted it in accordance with her softening of the Sermon on the Mount. Nonetheless, she keeps the ending of the story. This tension is a reminder that Proba, even when altering a text considerably, feels bound to follow the tradition transmitted to her. In this particular case, the result is a story afflicted with incoherence. Proba's version owes more to Roman ideals than to the radicality of Jesus' instruction in the biblical story; Jesus addresses the rich young man, urging him to practice the ideal of a frugal Roman home. *Aen.* 8.365 provides Proba with the wording, taken from a description of the welcoming house of poor Evander, where also Aeneas found a dwelling (*Aen.* 8.360–9). *Georg.* 2.524 adds to this picture; the line comes from Virgil's description of the farmer's house and family (2.513–31).

5.8   What has been proved by Proba's poem?

The first extant Christian cento was not made out of Homer, but of Virgil. Proba's cento enjoyed wide circulation; a fact proven both by Jerome's criticism aiming directly at her poem as well as the decision found in *Decretum Gelasianum.*[88] Proba wrote some time between 350–90, probably

---

[88] See Chapter 4.5.3 of this study.

shortly after Julian passed his law on Christian access to the classical literature. We saw that to some l. 23 was targeting precisely Julian's decree (Amatucci). Although the arguments, taken together, favour a post-Julian authorship, this is pushing the evidence. Proba's project is not unthinkable without Julian's law, but the pedagogical nature of the poem is well suited to this particular historical situation. At this point it might be helpful to compare with Apollinarius. His biblical paraphrase was written explicitly to replace what Julian did to the Christians, namely to restrict their access to literature and Greek *paideia*. Socrates says that Apollinarius' writings soon lost their impact, as though they had never been written (*Hist. eccl.* 3.16.7). He seems to imply that this was due to the fact that his paraphrases were devoted to the particularity of the situation. This being the case, Proba is different. However, the difference of the fate of their paraphrases may be due to the fact that Apollinarius later came to be considered a heretic, while the latter enjoyed much popularity, albeit that she was judged apocryphal. The difference between Apollinarius and Proba in terms of their effect on posterity may also indicate that Proba's *paraphrasis*—still triggered by the Julian context—was less situational. She turned a playful tradition into the very serious purpose of making sure that Christian children remained acquainted with Virgil, but in a way acceptable to Christian faith; and *vice versa*, that the Gospel was presented in the venerable form of the great poet of Rome's glorious past.

It is worth noticing that Proba's Virgilian story takes the Old Testament as its beginning. *Nova progenies* is indeed Virgilian, but it is from the Garden of Eden that this idea takes its significance in her cento. Her own conversion is described as a return precisely to that native land. She nicely brings out in Virgilian language a theology of *recapitulatio*, i.e. salvation is a completion of creation.[89] The prophetic perspective of her poem is also to be understood in this light. In this clearly Virgilian Gospel there is thus a true symbiosis, where the Old Testament informs the entire story. Since Proba has retained the playful form, and since the patchwork nature yields itself to amplifications and additions, it is necessary to see to what extent the form and genre of the cento made this happen here as well. The cento form made a deep impact on her story. The historical context of the story told is

---

[89] See Brox, ed. and trans., *Irenäeus*, 36, 55. Bengt Hägglund, *History of Theology*. Fourth Revised Edition (St. Louis: Concordia Publishing House, 2007), 46–50.

more or less removed. Biographical and geographical names are not
found; one senses an atmosphere of aristocratic life *in urbem* rather
than in Galilee and Judea. Proba's work is considerably shorter than
those of both Juvencus and Nonnus; much is missing in her poem. No
parable and no healing story are found, although some passages here
and there speaking about comfort and hope, as well as the summaries,
may be taken as more general hints. Two quite essential elements in
the Gospel tradition have thus been omitted from her cento, and witness to her free handling of the tradition.

One scene is clearly fabricated with no basis in either of the Gospels,
namely Jesus' furious words on the cross. The lines speak of Jesus
being chained [*vincula*] with his feet fixed (l. 621–4).[90] While bound
Jesus says:

621	Yet he, undaunted, said: 'What makes you tie these bonds?'	*Aen.* 10.717 + *Ecl.* 6.23
622	Has pride in your birth [*generis…fiducia*] possessed you?	*Aen.* 1.132
623	Some day, you will pay with punishment [*poena*] unlike this one to me	*Aen.* 1.136
624	Recounting this, he stood affixed and there remained [*talia perstabat memorans fixusque manebat*].	*Aen.* 2.650

L. 621 is from a battle-scene in which fearsome Mezentius, whom no
one dared to fight, meets fearless, undaunted enemies. The question
is taken from *Ecl.* 6.23; Silenus, a companion of Bacchus, has fallen
asleep. Someone found him and poked fun at him by fettering him
in his garlands. L. 622–3 are made up of lines from the same scene.
Both are sayings of Neptune. He finds Aeneas' fleet scattered over all
the sea because of a storm. In his anger he summons the winds of
East and West, addressing them with both a question and a threat. He
commands them to return to their lord, Aeolus, and tell him that sole
lord of the sea is Neptune. The mention of *genus* in l. 622 probably
reveals anti-Jewish sentiments here.[91] Proba has Jesus commenting on
his crucifixion in words taken from how angry Neptune addressed the
Wind for destroying Aeneas' fleet, thus making revenge and threat a
category from which to understand this incident. Ilona Opelt rightly calls

---

[90] This is the line quoted by Jerome in *Ep.* 53.7; see Chapter 4.5.3 in this study.
[91] I hold this to be Proba's rendering of the role of the Jews in the traditions of the
Passion Story.

this "die skandalöse Kreizigungsszene" of Proba.[92] She says that Proba "zeichnet also keinen leidenden Erlöser, sondern einen scheltenen und drohenden, einen beledighten und rächenden Gott".[93] There are clearly aspects of her theology supporting that conclusion,[94] but Opelt misses Proba's interpretation of the crucifixion as it appears in l. 598 (see 5.4 and 5.4.1 above), and also her own confession in l. 415–28. These passages leave a somewhat different picture.

There are other alterations worth noting as well, such as the softening of the radical discipleship taught by Jesus. However, it is difficult to claim that these alterations are due to the genre of paraphrasis itself. Often they seem caused rather by her own theological and practical agenda.[95] Generally speaking, I would say that the Gospel tradition has undergone a Virgilian transformation, but not to the extent that the Virgilian paraphrase invented texts *ex nihilo*. It is not the case that Proba needed Virgil to make up some of her scenes. The summaries given of Jesus' ministry seem to be the texts most freely composed, with no or little basis in the tradition. When she alters the biblical stories this is due to the need to bring the Bible and Virgil into harmony; this "negotiating" is necessary to cope with the Biblical text in a new setting. By necessity this implies that, even when she alters and invents, she is dependent upon the texts that Christian tradition transmitted to her. It is not the other way around.

5.8.1 *Virgil and the Christian Subject-Matter (Res)*

We have seen that Proba's cento is Virgilian and biblical simultaneously. With reference to current rhetorical terms we labelled the first *verba* and the second *res, sensus* or *materia*. The wording of Virgil put a restraint on Proba, but the biblical subject-matter also provided her with a new reading of Virgil. Is it possible to define the relationship between the two more precisely? The solutions that can be argued are the following. The traditions of *usus* (making proper use of)[96] and "the

---

[92] Opelt, "Der zürnende Christus," 115–6. She argues that it was this scene together with Proba's christology in general, that caused her work to be deigned apocryphal.

[93] Opelt, "Der zürnende Christus," 116.

[94] I agree with Opelt that her Virgilian constraint is not to be "blamed" for this; her own theology sets the agenda.

[95] This is pointed out also by Clarke and Hatch, *The Golden Bough. The Oaken Cross*, 125, 132–3.

[96] Gnilka, *ΧΡΗΣΙΣ*; Sandnes, *The Challenge of Homer*, 142–4, 174, 177–82, 241.

spoil of the Egyptians"[97] both represent an early Christian rationale for dealing with the pagan culture. These two traditions amount to much the same thing. This implies that Proba discriminates in her use of Virgil according to what is conformable or not with Christian faith and tradition. Proba's renouncing of pagan epic in l. 16–19 and 47–49 can be called upon as supportive evidence for this view. L. 47–49 are of less importance though, since they refer primarily to texts previously composed by Proba herself.[98] Compared to what we found in Juvencus' preface, there is less open criticism of Virgil in Proba's poem. There is, therefore, less reason with Proba than with Juvencus to explain the relationship to Virgil in terms of plundering him for things compatible with the Christian faith. This reasoning does not come to the surface, however. Furthermore, it is contradicted by the fact that Proba treated Virgil as a prophet.

Roger P.H. Green suggests that there is no attempt in Proba's poem at extracting from Virgil a deeper Christian sense. When Proba seeks divine help at the beginning of her poem, she is not praying for "help in divining the secrets of Vergil—that is not a problem—but for inspiration and illumination to put forward Christian truth in this strange garb."[99] Proba is then *imposing* upon Virgil a Christian meaning. It is thus due to the performance of Proba herself that Virgil is made to sing about Christ: "She will use the known schooltext to explain the unknown Christian mysteries."[100] There is no doubt that this happens in the poem; the role of Proba herself is crucial, as stated in l. 23 *loquar*. This might be a future indicative ("I will speak")[101] or present subjunctive ("let me speak").[102] I take the prayer genre of this particular passage to favour the latter; this being so, the creative role of Proba herself, albeit inspired, is emphasized. But is this the way Proba herself looked upon her reading of Virgil. Was it simply an imposing of something alien on him?

---

[97] Allen, *The Despoliation of Egypt*; Sandnes, *The Challenge of Homer*, 144–7, 222–6.

[98] See Chapter 5.3 in this study.

[99] Green, "Proba's Introduction to her *Cento*," 553; similarly on p. 556. "The point is not that Vergil is being mined for Christian truth (so Wiesen), or reinterpreted, but that he will be made or alleged to speak of 'the gifts of Christ,' a phrase which may be taken without difficulty to refer to both Old and New Testament."

[100] Green, "Proba's Introduction to her *Cento*," 556.

[101] Thus Green, "Proba's Introduction to her *Cento*," 556; McGill, "Virgil Christianity, and the *Cento* Probae," 188 n. 21.

[102] Thus Clark and Hatch, *The Golden Bough. The Oaken Cross*, 17 rendering this "Let me tell".

Some decades ago, David S. Wiesen argued that Proba read Virgil in a way comparable to how New Testament and Early Christian writers did exegesis with the help of their proof-texts. Proba held Virgil to be such a proof-text which, through help of the right methods, would unravel new dimensions of meaning in the pagan text: "…the serious biblical cento was used to support religious opinion."[103] This would be in accordance with how centonists generally viewed the classical texts they paraphrased, namely as open to yielding new and fresh meaning. Wiesen argues that centos were in vogue to support theological arguments by the allegorical method: "The Christian cento was a relative of allegorical exegesis."[104] According to Wiesen, the cento is a parallel to biblical typological exegesis. In spite of some undeniable affinities, I consider that he is neglecting the idiosyncrasy of the cento. Wiesen lumps together the present cento and what he calls "the many centos found scattered through the New Testament."[105] Although there are formal similarities between the cento form and the stitching together of biblical lines in New Testament scriptural argument, storied centos represent something else.[106] Furthermore, if allegorical exegesis is found in Proba—and I think it certainly is—it must be called what S. McGill labels "an idiosyncratic allegorical approach to the cento's hypotext."[107] While Green interpreted Proba as imposing Christian *res* on Virgil, Wiesen opens the possibility for "bringing out" from Virgil a Christian subject-matter present there already.

The scribe who composed the dedication expressed his view on the relationship between *verba* and *res* in terms of emulation. He conceived of this in competitive terms whereby Virgil is being improved, and the superiority of the Christian subject-matter is to be demonstrated. He is changed [*Maronem mutatum*] with a better *sensus*, i.e. in terms of *res* (Dedication l.3–4). This is *synkrisis* with advertised intertextuality on the macro level. The critical element involved in this brings to mind Jerome's criticism of Proba.[108] Since, however, this dedication was not written by Proba herself, it can hardly serve as a primary source to how *she* looked upon what she was doing to Virgil.

---

[103] Wiesen, "Virgil, Minucius Felix and the Bible," 88.
[104] Wiesen, "Virgil, Minucius Felix and the Bible," 85.
[105] Wiesen, "Virgil, Minucius Felix and the Bible," 90.
[106] See Chapter 4.5 of this study.
[107] McGill, "Virgil, Christianity, and the *Cento* Probae," 176.
[108] See Chapter 4.5.3; McGill, "Virgil, Christianity, and the *Cento* Probae," 177–9.

As pointed out above, l. 23 is key here. Worth noting is that Proba speaks in the past tense about Virgil: "he sang [*cecinisse*] about Christ". This implies that Virgil, so to say by himself, without Proba's efforts, is here claimed for Christ.[109] If this is so, Proba did not impose upon Virgil Christian *res*; the poem claims it was there beforehand. Although *synkrisis* is involved in Proba's bringing the two canonical bodies of texts together, there is less competition and claim of superiority; this is a difference from the scribe who wrote the dedication. The scribe may be closer to Jerome's attitude to Virgil than to Proba herself. We pointed out above that Virgil and Moses were both seen as having sung about Christ. In both instances *cecinisse* appears (l. 36), and both are conceived of as prophets. To put it in the words of Thomas Gärtner, commenting on Proba's claim to be inspired: "Hinter solcher Schreibweise steht die Auffassung, dass die christliche Heilswahrheit gleichwohl in gewissermassen verschlüsselter Form—latent bereits in Text des heidnischen Dichters enthalten ist."[110] Martin Bažil draws from this observation an important insight. While pagan centos, such as Ausonius, were a kind of amusement or game with Virgil, Proba considered her work

> ni de déconstruire Virgile, mais bien de le reconstruire. Cette reconstruction est une réinterprétation, en accord avec le but qu'elle affiche dans l'exorde général de son pòem.: *Vergilium cecinisse loquar pia munera Christi*, 'je montrerai que Virgile a chanté les actions salvatrices du Christ'.[111]

Virgil is thus brought to completion. This brings us somewhat closer to the view of Wiesen. This view can, however, only be adopted if combined with a distinction between levels of intertextuality in the cento. Not every intertextual link—numerous as they are—carry theological weight. Certainly, at some points a theologian at work is detectable in Proba's poem. Virgil's "Romeology" is transformed and Christianized. The concept of the Golden Age and its implications is a theological contribution. Sometimes the Virgilian context of the lines matters by deepening the implications in terms of contrast or transcendence, while

---

[109] McGill, "Virgil, Christianity, and the *Cento* Probae," 176 also gives emphasis to past tense here.

[110] Gärtner, "Die Musen im Dienste Christi," 426. Thus also Bažil, *Centones Christiani*, 196: "Proba utilise la Bible comme une clé herméneutique, qui lui sert à décoder Virgile, à trouver les vérités qu'il recèle, des vérités chrétiennes, bien entendu."

[111] Bažil, *Centones Christiani*, 196.

other times this context is of no meaning whatsoever. Proba very often looks up her "mental concordance" and finds a text suitable, simply because she found appropriate terms in it. It is then more a "seek and find" method than a full-fledged typology.

Harald Hagendahl has pointed out that Jerome is upset by Proba's citation of *Aen.* 1. 664 in l. 404, while the Vulgate's rendering of the Greek is *Tu es filius meus dilectus* (Mark 1:11);[112] the reason being that she uses a statement made by Venus to Cupid. Although Proba and Jerome embraced different ideals with regard to family life and asceticism, this is hardly the issue here, at least as seen from Proba's point of view. Jerome reacts because he takes the address and context of those words into consideration, while Proba has found wording enabling her to present the baptism of Jesus "according to Virgil", without being annoyed by the context. The example is, along with others mentioned above, revealing of her method. The links between the biblical stories and Virgil's lines are often limited to the verbal or external level. Her reading is not a method of inventing texts; it is rather a matter of finding ways to express an already given text within a new pattern. Gerard Genette stated that the relationship between a hypotext and its hypertext is always that the latter comments on the former.[113] If we apply this to Proba's cento, her poem is a comment upon Virgil. But her cento makes the rewriting of its hypotext known in a manner that has no analogy with how the New Testament interprets the Old Testament.

From her proem it is quite clear that Proba is unable to express her primary concern in lines taken from Virgil. In a prologue she, therefore, reverts to traditional Christian language and advertises that the story of Jesus' life is now to be recast in the light of Virgil and, of course, *vice versa*. The readers are not left uninformed about the task she has undertaken in her poem. Here she conforms to the practice found in Ausonius as well. The major difference between the two is, however, that while Ausonius made a text about sex out of Virgil, Proba made one of salvation out of the same text. Hence, she never calls her cento *ludus*, but rather a "sacred song" (l. 9) aimed at speaking about *res altae*, profound or deep things (l. 50–51).

---

[112] Hagendahl, *Latin Fathers and the Classics*, 189.
[113] Genette, *Palimpsestes*, 14–15.

We are therefore left with a somewhat complex picture. Proba is not imposing a Christian meaning on Virgil; it is there beforehand. On the other hand, this s advertised in language owing more to Christian tradition than to Virgil. Palatina Latina 1753 (foglio 62) recto as recorded in Schenkl (CSEL 16. 519–20), from sometimes between the 8th and 10th centuries C.E., says about Proba's poem that it was handed down to be read by all Christians, "showing that out of a foreign seer the truth, however obscured, the divine law is spoken in another sense and predicting with divine inspiration both his coming, passion and ascension as well as other things, even before the coming itself".[114] Worth noting is that this text makes a distinction between what I have called *verba* and *res* or *sensus. Inuolentes* means to be clothed or wrapped up,[115] thus referring to the outer appearance of the text, *verba* and style, while *mens* equals *sensus* here. I think this is in accordance with how Proba would describe her project vis-à-vis Virgil. Her proem reveals, however, that Virgil's divine inspiration can only be understood from a later Christian perspective.

---

[114] The Latin goes like this: *ostendens quia et alienigeni uates uera obscuris inuoloentes in alia mente legem divinum et aduentum passionem et ascensionem vel cetera ante aduentum divino inspirato praedixerunt.* My translation with some help from Menconi, "The Christian Cento and the Evangelization of Classical Culture," 112.

[115] OLD s.v.

CHAPTER SIX

EUDOCIA ATHENAIS:
THE GOSPEL "ACCORDING TO HOMER"

6.1 The Empress and Her Cento

These Homeric centos are attributed to the Empress Eudocia Athenais, who in 421 became the wife of Theodosius II.[1] For reasons that are now unclear, Eudocia fell out of favour and left the court, to settle finally in the Holy Land.[2] She thus followed in the footsteps, both historically and ideologically, Helena the mother of Constantine and Egeria from Spain. Jerusalem is probably the place where she composed her cento; in the midst of the biblical land this classical Greek text came to life. Eudocia also wrote a poem on the *Martyrdom of St. Cyprian of Antioch*.[3] Evagrius Scholasticus (527–65) provides some biographical information, concentrating on her achievements in the Holy Land (*Hist. eccl.* 1.20–22). She is introduced as a good speaker [καλλιεπῆ]; she was a daughter of the *rhetor* and philosopher Leontius. Evagrius does not, however, mention her cento. He says that she arrived at Antioch on her way to visit Jerusalem; she gave a speech and closed with a citation taken from Homer: "From your lineage and blood I boast to come" (*Il.* 6.211 = 20.241). Evagrius explains this as a historical reference to the Greek descent of Antioch's inhabitants. For our purpose, it is of interest to note her fondness of expressing herself in Homeric style.

In her cento she borrows lines from the *Iliad* and *Odyssey*, and reorders them to tell the Biblical story of the Paradise and Fall, and the Life of Jesus. She quotes Homer *verbatim*, with only slight modifications as may be necessary to fit the new story. Considerations of the original

---

[1] See Whitby, "The Bible Hellenized," 207–8; Sowers, *Eudocia. The Making of a Homeric Christian*, 3–4.

[2] For biographical information on Eudocia, see Alan Cameron, "The Empress and the Poet: Paganism and Politics at the Court of Theodosius II," *Yale Classical Studies* 27 (1982): 270–9. According to Zonaras *Epitome Historiarum* 13.23, a series of events led Eudocia to flee the court; mentioned in particular is the suspicion of a affaire that upset the emperor; and also the death of her protégé Paulinus.

[3] For this see Sowers, *Eudocia. The Making of a Homeric Christian*, 133–267.

Homeric context from where the lines are taken add new layers to the meaning of her text. The reader is thus invited to unearth the cento, and it by no means deserves the negative assessment often awarded it.[4] In the interplay between Homer and the Bible, particularly the Gospel stories, new meanings emerge. The limits of interpretation seem to be defined only by the competence of the reader.

6.1.1   *Outline and Structure of the Poem*

Here is an outline of Eudocia's poem, made with some aid from M.D. Usher's edition (the Iviron text), which is *Conscriptio Prima* in Rocco Schembra's edition. The lines in CP Schembra are numbered slightly differently.[5]

Preface	1–29
The Old Testament	
Paradise and Fall	30–87
On the Plan to bring Salvation	88–96
On the Father's Plan	97–174
The Obedience of the Son	175–201b
The Life of Jesus	
The Annunciation to Mary	202–67
Childhood of Jesus	
– Birth	269–81
– The Star	282–93
– The Magi	294–300
– On King Herod and the Killing of the Boys	301–39
– Flight to Egypt and Return from there	340–358
John the Baptist and Jesus' Baptism	359–454
Calling Disciples	455–66

---

[4] See Chapter 1.7; this applies to the judgement given by Pavlovskis, "Proba and the Semiotics of the Narrative Virgilian Cento," 72–75 as well.

[5] My discussion is throughout based on Usher's edition (i.e. CP in Schembra) unless otherwise indicated. I will occasionally mention the lines as they appear in CP Schembra.

On the Teaching of Jesus	467–81
On the Trinity	482–86
On the Resurrection	487–511
Followed by the Crowd	512–27
The wedding at Cana	528–627
The Lame	628–94
The Lame in Solomon's porticoes	695–727
The Daughter of the Centurion	728–816
The Crippled with the Withered Hand	817–51
The Blind	852–923
The Person possessed by a Demon	924–92
The Woman suffering from a Haemorrhage	993–1045
The Samaritan Woman	1046–1152
On the Seven Breads	1153–227
Lazarus	1228–99
The Woman who Anointed Jesus	1300–26
On the Betrayal	1327–44
On the Mystery (the final speech)	1345–84
The Lord's Supper	1385–1432
Washing the Feet of the Disciples	1433–69
On Judas the Betrayer	1470–1534
The Night The Lord was taken	1535–78
The Lord is praying (Gethsemane)	1580–1609
The Betrayal	1610–1728
The Arrest and the Mocking	1729–56
Peter's Denial	1757–814
On the Lashes before the Crucifixion	1815–53
The Crucifixion	1854–910
On the Centurion	1911–2007
On Judas' strangling	2008–29
Lamenting the Tomb	2030–73
Christ in the Tomb	2075–148
On the Resurrection	2149–268
On Thomas touching Jesus	2269–320
On the Ascension	2321–44

Eudocia's poem does not follow Proba's dual structure of giving the Old Testament and the story of Jesus in more or less equal length. Eudocia's Old Testament story is short, and concentrates on what she considers to be the key for understanding the Life of Jesus, namely the Fall (see below). From a theological point of view, the structure is determined by the idea of "Heilsgeschichte". Her presentation of the life of Jesus is located in the context of God's purpose.[6] The transitory role played by l. 202–67, on the obedience of the Son, is revealing. The theological rationale behind the poem is seen particularly in the Old Testament part. The focus is on humankind's need for salvation. This is further strengthened in l. 88–201b involving the Father's plan for how to bring about that salvation:

| l. 88 | But there was no one there to protect from the mournful destruction | *Il.* 6.16 |
| l. 89 | for blinded by their folly they perished | *Od.* 1.7[7] |

The salvation plan is here seen against the background of Odysseus, who saved himself and returned home; his crew,[8] however, he did not save [ἀλλ᾽ οὐδ᾽ ὣς ἐρύσσατο] (*Od.* 1.6). In l. 90, this contrast between Odysseus and Jesus is made explicit. L. 467–78 introduces the teaching of Jesus by citing from *Od.* 18.351–2, thus making his teaching directed against the "suitors," who, according to the Old Testament part, represent sinful humanity (see 6.2.1 below).

The narrative structure basically follows a Synoptic pattern, including some Johannine scenes and motifs, and coming to a close with the story of the Ascension. The poem is, therefore, in its narrative structure a Gospel harmony, bringing the four Gospels into one story. Included are also some scenes with no specific roots in the Gospels themselves, but which are derived from a confluence of various biblical texts or motifs; an obvious example is l.482–6 (Schembra CP 489–93) on the Trinity.

Since this procedure is a recurrent phenomenon in the cento, I will illustrate this with l. 1345–84 (Schembra CP 1352–91). These lines render a speech given to the twelve apostles, here presented in analogy with Odysseus' crew members [... κρίνας ἑτάρων δυοκαίδεκ᾽

---

[6] This is pointed out by Whitby, "The Bible Hellenized," 195 as well.

[7] As for Eudocia's *Homerocentones*, the translations are my own, made with the aid of A.T. Murray, ed. and trans. *Homer. The Iliad.* LCL 170–1 (Cambridge, MA, London: Harvard University Press, 1924) and A.T. Murray, ed. and trans., revised by George E. Dimock, *Homer. The Odyssey.* LCL 104–5 (Cambridge, MA, London: Harvard University Press, 1995). Quotations from Homer's texts are taken from LCL, or slightly altered.

[8] When MacDonald, *The Homeric Epics and the Gospel of Mark*, 21–23, 174 says that the disciples are depicted by analogy with Odysseus' companions, this observation does indeed find a parallel in Eudocia's poem.

ἀρίστους] before the Last Supper. It thus appears as a farewell speech where the content is taken from here and there in sermons given by Jesus according to the Gospels, and where some of the lines also represent inventions as well. The immediate context of these cento lines suggests that the Johannine idea of a farewell speech (chaps. 14–16) is placed within a Synoptic narrative scheme. The speech closes with l. 1380–4, which, in fact, introduce the next scene, the Last Supper. Jesus enters a house and sits down μετὰ δὲ μνηστῆρσι; the suitors here represent Judas the traitor. He is called thus also in l.1327 (Schembra CP 1334) and 1523 (Schembra CP 1530). Jesus commissions his disciples: "Go you and declare my message [ἀλλ᾽ ὑμεῖς ἔρχεσθε καὶ ἀγγελίην ἀπόφασθε] (l. 1364 = Schembra CP 1371).[9] This line is taken from Achilles in *Il.* 9.649. In these words, Achilles confirms that he remains wroth. In the cento this line is cut loose from the context, and given a meaning that recalls the words of the Resurrected Jesus about proclaiming the Gospel to all. Cutting loose the line from its Homeric context does not imply that this context is necessarily not present in Eudocia's mind. In this particular case, it makes perfect sense here to notice a contrasting transposition of Homer. Accordingly, l. 1365 (Schembra CP 1372) says: "to men and women over the much-nourishing earth," clearly echoing texts like Matt 28:19. In fulfilling this, the apostles are driven by ἀναγκαίη (l. 1366 = Schembra CP 1373), taken from *Il.* 6.85, but which also brings to mind Paul's ἀνάγκη γάρ μοι ἐπίκειται (1 Cor 9:16) on his commission to preach the Gospel. Thus Eudocia's creative mind draws on a plethora of biblical passages, and a combination of them as well.

Due to the restraints which cento composition in principle and by its very nature put upon style and composition, *Homerocentones* can hardly refer to places and names in the Gospel stories,[10] and characters are identified by Homeric circumscriptions. To take an example, Jesus is called "he who rules over all gods and men." Judas is called "he who did more harm than everyone else put together." Mary is called "the mother who bore him and nursed him when he was young." The statement about Patroclus in *Il.* 16.734 that "he grasped a stone (λάζετο πέτρον)" is used more than once for Πέτρος, which is, of course, in

---

[9] Cf. l. 1376 = Schembra CP 1383.
[10] This is definitely the case in Usher's text edition *Homerocentones Evdociae Augustae*; in Rey's edition, *Centons Homériques* (= *Conscriptio Secunda* in Scembra) there are some few examples.

accordance with Matt 16:18.[11] Exploiting Homer's text in this way is, in fact, an example of the omniscience attributed to his works. Homer's text is a quarry from which the biblical story can be mined.[12]

There is almost an obsession with Judas and his betrayal in the poem. Eudocia addresses this topic in three rather long sections, introducing Judas in l. 1327–30 with lines describing the shameful suitors in Penelope's house, and also in a line (1328) that narratively describes the disguised and cunning Odysseus. The hero of the *Odyssey* here lends words to the betrayer. Eudocia disregards the fact that she sometimes has noble figures serve a negative end in her poem.[13] L. 1330 describes Heracles, who killed Iphitos after having enjoyed his hospitality, thus recalling that Jesus and Judas reclined together.

6.1.2 *The Prefatory Poem*

A major problem is deciding upon which edition to make use of. In 1897 Arthurus Ludwich published his Teubner edition of Eudocia's *Homerocentones*. He left his task unfinished, because he did not find it worth his time, and he left it to be completed by more patient people.[14] The last decade has seen people more patient than Ludwich, and nowadays three modern editions are available.[15] To explain the situation that led to divergent manuscript traditions, it is necessary to look at the prefatory poem, which presumably stems from Eudocia herself.[16]

---

[11] For references and further examples, see Usher, *Homeric Stitchings*, 45–49.

[12] For this see Sandnes, *The Challenge of Homer*, 44–5.

[13] For further examples, see Usher, *Homeric Stitchings*, 132–3.

[14] See Arthurus Ludwich, ed., *Eudociae Augustae procli Lycii Claudiani Carminum Graecorum Reliquae Accedunt Blemyomachiae Fragmenta* (Leipzig: B.G. Teubner, 1897), 87–88 where he also describes the poem thus: *sterilis esse*; it does not yield anything. Ludwich thus encouraged the negative view commonly held on this genre.

[15] André-Louis Rey, ed. and trans. *Centons Homériques (Homerocentra). Introduction, Texte Critique, Traduction, Notes et Index* (Paris: Cerf, 1998); M.D. Usher, ed., *Homerocentones Evdociae Avgustae* (Stuttgart and Leipig: Teubner, 1999) (the new Teubner); Rocco Schembra, ed., *Homerocentones* (Turnhout, Leuven: Brepols, 2007). The latter presents four redactions of the *Homerocentones*. For a brief presentation of this situation, see Whitby, "The Bible Hellenized," 218–9.

[16] This preface is found in Rey, ed. and trans., *Centons Homeriques*, 518–21 with a French translation; Usher, ed., *Homerocentones*, IX–X. For an English translation, see Sowers, *Eudocia. The Making of a Homeric Christian*, 77–79, who uses Rey's text edition though. I follow Usher's Teubner edition. The argument that the Iverion recension, published in the Teubner edition, is Eudocia's reworked version appears plausible to me; see Usher, "Prolegomenon." A shorter prefatory poem is found in Rey, ed. and trans., *Centons Homeriques*, 516–8 and Schembra, ed., *Homerocentones*,

1   This is the account of a poem pleasing to God [θεοτερπέος ἐστὶν
    ἀοιδῆς].
2   Patricius, who sagaciously authored this book [βίβλον],
3   is eternally worthy of ever-flowing praise,
4   especially since he was the very first to plan the glorious work [κύδιμον
    ἔργον].
5   On the other hand, he didn't tell everything entirely truthfully,
6   nor did he preserve the complete harmony of the verses
7   nor in his singing [ἀείδων] did he keep in mind only the verses
8   which the brazen heart of blameless Homer sung [ἀμεμφέος εἶπεν
    Ὁμήρου].
9   But when I saw the glorious work of Patricius half-finished [ἡμιτέλεστον],
10 I took holy pages [σελίδας ἱερὰς] in hand,
11 whatever verses were not in order [οὐ κατὰ κόσμον]
12 I drew out *en masse* from his clever book,
13 what he left out, I reinscribed on his pages,
14 and conferred a holy harmony on the verses [γράψα καὶ ἁρμονίην ἱερὴν
    ἐπέεσσιν ἔδωκα].

28 But Patricius, who wrote this clever book,
29 rather than [ἀντὶ] the Argive army[17] recounted the race of Hebrews,
30 and, rather than [ἀντὶ] battle array, demonic and sacrilegous,
31 spoke of the son and begetter of the immortal one.[18]
32 Nonetheless, the work is shared
33 by both Patricius and myself, although I am a woman.
34 But he alone among men received great honor.

Judged from this prefatory poem, three basic observations are important
for the overall interpretation of the cento. In the first place, Eudocia
reworked an already existing poem composed by a cleric named
Patricius.[19] She points out some shortcomings in his work, which she
otherwise admires. His cento is said to be semi-finished; he did not tell
everything truthfully, he did not preserve the harmony of the verses,
and he seems to have mixed non-Homeric lines into the cento. Eudocia

---

CXXXVIII–CXIX with an Italian translation; see also the LCL edition *The Greek
Anthology* 1.119.

[17] The preceding lines have briefly summarized the plot of *the Iliad*.

[18] Ludwich's edition has plural here [ἀθανάτους]; the begetter of immortals.

[19] For the identification of Patricius, see Usher, "Prolegomenon," 316–7. According
to Zonaras, *Epitome Historiarum* 13.23, Eudocia's extraordinary ability περὶ λόγους
is seen from her composition of the Homeric centos. Zonaras refers to her adding
a prologue to the poem: "For a man named Patricius attempted in his zeal to do so.
He left the task unfinished [ἀτελὲς] and, so to say, unorganized [ἀνοργάνωτον]. She
brought it to completion and organized it. This can be seen by those approaching the
inscription [ἡ ἐπιγραφὴ] written by her in heroic verses (hexameter) and which has
been added to this poem." My translation.

brought Patricius' work into harmony with Homeric diction, thus indicating that he had been too free to add non-Homeric lines, probably in a way comparable to Juvencus' Virgilian paraphrase. Patricius' work was, therefore, in need of revision. This is why she took it upon herself to edit Patricius' work. She brought harmony to it.

This takes us to the next observation. There is a certain tension in this preface between its being bookish and oral at the same time. Patricius wrote a book—this is stated twice—and a song simultaneously. Usher emphasizes ἁρμονία as indicative of the aural dimension of the cento; it was performed orally.[20] That is, the cento was composed with performance in mind. In pointing out this, Usher takes up the playful nature of cento composition, as we pointed out in Chapter 4. The multiple references to songs in the preface adds support to this view. This must, however, not be urged in a way which neglects the bookish aspect emphasized in the preface.[21] Furthermore, the performance aspect is not to be mistaken; Eudocia does not write a poem for *ludus*; she considers the work a sacred song. The revision and also performance as its setting, together explain the circulation of various manuscript traditions and redactions. Such texts quite soon loose their authorial control and are prone to develop in either directions. Under such circumstances it is hardly possible to establish a reliable text claiming "authenticity;" the recensions are witnesses to a "living literature;"[22] i.e. an aggregation of material from different sources, maybe also from different times. To extract the oldest editorial layer is impossible.

Thirdly, this preface announces what the cento itself makes abundantly clear, namely that this is a Homeric poem. Thus this cento can be aligned with Ausonius and Proba who both prefaced their cento. With regard to Homer, an ambiguity can be discerned here. On the one hand, Homer is blameless. To judge from l. 8 (repeated in l. 27), Homer is blameless; line 9 goes on to say that shortcomings apply only to Patricius. Nonetheless, l. 29–30 bring a contrast into this harmonious picture. By reference to content, Patricius' project is separated

---

[20] Usher, *Homeric Stitchings*, 22 refers to Aristotle, *Rhet.* 1403b where ἁρμονία is essential as to the delivery of a speech; thus also LSJ s.v. It is not, however, a technical term.

[21] This is pointed out by Sowers, *Eudocia. The Making of a Homeric Christian*, 79–84.

[22] I borrow this term from liturgical studies, see e.g. Paul F. Bradshaw, Maxwell E. Johnson, L.Edward Phillips, *The Apostolic Tradition. A Commentary* (Minneapolis, MN: Fortress Press, 2002), 13–15.

from the wars told by Homer. While Homer told of armies and wars, Patricius told stories from the Old Testament and of Christ. The preface thus makes a distinction between *verba* and *res*, and thus provides the hermeneutical key for understanding the cento.

6.2   Gen 2–3 as Key to the Gospel "According to Homer"

Eudocia's poem begins in the Old Testament. All attention is directed to the story of Eden and the Fall (Gen 2–3) with emphasis on the Serpent and Eve. L. 33–67 (= Schembra CP) describe vividly the Serpent and the promises given to Eve. The pastiche of Homeric texts is a commentary on Gen 3:4–5: "But the serpent said to the woman, 'You will not die, for God knows that when you eat of it your eyes will be opened, and you will be like God, knowing good and evil.'" The Serpent is introduced as δράκων from the dream in *Il.* 2: "Then appeared a great portent [μέγα σῆμα]: a serpent [δράκων] bloodred on the back"(*Il.* 2.308 = l. 34). This is the Homeric text that seems to have enjoyed most popularity in the instruction given at school.[23] The lying dream of *Il.* 2 sets the scene for the Trojan War. In a deceiving dream, Zeus promises the Aechaeans a swift victory; hence the dream is called "great portent." The dream showed a snake devouring the children of the sparrow. This is the master scene of deception in the *Iliad* 2; likewise it forms the point of departure for Eudocia's Homeric paraphrase of Gen 3. The Serpent then takes on characteristics from many figures of the epic. It is dreadful like Charybdis (l. 35 = *Il.* 12.119), an enemy like Hector (l. 36 = *Il.* 22.380), tempts like Aphrodite (l. 37 = *Il.* 14.217 cf. 191–9), and rages like the wild beast of *Il.* 9.546 (l. 38). In Homer these figures represent temptation, danger and enmity; together they now draw a picture of Eudocia's Serpent from Gen 3.

Eve's meeting with the snake takes place at a well outside the city (l. 39). This is a good example of elements with no or little basis in the biblical story being invented from the Homeric text. A girl drawing water outside the city has no root in Gen 3—although there are many such scenes elsewhere in Genesis—but is taken from *Od.* 10.105

---

[23] See Cribiore, *Gymnastics of the Mind*, 194–5; MacDonald, *Does the New Testament Imitate Homer?*, 25–27. Christian criticism of Homer often took this deceptive dream given by Zeus as point of departure; see Sandnes, *The Challenge of Homer*, 43.

on the presentation of the daughter of Antiphates, the Laestrygonian.[24] Eve is given promises that together form an amalgamation of Homeric "Paradise" texts. Five Homeric scenes picture together the promises presented to Eve as temptation: The Elysion (l. 47–49 = *Od.* 4.565–7), the island of the Cyclops where growing is independent of sowing and plowing (l. 51–52 = *Od.* 9.108–9), the island Syria, a kind of utopia (l. 53–54 = *Od.* 15.407–8), the palace of the Phaeacians (l. 55–56 = *Od.* 7.114, 116), immortality expressed in the words of Calypso who saved Odysseus from shipwreck (l. 61 = *Od.* 5.136), home, children and harmony as pictured in the very plot of the Odyssey, his homecoming [νόστος], and in l. 62–66 expressed in words from Odysseus' blessing to Nausicaa for bringing him clothing (*Od.* 6.181–5). These are the Homeric scenes against which the Serpent's temptation is presented.

It is unusual in a cento, but more than once in the present one several lines in a row (here five!) are taken from the same Homeric text. Eudocia does not comply with Ausonius' rule on this particular point: "For to place two (whole) lines side by side is weak [*ineptum est*], and three in succession is mere trifling" (Ausonius' preface p. 133.24–28). Eudocia's prefatory poem addresses the question of "doubles" [δοιάδες] (l. 15–18). She is aware that her cento will be blamed for doing something that is not allowed [οὐ θέμις ἐστίν]. She excuses herself by saying that "we are all slaves of necessity [ἀνάγκη]." This is an interesting remark. She admits of violating accepted rules of cento composition, but implies that her cento must be adapted to her topic. We are thus reminded that the macro level of her cento is not taken from Homer but the Bible; this is the starting-point of her composition.

In l. 68–87 (Schembra CP 68–89), the focus is on Eve. The opening line from *Od.* 15.20 creates the misogynic atmosphere of the whole scene: "For you know what sort of a spirit there is in a woman's breast." This is the warning of Pallas Athene to Telemachus, saying that his mother Penelope may consider marrying one of the suitors. Eudocia does not succeed in explaining satisfactorily Eve's fall in the epic; the references to eating and drinking (l. 71, 76), which recall the biblical passage on the Fall, appear rather random. More important is the fact that at this point the cento leaves the reader in doubt, if

---

[24] This text appears not surprisingly, in Eudocia's paraphrase of the Samaritan woman in l. 1052.

not otherwise informed by the biblical text, as to the precise nature of Eve's sin. Eudocia's method is, therefore, to heap up lines about mischievous women in the epic, and the consequences humankind suffered from the failures of these women. The closing l. 87 puts it in this way: "upon all it brought toil, upon many it left woes" (*Il.* 21.524). This statement finds substantiation in what Homer says about the daughter of Tyndareus, who killed her husband (l. 77–79 = *Od.* 24.200–2): "killed her wedded husband, and hateful shall the song regarding her be among men, and evil repute she brings upon all womankind, even upon her who acts rightly." These are words spoken in Hades (*Od.* 24.203–4). This easily links up with Agamemnon's words about his wife Clytemnestra who killed him (*Od.* 11.427–9). In *Od.* 24 and 11, Eudocia found a type-scene of women killing their husbands that she found useful for picturing biblical Eve Homerically; from both texts she takes three lines in a row. L. 84 takes Oedipus' mother as a further example. In her ignorance she married her own son, and later killed herself and went to Hades (*Od.* 11.272–80). The fact that Hades appears in some of these texts on women demonstrates that the question of death in Gen 3 can be expressed in Homeric style and vocabulary. Finally, this leads Eudocia to the opening lines of the *Iliad* (1.3): "many valiant souls of warriors sent to Hades" (l. 86). This line summarizes the very plot of the Trojan War, and brings to mind the warlike story to be unfolded in the *Iliad*. Worth noting is that in Eudocia's centonizing of the fall, this war is caused by female frailties. This is also in accordance with the Fall in the biblical text.

The theological plot of Eudocia's cento is apparent from l. 84–92 (Schembra CP 86–94) following directly upon the fall of the woman:[25]

84	She unwittingly did a monstrous deed,	*Od.* 11.272
85	and, destructive, she caused many evils for men;	*Od.* 17.287
86	many strong souls she cast to Hades' abode,	*Il.* 1.3
87	wrought hardship for all, caused trouble for many.	*Il.* 21.524
88	But there was no one there to protect from mournful destruction	*Il.* 6.16
89	She did not save her comrades, for all her desires.	*Od.* 1.7
90	But He saved and gave a great profit [μέγ' ὄνειαρ]	*Od.* 4.444
91	He is lord over all mortals and immortals.	*Il.* 12.242
92	He raised his son, a beloved ruler of all people	*Od.* 7.170

---

[25] The translation of l. 84–87 is taken from Usher, *Homeric Stitchings*, 13. The rest is my own translation.

Eudocia makes two minor, but still important, modifications here. L. 89 is taken from Homer's account of Odysseus' failing to bring all his comrades back home; in Eudocia's text this must naturally be rendered in the feminine. In the second place, in the cento l. 92 Homer's Λαοδάμαντα (the name Laodamas) becomes λαομέδοντα ("ruler of all people"). Furthermore, Eudocia exploits the meaning of ὄνειαρ. In the Homeric setting from where Eudocia takes this line this refers to the leather couches provided by the goddess, in order to give Odysseus and his men rest. Eudocia allegorizes the rest provided for by the goddess to mean salvation. Homeric ἐσάωσε (l. 90) becomes Christian ἔσωσε[ν].[26]

It is a cento about salvation, understood against the background of humankind's need for help. This observation makes this rather awkward Christian text equally traditional when it comes to the foundational theological perspective that shaped it. The quotation is a summary of Gen 3, owing more to Christian tradition than to the source text itself, particularly so in the negative role assigned to women (1 Tim 2:14 cf. L.A.E. 3:1–2; 10:4, 15; 16:3.). Eudocia puts Gen 3 into a wider perspective, and thus reveals that the topic of her cento is about God's plan to remedy the Fall recounted in Gen 3.

6.2.1   A Divine Plan [μοῖρα and βουλή] for Salvation

A Johannine-sounding theologumenon enters the scene; father and son. L. 92–96 (Schembra CP 94–98) are taken from father and son scenes, such as Alcinous and his son (Od. 7.170–1), Odysseus and Telemachus (Od. 14.177) and Phylas nurturing Eudoros: "Eudoros did old Phylas nurse and cherish tenderly, loving him clearly, as he had been his own son" (Il. 16.191–2). The mention of 'beloved son' in these texts attracted the attention of a Homeric Christian like Eudocia. As pointed out by Hans Kvalbein, the idea of God's 'beloved son' flourishes in early Christian baptismal texts, inspired by the heavenly voice at Jesus' own baptism.[27]

That this is a cento about salvation is elaborated on in lines 97–174 (Schembra CP 99–176). A plan involving the son is now presented:

---

[26] LSJ s.v.
[27] See Hans Kvalbein, "The Baptism of Jesus as a model for Christian Baptism;" cf. Maxwell E. Johnson, The Rites of Christian Initiation. Their Evolution and Interpretation (Collegeville MN: Liturgical Press, 2007), 66.

"Will you now listen to me dear child, in what I will say?" (l. 97 = *Il.* 4.190). The dialogue between father and son implied in this scene has no biblical warrant in Genesis. It appears as a theological construct filled in imaginatively from the Johannine presentation of Father and Son, and probably taking the enigmatic plural "we" of Gen 1:26 as an invitation to do so. As pointed out by K. Smolak, this corresponds to the scene so familiar in Homer of the council of the Olympian gods; worth mentioning is also the idea of the heavenly *sôd* (Isa 6:8).[28] This is not a Homeric invention, but it is taken from a wider biblical tradition.

The best plan ever (l. 99–100) is now set in move, due to heavenly consultation, and presented to the son. A rather long section gives a catena of Homeric sins, not unlike Paul's Rom 1:18–3:20. In these lines the perspective is widened beyond the woman's sin in the fall; there is no loyalty, no truth, no kindness and hospitality. The shameful lifestyle of Penelope's suitors—all men, of course[29]—in *Od.* 22.230–2 (l. 108–10) and *Od.* 22.414–5 (l. 113–4) forms a climax of this catena. The plan implies that the son will suffer opposition, being slain and despised (l. 140–7). L. 166–8 elaborate on this by recalling the death of Hector (*Il.* 22.488–90), thus anticipating this event to appear later in the story. Not surprisingly, the analogy between Jesus and Hector appears in l. 1745 as well, when Eudocia sings the praise of Jesus' passion. In *Il.* 15.141, Eudocia found a helpful line to state the aim of Jesus' death (l. 134, Schembra CP 136): πάντων ἀνθρώπων ῥῦσθαι γενεήν τε τόκον τε ("to save lineage and offspring of all men"). The use of ῥῦσθαι or ῥύεσθαι in several New Testament texts to describe the salvation enjoyed by the believers[30] may have inspired the centonist to read this Homeric line contrary to its Homeric setting. In *Il.* 15, this is a line expressing the impossibility that all will survive. To Eudocia it becomes a precise description for what God's plan through Jesus' death did accomplish. Indirectly she is possibly conveying here that the original meaning of this Homeric line would come through, if God had not introduced a plan to alter this destiny. We can thus

---

[28] K. Smolak, "Beobachtungen zur Darstellungsweise in den Homerzentonen," *Jahrbuch der Österreichischen Byzantik* 28 (1979): 32; H.-J. Fabry, *sôd*, *TDOT* Vol. 10, 174–5.

[29] Here is an obvious contradiction to the role of women in Genesis, which Eudocia explored above.

[30] We noticed above that this verb was used in *Od.* 1.6, which formed the background against which Eudocia introduced the salvation plan of the Father.

observe that a theological endeavour is being unfolded here. This key line is repeated in l. 196 (Schembra CP 198), thus attesting its role as encapsulating the divine plan for salvation.

L. 169–70 state that the son, if turned down by men, may take vengeance. This brings to mind Proba's likewise ambivalent sayings on the death of Jesus.[31] L. 175–201b closes with the dialogue between father and son, clearly stated in l. 201a: ὡς οἱ μὲν τοιαῦτα πρὸς ἀλλήλους ἀγόρευον ("thus they spoke to one another"). In this section, the son's response dominates. His willingness is reiterated throughout, first in words of Aphrodite when asked by Hera to lend her the seducing power of love: "It is not right to deny you anything" (l. 176 = Il. 14.212). In words of Hector to Deïophobus, when fighting Achilles, the son says: "Now I deem to give you honour, more than ever" (l. 178 = Il. 22.235). The son's obedience means his willingly being slain; obedience and suffering are combined throughout in a way that brings to mind Phil 2:8, "obedient to the point of death—even death on a cross." Hence the son says: "It is indeed my destiny [μοῖρα] to die and meet the doom" (l. 191 = Il. 7.52).[32] Greek μοῖρα is the word for the destiny that emerges from the counsel of the deities in Homer;[33] in the cento it refers to the plan agreed between father and son.

The cento form of this Homeric line illustrates very well how centonists in general and Eudocia in particular adapts the Homeric text to form a new text (see Chapter 4). In the Iliad this is Pallas Athene reporting back to Hector about the decision made by the Olympian gods: his fight with Ajax will not be fatal for him. Upon these words, Hector confidently prepares for battle in Il. 7.52.

> The Iliad line goes like this: οὐ γάρ πώ τοι μοῖρα θανεῖν καὶ πότμον ἐπισπεῖν
> ("It is not yet your fate to die and meet your destiny/death.")[34]
>
> The cento line goes like this: εἴπερ[35] μοι καὶ μοῖρα θανεῖν καὶ πότμον ἐπισπεῖν
> ("Truly, it is my fate to die and face death.")

---

[31] Proba l. 623 speaking about poena ("punishment").
[32] CP Schembra l. 193.
[33] LSJ s.v.
[34] According to LSJ s.v. in Homer's writings this always means death.
[35] This is a strengthening or assuring word; see LSJ s.v.

Three important alterations occur here. In the first place, Eudocia changes the 2nd person to the 1st person, thus making it into a auto-biographical statement of the son. In Homer this is a comforting message to Hector from his brother Helenus who has received news from the council of the Olympian deities. Eudocia makes this a dictum of Christ about himself. In the second place, what is in Homer a promise that he will not yet die, becomes in the cento a statement that death is impending—thus bringing *Il.* 7 in to line with *Il.* 22 (Hector's death)—according to the divine plan. Finally, this fundamental alteration is emphasized by the assuring εἴπερ ("indeed/truly"); Eudocia is here informed by *Il.* 15.117 where εἰ πέρ μοι καὶ μοῖρα θανεῖν are words of Ares who willingly face death to save his son. This plan is to be made known to "all people," according to l. 193; words of Penelope to the suitors on announcing her plan to marry when she has finished weaving her web (*Od.* 2.112). Eudocia replaces "all Achaeans" with πάντες λαοὶ ("all people"). At first sight these minor changes appear as matters of style, relevant to the surface only, but in fact they reveal that another text is now being unfolded. The agenda is set by another text, and Homer's epics are made dependent upon it and altered according to it, namely the death of Jesus as the culminating point in the divine μοῖρα, i.e plan or destiny.

The sufferings of the son appear in the words of Odysseus about his readiness to fight and even die to eliminate the suitors from his house (l. 190 = *Od.* 16.107 cf. l. 200 = *Od.* 16.189). At this point it becomes clear that the cento exemplifies an idiosyncratic way of doing allegory. The suitors represent sinful humanity, and Jesus, the Son, is ready to fight like Odysseus. As a Christian, Eudocia feels obliged to clarify this allegory. Jesus is not fighting the sinners, as did Odysseus. She therefore has the son say: "I will rather that your people are saved than perish [βούλομ᾽ ἐγὼ λαὸν σόον ἔμμεναι ἢ ἀπολέσθαι]" (l. 199 = *Il.* 1.117).[36] The son prepares for fighting as did Odysseus against the suitors, but unlike Odysseus, Jesus' aim is not destruction, but for salvation. This runs contrary to the Odyssean story, but Eudocia here brings into her poem an Iliadic line taken from Agamemnon after he had sacrificed his daughter. In this way the son transvalues the example of Odysseus with the help of Iphigenia. Father and son have agreed on a plan to

---

[36] CP Schembra l. 201.

bestow favour on mankind [χάριν δ᾽ ἄνδρεσσι φέροντες] (l. 201b = *Il.* 5.874).

The stage is now set for this plan to be implemented:

| 202 | At that time he sent a herald to inform the woman | *Od.* 15.458 |
| 203 | of the plan [βουλὴν], since it pleased them who devised it | *Il.* 7.45 (Schembra CP 206–7) |

The noun βουλὴ, which appears in l. 261 as well, links the annunciation with the preceding section on the divine plan.[37] In the cento this is the angel announcing to Mary that she will give birth to Jesus (l. 202). Mary is not named; she is only called γυνή, in accordance with cento practice, and since Eudocia "is working from within a closed system (the actual Homeric texts)".[38] But this observation also has a bearing upon the question of how the biblical and Homeric texts relate. A reader unfamiliar with the Mary of Luke 1, will not grasp what woman the cento is now talking about. How is the reader to differentiate between Mary and Eve, who are both called γυνή? This leads to a fundamental observation, namely that the point of departure is the biblical texts, not the other way around. In pointing this out, I do not deny that within this foundational relationship of biblical dependence, the Homeric epics sometimes invent additions and information not yielded by the biblical texts. But it is unwarranted to say that the Homeric text is the source in the cento. This is one more example of how it is difficult to imagine that Christian Homeric interpretation made up texts in the way assumed by advocates of Mimesis Criticism. The Christian point of view of the centonist made her read Homer anew.

6.3   The Baptism of Jesus "According to Homer"

The fact that Homer was seen as an open text, of which the centonists took advantage in creating new texts, by necessity implies that the life of Jesus could draw upon support from Homeric lines lifted from

---

[37] The annunciation to Mary is given substantial place in the cento; see Usher, *Homeric Stitchings*, 90–93, where a translation is found. Mary's virginity is emphasized. Worth noting is that a seemingly ascetic tendency in l. 217 (Joseph had no desire for the things of marriage = sex) is rectified in l. 222 where it says that sex properly belongs in a marital relationship.

[38] Usher, *Homeric Stitchings*, 10

various places in his epics. Due to the playful nature of cento composition, which makes it a 'living tradition,' this is not surprising. In the
various recensions the same biblical story may be narrated with the
help of different Homeric lines; this adds nuances to the biblical story,
but within the variances a fixed pattern of some core lines is visible. I
intend to substantiate this by making a comparison here to the other
recensions.

The story of Jesus' baptism is preceded by John the Baptist, called
κῆρυξ. The hub of his message is that Jesus has returned home
[νόστησας] (l. 438); thus also in Conscriptio Secunda l. 364; Conscriptio
A l. 193; Conscriptio B l. 192 and Conscriptio Γ l. 195. Accordingly,
several lines are taken from *Od.* 24. This is a somewhat surprising
use of the νόστος motif since she later (see Chapter 6.8) depicts both
the Resurrection and the Ascension as the homecoming of Jesus. The
latter is more obvious; it also follows more naturally from Odysseus'
homecoming. But she might have found an echo of homecoming in
John's Gospel: "He came to what was his own [τὰ ἴδια], and his own
people [οἱ ἴδιοι] did not accept him" (John 1:11); implying that the
Incarnation is seen as a homecoming.

The baptism of Jesus is told in the following way in the Iviron recension (Usher 440–54 = CP Schembra 447–59):[39]

440	So saying he led the way, and Aias followed, a godlike man [ἰσόθεος].	*Il.* 11.472
441	He was pent into the deep-flowing and silver-eddying river	*Il.* 21.8
442	But when they now come to the ford of the fair-flowing river,	*Il.* 14.433
443	which is the far most beautiful river sending forth its streams upon the earth,	*Od.* 11.239
444	borne from far away, he bathed [λοῦσεν] in the streams of the river.	*Il.* 16.679
445	Hiding him in the eddies deep and wide	*Il.* 21.239
446	He clothed [ἕννυτο] himself in a cloak of divine gold	*Od.* 5.230
447	finely woven and beautiful, and about his waist he throws a girdle	*Od.* 5.231

---

[39] Rey, ed. and trans., *Centons Homeriques*, 196–205 gives another and longer collection of lines on Jesus' baptism (Chapter 11). The translation is my own, done with
some help from the LCL's edition of the Homeric epics.

448	straightaway he bound beneath his feet his beautiful sandals.	*Il.* 24.340
449	When washed in deep-flowing river,	*Od.* 6.210
450	he took around himself the clothing which the virgin [παρθένος] gave.	*Od.* 6.228
451	He prayed, stretching hands to the starry heaven.	*Il.* 15.371
452	High up beneath the clouds he saw the timorous dove	*Il.* 23.874
453	And the gleam thereof went up to heaven, all the earth around smiled,	*Il.* 19.362
454	and again the flood streamed down the fair river-bed	*Il.* 21.382

This patchwork of Homeric lines is united by motifs and terms that can easily be associated with baptismal texts. The opening statement about a godlike man is terminologically quite close to Phil 2:6 [τὸ εἶναι ἴσα θεῷ]. In the first part of l. 444 we are, therefore, reminded of the pre-existence of Jesus. If this is correctly understood, it is possible to read this line as a voice critical of adoptionist christology, which sees the baptism of Jesus as an act of adoption; Jesus thus becomes what he had *not* been before His baptism. The Iviron version has καί μιν ἀποπρὸ φέρων.[40] At this point there are minor differences between the versions; some read καί μιν ἄπο προφέρων (Schembra CS 376), while Rey XI.42 has πολλὸν ἄπο προφέρων, which seems to strengthen the preexistence through πολλὸν, equivalent to πολύς or πολύ.[41]

The Homeric lines are held together by the fact that they all deal with rivers and water, which Eudocia could easily associate with the River Jordan. In two of the lines, traditional baptismal vocabulary appears; λούειν often refers to the baptismal bath,[42] and the concept of "being clothed" is baptismal language rooted in the Pauline tradition[43] and taken up in liturgies.[44] The vision of Christ wearing a robe with

---

[40] Thus also Conscriptio A l. 196; Conscriptio B l. 195; Conscriptio Γ.

[41] LSJ s.v.

[42] E.g. John 13:10; Heb 10:22. This is amply demonstrated in Lampe, *A Patristic Greek Lexicon* s.v. See also Everett Ferguson, *Baptism in the Early Church. History, Theology, and Liturgy in the First Five Centuries* (Grand Rapids, MI, Cambridge, U.K.: Wm. B. Eerdmans Publishing Co., 2009), 267–8.

[43] E.g. Gal 3:27; Col 3:10.

[44] From this figurative speech developed a ceremony of initiation, the putting on of a robe or tunic by the baptizand. This is possibly assumed in *Apostolic Tradition* chaps. 20–21 where the baptizand's being naked in the bath is emphasized. See also Lampe, *A Patristic Greek Lexicon*, s.v. ἔνδυμα.

a golden sash (Rev 1:13–15) may also have inspired Eudocia's transposition of Homeric texts. Finally, the mention of the sandals brings to
mind the witness of John the Baptist concerning Jesus, which is intimately connected with the tradition of Jesus' baptism. Jesus stretching
forth his hands to heaven in prayer is a detail found only in Luke's
version of Jesus' baptism (Luke 3:21), and demonstrates how the centonist constantly moves between larger theological motifs and minute
details. L. 452 on the dove also demonstrates familiarity with Luke's
version; according to Luke 3:22 the dove appeared in a physical form
[σωματικῷ εἴδει]. From this recension, as in most of the others, it is
difficult to see why παρθένος is mentioned in l. 450. In Homer this
clearly refers to Nausicaa, the daughter of Alcinous. In *Conscriptio
Prima*, the reference remains unclear, but will be clarified in other
recensions (see below).

A reasonable assumption is that Eudocia formed this baptismal
scene, as it appears in CP, out of the bath scene in *Od.* 6.198–238
in particular, but also *Il.* 16. Odysseus enjoys the hospitality of the
Phaeacians and Nausicaa in particular. He is given a bath, clothing
and food.[45] The bath scenes can easily be transposed into a classical
baptismal scene, because obviously the latter resembles the former:
nudity, water, oil and clothing.[46] It is to be noted though, that oil does
not appear here; it certainly does, however, in *Conscriptio Secunda*
(see below). *Il.* 16.680, the line following upon 16.679, cited in CP,
does mention oil within a bath scene, but CP has not included that
particular line. In Homer, the bath scene is preceded by the vision of
Odysseus' homecoming, a text we have seen that Eudocia incorporated
in her eschatological language.[47] It seems that *Od.* 6 provided this centonist with a model scene that, together with the vision of Odysseus'
homecoming, forms a baptismal theology *par excellence*.[48]

Again it is possible to explore the open-endedness of the cento. It
is possible that Eudocia is here dependent on the practice attested
in early Christian texts, about the baptizands being given milk and

---

[45] *Od.* 6.208 about providing the guest with food and drink appear in l. 1182 on
Eudocia's rendering of the bread miracle.
[46] See Ferguson, *Baptism in the Early Church*, 34–36, 341–2.
[47] See chaps. 6.2 and 6.3 in this study.
[48] This corresponds to Proba's presentation of her own conversion (l. 415–428)
against the background of baptismal theology; see Chapter 5.4.1 in this study.

honey after the bath.[49] The relevant sources speak of this in a double
way, as being both nutrition for newborn children and the food of the
Promised Land in biblical language.[50] In Eudocia's world the Homeric
homecoming and the biblical "Promised Land" are easily merged. In
my view this demonstrates that Eudocia's *Homerocentones* is not an
uninteresting piece, as stated so often.[51] The baptism of Jesus is presented as his νόστος. He came to his own, and was welcomed by his
Father, for which the heavenly voice can easily be called upon as sup-
portng evidence. Likewise, Christian baptism is often seen as an anticipated "homecoming," signalled by milk and honey, as well as in the
kiss and the first eucharist.[52] This logic depends on the view that the
cento combines Jesus' baptism and Christian baptism. In *Conscriptio
Secunda* this is, I think, apparent (see below).

Identifying the key scene is crucial for understanding Eudocia's
Homeric version of Jesus' baptism. Once this model scene is found,
Eudocia is able to incorporate lines taken entirely out of their context. One example is l. 452 on Jesus seeing a dove beneath the clouds.
In Homer this is a dove shot down by Teucer, but read in the light
of the bath scene in *Od.* 6, the dove of Teucer becomes helpful. The
patchwork of Homeric lines given here form together a mosaic held
together by a story found *not* in Homer but in the Gospels. Imagining
that things developed the other way around is extremely difficult if
judged by the cento itself.[53]

6.3.1   *The Baptism of Jesus in* Conscriptio Secunda

In *Conscriptio Secunda* (= Rey's text), the story of Jesus' baptism is considerably enlarged (l. 341–99), and it is embedded in a context empha-

---

[49] E.g. *Barn.* 6.8–19; *Trad.ap.* 21.48; Tertullian *Cor.* 3; see N.A. Dahl. "La terre où coulent le lait et le miel selon Barnabé 6.8–19," in *Aux Sources de la Tradition Chrétienne.
Mélange offertts à M. Maurice Goguel* (Neuchatel, Paris: Delachaux & Niestlè, 1950).
[50] "The land flowing with milk and honey"; see e.g. Exod 3:8, 17; 13:5.
[51] See Chapter 1.7 in this study.
[52] See e.g. Justin Martyr *1 Apol.* 65; for further references, see Hans-Ulrich
Weidemann, "Taufe und Taufeucharistie", in *Ablution, Initiation, and Baptism in
Early Judaism, Graeco-Roman Religion, and Early Christianity*, ed. David Hellholm,
Øyvind Norderval and Tor Vegge (Berlin: Walter de Gruyter 2011).
[53] In his comments on Mark's Homeric version of Jesus' baptism, MacDonald, in
Homeric Epics and the Gospel of Mark 195–6, does not mention the Homeric centos.
Generally speaking, there seems to be little connection between MacDonald's sugges-
tion that the Homeric centos are relevant analogies for how the Gospels came into
being and his actual exegesis of Mark's Gospel.

sizing christology (l. 341–52). These lines seem inspired by the heavenly voice at Jesus' baptism, declaring Jesus as God's beloved Son. It says that people marvelled at the sight of Jesus, and "they said to each other 'who is he and from where does he come [τίς εἴη καὶ πόθεν ἔλθοι]" (l. 348 = *Od.* 17.368). This is expressed in typical Johannine terms of Jesus coming from above.[54] "He was not like the son of a mortal man, but of God" (l. 349–50 = *Od.* 9.190 + *Il.* 24.259), clearly echoing Homer's Hector. Eudocia's name for Jesus was, therefore, Theoclymenos;[55] meaning "he who hears God." L. 351 says: "His son it was, Theoclymenos by name;" clearly a Homeric paraphrase of the heavenly voice at Jesus' baptism declaring him to be the beloved son. This name makes sense in the light of the intimate relationship announced in the heavenly voice.

Another peculiar thing compared to CP, is that CS emphasizes strongly the saving ministry of Jesus within the framework of this story. In words recalling the βουλή (see above) and anticipating the death of Jesus, it is said thus by John (l. 356–60):

356	Near by is the man. Not long do we need to seek if you will	*Il.* 14.110
357	escape from evil death and black fate	*Il.* 21.66
358	and noone at all can match oneself with him in might.	*Il.* 6.101
359	Like a ram he seems to me, a ram of thick fleece.	*Il.* 3.197
360	For the ram was the far best of the flock.	*Od.* 9.432

L. 356–8 appear in Iviron (l. 432–4) as well, but l. 359–60 are not found there. These lines pick up from CS l. 334, thus making it clear that in His baptism Jesus embarks upon His saving ministry. In l. 344 this is stated in words taken from *Il.* 15.141: "to save the lineage and offspring of all men."[56] L. 359–60 do appear in Iviron's crucifixion scene (l. 1864

---

[54] Karl Olav Sandnes, "Whence and Whither. A Narrative Perspective on Birth ἄνωθεν (John 3,3–8)," *Bib* 86 (2005).

[55] This name is used thirteen times in Iviron; see Usher, *Homeric Stitchings*, 46. Heraclitus *Homeric Problems* 75.2 gives this explanation: ὁ τὰ θεῖα κλύων, "the man who hears divine things." He says that this was a suitable name for his scientific speculation [ἡ φυσικὴ θεωρίας], which implies that the meaning of this name is intimately connected to the allegorical approach and interpretation given throughout *Homeric Problems*. The Homeric text is open to be exploited in various ways.

[56] This line is found in Iviron l. 134 (Schembra CP 136) and 196 (Schembra 198) and in CS l. 36 and 76, as well as in the other recensions. It was clearly a favourite Homeric line for the centonists.

and 1866), thus strengthening the impression that CS interprets the baptism in the light of the crucifixion scene.[57]

In bringing together Jesus' baptism and the divine plan for saving humankind, Eudocia seems inspired by John 1:29–34, where this happens more pointedly than in the Synoptic tradition: "Here is the lamb of God who takes away the sin of the world" (v.29). According to the Homeric texts, the cento has ἀρνειὸς, not ἀμνὸς as in John. In the Apocalypse, however, ἀρνίον is a favourite designation for Christ in precisely the role attributed to him by John the Baptist in John 1:29.

L. 363–6 correspond to *Prima* (= Iviron) l. 437–9 where the coming of Jesus to the Baptist is described in lines taking from the homecoming of Odysseus. This motif is clearly seen at work in l. 363–71 preceding the story about the bath itself. Clearly this story is a recognition scene in which the true identity of Jesus is revealed, in words primarily taken from the recognition of Odysseus at his homecoming. Lines taken from *Od.* 24 dominate the passage. It is worth noting that the centonist in *Od.* 10.453 (l. 368) found a helpful line of recognition within the context of a bath scene: "They saw and recognized each other, face to face." Furthermore, in *Od.* 8.453 another bath scene becomes helpful, since in it is found a line about divine appearance. The heavenly voice and Homeric bath and recognition scenes were thus mutually illuminating to the centonist.

Upon this follow the baptismal bath itself in l. 372–89. A comparison between the way in which CP and CS describe Jesus' baptism is illuminating as to demonstrate the nature of the cento: flexibility within a pattern of some core lines taken from type scenes. The core lines are *Il.* 14.433; *Od.* 11.239; *Il.* 16.679; *Od.* 6.228; *Il.* 15.371; *Il.* 23.874 and *Il.* 21.382. These are the lines making up the narrative plot of the event. As will become clear when *Secunda* is seen in the light of recensions other than *Prima*'s, *Il.* 1.201 + 7.135 are to be added to these core lines. Together these lines express key elements of the biblical story: river, bathing, clothing, praying, dove. In *Conscriptio Prima*, we noticed that the bath scene of *Od.* 6 held a key position, as well as *Il.* 16. *Secunda* includes lines taken from the bath scene where Telemachus is given a bath followed by his being anointed in *Od.* 3. This illustrates how the

---

[57] This is in accordance with the heavenly voice declaring Jesus to be God's Son in words taken from Isa 42:1; see Ulrich Luz, *Das Evangelium nach Matthäus* (Mt 1–7) EKK 1.1 (Düsseldorf, Zürich: Benziger Verlag und Neukirchener Verlag, 2002), 214–8.

centonist proceeds, taking as its point of departure scenes analogous to the biblical text.

Peculiar to *Conscriptio Secunda* is an attempt to introduce biblical geography into Homer (l. 373), such as "Jordan where the Sidonians live". Jordanus is a minor modification of the river Jardanus at Crete (*Od.* 3.292). Homer's text has Κύδωνες here; thus also Rey's edition,[58] while Scembra has Σιδόνες, which makes sense as a biblically-motivated modification. This minor detail is worth pondering upon. It shows that the centonist is proceeding not from Homer, but from the biblical texts as available in her tradition. This geographical alteration demonstrates that the biblical stories determine the entire project, and are the basis from which the selections of Homeric texts are lifted and the alterations made. A second characteristic of *Secunda* on Jesus' baptism is the anointing, mentioned twice: "and anointed [χρῖσεν] him with ambrosia" (l. 378 taken from *Il.* 16.680) and in l. 383 (= *Od.* 3.466): "when he had bathed [λοῦσέν] him, anointed him with oil [ἔχρισεν λίπ' ἐλαίῳ]"—both lines taken from bath scenes. I think baptismal practice known to the centonist sets an agenda for the poem here, but I consider it unlikely that the mention of a double anointing reflects that particular practice, although a double anointing is witnessed to in some sources.[59] The New Testament evidence for Jesus' baptism as an anointing is limited to Acts 10:37 [ἔχρισεν αὐτὸν].

I have already indicated a possible connection between the baptism of Jesus and Christian baptism as a background against which to understand the cento at this point. The emphasis on the anointing definitely goes beyond the New Testament evidence, and is, I think, to be explained by the role of anointing in Christian baptismal theology.[60] This finds a possible corroboration in l. 390–9 representing a somewhat unexpected closing of the baptismal story. According to these lines, Jesus entered the holy city (= Jerusalem?), and people followed him like a flock following a ram [μετὰ κτίλον]. In *Il.* 13.492, the aim is to find water to drink, which makes a baptismal reference appear likely

---

[58] Rey, ed. and trans., *Centons Homérique*, 194 says that he doesn't know what to make of the Cydonians here.

[59] Both before and after the bath; see e.g. *Trad. ap.* 21; Johnson, *The Rites of Christian Initiation*, 41–114.

[60] Karl Olav Sandnes, "Seal and Baptism in Early Christianity," in *Ablution, Initiation, and Baptism in Early Judaism, Graeco-Roman Religion and Early Christianity*, ed. David Hellholm. Berlin: Walter de Gruyter 2010; for Christian baptism as "our Jordan", see Johnson, *The Rites of Christian Initiation*, 57–60 and 6.2.1. above.

(cf. 1 Cor 12:13). The city was full: "everyone with his language among
the many races of humans" (l. 394 = *Il.* 2.804). André-Louis Rey is in
some doubt here: "*Est-ce un simple moyen de renforcer l'évocation de
la foule ou l'indication que des personnes issues de peuple divers suiv-
ent le Christ? La deuexième interprétation est probablement la bonne.*"[61]
He then refers to texts about the rumour about Jesus spreading (Matt
4:25; Mark 3:7–8; Luke 6:17); Rey also includes here a prefiguration of
"*l'expansion apostolique.*" A combination of baptism and Acts 2 seems
likely here, and is in line with what Rey says. Acts 2 takes place in
the city, languages are involved, and it is about salvation, as is l. 395
[ἐσάωσε]. The unexpected closing of the baptismal story is then due to
Christian theology on baptism as an act of following Jesus.

6.3.2   *The Baptism of Jesus in* Conscriptio A, B *and* Γ

Conscriptio A is a rather short version of Jesus' baptism, consisting
only of seven lines (l. 195–201). It is worth noting that these are made
up the core lines: *Il.* 14.433 (fair-flowing river), *Il.* 16.679 (bathing),
Od. 11.239 (the most beautiful river), *Il.* 7.135 (Jordanus), *Od.* 6.228
(bathing and clothing). *Od.* 8.453 which closes the event in l. 201 is
also found in *Secunda* l. 371. In this version the dove is unmentioned,
and also the anointing.[62] Most interesting is, however, l. 199–200: "he
took around himself the clothing which the unwed virgin [παρθένος]
gave, his mother who gave birth to him and nursed him when a child"
(*Od.* 6.228 + *Od.* 23.325). The latter reference appears in the Ascension
also; Jesus' mother is present there as well (CP l. 1910). On that occasion this is not surprising, due to the fact that his mother is mentioned
in Acts 1:14, the immediate context of the text that Eudocia obviously
depends upon in her Homeric version of the Ascension; see Chapter
6.8 in this study. Thus *Conscriptio A* solves the riddle of παρθένος in
the baptism story (see above). It is simply assumed that Jesus' mother
was present. At Jesus' baptism both his heavenly father—not mentioned
in particular in this recension though—and also his earthly mother are
present. This seems a perfect example that the Homeric lines drawn
upon are not "innocent" when it comes to how they affect the biblical
story. There is no biblical warrant for the presence of Jesus' mother

---

[61] Rey, ed. and trans., *Centons Homériques*, 205.
[62] *Il.* 16.680 has anointment following upon the bath, but this line is not included
in *Conscriptio A*.

at his baptism. A fair guess is that the presence of both the heavenly father and his mother together expresses his dual identity, human and divine. We have already observed that christology developed from the heavenly voice at Jesus' baptism, and is therefore an appropriate place for voicing a position on the much-discussed issue of the christology of the time. *Conscriptio B* (l. 194–200) and Γ (l. 197–203) follow A closely, and have the same Homeric lines.

6.4 THE BEST VISION [μέγα θαῦμα]

After the baptism of Jesus follows the election of twelve disciples, called ἑταῖροι like the crew of Odysseus (l. 455–66) upon which Eudocia presents Jesus' teaching (l. 467–511), before she again picks up the narrative. A summary of Jesus' teaching is introduced in the words of Odysseus: "Hear me, suitors of the glorious queen, that I may say what the heart in my breast bids me (l. 467–8 = *Od.* 18.351–2)". The mention of the suitors forms a bridge to l. 455–66 which summarize the ministry of Jesus by recapitulating the Old Testament part of the poem where the suitors allegorically represent the sin Jesus has come to remedy (see above). Furthermore, these lines also pick up from the story of Jesus' baptism and the relationship between Father and Son developed from the heavenly voice:

477	I am his son, and he declares himself my father	*Od.* 9.519
478	For this cause he sent me to instruct you in all things	*Il.* 9.442
479	for he have signs which we two alone know, signs hidden from others,	*Od.* 23.110
480	and we know all things that will come to pass upon the fruitful earth	*Od.* 12.191
481	the happiness and misfortune of mortal men	*Od.* 20.76[63]

The son has been sent by his Father to instruct the people in hitherto hidden divine knowledge. This includes instruction about the doctrine of the Trinity:

484	Three, turning all ways from one neck	*Il.* 11.40
485	equal in age and strength, their power not easily exhausted	*Od.* 18.373

---

[63] CS adds here a line (l. 434), cited from *Od.* 17.487: "beholding the violence and righteousness [ὕβριν τε καὶ εὐνομίην] of men," which confirms that this is a summary.

The first line is taken from the description of Agamemnon's armour as he prepares for battle; the second is taken from Odysseus' words to one of the suitors in his house. Both lines are taken from descriptions of preparation for fighting. Together these two lines present the Trinity embarking upon a battle. As a presentation of Jesus' teaching, the role of the Trinity is unexpected. Less unexpected are the other topics emerging in this section, such as the relationship between Father and Son, and doing good versus evil, which echoes traditional paraenetical language, found in e.g. the Sermon on the Mount and the *Didache*, and the raising of the dead. L. 467–511 appear as a summary of Jesus' teaching centred around the Trinity and the Resurrection, thus reminding us that Eudocia's cento owes as much to Christian tradition as to the Biblical texts themselves, strictly speaking.

In *Il.* 21.111, Eudocia found a biblically-sounding formulation that invited an eschatological perspective: "There shall come a dawn or eve or midday" (l. 492).[64] Employing a Homeric line about those residing in Hades, Jesus says in l. 490: "They shall rise up and return from the realms of misty darkness." This is said by Achilles after he has killed many Trojans on the river Xanthus (*Il.* 21.56), remarking that it is the best vision [μέγα θαῦμα] given to his eyes (*Il.* 21.54). Vengeful, Achilles thus sees an opportunity to kill his enemies a second time. In its Homeric setting this line is, therefore, testimony to the unaltered wrath of Achilles. In Eudocia's text this grim line becomes an opportunity to present the true μέγα θαῦμα, a line about the resurrection, even though the phrase μέγα θαῦμα is not found in the cento. There is every reason to believe that Eudocia knew perfectly well that this line engaged her with a major plot in the *Iliad*. Wrathful Achilles unceasingly unleashed war and revenge. A line taken from that particular context attests resurrection. This must have appeared to her as a fundamental example of the outstanding role of Christian faith,[65] a transvaluation of a recurrent theme in the *Iliad*.

Another Homeric vision that Eudocia transposes in her presentation of the instruction given by Jesus is farewell words to Odysseus from Alcinous, the king of the Phaeacians. He envisages Odysseus' homecoming in a vision of ships in no need of a pilot or steering oars

---

[64] The biblical counterpart is the statement which often introduces prophecies in the Septuagint, and which is taken over also in the New Testament; e.g. Matt 9:15; Luke 17:22.

[65] Another example is commented upon in Chapter 6.2s.1. above.

since they by themselves find their way, "nor ever have they fear of damage or shipwreck" (l. 508 = *Od.* 8.563).[66] The νόστος motif, elsewhere used christologically,[67] is here used to depict Christian hope. This is no surprise, if seen in the light of the observations above about baptism as an anticipated "homecoming". It is possible that Eudocia's use of this motif also owes much to the common Christian simile of life as sailing towards harbour.[68] This is an example where it is difficult to decide on the intention of the centonist, but where the cento itself opens up a wider horizon.

6.5   The Crucifixion "According to Homer"

1854	Above the earth is raised a dry piece of wood [ξύλον] with length about six feet	*Il.* 23.327
1855	of oak or pine; in the rain it does not rot.	*Il.* 23.328
1856	The mark showing [σῆμα] a man that died in time past	*Il.* 7.89
1857	so huge it was in length and breadth to look upon.[69]	*Od.* 9.324
1858	They bound around the man a twisted rope	*Od.* 22.175
1859	Forcefully they pulled, trusting their strength and power of their hands.	*Il.* 11.9
1860	Men of the people, who at games arranged everything well.	*Od.* 8.259
1861	Fools, who thus prepared these naught [μήδεα].[70]	*Il.* 8.177
1862	The labourers [δρηστῆρες][71] on the other hand shouted aloud in the hall,	*Od.* 22.211

---

[66] In the utopian hopes for a new world, the end of the dangers inherent in sailing is a recurrent motif; see Sandnes, "Markus—en allegorisk biografi?," 294–5.

[67] See Chapter 6.8 of this chapter.

[68] According to Clement Alexandria *Protr.* 12.118.4/GCS p. 83.25–27, salvation is "to anchor in the harbours of heaven [τοῖς λιμέσι καθορμίσει τῶν οὐρανῶν]." This is depicted in analogy with Odysseus' homecoming. He passed the threatening Charybdis and the tempting Sirens. As he survived bound to the mast, so shall the Christians arrive their home safely bound to the cross [τῷ ξύλῳ προσδεδεμένος]. For further references, see Sandnes, "Markus," 290–5.

[69] The line immediately following upon this (*Od.* 9.325) has terminology found also in the Homeric cento l. 1854, thus suggesting that the centonist is here combining texts with the help of the same key terminology.

[70] The Homeric text here has walls [τείχεα].

[71] The Homeric text here has suitors [μνηστῆρες]; quite naturally since this is what the Homeric story is really about.

1863	Straight on they charged like wolves ready to devour.	*Il.* 17.725 +5.782
1864	Like a ram [ἀρνειῷ] he seemed to me, a ram of thick fleece	*Il.* 3.197
1865	walking through a great flock of white sheeps.	*Il.* 3.198
1866	A ram, far best of the flock	*Od.* 9.432
1867	And he moved among them, confidently in his purpose	*Il.* 2.588
1868	bound with bitter bond, suffering hardships [ἄλγεα πάσχων].	*Od.* 15.232
1869	They bound feets and hands together in the anger of their hearts,	*Od.* 22.189+477
1870	led him into the midst, and put up both hands.	*Od.* 18.89
1871	Swiftly laid down his cloak of purple.	*Od.* 14.500
1872	And when the sun had come round to mid-heaven	*Il.* 8.68
1873	they took him, stood apart and stretched him out	*Il.* 17.391
1874	with stake after stake, now here, now there, incessant,	*Od.* 14.11
1875	naked body, since clothes lay in the palace	*Il.* 22.510
1876	straight up at the foot of the mast-beam, then fastened cables around him	*Od.* 12.179
1877	very high up in the air, while the mob was shouting behind him.	*Il.* 17.723[72]
1878	Like this he was left there, stretched in deadly bond [δεσμῷ]	*Od.* 22.200
1879	between earth and starry heaven	*Il.* 5.769
1880	in spring-time, when days are long	*Od.* 18.367
1881	that he may stay alive a long time, and suffer harsh torment [ἄλγεα πάσχων],[73]	*Od.* 22.177
1882	not a limb to move nor to raise up	*Od.* 8.298
1883	nowhere to put firmly the feets or to sit steadfast.	*Od.* 12.434[74]

This part of the crucifixion scene, which takes its start in l. 1815 (Schembra CP 1825) illustrates the way Eudocia is stitching together her cento. In the first place, beneath the Homeric surface level lies a narrative plot easily recognizable from the passion stories of the New

---

[72] The translation of l. 1872–7 is taken from Usher, *Homeric Stitchings*, 70.

[73] This phrase was also used in l. 1868, taken from *Od.* 15.232, demonstrating how Eudocia proceeds with the aid of key terminology.

[74] The lines cited here are found in Schembra CP as l. 1864–93.

Testament. The starting point for the composition is the New Testament stories and Christian traditions developed from them. The crucifixion scene known from there creates the structure into which the Homeric lines are then fitted. The biblical scenes of the crucifixion are recalled in Jesus being surrounded by enemies and the mob, the mention of his clothes and in particular his purple cloak.

Furthermore, Jesus is called a ram or lamb. Its Homeric background is Priam's simile about Odysseus, and the favourite sheep in the flock of the Cyclops, under which Odysseus was able to hide. M.D. Usher considers this an example of the "considerable *Verfremdung*" accompanying the cento throughout,[75] but he does not explain how. A key to understanding this may possibly be found in the combination of the fact that "Jesus as a lamb" is at home in the interpretative traditions that accompanied the passion stories, and the story of the Cyclops' favourite sheep. Odysseus escaped from the cave thanks to his hiding beneath this sheep. For a theologically and homerically creative mind like that of Eudocia, it is not inconceivable that she her found a line aptly describing the salvation-plan [βουλὴ] at work. In The Book of Revelation ἀρνίον is a favourite term for Christ, intimately connected to his sufferings (Rev 5:6; 6:1; 7:14 etc.). The idea of Jesus as the Lamb of God is found also in John 1:29, 36 and in Christian theology derived from Isa 53:7, as in e.g. Acts 8:32 and 1 Pet 1:19. L. 1864–8 in the midst of the crucifixion scene bring to mind Isa 53:7: "Like a lamb that is led to the slaughter." This life-saving effect of Jesus' death as a sacrificial lamb, Eudocia saw at work in Odysseus finding rescue under the sheep of the Cyclops.

In the second place, when Eudocia's poem differs from the New Testament, that is not necessarily due to Homeric influence or metre; sometimes it is because she follows the Christian tradition that by her time has developed. In other words, Homer brings into being (cf. "open" to yielding new texts, Chapter 4) a version of the crucifixion that owes as much to Christian tradition as it does to the New Testament itself. The emphasis on the binding of Jesus represents a Homeric invention, since this is not mentioned anywhere in relevant New Testament passages,[76] not directly at least. In the third place,

---

[75] Usher, *Homeric Stitchings*, 133–4.
[76] As I have pointed out in Chapter 5, Melito of Sardes, *Pascha* 96 may be a witness to this concept of the crucifixion.

some Homeric scenes form a key bridge between the two canonical texts involved. We have seen above that the bath scene of *Od.* 6 is a source from which Eudocia lifts lines of importance for the making of her poem, and also a scene into which lines taken from elsewhere are fitted.

The crucifixion scene similarly draws particularly on some Homeric type-scenes. I restrict myself to pointing out four such scenes. *Il.* 17 provides Eudocia with battle-scenes and lines picturing enemies. There she finds appropriate lines for describing the Roman soldiers. They are compared to wolves ready to devour. It is indeed worth noting that the Homeric text, from which l. 1863 is made, has κύνεσσιν (dogs), not wolves.[77] Why wolves then? Obviously, because the Homeric texts do not represent the sources here. It is reasonable to assume that the Roman soldiers are presented as wolves because they are contrasted with the sheep as their enemies.[78] It thus becomes clear that the concept of sheep was dominant here, and therefore guided the centonist to speak of wolves instead of dogs. This minor detail is, in fact, quite significant; it challenges the position of Mimesis Criticism, namely that Homeric scenes are sources for the Gospel stories. The biblical idea of lamb or sheep here takes control over the Homeric text, not the other way around.

The second scene is Achilles' killing of Hector and the burial of Patroclus (*Il.* 22–23). The crucifixion scene is introduced with two lines about the marking of Patroclus' burial place. The Achilles/Hector scene in particular has provided Eudocia with many lines as she centonizes the death of Jesus.[79] L. 1875 describes Jesus on the pole in terms taken from descriptions of Hector's naked body by the women lamenting his death.

The third scene is Odysseus' fighting the suitors in *Od.* 22, a scene we have seen was important also for the cento's presentation of sinful humanity in the Old Testament part. L. 1862 replaces the suitors with labourers. Eudocia's use of this scene demonstrates how slippery and inconsistent her use of Homer can be. In l. 1862 the suitors of the Homeric text form the background against which Jesus' enemies and the Romans are depicted. This makes sense in the light of her use

---

[77] *Il.* 578 has lions.
[78] Thus also Usher, *Homeric Stitching*, 134.
[79] See l. 1930, 1931, 1956, 1990, 2140; for further details see Usher, *Homeric Stitching*, 45, 93, 139–41.

of the suitors in the beginning of the cento. Then appears a somewhat surprising shift, where the binding of the suitors, commanded
by Telemachus and Odysseus, serves to describe Jesus on the pole
(l. 1869). Obviously, Eudocia is not concerned with appropriate characters, but with finding appropriate terms.

The fourth scene is a double one, both taken from *Od.* 12, where
Odysseus first had to stand firm against the temptations of the Sirens
(l. 1876), and then to escape from Scylla and Charybdis (l. 1883).
Odysseus binding himself to the mast of his ship pictures Christ's
crucifixion. In Christian theology this scene was from quite early on
taken to speak about the crucifixion.[80] This may explain why Eudocia
so consistently depicts crucifixion as binding to a pole. This invention,
therefore, probably comes not from Homer direct, but rather from an
already established *topos* originally taken from Homer. What to modern readers appears as an invention, to Eudocia was probably a piece
of mainstream Christian tradition.

6.5.1 *Jesus and Hector (Il. 22)*

Dennis R. MacDonald has drawn attention to Mark's Jesus as an imitation of Hector in the passion story.[81] Despite some obvious influence
from the Jewish scriptures, "these text *eis ipsis* cannot account for the
Passion Narrative as we have it...Mark seems to have created much of
the Passion Narrative in imitation of the Homeric epic."[82] MacDonald
points to the death of Hector in *Il.* 22 as the model, which makes perfect
sense in the light of the fact that this is a type-scene applied in the cento
itself. His claim is substantiated though, not by reference to the use of
Il. 22 in the cento itself, but by the following observations. Both Hector
and Jesus are forsaken by the gods. When Jesus cites from Ps 22, he
resembles Hector in recognizing that he has been abandoned by the deities (*Il.* 22.297–9): "Both heroes soliloquize their dooms."[83] Secondly, the
deaths of both heroes bring about the fall of a city, Troy and Jerusalem
respectively. Thirdly, both are subjected to gloating by officers. Regarding
this last, we saw in Chapter 1.5 that Dennis R. MacDonald suggested

---

[80] For references see Rahner, *Griechishen Mythen in christlicher Deutung*, 281–328;
Sandnes, *The Challenge of Homer*, 134–40, 177.
[81] MacDonald, *The Homeric Epics and the Gospel of Mark*, 136–47.
[82] MacDonald, *The Homeric Epics and the Gospel of Mark*, 135–6.
[83] MacDonald, *The Homeric Epics and the Gospel of Mark*, 139.

that Mark 15:39 was ironic, and so not unlike Achilles' gloating over his fallen enemy Hector (*Il.* 22.393–4). It might be worthwhile to see how this Markan text is interpreted by those who really undertook the task of presenting this story Homerically. Did Eudocia also take it as gloating? It seems not. L. 1911–2007 (Schembra CP 1921–2017) has this event in its Homeric version. The text is introduced like this:

1911	Thus spoke a man as he was looking up into heaven	*Il.* 7.201
1912	"Truly, he is the son of Him, as he says.	*Od.* 4.157
1913	For he speaks wise words, of the kind which also comes from the Father.	*Od.* 4.206
1914	He is prudent and feels righteous indignation in his mind,	*Od.* 4.158
1915	in utter obedience [ἐν πείσῃ κραδίη] he remained enduring	*Od.* 20.23

The centurion here gives his assent to the Son's obedience, which was so important in the first part of the poem. The centurion utters a confession in words taken from *Od.* 4, in which Menelaus recognizes Telemachus from his resemblance to his father, Odysseus. Anyway, there is no indication of gloating here. Furthermore, according to l. 1917 it is a vision of μέγα θαῦμα, which makes gloating impossible here.

Finally, women are watching the deaths from afar. MacDonald is fundamentally right in pointing to Hector's death as a scene from which Eudocia takes her lines, although he makes no use of the cento itself to prove his case. It is unwarranted though that this scene is the source of Markan story.

Let us now see in what way the death scene of Hector in *Il.* 22 has influenced Eudocia's poem on Jesus' death. In addition to the lines mentioned above, the following lines are taken from *Il.* 22:

1890	the lips he wetted, but palate he did not wet	*Il.* 22.495
1930	thus he spoke and the end of death enfolded him.	*Il.* 22.361
1931	His soul, fleeting from his limbs, went to Hades.	*Il.* 22.362
1956	Thus he spoke and draw near to deal a wound.	*Il.* 22.375

The first line is about Hector's wife, lamenting her dead husband. The two following lines are taken from the moment of Hector's death. The final line describes Achaeans demonstrating their superiority over their fallen enemy when Hector is finally dead. The lines taken from *Il.* 22 are fitted into an already existing story; in no way are they making up the story. Each line taken from *Il.* 22 finds its meaning in the framework of the Passion Narratives, as we know them from the Gospels. L. 1890 corresponds to Mark 15:36parr; 1930–1 correspond to Mark 15:37parr. L. 1956 correspond to John 19:34 about the Roman soldier who pierced Jesus with his spear.

These findings in the Iviron recension find corroboration in the other recensions as well. The appearance of *Il.* 22 in the death scene of Jesus can be listed like this:[84]

Conscriptio Prima	Conscriptio Secunda (= Rey)	Conscriptio A	Conscriptio B	Conscriptio Γ
1885 *Il.* 22.510				
1900 *Il.* 22.495				
1908 *Il.* 22.185	1679 *Il.* 22.185 534	*Il.* 22.185 580	*Il.* 22.185	
	1684 *Il.* 22.375 535	*Il.* 22.375 581	*Il.* 22.375 603	*Il.* 22.375

The picture emerging from this is that all versions except *Prima* quote from *Il.* 22.375. *Il.* 22.185 is quoted by all, except Iviron (Usher's text) and Γ. *Prima* and Iviron make use of *Il.* 22.495. Iviron is alone in drawing upon *Il.* 22.361–2, and Prima (and Usher l. 1875) draw upon *Il.* 22.510. What does this bring to the picture? *Il.* 22 is a key text, but from this type-scene some variations occur. *Il.* 22.185 and 510, as they appear in the cento, need some comments.

Il. 22.185 "Do as your pleasure is, and do not hold back." The Homeric context for this is the heavenly council between Pallas Athene and Zeus; the question is the fate of Hector. Pallas blames Zeus for protecting Hector against the will of the other gods. Zeus' answer is the line in question; in practice this means that Hector's destiny is sealed. Viewed through its Homeric background, this line adds support to MacDonald's emphasis on Jesus being abandoned by God (Ps 22). This is, however, not the use made of this Homeric line in the cento. In the cento this becomes an ironical statement uttered by an arrogant young man; i.e. one of the robbers crucified with Jesus. Indirectly, this echoes Mark 15:27, but more important is Luke's version of this incident, since he has one of the robbers mocking Jesus. If

---

[84] This table is made with the help of Scembra, ed. and trans., *Homerocentones*.

Jesus is really divine, and has attended to the divine voice, he should act as he wants to, and hold back no more.

Il. 22.510 says: "naked body, for clothes lie in the halls." In Homer, this forms the climax of the lamentation of Hector's wife. Andromache realizes that Hector will never return to what is ready for him at home. His awaited homecoming will never occur. This line describes the destiny of Jesus as well; thus the fatal destiny of the two heroes is compared. But a transpositional meaning appears since Jesus did return "home." This is yet to be unpacked. The end of the cento in *Prima* depicts— as does Iviron (see Chapter 6.8)—the Ascension as his homecoming. A contrast between Hector and Jesus is therefore apparent. Eudocia knows of another hero who returned home, namely Odysseus. Just as Odysseus finally reached home [εἰσαφίκανεν] (*Prima* l. 2353 = Iviron l. 2343), so too does Christ. He is seated in the throne he once left (*Prima* l.2534 = Iviron l.2344); a line taken from Telemachos coming home. This means that Eudocia, according to *Conscriptio Prima*, combines Hector and Jesus in such a way that the transposition mirrors the fate of Odysseus. Hector failed to return home, whereas Odysseus did. And so did Jesus. This demonstrates how slippery the comparisons in the cento are. What starts out as a Hector/Jesus analogy, turns into an Odysseus-like interpretation.

It takes more than what I have done here to discuss sufficiently MacDonald's claim on Markan dependence on Hector's death. My point is a very simple one, but nonetheless significant: Taking the cento, in all available recensions, as a point of departure, the similarities pointed out by MacDonald are *his* inventions, with no support in the cento itself, besides, of course the correspondence between the two scenes as death scenes. By no means would I deny that MacDonald's observations make sense of the Passion narrative if read against a Homeric background. But if the Homeric centos are really important analogies for how Mark treated Homer's epics, it is worth pondering why Eudocia's use of *Il.* 22 does not support the observations made by MacDonald. One also wonders why he does not mention this since he calls upon precisely this analogy.

6.6   *Descensus ad Inferos*

The lines about Christ visiting the kingdom of the dead prior to his being resurrection (l. 2105–48) are worth considering as an example of a real invention based on Homer alone. The *Odyssey* 11 describes Odysseus visiting the dead:

> Then there gathered from out of Erebus the ghosts of those that are dead, brides, and unwed youths, and toil-worn old men, and frisking girls with hearts still new to sorrow, and many, too, that had been wounded with bronze-tipped spears, men slain in battle, wearing their blood-stained armor. These came thronging in crowds about the pit from every side, with an astounding cry; and pale fear seized me.... (*Od.* 11.36–43)
>
> And I should have seen yet others of the men of former times, whom I was eager to behold, but before that the myriad tribes of the dead came thronging up with an eerie cry, and pale fear seized me, that august Persephone might send upon me out of the house of Hades the head of Gorgon, that terrible monster (*Od.* 11.630–5)

In *Od.* 11, death is described as foggy darkness and shades, and Eudocia finds appropriate lines for her Jesus poem here. This story inspired Virgil's *Aen.* 6. Did it also inspire Eudocia to bring Jesus visiting the House of Hades into her Homeric Gospel? L. 2130 and 2132 are taken from the classical scene in *Od.* 11 and might indicate such a connection. In the later *Gospel of Nicodemus* (see below) this *topos*, *descensus ad inferos*, known from *The Apostolic Creed*, is narrated. Dennis R. MacDonald takes this as an example of how Homer was the primary source for stories known from the Gospels.[85] Eudocia includes a dialogue between Jesus and Hades for which there is no biblical analogy. We have seen though, that she did the same thing in l. 88–201, with the heavenly conversation between Christ and the Father. However, that purely imaginative dialogue was not without any basis in the Bible, particularly if read in a holistic way, i.e. reading together texts from various parts of the Bible. I suggest that something similar is the case here as well. Before answering the question of invention, it is worth looking into what Eudocia actually does here.

2136	Thus Aidoneus (= Hades), lord of those under the earth addressed him	cf. *Il.* 20.61
2137	entreating, but harsh was what he heard:	*Il.* 21.98
2138	'Now I must say and announce my word,	*Il.* 9.309
2139	what I have in mind, and how it shall come to pass.	*Il.* 9.310
2140	A man mortal, appointed long ago for his destiny	*Il.* 22.179
2141	both well-girdled women and small children	*Il.* 23.261 + 22.63

---

[85] MacDonald, "My Turn," 21–22; only tentatively and preliminary presented there.

2142	I will deliver again from painful death.	*Il.* 16.442
2143	Put to your heart, I demand you to withdraw	*Il.* 20.196
2144	into the crowd, and not to oppose me.	*Il.* 20.197
2145	You shall in no way have power to accomplish anything, but from my heart	*Il.* 1.562
2146	you shall be further. That will become you worse.'	*Il.* 1.563
2147	He left him having spoken thus all	*Il.* 20.340
2148	threats, for Mighty fear from the man's rebuking words.	*Il.* 6.137

This is not a dialogue between equals. Hades appears terrified and Jesus announces his superiority. The overall focus is Christ subduing and rebuking Hades. The climax of this perspective is reached in l. 2148, taken from Diomedes' conversation with Glaukos, implying that it is impossible to fight the gods. Likewise, Christ is not to be defeated by anyone, not even Death. This point is made also in Eudocia's slight but quite significant modifications in l. 2140 and 2142. These lines from *Il.* 22.179 about Hector and *Il.* 16.441–2 about Sarpedon are intimately related in terms of theme and motif, even having the same vocabulary [ἄνδρα θνητὸν ἐόντα]. These are Homeric types of fallen heroes. In both instances there is a dispute among the gods over the fate of these heroes. In both instances, Zeus is opposed by Hera or Pallas Athene with a rhetorical question: If Sarpedon and Hector are saved, how will Zeus then appear righteous? The other inhabitants on Mt. Olympus will be tempted to intervene in like manner on behalf of their endangered offspring. In other words, in their Homeric setting, these lines seal the fates of Sarpedon and Hector. Eudocia makes these rhetorical questions, to which the expected answer is no, into statements or promises. It follows naturally that the 2nd person is replaced with the 1st person, thus affirming what the Homeric texts deny; and of course, these lines are here given a general application to men in general: Christ is intervening on behalf of the endangered and the dead. This is the theologian Eudocia at work, only slightly modifying Homer, if judged by what she does to his *verba*, but significantly altering it with regard to its *res* or *sensus*.

L. 2141 consists of two half-lines; the first taken from Achilles collecting the spoils after his killing of Hector, and the latter from Priam lamenting his fallen children. The line is an example of how Eudocia proceeds by bringing together texts joined by similarity in scene, terminology or motif. *Il.* 22.179, which forms the basis of l. 2140, equals *Il.* 16.441, the immediately-preceding line of the Homeric text quoted in l. 2141, thus making it natural to bring together Hector and Sarpedon.

The threatening words against Death are taken from Achilles' warning of Aeneas (*Il.* 20) and Zeus rebuking Achilles (*Il.* 1).

This dialogue proclaiming Jesus victorious over Hades is thus inspired by Homeric scenes, of which *Od.* 11 is most important. The New Testament basis is indeed scant. While *Od.* 11 closes with Odysseus being seized by fear and running to his ships, Christ, however, speaks victoriously to Hades. This is an example of transvaluation, not necessarily an argument though that *Od. 11* is the proper source here. There are numerous texts in the New Testament that Eudocia might have drawn upon to create Christ encountering Hades directly. In my view, these cento lines represent a Homeric version coming out of the very centre of early Christian conviction that Christ is risen from the dead. Relevant New Testament passages are the many texts where Ps 110:1–2 is quoted; e.g. 1 Cor 15:54–55; Rom 8:37–39; 10:7 [εἰς τὴν ἄβυσσον]; Luke 16:23: Ephes 4:8–10 [κατέβη εἰς τὰ κατώτερα μέρη τῆς γῆς] and 1 Pet 3:19 and 4:6. Most of these are about the resurrection, but some were early on taken to address what happened after Christ's death and prior to His resurrection. 1 Pet 3:19 is of special interest since in this text there is a combination of πορευθεὶς and τῷ ᾅδη in some mss.[86] This is hardly the better interpretation of that passage, judged from the epistle itself, but a widely accepted interpretation that eventually led to Christ's *descenus ad inferos* as we have it in the creed. This is likely a basis upon which Eudocia could include this in her Homeric paraphrase of the life of Jesus.

The story of *Christ's Descent into Hades* takes up chaps. 17–27 of *The Gospel of Nicodemus* (*Acta Pilati*).[87] The genesis of this text is indeed complex, as it is made up of different sources and versions in

---

[86] See Nestle-Aland's text-edition mentioning minuscle 614 and few other mss (*pc*) and Ambrosiaster. Worth mentioning here is also 2 Pet 2:4 [σειραῖς ζόφου ταρταρώσας]; Jude 6 [δεσμοῖς ἀϊδίοις ὑπὸ ζόφον] cf. 2 Pet 2:17, Jude 13. All these texts speak of death as imprisonment in the House of Hades. This way of talking about death has its Old Testament analogies as well; see e.g. Gen 37:35 [καταβήσομαι εἰς ᾅδου]; Num 16:35 [κατέβησαν εἰς ᾅδου].

[87] For the Latin and Greek texts, see Constantinus de Tischendorf, ed., *Evangelia Apocrypha. Adhibitis Plurimis Codibus Graecis et Latinis Maximam Partem nunc Primum Consultis atque Ineditorum Copia Insignibus* (Lipsiae: Hermann Mendelssohn, 1876) in which this part is reckoned as *pars altera* of the *Gospel of Nicodemus*. A more recent Latin edition is given by H.C. Kim, ed., *The Gospel of Nicodemus Gesta Salvatoris. Edited from Codex Einsidlensis. Einsideln Stiftsbibliothek, MS 326* (Toronto: Pontifical Institute of Medieval Studies, 1973).

both Greek and Latin, and was later also translated into many other
languages. The longer Greek version, in which the alleged Homeric
comparisons are found, is an early medieval reworking of a shorter
version;[88] it is probably to be dated to the fifth or sixth centuries.[89] There
is no biblical warrant for a story about Christ visiting Hades, but there
are references that, if put together, might form the building-blocks of
such a story, as pointed out above.[90] This is exactly what happens in
Acta Pilati. It sets out as a story that develops from Matt 27:52–53,
about the dead who were seen alive in Jerusalem. The story is presented as a written report about the incident from two of those who
were raised from the dead on this occasion.

As this story is told by the *Gospel of Nicodemus*, it represents a miscellany of biblical texts, some of which are the following:

- Isa 9:1–2: light is brought to those who walk in the darkness, to those
  who live in the land and shade of death (*Gos. Nic.* 18.1). The Latin
  version A is here most explicit: *populus qui sedet in tenebris viudebit
  lucem magnam, et qui sunt in regione umbrae mortis lux fulgebit super
  eos.*[91] This Old Testament text comes into play since it corresponds
  nicely to descriptions of death commonly found in antiquity.[92]
- Ps 24:7: The text about lifting up the gates of hell so the Lord of Glory
  may enter is addressed to Satan and Hades. (*Gos. Nic.* 21.1).
- Ps 107:15–17: This text is seen in tandem with Ps 24:7, since it speaks
  about gates of brass and bars of iron to be broken. This interpretation might be influenced by the concept of the House of Hades as a
  prison.[93]
- Hab 3:13 about God who went out to rescue His people is cited in
  the Latin version A:... *ad liberandum electos tuos.*

---

[88] J.K. Elliott, trans., *The Apocryphal New Testament. A Collection of Apocryphal
Christian Literature in an English Translation based on M.R. Jones* (Oxford: Clarendon
Press), 165–6. The longer Greek version is found in Tischendorf, ed., *Evangelia
Apocrypha*. For an introduction to this work, see Zbigniew Izydorczyk and Jean-
Daniel Dubois, "Nicodemus' Gospel Before and Beyond the Medieval West", in: *The
Medieval Gospel of Nicodemus. Texts, Intertexts, and Contexts in Western Europe*, ed.
Zbigniew Izydorczyk (Tempe: Arizona State University, 1997).
[89] Elliott, trans., *The Apocryphal New Testament*, 165–6.
[90] Kim, ed., *The Gospel of Nicodemus*, 5 gives some of these texts.
[91] The Latin text is from Kim, ed., *The Gospel of Nicodemus*, 36.
[92] As for *Od.* 11, see above.
[93] See above.

- The Lazarus story (John 11) plays an important role, due to the fact that Hades is here described, and the appearance of the Greek ἐν τῷ ᾅδῃ (Luke 16:23–6) (*Gos. Nic.* 20). Lazarus is taken as an example of someone who escaped Hell. This biblical narrative, therefore, becomes a paradigm story here. The text is combined with the other Lazarus story found in the Bible; the two are linked not only by the appearance of the same name, but also by Hades. Hades speaks up, commenting on the Lazarus event in a way that also explains why the two biblical texts mentioned above belong together: "So now I know that the man who could do these things (= the raising of Lazarus) is God, powerful in dominion, mighty in humanity, and is the saviour of the human race. And if you bring him to me he will release all who are here shut up in the cruelty of prison and fettered with the unbreakable chains of their sins, and will bring them to life of his divinity for ever" (*Gos. Nic.* 20.3).[94]

The story of Jesus' descent to the House of Hades, therefore, appears as a kind of a "midrash," based on a miscellany of biblical texts. But does this necessarily exclude Homer' role here? The question can be put like this: What brings these biblical texts together to form a *story* about a descent into Hades? This is a pertinent question since the New Testament never tells such a story. It is not impossible that famous *Od.* 11 brought together biblical texts to create a counter-story of *Christ's Descensus*. When Odysseus paid a visit to the realm of the dead, he met the heroes of old. According to *The Gospel of Nicodemus*, Jesus likewise meets the patriarchs and prophets while in Hades. *Od.* 11 might well have instigated such a story, but it did not take *Od.* 11 to come up with this idea of Christ visiting Hades. I think Eudocia's inclusion of this event in the life of Jesus demonstrates that her cento is informed not only by the canonical gospels, but also by non-canonical Christian traditions available to her. She, therefore, reads Homer through the lenses not only of the Gospels, but also of the wider Christian tradition.

---

[94] Quoted from Elliott, trans. *The Apocryphal New Testament*, 193.

6.7 The Resurrection of Jesus "According
to Homer" (L. 2149–68)

The section on the Resurrection is rather lengthy compared to the New
Testament texts relevant here. The substructure of the passage is seen
by the fact that it includes important elements recognizable from the
biblical narratives: the third day, dawn, wailing women, the removal of
a stone, messengers [ἄγγελοι], reunion, joy and commission. But all this
is steeped in a Homeric universe. The idea of Jesus being raised from
the dead, Eudocia finds in *Il.* 15.286–7 where it says about Hector in
the midst of a battle: "Now, look you, a great miracle [θαῦμα][95] my eyes
behold, that he has risen again [ἀνέστη] and avoided death" (l. 2235),
and in *Il.* 1.57 (= l. 2248) about Achilles who stood up [ἤγερθεν] to
speak (see below). To Eudocia, a simple standing up becomes a line
appropriate for expressing resurrection, since she is familiar with this
terminology as being 'at home' in Christian belief. It is hardly possible
to imagine such Homeric lines as the formative basis for the stories of
Jesus' resurrection found in the Gospels. The only link is the appearance of key terms. These Homeric lines can only work as witnesses to
the resurrection if this is already established as a story within which
this terminology is fixed. In these Homeric lines, Eudocia found key
terminology from the New Testament traditions on the resurrection.

The fact that the Homeric support for the idea is taken from the two
arch-enemies in Homer's story seems not to have troubled her; thus
exemplifying how accidentally she sometimes brings texts together,
or maybe Eudocia would consider this a double witness. The glue of
her cento is found in the biblical texts and Christian traditions. L. 2152
speaks of Jesus' resurrection in terms of awakening from a dream (*Il.*
2.41): "Then he awoke from sleep; the divine voice [θείη ὀμφή] was
ringing in his ears." As pointed out by André-Louis Rey, the idea seems
to be the Father calling Jesus forth out of his grave, very much in
analogy with Lazarus in John 11:43: φωνῇ μεγάλῃ ἐκραύγασεν Λάζαρε,
δεῦρο ἔξω.[96] The removal of the stone is described in accordance with
Odysseus, the athlete, throwing a discus in a competition (*Od.* 8.189–
90 = l. 2186 + 2188), and Sisyphos in Hades, who continuously rolls

---

[95] This is also elsewhere a reference to the belief in resurrection in general; see
Chapter 6.4 of this study.
[96] Rey, ed. and trans., *Centons Homériques*, 484.

the stone upward only to see it roll back down again (*Od.* 11.589). The wailing women are given a role that far exceeds the New Testament testimony. The identity of the women is far from clear. Compared to the New Testament it is surprising that the mother of Jesus is given such a prominent place. Her grief is described with lines taken from the Trojan women bewailing the fallen Hector (*Il.* 24) and Penelope's tears for her husband (*Od.* 19).

2248	When they were assembled he raised up [ἤγερθεν].	*Il.* 1.57
2249	They were glad, and the heart in the breasts of all were filled with joy	*Od.* 15.165
2250	as they saw him come to join them alive [ζωόν] and safe.	*Il.* 5.515
2251	When they joyfully had looked upon each other	*Il.* 24.633
2252	they greeted him in speech and took his hands.	*Od.* 24.410
2253	With welcoming love they kissed his head and shoulders.	*Od.* 17.35
2254	Godlike [θειοειδής] Theoclymenus then spoke to them	*Od.* 20.350
2255	'My child(ren), I have come as an immortal God	*Il.* 24.460
2256	As I was yesterday in our home	*Od.* 24.379
2257	so I will become, thus was my first pledge and promise.	*Il.* 4.267
2258	Now finally, has your desire been fulfilled	*Od.* 23.54
2259	But I am present, having suffered pain and endured much,	*Od.* 16.205
2260	winning my Father's great glory as well as mine own.'	*Il.* 16.446

The passage addresses the joyous reunion after the resurrection with the help of *Il.* 24.633 (l. 2251) about Priam, who approached the enemy camp to see and to lament the dead body of his son Hector. He found that Achilles, the man who killed Hector, showed him the kindness of allowing him to mourn his dead son. This is also the Homeric scene from which l. 2255 is taken. Hermes took care of Priam in this danger-ous attempt to enter the camp of the enemy, and his self-presentation becomes words in the mouth of the resurrected Jesus. Against this background, Jesus' resurrection in the cento is, in fact, described by analogy with an act of reconciliation. Lines from *Od.* 23 and 24 make the resurrection scene a homecoming as well. Jesus has finally arrived where he is at home (l. 2255-8). L. 2256-7 taken together put in Homeric words the Christian belief in Christ's pre-existence and the Parousia.

Jesus addresses his companions in the name of Theoclymenus, the prophet from Argos. The epithet given him by Homer ("godlike") is a natural point from which Eudocia proceeds. Jesus speaks under this name elsewhere in her cento;[97] in these instances *Od.* 20.350 = *Od.* 15.271 is quoted. Adding adjectives to the presentation of the figures is a typical and recurrent Homeric feature. To mention some examples, *Il.* 22.294 ("Deïphobus of the white shield"); *Od.* 21.74 ("godlike Odysseus"); *Od.* 21.384 ("wise Eurycleia"). M.D. Usher points out that this was of much help for Eudocia who could not use names for the individuals in the Gospel story. Naming Jesus "godlike" is an example of this.[98]

6.8 THE νόστος ("HOMECOMING") OF JESUS: THE CLOSING OF THE POEM

The so-called νόστος motif, so important in the *Odyssey*, comes to fruition in Eudocia's cento. We have already come across the homecoming motif in the heavenly voice at Jesus' baptism. I there interpreted this as a reference to the Incarnation, probably inspired by John 1:11. We will now see that this motif is not uniform in the cento. Of particular importance here is that Christ's resurrection in this passage is described in accordance with Odysseus' homecoming. This is a recurrent motif guiding the whole story of the *Odyssey*. The starting point is Odysseus longing for his return (*Od.* 1.13). He is throughout the story on his way home [οἴκαδε].[99] This plot reaches its fulfilment in Chapter 23, where it is stated that Odysseus has finally arrived at his home: οἶκον ἱκάνεται (*Od.* 23.7, 27, 108).[100] The passage quoted above has several lines that are all in different ways associated with the νόστος motif— not to speak of the other occurrences in the resurrection section seen as a whole. L. 2259 is taken from Odysseus making himself known to his son Telemachus. The cento line continues in Homer thus: "I have come in the twentieth year to my native land [ἐς πατρίδα γαῖαν]". L. 2253 is taken from Odysseus being welcomed back to his home by Telemachus, Eurycleia and his servants. L. 2258 is taken from the very climax of Odysseus' homecoming; he is now recognized by Penelope,

---

[97] E.g. l. 1648 and 2330.
[98] Usher, *Homeric Stitchings*, 45–46.
[99] See e.g. *Od.* 1.326–7, 350; 5.19; 12.345; 13.130–9, 305; 19.85; 24.400.
[100] For the importance of this motif in ancient literature, see MacDonald, *Christianizing Homer*, 113–75.

his wife: "Finally, has this your long desire been fulfilled [ἐκτετέλεσται]."
This cento line is in Homer immediately followed by this line: "he has
come himself, alive to his own hearth [ἐφέστιος]"[101] (*Od.* 23.55). L. 2252
and 2256 are taken from the immediate context of the celebration of
Odysseus' homecoming in *Od.* 24.400: "You finally reached home [ἐπεὶ
νόστησας]."

The homecoming hero provides Eudocia with both a Homeric scene
and language in which to recount Christ's resurrection.[102] By bringing
the two together, Eudocia comes quite close to the Johannine perspective of the Son returning to his Father (John 13:1–3; 14:12, 28; 16:28;
20:17). This becomes very clear as the cento comes to a close with the
following lines from the ascension, inspired by Luke-Acts:

2337	He went to his mighty Father's well-built house [πρὸς πατρὸς ἐρισθενέος πυκινὸν];	*Il.* 19.355
2338	he went amid the clouds up to heaven broad	*Il.* 5.867
2339	imperishable, decked with stars, pre-eminent among the immortals.	*Il.* 18.370
2343	He started running, and eagerly he arrived with his beloved Father [μάλα δ' ὦκα φίλον πατέρ εἰσαφικανεν]	*Od.* 22.99
2344	and then sat down again at the seat [ἐπὶ θρόνου] from which he had once left.	*Od.* 21.139 = *Od.* 18.157

Eudocia's cento closes with a Homeric line which echoes John 17:5, 24
about Jesus receiving from his Father the glory he once enjoyed with
him, before his coming to the world. L. 2337 is about Pallas who returns
to Mt. Olympus, the abode of the gods; for natural reasons, Eudocia
therefore changes the feminine into αὐτὸς. L. 2338 describes a similar
departure, now with regard to Ares. The two last lines are especially
interesting since they alter the Homeric homecoming motif in accordance with biblical thought, particularly in its Johannine version. The
homecoming Odysseus, obviously the father of his house, becomes in
these two lines the son returning to his Father. Both lines are really
about Telemachus. L. 2343 is about Telemachus embracing his father,
and l. 2344 is about his sitting down in the house of his father. This
example demonstrates how the classical homecoming motif is altered

---

[101] *LSJ* s.v. renders this "at one's fireside, at home."
[102] This is prepared in her *paraphrasis* of Christ meeting Thomas, John 20, where
lines from *Od.* 23 and 24 abound towards the end of her story.

by the biblical idea to be expressed, or in other words, how the macro level bends the micro level.

6.8.1   *The Ascension in the other Recensions*

While in *Prima* the cento closes with *Od.* 18.157 = 21.139, on Jesus sitting down on the chair from which he once rose, *Secunda* has a different ending. This line is found here in l. 1915 followed by *Od.* 1.257 (l. 1916). Pallas Athene expresses to Telemachus the grief over Odysseus who have left his home, and the hope that he will one day return: "such a man as he was when I first saw him." In *Secunda* this becomes the fulfilment of this hope, thus strengthening the νόστος motif. The gates of heaven [πύλαι οὐρανοῦ][103] opened to receive Jesus (l. 1913–14), and

1918	He sat down [καθέζετο] before his face (i.e. Father), exulting his glory.	*Il.* 1.360 + *Il.* 1.405
1919	He appeared on the right, and all earth round about laughed [δεξιὸς ἀΐξας ἐγέλασσε δὲ πᾶσα περὶ χθών]	*Il.* 24.320 + 19.362

These lines are the Homeric version of Ps 110:1 (LXX 109) [κάθου ἐκ δεξιῶν μου] as it appears in the New Testament. Christ is pictured as the ruler of Olympus (l. 1920), given the sceptre and the law (l. 1921), words describing powerful Agamemnon in *Il.* 9.99. Many lines describe Jesus' power to rule (l. 1922–49),[104] bringing to mind Phil 2 saying that every knee in heaven and on earth and under the earth shall bend to the glory of Jesus the Lord (Isa 45:23). After a number of lines indicating the overall rulership of Jesus, a shift takes place in l. 1941; now enters ἐγὼ referring to the centonist, or at least someone commenting upon the poem, but unlike the preface the lines are here taken from Homer, somewhat, but still significantly, modified:[105]

1941	Indeed, I will prophesy [μαντεύσομαι] to you, and I will hide nothing	*Od.* 1.200 + 17.154
1942	Jesus shall return; that shall be a good tiding to you [ὡς νεῖτ' Ἰησοῦς εὐαγγέλιον δέ τοι ἔστω]	*Od.* 14.152

---

[103] Justin takes Ps. 24:7 on "the gates of heaven [πύλαι αἰώνιοι]" to refer to the ascension (*1Apol.* 51.7) In *Dial.* 36.5 and *Dial.* 127.5; Ps 24 and Ps 110:1 are combined in a way similar to what Eudocia does here. I owe this observation to my colleague Oskar Skarsaune.

[104] Thus also in *Conscriptio B* l. 632–3.

[105] Rey, ed. and trans., *Centons Homériques*, 504–5.

L. 1942 replaces Odysseus with Jesus, thus making the homecoming motif explicit. Eumaeus complains to the stranger, whom he does not recognize, as Odysseus returned. The stranger, Odysseus in disguise, answers with the lines cited here. The Ascension is clearly a homecoming. However, the future tenses in l. 1941 raise some doubt here. It is possible that this is a prophecy of the Parousia.[106] This will then imply yet another aspect of the νόστος motif; the incarnation, resurrection and ascension, and Christ's return. I admit uncertainty here. It would certainly fit the Odyssean context better to take this as a statement of presence rather than future coming. *Conscriptio B* and *Γ* have these two lines forming the end of the cento. In fact, this is in accordance with Acts on the Ascension. That story ends with the angels' saying: "This Jesus, who has been taken up from you into heaven, will come in the same way as you saw him go into heaven" (Acts 1:11). The Ascension as homecoming makes the best sense as a Homeric reading of Jesus' story, but Eudocia does not, as we have seen, limit herself to this use of this important Homeric motif.

Compared to these two recensions, *Secunda* adds some lines (1943–8). In Homeric style and vocabulary, the "epilogue" picks up the prefatory preface and addresses the project as such. Generations will speak of a sacred song given by the Deity [ὤπασε θέσπιν ἀοιδὴν]. L. 1953 comes from *Od.* 8.498, where Odysseus challenges Demodochus to sing about the Trojan War to the Phaeacans. So he did, with a song inspired by god [ὁρμηθεὶς θεοῦ ἤρχετο] (*Od.* 8.499, which is not cited however. The poem, called "a sacred song", closes in the following way

1945	late in coming, late in fulfillment, its fame,	
	however, shall never perish.	*Il.* 2.325
1946	He dwelt in Phrygia by the streams of Sangarius,	*Il.* 16.719
1947	preeminent [ἄριστος] among all the heroes,	*Il.* 2.579
1948	they were leaders of the Danaans and their masters	*Il.* 2.760

Demodochus' song about the Trojan War and the heroes becomes a paradigm for the cento itself. It is a Trojan song in style, but not in content. Surprisingly, in l. 1945 *Secunda* picks up a line about the lying portent, the deceiving dream that started the Trojan War. The last part of the sentence probably attracted the attention of the centonist. The three closing lines in *Secunda* are indeed enigmatic. The key question is to whom the relative pronoun ὃς of l. 1946 refers. André-Louis Rey

---

[106] Rey, ed. and trans., *Centons Homériques*, 506.

takes it as a reference to Eudocia's poet colleague Cyrus of Panoplis, who was exiled to Phrygia due to accusations not unlike those she herself had suffered.[107] In the light of the cento elsewhere it appears more likely that ἄριστος is more likely to have a christological implication, but this leaves Phrygia void of meaning. Since these lines work as a metatext, somehow set apart from the cento, they may well find an interpretation not prepared for in the cento proper.

An investigation of the recensions of the Ascension comes to the same conclusion as regards how the centonist is working: a core of Homeric lines is found, picked according to type scenes. The order of these lines is, however, flexible. In addition to this a number of other lines are added—more or less at random, it seems. The key scenes are about the power to rule, and in particular the homecoming of Odysseus. Two other key lines are taken from *Od.* 10.97 (climbing a height), *Il.* 19.355 (going to the Father's house) and *Il.* 5.867 (going up to heaven amid the clouds). A most important line is taken from *Od.* 18.157 = *Od.* 21.139: "And he sat down again on the chair from which he had risen." The cento in *Prima* closes with this climax. The line is found in all versions; in *Secunda* l. 1915, *Conscriptio A* l. 614, *Conscriptio B* l. 629, *Γ* l. 714.

Conscriptio A gives a special emphasis to this homecoming motif. In addition to the line just mentioned (l. 614), l. 613 (*Od.* 22.99), 615 (*Od.* 24.413) and 620 (*Od.* 18.36) clearly echo this Odyssean motif. The latter says: "Friends, never before has such a thing come to pass". The Homeric context for this line is Odysseus returning home disguised as an old beggar and now being challenged to fight.

The homecoming of Odysseus marks the climax and fulfilment of the Odyssean story. *Conscriptio A*, therefore, has the cento ending in this way:

622   Thus he spoke, and now all this is fulfilled
      [τὰ δὴ πάντα τελεῖται]   *Il.* 2.330

Enters now transvaluation. The climax of the *Odyssey* is not only his coming home in itself, but returning home in order to take revenge. These are twin motifs in the story, and hence not to be separated.[108] It is against this background that the τελεῖται of l. 622 is to be understood.

---

[107] Rey, ed. and trans., *Centons Homériques*, 505.
[108] See e.g. *Od.* 14.110, 163; 16.91–110; 18.345–8; 19.51–52, 409.

It links up with l. 609 where the Ascension is introduced by quoting
Od. 11.246: "When God had finished his best acts [ἐτέλεσσε θεὸς
πανυπέρτατα[109] ἔργα]." The adjective used in Homer is an amorous
term. This line is taken from an erotic scene where Enipeus, later identified as Poseidon, makes love to Tyro; the sentence above introduces
his promise to Tyro that she will give birth to sons. Eudocia alters the
Homeric story considerably by using this sentence within a context of
Odysseus' homecoming. By placing this utterance of Poseidon's love
within this context, the twin motif of homecoming and revenge is torn
apart. The entire cento of Eudocia adds proof to this transformation
of the homecoming motif. *Conscriptio A* probably found this transformation witnessed in the last words of Jesus according to John 19:30:
τετέλεσται. In John's Gospel this marked the end of a life full of love
(John 3:16; 10:15; 13:1; 15:13). L. 621 quotes *Il.* 15.287 about Hector and
speaks of ascension in terms of rising from death [ἀνέστη]. It may be
stretching the point here, but it is worth considering that l. 622 taken
from *Il.* 2.330 is a comment on the vision which deceives the Achaeans
into trusting in victory, a confidence that led to years of war. The story
told by Eudocia is indeed different; it is not about deception, nor is it
about war and revenge.

At the centre of Dennis R. MacDonald's Homeric reading of Mark's
Gospel is the plot of the returning home of the hero: "Both heroes
return home to find it infested with murderous rivals that devour the
houses of widows."[110] In *Does the New Testament Imitate Homer?*,
MacDonald puts it like this: "Like Odysseus, Jesus comes to his 'house,'
the Jerusalem temple, which has fallen into the hands of rivals, who, like
Penelope's suitors, devour widow's houses."[111] I have elsewhere argued
against this reading on the basis of Mark's Gospel itself.[112] The presentation given above of Christ's resurrection and ascension according to
the Homeric cento, one of the analogies claimed by MacDonald, does
not support his reading of Mark. The νόστος motif, so richly used in
the cento, is—even when applied to Jesus—indeed slippery, referring
as it does to the Incarnation, the Ascension and even the Parousia.
Eudocia simply uses the motif of the homecoming hero in different

---

[109] This adjective means "the highest" or "best"; see LSJ s.v.; Homer has φιλοτήσια
("acts of love").
[110] MacDonald, *The Homeric Epics and the Gospel of Mark*, 3 cf. 17.
[111] MacDonald, *Does the New Testament Imitate Homer?*, 172.
[112] Sandnes, "Imitatio Homeri?," 719–22.

ways, the most important however being the Ascension. In fact, she
turns to John's Gospel and Luke's writings to find the proper place
for this motif in the story of Jesus. One final observation substantiates
this further. According to MacDonald, in Mark's Gospel the suitors
equal the merchants of the Jerusalem temple, who threaten widows.
We have seen that the suitors in Eudocia's cento are introduced for
the first time already in the Old Testament part, representing allegorically the power of sin which Jesus had to put right. It is worth noticing
that the suitors appear again now at the very end of her cento, in line
2335: "The suitors were troubled and downcast in spirit." Against the
background of Eudocia's use of the suitors in the beginning of her
cento (see above), this line appears as a summing up the message of
her poem. Finally, the suitors are defeated. This is, of course, not necessarily an argument against MacDonald's reading of the homecoming
motif in Mark's Gospel. We have seen that Homeric motifs may be
cast in quite various ways. It is worth noting though, that the analogy
claimed by MacDonald has a different reading of the homecoming
motif, the very plot of the *Odyssey*.

CHAPTER SEVEN

SUMMARY

Throughout antiquity, Christians took different views of pagan literature. The positions held ranged from abandoning this body of literature entirely, thereby cutting themselves off from the legacy of the past, to making use of this legacy in a proper way; i.e. discriminating between good and bad. Christian advocates of pagan literature often took advantage of the interpretational discourse and methods developed by the nurturing of this legacy in antiquity in general, of which Heraclitus the Grammarian's *Homeric Problems* is an outstanding example, as we have seen.[1] In the fourth century C.E., some elite Christians took upon themselves to paraphrase the life of Jesus according to the standards of the pagan literature which made up this legacy, mostly Homer and Virgil. They composed what I have labelled "Gospels according to Homer and Virgil." These are idiosyncratic versions of methods held by Christian advocates of this legacy. The first known to have done this was Juvencus, later followed by Proba and Eudocia. The two women composed centos, imposing on themselves the restraint of using Homeric or Virgilian lines verbatim, with only minor modifications. When the lines and half-lines are reorganised according to a substructure taken from the Gospels or from Christian theology in general, new texts emerged from the classical canon. From the classical legacy the centonists were able to cull a new text, epic and biblical *simultaneously*. Their poems represent examples of truly extreme intertextuality. This book has focused on Christian cento composition of the life of Jesus, by putting this phenomenon into the wider context of rhetoric and literary amusement in antiquity.

---

[1] For this discourse, see the contributions found in Robert Lamberton and John J. Keaney, *Homer's Ancient Readers. The Hermeneutics of Greek Epic's Earliest Exegetes* (Princeton, NJ: Princeton University Press, 1992). The debate among Christians on encyclical studies and Homer is presented in Sandnes, *The Challenge of Homer*.

7.1   Bringing Homer and Virgil to their Completion

The undertaking of Proba and Eudocia should be seen within the framework of ancient rhetoric, the recycling of texts in education and also the playing with texts of authority as means of amusement. Antiquity was a culture that traded in its "canonical" texts. The Christian centos came to life as part of this culture of playing with, altering and bending the canonical texts. The epics of Homer and Virgil were seen as open texts which, given some reworking, were able to yield new texts. They were manipulable in a way that could turn their readers into authors of fresh texts with regard to content, but still kept within the old style and in the venerated words of the poets. Homer's and Virgil's epics were deconstructed, not to say distorted, in order to bring to life new texts, be they about sex (*Cento Nuptialis*), bread (*De Panificio*), dicing (*De Alea*) or salvation in Christ. Furthermore, what appears to modern readers, as well as to ancient critics, as deconstruction, might rather be classified as a reconstruction—in the view of the Christian centonists themselves. These considered the classical texts as buried treasures of wisdom; it had become merely a matter of unearthing it. Homer and Virgil were thus brought to their completion in a Christian rearranging of their texts. Seen in the light of ancient rhetoric this is not artificial, as it may easily appear to a present-day reader, a fact witnessed to in the many negative views expressed by scholars on cento composition. Rather, the centonists are standing on the shoulders of the ancient culture's trading in the same texts.

In fact, Christian cento composition can be seen as fulfilment, highly idiosyncratic, of some very important attitudes to the classical poets in antiquity. In the first place, we have noted that poets, and Homer and Virgil in particular, were considered to have been inspired by the Muses.[2] Accordingly, they could be seen as prophets; hence *vates* often has this dual meaning. Their epics were therefore seen as pools from which divine answers could be drawn. In fact, these two great poets served as a means of divination. Random passages from their works were read to predict the future and address present situations, very much like an oracle.[3] This is called *sortes* since the texts were written

---

[2] For the inspiration of Homer, see Sandnes, *The Challenge of Homer*, 45–47. See Chapter 1.2 of this study.

[3] For the relevance of this for understanding Christian centos, see Bažil, *Centones Christiani*, 104. Christians took over this practice and used the Bible in the same way

on tablets or counters drawn from a vessel or chest or thrown like dice (Cicero, *Div.* 1.74). *Scriptores Historiae Augustae*, a collection of imperial biographies modelled on Suetonius' *Lives of the Caesars*, give examples of this practice. Hadrian, anxious about Trajan's attitude to him, consulted the oracle [*Virgilianas sortes consuleret*], which means that he took a random text to indicate his fate. The text referred to is *Aen.* 6.808–12 of Numa Pompilius, where it says that a man with a hoary head and beard will establish Rome anew (*Had.* 2.8).[4] Thus the text becomes an *omen*. Cicero compares the diviners to *grammatici* who are able to interpret the poets (*Div.* 1.34). This attitude naturally paved the way for looking upon the classical epics as open to exploitation by Christians interpreters like the centonists.

In the second place, Homer was omniscient: "Homer's epics were held to be encyclopaedic; with the help of interpretation, everything could be extracted from his writings."[5] Plato ironizes, but nonetheless attests how widespread this idea was, that Homer knew all things, human and divine [καὶ τά γε θεῖα] (*Resp.* 598E). It is not difficult to imagine that this suggested the notion of digging into Homer to find Christian truth there as well. No topic was left unaddressed by the great poet. Thirdly, another means of extracting meaning from the epics was allegory. Fourthly, another hermeneutic approach, sometimes seen as an alternative to allegory, was expressed in the maxim "to elucidate Homer by Homer;"[6] a principle proceeding from the conviction that Homer was divinely inspired. These points are just a summary of commonly held opinions on the great poets. These hermeneutical principles may individually, not to say when taken together, easily further a renewed reading of Homer and Virgil. As a matter of

---

(bibliomancy); see Pierre Courcelle, "L'enfant et les 'sorts virgiliens'," *VC* 7 (1953) who takes Augustine's famous *tolle lege* (*Conf.* 8.12.29) as an example of this. This example is revealing as to a reading done according to an unsystematic attitude taken to the text; see Sandnes, *The Challenge of Homer*, 214–5.

[4] See also *Clodius Albinus* 5.4 who made an inquiry [*sortem tollere*] to the oracle of Apollo in Cumae about his fate. The answer given to him was *Aen.* 6.857–8 cf. *Severus Alexander* 14.5 where a Virgilian text is seen as a sign [*signum*] that he will become emperor.

[5] Sandnes, *The Challenge of Homer*, 45.

[6] For this maxim, see James I. Porter, "Hermeneutic Lines and Circles: Aristarchus and Crates on the Exegesis of Homer", in *Homer's Ancient Readers. The Hermeneutics of Greek Epic's Earliest Exegetes,*" ed. Robert Lamberton and John J. Keaney (Princeton, NJ: Princeton University Press, 1992), 70, 76–77; Sandnes, *The Challenge of Homer*, 53–54.

fact, in this perspective Christianizing their epics is no less than bringing to completion how the great poets were commonly construed in antiquity. The centonists' claim that Homer and Virgil prefigured the story of Christ is definitely a Christian idea, but in making this claim they were in fact aligning themselves structurally with more common ways of reading and making use of the poets. What appears rather awkward to a modern interpreter, therefore, makes perfect sense from the perspective of the ancient reception of the poets. Furthermore, the cento genre itself contributed further to this potential for reading the poets in a Christian way, by its very nature of considering the classical epics texts open to be bent.

7.2 MICRO AND MACRO LEVELS

The centos we have been looking at keep very close to Homer's and Virgil's texts, almost verbatim. This applies to the micro level of the centos in which the detailed *mimesis* of the classical texts is unfolded. At the micro level, the centonists interfere only slightly with the inherited text. Finding the appropriate wording in Homer or Virgil to tell the story of Jesus is a key occupation for centonists working on the micro level. It happens quite often that finding the right terms and lines is so dominant that the centonists seem not to have paid attention to the fact that the context and the figure from where they took the wording must have been offensive to Christian sentiments; wording is then more important than context or the figure to whom the wording is applied in the hypotext. We noted that this might have been one of the reasons that Jerome found Proba's cento offensive.

At the macro level, however, things look very different. This level is not equally visible, and it therefore takes a reader familiar with both texts to get at it. This "hidden" text informs the reader how the lines are organized to make a new text. The macro level in Christian centos does not come from Homer or Virgil; it is biblical texts and traditions attached to them.

This means that one of the critical points raised by Margaret Mitchell and myself against Dennis R. MacDonald misses its target. We both criticized MacDonald for claiming analogies which were slippery, abruptly jumping from the one to the other: "What began as a Jesus—Odysseus parallel emplotment becomes a Jesus—Hector one, even as sometimes it is Telemachus the son, not Odysseus, whose career Mac-

Donald regards as parallelled by the Markan Jesus".[7] Such a critique assumes comparisons of plots. At the micro level plots are not decisive; the centonists move freely, seemingly undisturbed by the fact that they proceed in a concordance-like way.

At the macro level, however, things look different. In order to make a new text, the centonists did indeed interfere at the macro level, and in a way that entirely altered the very plot of the epics. This applies to the narrative substructure providing the cento with its organizing principle and chronology. We saw that the macro level for both Proba and Eudocia was a Christian "Heilsgeschichte" culminating in the life of Jesus. It is at the macro level that it is decided whether it is a cento about sex, bread, dicing or salvation. The reciprocity between the two levels is precisely what the centos aim at, and is also the point where "Verfremdung" takes place.

The Christian centonists relate to their hypotexts, be they Homer or Virgil, in various ways. They sometimes approach the hypotext as a quarry from where more or less isolated units are found appropriate; it is then simply a matter of coincidence in language. At other times, they engage with the wider context in more conscious ways, often in a contrasting or transcending way. This has been labelled "Kontrastimitation," "transformation," "transvaluation," "transposition" or "Verfremdung." Through contrasts, unexpected bendings, astonishments and curiosity, a heightened understanding of the hypotext is achieved. Dennis R. MacDonald has rightly called this a *Kulturkampf*, and I have argued that this corresponds to a hermeneutical *synkrisis* at home in rhetorical criticism. Canonical texts are compared, juxtaposed, evaluated, and finally ranked.

7.3   Mimesis Involving two "Canonical" texts

In the Christian centos, the centonists succeeded in keeping the two canonical bodies together. The hypotext represents *verba* with rhythm and style, while the biblical text furnishes the *res* or *sensus*; thus creating

---

[7] Mitchell, "Homer in the New Testament," 249; similarly Sandnes, "Imitatio Homeri?." This is also pointed out by Usher, *Homeric Stitchings*, 144: "the referents in Cento appropriation are not stable, nor the grounds for comparison consistent: Judas, the demoniac, and Jesus are all compared to Ajax; both Christ and the demoniac are compared to Hector." Confer the flexibility we have observed with regard to the homecoming motif.

a cultural symbiosis. In this symbiosis, the hypotext is being fulfilled, a heightened understanding of the classical text is reached, and the biblical text is improved upon in outer appearance. The hypotext is thus given a place within a greater divine plan. This happens in a steady oscillation between patterns of intertextual consonance and dissonance, continuity and discontinuity.[8] These two work together and bring about surprises, irony and idiosyncratic allegory. This implies that the allegory is not primarily a point-by-point allegory, but includes narrative plots as well. We have seen that this sometimes appears as an analogical imitation, implying a simple comparison. On other occasions, the imitations are contrastive, marking differences or alterations. At the end of the day, all imitations serve within a pattern of comparison where the hypertext surpasses what the hypotext is about.

Comparison of canonical texts is a speciality within rhetorical comparison or *synkrisis*. It tends to be less triumphalist and arrogant than the typological exegesis where Christians oppose both the Jewish and Graeco-Roman contexts. In the centos this takes a different form, since there is a fundamental acceptance of comparing *two* canonical bodies; both are assigned dignity and authority, albeit in quite different ways. This investigation has formulated this as the play between content or matter and style, rhythm and vocabulary; *res* or *sensus* versus *eloquentia*. The Christian centonists held a view of canon that differed somewhat from that of Irenaeus and Tertullian. To the two Church Fathers, canon was primarily seen as conveying doctrine. The centonists fundamentally shared their view on *res*, since this is the decisive point in their poems. But through *res* they were involved in a creativity separating them from Tertullian and Ireneaus. To the centonists, the power of canonicity was not limited to doctrine.[9] They certainly cared about the doctrine, but they did not work only with that, as they engaged in a work of creativity inspired by the biblical stories themselves.[10] According to the centonists, Christian truths lent themselves to be formulated in the venerable words of the past, thus forming a

---

[8] Schnapp, "Reading Lessons," 112.

[9] For this view on canonicity, see Alter, *Canon and Creativity*, 4–5, 57, 60–61.

[10] Scott Fitzgerald Johnson, *The Life and Miracle of Thecla. A Literary Study* (Cambridge, MA and London: Harvard University Press, 2006), 78–86 argues that the canon became a starting-point for a rewriting, a practice rooted in the idea of the "Rewritten Bible" in Judaism, i.e. the interpreted Bible.

symbiosis with the classical texts. Frances Young aptly describes the reaction of some Christians to the crisis caused by Julian: "In the first, place, Christian rhetoricians began to produce a new literature which had classical styles and genres but Christian content."[11] From the perspective of the centonists the idea of *Kulturkampf* is somewhat misleading. They are certainly not involved in an eristic enterprise against the epics. Christian centonists did not approach the epics as texts in which dangers were lurking.

Although all centos are ludic by nature, Scott McGill makes a helpful distinction between those where Virgil's *res*—this applies to Homer as well—is altered to a "content that is itself serious in nature and that belongs to the high literary tradition".[12] Hosidius Geta's *Medea*, a tragic Virgil, is a good example, but even Ausonius's cento "deals with highborn marriages."[13] The *res* of *Cento Nuptialis* no doubt has shock value, and it provokes laughter,[14] but "the Virgilian material is not degraded."[15] Hence it is ludic but not parodic. McGill points out that it is different with *De Alea* and *De Panificio*, where subjects are breadmaking and dicing respectively: "This content is certainly lower than the *Aeneid* and lower than even the most modest content found in the *Eclogues* and *Georgics*."[16] They apply high poetry to a low content, in order to evoke laughter. How do Proba and Eudocia fit this distinction between centos with a serious *res* and those with a parodic *sensus*? There is no doubt that these two Christian centonists would consider their poems in themselves serious, and worthy of Virgil's high poetry. But how would a person of Julian's mind view them? His evaluation would certainly be more sinister, claiming the whole enterprise to be unjustified. Very likely, such a person would judge them in ways comparable to how Tertullian and Irenaeus regarded the deconstructional power of cento composition. In other words, from this perspective, Christian centos would be considered impossible, simply because they

---

[11] Frances Young, "Classical Genres in Christian Disguise, Christian genres in Classical Guise", ed. Frances Young, Lewis Ayres, Andrew Louth, *The Cambridge History of Early Christian Literature* (Cambridge: Cambridge University Press, 2004), 251.

[12] McGill, *Virgil Recomposed*, 54.

[13] McGill, *Virgil Recomposed*, 54.

[14] I do not understand why McGill, *Virgil Recomposed*, 55 says that it does not possess a comic character.

[15] McGill, *Virgil Recomposed*, 55.

[16] McGill, *Virgil Recomposed*, 55.

distorted the given *res*. Julian, together with Irenaeus and Tertullian, held a different view of authorial respect than did the centonists.

7.4 WHY CHRISTIAN CENTOS?

What brought biblical epics and centos in particular into being? My investigation has suggested two answers to this, one literal and one historical. A sense of embarrassment on behalf of the Gospels and Christian literature in general is felt throughout. Compared to the classical legacy, Christian texts appeared crude in both style and embellishment. The fictitious correspondence between Paul the Apostle and Seneca the Younger, written in the 4th century C.E.,[17] is a contemporary parallel example of the effort to deal with the cultural poverty of Christian texts. These apocryphal letters highlight this phenomenon, and represent an attempt at dealing with the problem of embarrassment in its own way.[18] "Seneca" wrote the following to Paul:

> For the Holy Spirit is in you and above all exalted ones gives expression by your sublime speech to the most venerable thoughts. I could wish therefore [*vellem itaque*] that when you express such lofty thoughts a cultivated form of discourse should not be lacking to their majesty [*ut maiesti earum cultus sermonis non desit*]. And that I may conceal nothing from you, brother, or burden my conscience, I confess that the emperor was moved by your sentiments. When I had read to him about the origin of power in you, he said that he could only wonder that a man who had not enjoyed the usual education should be capable of such thoughts [*qui non legitime imbutus sit taliter sentiat*]. To which I answered that the gods are wont to speak through the mouths of the innocent [*ore innocentium*], not of those who by their education are able to prevaricate. I gave him the example of Vatienus, an educated countryman [*hominis rusticuli*], to whom two men appeared in a field at Reate who afterwards are named Castor and Pollux; with that he seems sufficiently instructed (*Ep. 7*).

---

[17] See Cornelia Römer, "The Correspondence between Seneca and Paul", in *New Testament Apocrypha Vol. 2*, ed. Edgar Hennecke, Wilhelm Schneemelcher and R. Mcl. Wilson (Louisville, KE: Westminster John Knox Press, 2003), 46–47; Alfons Fürst, Therese Fuhrer, Folker Siegert, Peter Walter, ed. and trans., *Der apokryphe Briefwechsel zwischen Seneca und Paulus* (Tübingen: Mohr Siebeck, 2006), 6–10, 69–70.

[18] This was pointed out to me by the anonymous reader who commented upon my manuscript.

This letter addresses a lack of correspondence between content and style in the letters of the Apostle, drawing on the well-known rhetorical distinction between *res* and *verba*.[19] Precisely because they contained lofty thoughts [*virtus*], the philosopher wished [*vellem itaque*] them to have a corresponding style. The incongruity between *res/sensus* and *verba*, with which this Christianised "Seneca" is concerned, is due to Paul being both *innocens* and *risticulus*,[20] which implies his lack of proper education.[21] A theological construct develops from this incongruity; namely that God reveals hidden mysteries to simple people.[22] *Ep.* 13 speaks very much in the same vein. The great power at work in the Apostle's thoughts [*rerum tanta vis*] is, according to the philosopher, "to be adorned not with verbal trappings but with a certain refinement [*non ornamento verborum, sed cultu quodam decoranda est*]." The Apostle should have no fear that his *res* will be affected by rhetorical refinement. The task entrusted to him is well fulfilled even if regard is given to correct Latin,[23] "noble words and proper form [*honestis vocibus et speciem*]." Accordingly in *Ep.* 9 "Seneca" says that he has sent to Paul *librum de verborum*. Cornelia Römer renders this "a book on verbosity," while Fürst renders it "ein Buch 'Über den reichen Wortschatz;'" the aim of which is to have Paul alleviating the verbal and rhetorical deficit of his texts.

This Correspondence is of great value for understanding the atmosphere that brought forth various ways of coping with what many intellectual Christians found to be the deficit of their literary legacy in

---

[19] For the rhetorical currency of this distinction, see Fürst, Fuhrer, Siegert, Walter, *Der apokryphe Briefwechsel zwischen Seneca und Paulus*, 60–61.

[20] Clearly echoing allegations made against the Christians from early on; see Sandnes, *The Challenge of Homer*, 149–58.

[21] Contrary to e.g. Jerome's *Ep.* 49.13 where it says that Paul's letters appear to be *verba simplicia et quasi innocentis hominis ac rusticani* ("simple words of an innocent and uneducated person"). To Jerome they are, however, compared to lightning [*fulmina sunt*]; this is pointed out by Fürst, Fuhrer, Siegert, Walter, ed. and trans. *Der apokryphe Briefwechsel zwischen Seneca und Paulus.* 48. To what extent Jerome thereby intends to say something about the rhetorical standard remains unclear to me; it seems rather to be about the power inherent in his message. The view expressed on Paul's education runs contrary to much contemporary exegesis as well; see e.g. Vegge, *Paulus und das antike Schulwesen*, 345–75.

[22] Fürst, Fuhrer, Siegert, Walter, *Der apokryphe Briefwechsel zwischen Seneca und Paulus*, 48 rightly draws attention to Matt 11:25; Luke 10:21, Ps 8:3 as well as to the role attributed to children in Roman divination (Cicero, *Div.* 2.86).

[23] This mistake, Paul writing in Latin, is due to the ignorance of the writer and his living distant from the real Paul, or the fact that his access to Paul's text is through a Latin translation, which still makes this an awkward statement.

the era when Christian centos came to life. In the texts just mentioned, "Seneca" is the mouthpiece of representative of attitudes that fostered texts like the centos.

From a historical perspective, Juvencus' attempt took place during Constantine and was therefore not affected by Julian's decree to keep Christians away from education and hence from classical texts. But "a drift into a respectable Christianity," as Peter Brown puts it,[24] was already on its way. Nonetheless, Julian's edict of 362 caused panic among Christians, particularly among the intellectuals who were thereby cut off from the inheritance in which the *logos* expressed itself. Christian sources almost unanimously claim that the imperial decree targeted not only teachers but also students and children. As for the latter, there is some historical doubt. This does not affect, however, the importance of this decree for the present study, namely that Christians acted upon their understanding of the law issued. Apollinarius for one did so; although he did not compose a Homeric Gospel, but rather Platonic dialogues.

7.5 Gospel Composition and Centos

Throughout this investigation, we have also been commenting upon Mimesis Criticism generally and the contributions of Dennis R. Mac-Donald in particular. He argues that the Gospels, especially Mark, as well as the Book of Acts are emulations of Homer. Marianne Palmer Bonz emphasized the role of Virgil in the Book of Acts. Mimesis Criticism rightly argues that New Testament dependence on the pagan literature cannot be limited to the quotations identified there; there is certainly a much wider dependence. Looking at Homer and Virgil from this perspective is, therefore, a most natural thing to do. Mac-Donald claims that the biblical epics of the 4th and 5th century are relevant analogies for how the above-mentioned biblical narrative texts came into being. The idea is that, just as Eudocia rewrote the life of Jesus in Homeric style, so did Mark as well—at least similarly enough to justify a comparison. A major difference is that while she had two texts to reconcile, Mark invented larger parts of his story on the basis

---

[24] Peter R.L. Brown, "Aspects of the Christianization of the Roman Aristocracy," *JRS* 51 (1961): 9.

of Homeric parallels he found it worthwhile to transvalue in light of Christian faith.

In my view, this is a fundamental difference. The centos are indeed examples that biblical texts were altered, embellished, expanded on, and sometimes even invented, but the centonists had at their disposal biblical texts from which to proceed. The alterations and inventions are often comprehensible in the light of the wider Christian tradition, which implies that the hypertexts in Christian centos are something more than merely transmitted texts. On the basis of the accessibility of Homer in Antiquity, MacDonald argues that Homeric allusions are there, albeit in a subtle and concealed form. He may well be right that readers well-versed in Homer may find allusions to his epics, perhaps most densely in the passion story as a Jesus—Hector comparison. But judged by what we have learned from the nature of the centos and MacDonald's claim that a cultural struggle between two legacies is going on here, the absence of advertised intertextuality is indeed problematic. Cultural struggle between texts requires identification far beyond general accessibility in the culture. This is what we learn from the very analogies he claims. In my opinion it is necessary to distinguish between on the one hand *mimesis* performed in order to embellish a text or to present the author as an erudite and culturally-trained person, and on the other hand *mimesis* as a means of cultural struggle. In fact, concealed intertextuality and claiming that centos are analogies to the Gospels are contradictory viewpoints. There is certainly much concealed interpretation going on in the centos; there are layers of meaning to explore. But one thing is sure: There is no concealment with regard to the bodies of texts involved.

In addition to using their hypotext verbatim, the centonists also added a poem or a prologue to their poems; not a proper part of the cento itself however, but working as a metatext. Proba and Eudocia did this; so did Ausonius, and also Juvencus. The centonists considered it necessary to instruct their audience how to read their epics. The introduction serves to notify the reader and to guide her to the macro level in the centos and to the canonical texts involved. The prologue gives the macro perspective from which the micro level is to be understood; in other words, the level from which the deconstruction of the hypotext gives way to a new text. The prologue advertises the perspective from which Virgil or Homer will be read, be it about sex or salvation. In my opinion, the fact that these two great poets were generally accessible cannot make up for the lack of advertising, especially if the purpose is to embark upon a *Kulturkampf.*

Tracing the Homeric or Virgilian imitation demonstrated in the biblical epics of the 4th and 5th century back to Mark and Acts is indeed difficult, since they belong so much further down the road. In addition to the historical distance, three important observations substantiate this difficulty. In the first place, biblical epics and centos came to life among Christians who found the literary style of the Gospels cruder than the classical literature. By necessity, this implies that the Gospels were there already. Using texts which came into being in order to address precisely this problem as analogies for the genesis of the Gospels themselves, is circular logic. Secondly, Julian created a situation that called for a response. It is a riddle why Julian's edict made it necessary to rewrite biblical texts in a classical style if the Gospels were already soaked in Homer. The response to Julian's law is hardly evidence for what happened about three centuries earlier; here chronology matters. Thirdly, the centos came to life among the senatorial class of Roman society. The analogy claimed by Mimesis Criticism involves a picture of the Gospels and of Acts as composed by a similar elite. The social milieu behind the poems raises questions about the Gospels' social context that calls for more consideration than hitherto given to it.

In his "My Turn," published on his homepage, MacDonald presents what he considers a parallel that would satisfy those who found his examples from Mark's Gospel less than convincing, namely the Passion Narrative in the *Gospel of Nicodemus.* He builds on observations made by J. Rendel Harris in 1898 (*The Homeric Centones and the Acts of Pilate*), and says that he is presently writing a book on the topic: "The links I made in my book between Mark's Passion and the *Iliad* are largely congruent with those in recension M of the Gospel of Nicodemus. Jesus plays a role similar to that of Hector, and Pilate that of Achilles. Joseph of Arimathea, not Joseph of Nazareth, plays the role of Hector's father, Priam. The Theotokos resembles Hecuba and Mary Magdalene resembles Andromache. One simply cannot say that no one recognized the similarities between the deaths of Jesus and Hector that ultimately trace back to Mark."[25] It is not quite clear yet how MacDonald will consider this narrative Homeric Gospel vis-à-vis the centos, but it seems that he is arguing that it is inspired by

---

[25] MacDonald, "My Turn," 22.

the cento's bringing together of Homer and the Gospels. We are now well into the 6th century. It is possible that this narrative has a relationship to the centos, although that remains to be worked out. Even if that claim can be substantiated, this hardly takes us further back than to the centos themselves. My investigation argues that the centos are a phenomenon, not only by accident, but by necessity, of the 4th and 5th centuries. Arguing that the *Gospel of Nicodemus* is dependent upon the centos brings nothing to the question of Mark as such.

From the idea that the classical epics are "open," and therefore to be interpreted and reconfigured, it follows naturally that there is no one fixed "Gospel according to Homer or Virgil." This has become very clear with regard to the *Homerocentones*. The different recensions are to some extent optional Homeric versions of the Life of Jesus, which is here more or less a harmony of the four canonical Gospels. It seems that lines were added more or less randomly to some core texts related to type scenes. This observation proves that Homer is not the text which brought the story into being. The life of Jesus is the primary, Homer the secondary. When for example Hector's rising up in the middle of a battle, or Achilles standing up to speak, become witnesses of the Resurrection, this is only possible if the biblical texts and traditions on the Resurrection are well established *independent of* the Homeric lines. The lines themselves do not create the story. There is a framework, an overarching plot, a macro level, into which the lines are fitted. It hardly makes sense to claim this literature as analogous to how the texts, from which this overarching plot is made up, came into being. What Christian cento composition, therefore, attests is that biblical faith informs a reading of Homer not possible on the basis of the Homeric texts themselves.

They represent attempts to bring together *eloquentia* and *veritas*. In my view it is a misunderstanding of the nature of the Christian centos to consider them paradigms for how Mark's Gospel or other Christian narratives came into being. The centos belong much further down the road. They belong in the time where attempts were made at "converting the culture", to borrow Jean-Claude Fredouille's description of how Christians of the third and fourth century came to terms with the classical legacy.[26] The very nature of the centos assumes the biblical texts or Christian traditions. No doubt these were embellished

---

[26] Jean-Claude Fredouille, *Tertullien et la Conversion de la Culture Antique* (Paris: Études augustiniennes, 1972).

and expanded, but the centos proceed from the fact that they have a given *res*, i.e. biblical tradition, which is now to be unfolded in a new way. Gregory Nagy in his foreword to Usher's *Homeric Stitchings*, says that this cento was "intended for performance before audiences who were intimately familiar with both Homer and the Bible. To say 'familiar' may well be an understatement. The Homeric Centos presuppose a veritable internalization of both Homer and the Bible for both the composer and the audience."[27]

This book was introduced by a reference to how Christians in various ways coped with the great epics of antiquity. The Christian centos represent a view where the epics were not longer only the text ἔξωθεν, coming from the outside;[28] they were not texts from which "spoils" were to be taken, in analogy with the "spoil of the Egyptians". Although competition and transvaluation are important in the *synkrisis* as it is unfolded in the centos, the centonists were at home in both bodies of literature; they had internalized both epics and Gospels. David Vincent Menconi presents the Christian cento as found in Proba in a way that calls for some comments. He considers the nature and aim of the Christianization of this genre to belong within "evangelisation" of the classical culture: "It is the perfect symbol of what was transpiring in the early Church: utilizing the best of non-Christian culture to argue that all that was good and true and beautiful in the ancient world spoke of Christ when understood correctly."[29] This means that he considers the Christian centos as apologetic literature using well-known strategies such as "making right use of" (usus or χρῆσις), "acting like bees," "the spoil of the Egyptians," and a propaideutic rationale.[30] All these hermeneutic models imply in some way that tribute is paid to the ancient culture with its texts, but they also involve a critical element of leaving something behind. It is primarily a matter of extracting from these things what is useful. To distinguish between good and bad is

---

[27] Usher, *Homeric Stitchings*, IX–X; cf. Pucci, *The Full-Knowing Reader* who emphasizes a learned readership, an observation which finds support in the Christian centos we do know.

[28] In my *The Challenge of Homer* I demonstrate that this was a common way of describing pagan literature in the debate on encyclical studies and Homer in particular.

[29] Menconi, "The Christian Cento and the Evangelization of Classical Culture," 110–1.

[30] All these models are presented throughout Gnilka, *CHRÊSIS*; Allen, *The Despoliation of Egypt* and Sandnes, *The Challenge of Homer*.

essential for the hermeneutics involved here. The Christian centos cannot be separated from this effort to cope with the culture. Nonetheless, I think Menconi is too easily fitting the centos into these models. The present study has argued that they have a idiosyncrasy that amounts to a *reciprocity* with regard to both the epics and the Bible. There is a need of ameliorating both canonical texts, in different ways though, one with regard to meaning and sense, and the other with regard to words and style.

The commingling of Jesus' life and ministry and the great epics of antiquity on the other hand, demonstrates the "trafficking in Homer and Virgil" also among Christians. It is the merit of Dennis R. MacDonald to have raised the question of how this might have affected how the Gospels were read in antiquity. The material presented in the present study sheds a fascinating light on how the Gospels may possibly have been read, when seen from this angle. But the nature of the centos makes it impossible to perceive them or their genre as in any way being a source or inspiration for the composition of the canonical Gospels.

The suggestions of Homeric imitations made by MacDonald have preoccupied me for some time now, particularly his suggestion that the Homeric epics form sources of the Gospel stories. I am far from convinced on that point, particularly in the light of the biblical epics addressed in this study. It seems to me that MacDonald, so far, is less dependent upon the analogy he claims for how Mark composed his Gospel. In my view, this claim is a blind alley, but a fascinating blind alley, well worth strolling down, and yielding much new insight into the world in which the Gospels were interpreted. It opens up a new world, not of how the Gospels and Acts came into being, but of a reception history largely unnoticed by New Testament scholarship.

BIBLIOGRAPHY

1. Tools

Dutripon, F.P. *Vulgatæ Editionis Bibliorum Sacrorum Concordantiæ*. Editio Quinta. Barri-ducis: RR. PP. Coelestini Successors, 1874.

Frisk, Hjalmar. *Griechisches Etomologisches Lexicon Band 1. A-Ko*. Heidelberg: Carl Winter Universitätsverlag, 1960.

Glare, P.G.W., *Oxford Latin Dictionary*. Oxford: Clarendon Press, 1982.

Hornblower, Simon and Spawforth, Anthony. *Oxford Classical Dictionary 3rd Edition*. Oxford University Press, 1996.

Lampe, G.W.H. *A Patristic Greek Lexicon*. Oxford: Clarendon Press, 1961.

Liddell, Henry George, Scottt, Robert; Jones, Henry-Stuart. A Greek-English Lexicon. Oxford: Clarendon Press 1996.

Passow, Franz. *Handwörterbuch der Griechischen Sprache*. Leipzig: Fr. Chr. Wilh. Vogel, 1841.

Suidae Lexicon, Graeca et Latine ad Fidem Optimorum Librorum Exactum post Thomam Gaisfordum Recensuit et Annotatione Critica Instruxit Godofredus Bernhardy, Tomus Prior. Halis et Brunsvigae: M. Bruhn, 1853.

2. Primary Sources

The Greek Anthology

W.R. Paton, ed. and trans., *The Greek Anthology in Five Volumes Vol. 1*. LCL. Cambridge MA and London: Harvard University Press and William Heinemann Ltd., 1980.

Anthologia Latina

Buecheler, Franciscus et Riese, Alexander, ed., *Anthologia Latina Pars Prior. Carmina in Codicibus Scripta Fasc 1*. Teubner: Leipzig, 1894.

Apollinarius

Ludwich, Arthurus, ed., *Apolinarii Metaphrasis Psalmorum*. Leipzig: B.G. Tevbneri, 1912.

Augustine

Chadwick, Henry, trans. *Saint Augustine. Confessions. A New Translation*. Oxford, New York: Oxford University Press, 1991.

Christopher, Joseph P., trans., *St. Augustine. The First Cathecetical Instruction* [*De Catecechizandis Rudibus*]. ACW 2. Westminster ML: The Newman Bookshop 1946.

Madec, Goulven, ed. and trans., *La Première Catéchèse. De cathecizandibus rudibus*. Bibliothèque Augustinienne. Études Augustiniennes 1991.

Green, Roger P.H., *Augustine*. ed. and trans., *De Doctrina Christiana*, Oxford: Clarendon Press, 1995.

Hill, Edmond, trans., *Sermons III (51–94). The Works of Saint Augustine. A Translation for the 21st Century*, Brooklyn, New York: New City Press, 1991.

Ausonius

Green, Roger P.H., ed. *The Works of Ausonius. Edited with Introduction and Commentary*. Oxford: Clarendon Press, 1991.
White, Hugh G. Evelyn, ed. and trans., *Ausonius with an English translation in two volumes*. LCL. London and New York: William Heinemann and G.P. Putnam's Sons, 1919–1921.

Clement of Alexandria

Stählin, Otto, ed., *Clemens Alexandrinus. Erster Band. Protrepticus und Paedagogos*, GCS 12a, Berlin: Akademie Verlag, 1972.

Decretum Gelasianum

Von Dobschütz, Ernst, ed., *Das Decretum Gelasianum De libris recipiendis et non recipiendis*, TUGAL 38, Leipzig: J.C. Hinrichs'sche Buchhandlung, 1912.

Dionysius of Halicarnassus

Usener, Hermann and Radermacher, Ludwic, ed., *Dionysii Halicarnasei Opuscula. Volumen Quintum*, Leipzig: B.G. Teubner, 1899.
——. ed., *Dionysii Halicarnasei Opuscula. Volumen Sextum*, Leipzig: B.G. Teubner, 1904–29.
Pritchett, W. Kendrick, trans., *Dionysios of Halicarnassus: On Thucydides. English Translation based on the Greek text of Usener-Radermacher with Commentary*, Berkely, Los Angeles, London: University of California Press, 1975.
Aujac, Germaine, ed. and trans, *Denys D'Halicarnasse Opuscules Rhetorique Tome V. L'Imitation (Fragments, Épitomé), Prémière Lettre à Ammee, Lettre à Pompée Géminos, Dinarque*. Opuscules rhetoriques. Paris: Les Belles Lettres, 1992.

Evagrius Scholasticus

Hübner, Adelheid, trans., *Evagrius Scholasticus. Historia Ecclesiastica*, FC 57/1–2, Turnhout: Brepols Publishers, 2007.

Heliodorus

Hadas, Moses, trans. *An Ethiopian Romance*, Westport Connecticut: Greenwood Press, Publishers, 1976.

Heraclitus

Russell, Donald A and Konstan David, ed. and trans. *Heraclitus: Homeric Problems*. SBLWGRW 14. Atlanta, GA: Society of Biblical Literature, 2005.

Homer

Murray, A.T., ed. and trans., *Homer. The Iliad Books 1–12*. LCL 170. Cambridge, MA and London: Harvard University Press, 1998 (= 1924).
——. *Homer. The Iliad. Books 13–24*. LCL 171. Cambridge, MA and London: Harvard University Press, 1993 (= 1925).
Murray, A.T.; Dimock, George E., ed. and trans., *Homer. The Odyssey Books 1–12*. LCL 104. Cambridge, MA and London: Harvard University Press, 1995.
——, *Homer. The Odyssey Books 13–24*. LCL 105. Cambridge MA and London: Harvard University Press, 1995.

Homerocentones

Ludwich, Arthurus, ed., *Eudociae Augustae Procli Lycii Claudiani Carminum Graeco-rum Reliquiae accedunt Blemyomachiae Fragmenta*, Leipzig: B.G. Teubner, 1897.

Rey, André-Louis, ed. and trans., *Patricius, Eudocie, Optimus Côme de Jerusalem. Centons Homerique (Homerocentra). Introduction. Texte Critique, Traduction, Notes et Index*. SC 437. Paris: Cerf, 1998.

Schembra, Rocco, ed. *Homerocentones*. CCSG 62. Turnhout & Leuven: Brepols Publishers & Leuven University Press, 2007.

Usher, M.D., ed. *Homerocentones Eudociae Augustae*. Stuttgart: Teubner, 1999.

Hosidius Geta

Lamacchia, Rosa, ed., *Hosidii Getae Medea Cento Virgilianus*. Bibliotheca Scriptorum Graecorum et Romanorum Tevneriana, Leipzig: Teubner Verlagsgesellschaft, 1981.

Irenaeus

Rousseau, Adelin, ed. trans., *Irenee de Lyon, Contre Les Hérésies Livre 1*. SC 264. Paris: Cerf, 1979.

Brox, Norbert, ed. and trans., *Irenäus von Lyon. Epideixis, Adversus Haereses. Darlegung der apostolischen Verkündignung. Gegen die Häresien. Griechisch, Lateinisch, Deutsch I*. FC 8/1. Freiburg etc.: Herder, 1993.

——. ed. and trans., *Irenäus von Lyon. Adversus Haeresis. Gegen die Häresien II*. FC 8/2. Freiburg. etc.: Herder, 1993.

Isidore of Seville

Lindsay, W.M., ed., *Isidori Hispalensis Episcopi Etymologiarum sive Originum*. Oxford: Clarendon Press 1987 (reprint 1911).

Itala

Jülicher, Adolf, ed. *Itala. Das Neue Testament in altlateinischer Überlieferung* 1–4. Berlin: Walter de Gruyter, 1938–63.

Jerome

Bonnard, Émile, ed. and trans., *Saint Jérôme Commentaire sur S. Matthieu Tome 1 (Livres 1–11)*. SC 242. Paris: cerf, 1977.

Helm, Rudolf, ed., *Die Chronik des Hieronymus. Eusebius Werke Siebenter Band, Hieronymi Chronikon*. GCS 47, Berlin: Akademia Verlag, 1956.

Halton, Thomas P., ed. and trans., *Saint Jerome On Illustrious Men, The Fathers of the Church. A New Translation*. Washington D.C.: The Catholic University of America Press, 1999.

Richardson, Ernest Cushing, *Hieronymus Liber De Viris Inlustribus. Gennadius Liber De Viris Inlustribus*. TU 14/1. Leipzig: Hinrichs'sche Buchhandlung 1896.

Julian Emperor

Bidez, J. ed., *L'Empereur Julien. Oeuvres Complètes. Tome 1.2 Lettres et Fragments*. Paris: Les Belles Lettres, 1924.

Hoffmann, R. Joseph, trans., *Julian's Against the Galileans*, New York: Prometheus Books, 2004.

Wright, Wilmer Cave, ed. and trans., *The Works of the Emperor Julian in Three Volumes*. LCL 13; 29; 157. Cambridge MA and London: Harvard University Press and William Heinemann Ltd., 1980 (= 1913); 1992 (= 1913); 1993 (= 1913).

Justin Martyr

Goodspeed, Edgar J., ed., *Die ältesten Apologeten. Texte mit kurzen Einleitungen.* Göttingen: Vandenhoeck & Ruprecht 1984.

Juvencus

Hvemer, Iohannis, ed., *Gai Vetti Aqvilini Ivvenci Evangeliorum Libri Quatvor.* CSEL 24. Wien, Leipzig: F. Tempsky; G. Freytag, 1891.

Lactantius

Brandt, Samuel, ed., *L. Caeli Firmiani Lactanti, Diviniae Institutiones et Epitome Divinarum Institutionum.* CSEL 19. Prague, Vindobonae, Lipsiae: F. Tempsky; G. Freytag, 1890.
Monat, Pierre, ed. and trans., *Lactance. Institutions Divines. Livre V. Tome I et II.* SC 204–5. Paris: Cerf, 1973.
Ingremeau, Christiane, ed. and trans., *Lactance. Institutions Divines. Livre VI.* SC 509. Paris: Cerf, 2007.
Bowen, Anthony and Garnsey, Peter, trans., *Lactantius. Divine Institutes. Translated with an introduction and Notes*, Liverpool: Liverpool University Press, 2003.

Melito of Sardes

Hall, Stuart G., ed., *Melito of Sardes On Pascha and Fragments*, Oxford: Clarendon Press, 1979.

Macrobius

Willis, Jacob, ed., *Ambrosii Theodosii Macrobii Saturnalia.* Teubneriana, I–II. Leipzig: B.G. Teubner, 1963.
Davies, Percival V., trans., *Macrobius. The Saturnalia translated with an Introduction and Notes*, New Yorn and London: Columbia University Press, 1969.

Marcellinus

Seyfarth, W., ed. *Ammianus Marcellinus Rerum Gestarum quae supersunt Vol. 1. Libri XIV–XXV*, Stuttgart and Leipzig: Teubner 1999.

New Testament Apocrypha

Wilson, R. Mcl., trans., *New Testament Apocrypha. Vol. 2. Writings Relating to the Apostles; Apocalypses and Related Subjects. Revised Edition.* Louisville, KE: Westminster John Knox Press, 2003.

The Gospel of Nicodemus (Acta Pilati)

Tischendorf, Constantinus de, ed., *Evangelia Apocrypha. Adhibitis Plurimis Codibus Graecis et Latinis Maximam Partem nunc Primum Consultis atque Ineditorum Copia Insignibus*, Lipsiae: Hermann Mendelssohn, 1876.
Kim, H.C., ed., *The Gospel of Nicodemus. Gesta Salvatoris. Edited from Codex Einsidlensis. Einsideln Stiftsbibliothek, MS 326*, Toronto Medieval Latin Texts. Toronto: Pontificial Institute of Medieval Studies, 1973.
Elliott, J.K., trans., *The Apocryphal New Testament. A Collection of Apocryphal Christian Literature in an English Translation based on M.R. Jones*, Oxford: Clarendon Press, 1993.

Origen

Chadwick, Henry, trans., *Origen Contra Celsum*, Cambridge; Cambridge University Press, 1965.

Crouzel, Henri et Simonetti, Manlio, ed. and trans., *Origène Traité de Principes Tome III; Tome IV*. SC 268–9. Paris: Cerf, 1980.

Gürgemanns, Herwig und Karpp, Heinrich, ed. and trans., *Origenes Vier Bücher von den Prinzipien*. Texte zur Forschung 24. Darmstadt: Wissenscaftliche Buchgesellschaft, 1976.

Orosius Paulus

Arnaud-Linet and Marie-Pierre, eds., *Orose. Histoires (Contre les Païens) Tome III. Livre VII*, Paris: Les Belles Lettres, 1991.

Deferrari, Roy J., trans., *Paulus Orosius. The Seven Books of History Against the Pagans*, The Fathers of the Church. A New Translation, Washington: The Catholic University of America, Press 1981.

Petronius

Heseltine, Michael and Warmington, E.H., ed. and trans., *Petronius*, LCL. Cambridge MA and London: Harvard University Press and Wm. Heinemann, 1987.

Philostorgius

Bidez, Joseph und Winkelmann, Friedrich, eds., *Philostorgios Kirchengeschichte*. GCS. Berlin Akademia Verlag, 1972.

Pompei

Pompei: Pitture E Mosaici. Vol. 1. Regio I Parte Prima, Roma: Istituto della Enciclopedia Italiana, 1990.

Proba

Elizabeth A. Clark and Diane F. Hatch, ed. and trans., *The Golden Bough. The Oaken Cross. The Virgilian Cento of Faltonia Betitia Proba*. Text and Translations Series 5. Chico: Scholars Press, 1981.

Schenkl, Carolus, ed., *Poetae Christianae Minores* Pars 1. CSEL 16. Mediolani, Vlricvs Hoeplivs, Edidit 1888, pp. 511–609.

Progymnasmata

Kennedy, George A., trans., *Progymnasmata. Greek Textbooks*. SBLWGRW 10. Leiden, Boston: Brill, 2003.

Hock, Ronald F.; O' Neill, Edward N. trans., *The Chreia and Ancient Rhetoric. Classroom Exercises*. SBLWGRW 1. Atlanta. Society of Biblical Literature, 2002.

Rufinus

Amidon, Philip R., trans., *The Church History of Rufinus of Aquileia Books 10 and 11*. New York, Oxford: Oxford University Press 1997.

Scwartz, Eduard; Mommsen, Theodor, ed., *Eusebius Werke. Zweiter band. Die Kirchengeschichte. Die Lateinische Übersetzung des Rufinus*. GCS. Leipzig: J.C. Hinrichs'sche Buchhandlung, 1903–8.

Seneca and Paul

Fürst, Alfons; Fuhrer, Therese; Siegert, Volker; Walter, Peter. *Der apokryphe Brief-wechsel zwishen Seneca und Paulus.* SAPERE 11. Tübingen. Mohr Siebeck, 2006.
Römer, Cornelia. "The Correspondence between Seneca and Paul." In Edgar, Hen-necke, Wilhelm Schneemelcer, R. Mcl. Wilson, trans., *New Testament Apocrypha Vol. 2.* Louisville, KE: Westminster John Knox Press, 2003, 46–53.

Socrates, Church Historian

Hansen, Günther Christian and Manja Širinjan, ed. *Kirchengeschichte Socrates Scho-lastikus.* GCS. Berlin: Akademie Verlag 1995.
Périchon, Pierre; Maraval, Pierre, ed. *Socrate de Constantinople Histoire Ecclesiastique Livres II–III. Texte Grec de l'Edition G.C. Hansen (GCS).* Paris: Cerf, 2005.

Sozomen

Bidez, Joseph; Hansen, Günther Christian, eds., *Sozomenus Kirchengeschichte,* GCS 50, Berlin: Akademie Verlag, 1960.
Hansen, Günther Christian, ed. and trans. *Sozomenos. Historia Ecclesiastica. Kirch-engeschichte,* FC 73.2 and 4. Turnhout: Brepols 2004.
Sabbah, Guy, ed. and trans., *Sozomene. Histoire Ecclesiastique Livres V–VI.* SC 495. Paris: Cerf, 2005.

Suetonius

Kaster, Robert, ed. and trans., *C. Suetonius Tranquillus, De Grammaticis et Rhetoribus. Edited with a translation, introduction, and Commentary,* Oxford: Clarendon Press, 1985.

Tertullian

Schleyer, Dietrich, ed. and trans., *Tertullian: De Praescriptione Haereticorum, übersetzt und erklärt.* FC 42. Turnout: Brepols, 2002.
Willems, R., ed. *De Testimonio Animae.* CCSL 1. Turnout: Brepols 1954.

Theodoret

Parmentier, Leon, Günther Christian Hansen, eds., *Theodoret Kircehengeschichte.* GCS. Berlin: Akademie Verlag 1998.

Virgil

Fairclough, H. Ruston, ed. and trans. *Virgil. Eclogues. Georgics. Aeneid 1–6.* LCL 63. Cambridge, MA and London: Harvard University Press, 1994 (= 1935).
Fairclough, H. Ruston, ed. and trans., *Virgil. Aeneid 7–12. The Minor Poems.* LCL 64. cambridge MA and London: Harvard University Press and William Heinemann Ltd., 1986 (= 1934).

Zonaras

Dindorfius, Ludovicus, ed., *Iohannis Zonarae Epitome Historiarum,* Lipsiae: B.G. Teu-bneri, 1870.

Literature

Agosti, G. "L'epica biblica nella tarda antichità greca: autori e lettori nel IV e V secolo." In *La Scrittura infinita. Bibbia e Poesia in Età Medievale e Umaniscita.*

Atti del Convegno Internazionale (Firenze 26–28 giugno 1997), edited by Francesco Stella, 67–80. Florence: Sismel, 2001.

Aland, Barbara. "Christentum, Bildung und römische Oberschicht. Zum 'Octavianus' des Minucius Felix." In *Platonismus und Christentum. In Honour of H. Dörrie*, edited by Barbara Aland und Friedhelm Mann, 11–30. JAC Ergänzungsband 10. Münster: Aschendorff, 1983.

Alexander, Loveday. *Acts in its Ancient Literary Context. A Classisist Looks at the Acts of the Apostles*. Early Christianity in Context 289. London and New York: T&T Clark, 2005.

Allen, Joel S. *The Despoliation of Egypt in Pre-Rabbinic, Rabbinic and Patristic Traditions*. Supplements to VC 92. Leiden: Brill, 2008.

Alter, Robert. *Canonical Creativity. Modern Writing and the Authority of Scripture*. New Haven and London: Yale University Press, 2000.

Amatucci, A.G. *Storia della Letterature Latina*. Bari: G. Laterza, 1929.

Athanassiadi, Polymnia. *Julian. An Intellectual Biography*. London and New York: Routledge, 1992.

Balch, David L. "Paul's Portrait of Christ Crucified (Gal. 3.21) in Light of Paintings and Sculptures of Suffering and Death in Pompeiian and Roman Houses." In *Early Christian Families in Context. An Interdisciplinary Dialogue*, edited by David L. Balch and Carolyn Osiek, 84–108. Grand Rapids: Wm. B. Eerdmans, 2003.

——. *Roman Domestic Art and Early House Churches*. WUNT 228. Tübingen: Mohr Siebeck, 2008.

Banchich, Thomas M. "Julian's Schools Laws: Cod. Theod. 13.3.5 and *Ep.* 42." *The Ancient World* 24 (1993): 5–14.

Bartelink, G.J.M. "Sermo Piscatorius. Die 'Visserstaal' van den Apostelen." *Studia Catholica* 35 (1960): 267–77.

Bažil, Martin. *Centones Christiani. Métamorphose d'une Forme Intertextuelle dans la poési Latine Chrétienne de l'Antique Tardive*. Collection des Etudes Augustiennes. Série Moyen Âge et Temps Modernes 47. Paris: Institut d' Études Augustiennes, 2009.

Benko, Stephen. "Virgil's Fourth Eclogue in Christian Interpretation." *ANRW* II.1: 646–705.

Bonz, Marianne Palmer. *The Past as Legacy. Luke-Acts and Ancient Epic*. Minneapolis, MN: Fortress Press, 2000.

Bradshaw, Paul F.; Johnson, Maxwell E.; Phillips, L. Edward. *The Apostolic Tradition. A Commentary*. Hermeneia. Minneapolis: Fortress Press, 2002.

Braun, Ludwig and Engel, Andreas. "'Quellenwechsel' im Bibelepos des Iuvencus," *ZAC* 2 (1998): 123–38.

Brilliant, Richard. *Visual Narratives. Storytelling in Etruscan and Roman Art*. Ithaca and London: Cornell University Press, 1984.

Brown, Peter R.L. "Aspects of the Christianization of the Roman Aristocracy," *Journal of Roman Studies* 51 (1961): 1–11.

Browning, Robert. "The Byzantines and Homer." In *Homer's Ancient Readers. The Hermeneutics of Greek Epic's Earliests Exegetes*, edited by Robert Lamberton and John J. Keaney, 134–48. Princeton, NJ: Princeton University Press, 1992.

Bruce, F.F. *Commentary on the Book of Acts*. NICNT. Grand Rapids: Eerdmans Publishing Co., 1965.

Byrskog, Samuel. "The Early Church as a Narrative Fellowship. An Exploratory Study of the Performance of *Chreia*." *Tidsskrift for Teologi og Kirke* 78 (2007): 207–26.

Cameron, Alan. "The Empress and the Poet: Paganism and Politics at the Court of Theodosius II." *Yale Classical Studies* 27 (1982): 217–89.

Cancik, Hubert. "Standardization and Ranking of Texts in Greek and Roman Institutions." In *Homer, the Bible and Beyond. Literary and Religious Canons in the Ancient World*, edited by Margalit Finkelberg and Guy G. Stroumsa, 117–30. Jerusalem Studies in Religion and Culture 2. Leiden, Boston: Brill, 2003.

Chadwick, Henry, "Florilegium," *RAC* 7: 1131–60.
Coarelli, Filippo, "The Odyssey Frescoes of the Via Graziosa: A Proposed Context." *Papers of the British School at Rome* 66 (1998): 21–37.
Conte, Gian Biagio. *The Rhetoric of Imitation. Genre and Poetic Memory in Virgil and Other Latin Poets*. Ithaca and London: Cornell University Press, 1986.
Cook, John G. "Some Hellenistic Responses to the Gospels and Gospel Tradition." *ZNW* 84 (1993): 233–54.
——. "The Protreptic Power of Early Christian Language from John to Augustine." *VC* 48 (1994): 105–34.
——. *The Interpretation of the New Testament in Graeco-Roman Paganism*. Peabody MA: Hendrickson Publishers, 2002 (originally published Tübingen: Mohr Siebeck, 2000).
Courcelle, Pierre. "L'enfant et les 'Sorts Virgiliens'." *VC* 7 (1953): 194–220.
Cribiore, Raffaella. *Gymnastics of the Mind. Greek Education in Hellenistic and Roman Egypt*. Princeton, Oxford: Princeton University Press, 2001.
Dahl, Nils A. "La Terre où coulent le Lait et le Miel selon Barnabe 6.8–19." In Aux Sources de la Tradition Chrétienne. Mélanges offerts à M. Maurice Goguel, 62–70. Neuchatel/Paris: Delachaux et Niestlé, 1950.
——. "The Story of Abraham in Luke-Acts." In *Studies in Luke-Acts. In Honor of Paul Schubert*, edited by Leander E. Keck and J. Louis Martyn, 139–58. London: SPCK 1968.
Daniélou, Jean. *Gospel Message and Hellenistic Culture. A History of Early Christian Doctrine before the Council of Nicea Vol. 2*. London & Philadelphia: Darton, Longman & Todd and the Westminster Press, 1973.
Den Boeft, J., Drijvers, J.W., Den Hengst, D. Teitler, H.C., *Philological and Historical Commentary on Ammianus Marcellinus XXII*. Groningen: Egbert Forsten 1995.
Droge, Arthur. *Homer or Moses? Early Christian Interpreters of the History of Culture*. Tübingen: J.C.B. Mohr (Paul Siebeck), 1989.
Elm, Susanna. "Hellenism and Historiography: Gregory of Nazianzus and Julian in Dialogue." *Journal of Medieval and early modern Studies* 33 (2003): 493–515.
Ermini, Filippo. *Il Centone di Proba e la Poesia Centonaria Latina*. Roma: Ermanno Loescher, 1909.
Evenepoel, W. "The Place of Poetry in Latin Christianity." In *Early Christian Poetry. A Collection of Essays*, edited by J. den Boeft and A. Hilhorst, 35–60. Suppl. *VC* 22. Leiden etc.: Brill, 1993.
Fabry, H.-J. "*Sôd.*" *TDOT* 10: 171–8.
Ferguson, Everett. *Baptism in the Early Church. History, Theology, and Liturgy in the First Five Centuries*. Grand Rapids, MI: Wm. B. Eerdmans. 2009.
Finkelpearl, Ellen. "Pagan Traditions of Intertextuality in the Roman World." In *Mimesis and Intertextuality in Antiquity and Christianity*, edited by Dennis R. MacDonald, 78–90. Studies in Antiquity & Christianity. Harrisburg PA: Trinity Press International, 2001.
Focke, Friedrich. "Synkrisis," *Hermes* 58 (1923): 327–68.
Foley, John Miles. *A Companion to Ancient Epic, Blackwell Companion to the Ancient World*. Oxford: Blackwell Publishing, 2005.
Fredouille, Jean-Claude. *Tertullien et la Conversion de la Culture Antique*, Paris: Études augustiniennes, 1972.
Frisk, H. "Cento," *Griechisches Etymologisches Lexicon*, Vol. 1: 820–1.
Freund, Stefan. *Vergil im frühen Christentum. Untersuchungen zu den Vergilzitaten bei Tertullian, Minucius Felix, Novatian, Cyprian und Arnobius*. Studien zur Geschichte und Kultur des Altertums NF 16. Paderborn: Ferdinand Schöning, 2000.
Gärtner, Thomas. "Die Musen im Dienste Christi. Strategien der Rechtfertigung Christlicher Dichtung in der Lateinischen Spätantike." *VC* 58 (2004): 424–46.

Gemeinhardt, Peter. *Das lateinische Christentum und die antike pagane Bildung*. Studien und Texte zu Antike und Judentum 41. Tübingen: Mohr Siebeck, 2007.

Genette, Gérard. *Palimpsestes. La littérature au second degré*. Paris: Seuil, 1982.

Gilbert, Gary. "Roman Propaganda and Christian Identity in the Worldview of Luke-Acts." In *Contextualizing Acts. Lukan Narrative and Greco-Roman Discourse*, edited by Todd Penner and Caroline van der Stichele, 233–56. Atlanta: Society of Biblical Literature, 2003.

Gnilka, Christian. *ΧΡΗΣΙΣ. Die Methode der Kirchenväter im Umgang mit der antiken Kultur I. Der Begriff des ' rechten Gebrauches,'* Basel, Stuttgart: Scwabe, 1984.

Golega, Joseph. *Der Homerische Psalter. Studien über die dem Apollinarios von Laodikea zugeschribenenen Psalmenparaphrase*. Ettal: Buch-Kunstverlag Ettal, 1960.

Guyot, Peter; Klein Richard, *Das frühe Christentum bis zum Ende der Verfolgungen. Eine Dokumentation* Bd. 2, Darmstadt: Wissenschaftliche Buchgesellschaft, 1997.

Green, Roger P.H. "Proba's Cento: Its date, Purpose, and Reception." *Classical Quaterly* 45 (1995): 551–63.

——. "Proba's Introduction to her Cento." *Classical Quarterly* 47 (1997): 548–59.

——. *Latin Epics of the New Testament. Juvencus, Sedulius, Arator*. Oxford: Oxford University Press, 2006.

——. "The *Evangeliorum Libri* of Juvencus: Exegesis by Stealth?" In *Poetry and Exegesis in Premodern Latin Christianity. The Encounter between Classical and Christian Strategies of Interpretation*, edited by Willemien Otten and Karla Pollmann, 65–80. Supplements to VC. Leiden, Boston: Brill, 2007.

Hagendahl, Harald. *Latin Fathers and the Classics. A Study on the Apologists, Jerome and other Christian Writers*. Studia Graeca et Latina Gothoburgensia 6. Göteborg: Almquist & Wiksell, 1958.

——. *Augustine and the Latin Classics* Vol. II., Studia Graeca et Latina Gothoburgensia 22.II, Stockholm: Almqvist & Wiksell, 1967.

Hargins, Jeffrey W. *Against the Christians. The Rise of Early Christian Polemic*. Patristic Studies 1. New York, Bern: Peter Lang, 1999.

Harrison, Stephen J., "Palinurus," *Oxford Classical Dictionary*, 1100.

Harvey, Susan Ashbrook. "Women and words: Texts by and about Women." In *The Cambridge History of Early Christian Literature*, edited by Frances Young, Lewis Ayres, Andrew Louth, 382–90. Cambridge: Cambridge University Press, 2004.

Hägglund, Bengt. *History of Theology. Fourth Revised Edition*. St. Louis: Concordia, Publishing House, 2007.

Hägerland, Tobias. *Jesus and the Forgiveness of Sins. An Aspect of His Prophetic Mission*. D.D. dissertation at University of Gothenburg, Sweden 2009.

Hägg, T. "Hierocles the Lover of Truth and Eusebius the Sophist." *SO* 67 (1992): 138–50.

——. "Canon Formation in Greek Literary Culture." In *Canon and Canonicity. The Formation and use of Scripture*, edited by Einar Thomassen, 109–28. Copenhagen: Museum Tusculaneum Press 2010.

Heckel, Hartwig. "Zeitalter," *Der Neue Pauly* 12.2: 706–9.

Herzog, Reinhart. *Die Bibelepik der Lateinischen Spätantike. Formgechichte einer erbaulichen Gattung*. Texte und Abhandlungen 37. München: Fink, 1975.

——. *Restauration und Erneuerung die Lateinischen Literatur con 284 bis 374 n. Chr.* München: C.H. Beck'sche Verlagsbuchhandlung, 1989.

Hinds, Stephen. *Allusion and Intertext. Dynamics of Appropriation in Roman Poetry*. Cambridge: Cambridge University Press, 1998.

Hock, Ronald F. "Homer in Greco-Roman Education." In *Mimesis and Intertextuality in Antiquity and Christianity*, edited by Dennis R. MacDonald, 56–77. Studies in Antiquity and Christianity. Harrisburg PA: Trinity Press International, 2001.

——. "Paul and Greco-Roman Education." In *Paul in the Greco-Roman World. A Handbook*, edited by J. Paul Sampley, 198–227. Harrisburg, PA: Trinity Press International, 2003.

Hoffmann, R, Joseph. *Julian's Against the Galileans*. New York: Prometheus Books, 2004.

Iverson, Kelly R. *Gentiles in the Gospel of Mark. 'Even Dogs under the Table Eat the Children's Crumbs'*. LNTS 339. New York, London: T & T Clark International, 2007.

Izydorczyk, Zbigniew and Dubois, Jean-Daniel. "Nicodemus' Gospel Before and Beyond the Medieval West." In *The Medieval Gospel of Nicodemus. Texts, Intertexts, and Contexts in Western Europe*, edited by Zbigniew Izydorczyk, 21–41. Medieval & Renessaince Texts & Studies 158. Tempe: Arizona State University, 1997.

Janka, Markus. "*Quae philosophia fiut, satura facta est*. Julians 'Misopogon' zwischen Gattungskonvention und Sitz im Leben." In In *Kaiser Julian 'Apostata' und die philosophische Reaktion gegen das Christentum*, edited by Christian Schäfer, 177–206. Millenium Studies 21. Berlin: Walter de Gruyter, 2008.

Jervell, Jacob. "The Future of the Past: Luke's Vision of Salvation History and its Bearing on his Writing of History." In *History, Literature, and Society in the Book of Acts*, edited by Ben Witherington III, 104–26. Cambridge: Cambridge University Press, 1996.

Johnson, Scott Fitzgerald. *The Life and Miracles of Thecla. A Literary Study*. Hellenic Studies 13. Cambridge, MA and London: Harvard University Press, 2006.

Johnson, Maxwell E. *The Rites of Christian Initiation. Their Evolution and Interpretation. Revised and Expanded Edition*. Collegeville MN: Liturgical Press, 2007.

Jones, Christopher P. "Dinner Theater." In *Dining in a Classical Context*, edited by William J. Slater, 185–98. Ann Arbor: The University of Michigan Press, 1991.

Kallendorf, Craig. "Virgil's Post-Classical Legacy." In *A Companion to Ancient Epic, Blackwell Companion to the Ancient World*, edited by John Miles Foley, 574–88. Oxford: Blackwell Publishing, 2005.

Kaster, Robert A. *Guardians of Language. The Grammarian and Society in Late Antiquity*. Berkeley, CA: University of California Press, 1988.

Kennedy, George A. *Greek Rhetoric under Christian Emperors*. Princeton, NJ: Princeton University Press, 1983.

——. *New Testament Interpretation through Rhetorical Criticism*. Chapel Hill N.C. & London: University of North Carolina Press, 1984.

Klein, Richard. "Kaiser Julian's Rhetoren- und Unterrichtsgesetz," *RQ* 76 (1981): 73–94.

Kobusch, Theo. "Philosophische Streitsachen. Zur Auseinandersetzung zwischen christlicher und griechisher Philosophie." In *Kaiser Julian 'Apostata' und die philosophische Reaktion gegen das Christentum*, edited by Christian Schäfer, 17–40. Millenium Studies 21. Berlin: Walter de Gruyter, 2008.

Krestan. L. "Commodianus," *RAC* 3:248–52.

Kunzmann, F. & Hoch C. "Cento." In *Historisches Wörterbuch der Rhetorik* 2:148–57.

Kvalbein, Hans. "The Baptism of Jesus as a Model for Christian Baptism. Can the Idea be traced back to New Testament times?" *ST* 50 (1996): 67–83.

Lamberton, Robert. *Homer the Theologian. Neoplatonist Allegorical Reading and the Growth of the Epic Tradition*. Berkeley, Los Angeles, London: University of California Press, 1989.

Lamberton, Robert and Keaney John J. *Homer's Ancient Readers. The Hermeneutics of Greek Epics Earliest Exegetes*. Princeton, NJ: Princeton University Press, 1992.

Larsen, Kasper Bro. *Recognizing the Stranger. Recognition Scenes in the Gospel of John*. Biblical Interpretation Series 93. Leiden: Brill, 2008.

Lee, A.D. *Pagans & Christians in Late Antiquity. A Sourcebook*. London and New York: Routledge, 2000.

Lies, Lothar. *Origenes' 'Peri Archon.' Eine undogmatische Dogmatik*. Darmstadt: Wissenschaftliche Buchgesellschaft, 1992.

Lietzmann, Hans. *Apollinaris von Laodicea und seine Schule*. TU. Hildesheim, New York: Georg Olms Verlag, 1979 (= Tübingen: J.C.B. Mohr (Paul Siebeck), 1904).

Lim, Richard. "Augustine, the Grammarians and the Cultural Authority of Vergil." In *Romane Memento. Vergil in the Fourth Century*, edited by Roger Rees, 112–27. London: Gerald Duckworth & Co., 2004.

Lona, Horacio E. *Die 'wahre' Lehre des Kelsos. Übersetzt und erklärt, Kommentar zu frühchristlichen Apologeten*. Ergänzungsband 1. Freiburg: Herder, 2005.

Luz, Ulrich. *Das Evangelium nach Matthäus (Mt 1–7)*. EKK 1.1. Düsseldorf und Zürich: Benziger Verlag und Neukirchen Verlag, 2002.

MacCormack, Sabine. *The Shadows of Poetry. Vergil in the Mind of Augustine*. Transformation of the Classical Heritage 26. Berkeley, CA: University of Californisa Press, 1998.

MacDonald, Dennis R. *Christianizing Homer. The Odyssey, Plato, and The Acts of Andrew*. New York, Oxford: Oxford University Press, 1994.

——. "The Shipwrecks of Odyssey and Paul." *NTS* 45 (1999): 88–107.

——. *The Homeric Epics and the Gospel of Mark*. New Haven, CT and London: Yale University Press, 2000.

——. *Does the New Testament Imitate Homer? Four Cases from the Acts of the Apostles*. New Haven, CT and London: Yale University Press, 2003.

——. "The Breasts of Hecuba and those of the Daughters of Jerusalem. Luke's Transvaluation of a Famous Iliadic Scene." In *Ancient Fiction. The Matrix of Early Christianity and Jewish Narrative*, edited by Jo-Ann A. Brant, Charles W. Hedrick, Chris Shea, 239–54. SBLSymS 32. Atlanta: Society of Biblical Literature, 2005.

——. "A Categorization for Antetextuality in the Gospels and Acts: A Case for Luke's Imitation of Plato and Xenophon to Depict Paul as a Christian Socrates." In *The Intertextuality of the Epistles. Explorations of Theory and Practice*, edited by Thomas L. Broodie, Dennis R. MacDonald and Stanley E. Porter, 211–25. Sheffield: Sheffield Phoenix Press, 2006.

——. "Imitations of Greek Epic in the Gospels." In *The Historical Jesus in Context*, edited by Amy-Jill Levine, Dale C. Allison Jr., John Dominic Crossan, 372–84. Princeton Readings in Religion. Princeton and Oxford: Princeton University Press, 2006.

——. "My Turn. A Critique of Critics of 'Mimesis Criticism." www.iac.cgu.edu (printed May 2008).

Mack, Burton L. and Robbins, Vernon K. *Patterns of Persuasion in the Gospels*. Sonoma, CA: Polebridge Press, 1989.

Malamud, Martha A. *A Poetics of Transformation. Prudentius and Classical Mythology*. Ithaca and London: Cornell University Press, 1989.

Malbon, Elizabeth Struthers. "Ending at the beginning: A Response," *Semeia* 52 (1991) 175–84.

Malley, William J. *Hellenism and Christianity. The Conflict Between Hellenic and Christian Wisdom in the Contra Galilaeos of Julian the Apostate and the Contra Julianum of St. Cyril of Alexandria*. Analecta Gregoriana 68. Roma: Universita Gregoriana Editrice, 1978.

Markus, R.A. "Paganism, Christianity and the Latin Classics in the Fourth Century." In *Latin Literature of the Fourth Century*, edited by J.W. Binns, 1–21. Greek and Latin Studies Classical Literature and its Influence, London and Boston: Routledge & Kegan Paul, 1974.

Marrou, Henri-Irénée. *Saint Augustine et la Fin de la Culture Antique*. Paris: E. De Boccard, 1938.

McGill, Scott. *Virgil Recomposed. The Mythological and Secular Centos in Antiquity*. American Clasical Studies 48. Oxford, New York: Oxford University Press, 2005.

——. "Virgil, Christinanity, and the Cento Probae." In *Texts and Culture in Late Antiquity. Inheritance, Authority, and Change*, edited by J.H.D. Scourfield, 173–93. Swansea: The Classical Press of Wales 2007.

Meconi, David Vincent. "The Christian Cento and the Evangelization of Classical Literature." *Logos* 7 (2004): 109–32.

Mitchell, Margaret M. "Homer in the New Testament." *JR* 83 (2003): 244–60.

Morgan, Teresa. *Literate Education in the Hellenistic and Roman World*. Cambridge: Cambridge University Press, 1998.

Mühlenberg, Ekkehard. "Apollinaris." *TRE* 3:362–71.

——. *Apollinaris von Laodikea*. Forschungen zur Kirchen- und Dogmengeschichte 23. Göttingen: Vandenhoeck & Ruprecht, 1969.

Nestle, W. "Anklänge der Euripides in der Apostelgeschichte." *Philologus* 59 (1900): 46–57.

Opelt, Ilona. "Der zürnende Christus im Cento der Proba." *JAC* 7 (1964): 106–16.

Pavlovskis, Zoja. "Proba and the Semiotics of the Narrative Virgilian Cento." *Vergilius* 35 (1989): 70–84.

Penner, Todd and van der Stichele, Caroline. *Contextualizing Acts. Lukan Narrative and Greco-Roman Discourse*. SBL Symposium 20. Atlanta: Society of Biblical Literature, 2003.

Phillips, Peter. "Biblical Study and Intertextuality: Should the Work of Genette and Eco Broaden our Horizons?" In *The Intertextuality of the Epistles. Explorations of Theory and Practice*, edited by Thomas L. Broodie, Dennis R. MacDonald and Stanley E. Porter, 35–45. Sheffield: Sheffield Phoenix Press, 2006.

Plümacher, Eckhard. *Lukas als hellenistischer Schriftsteller. Studien zur Apostelgeschichte*. Göttingen: Vandenhoeck & Ruprecht, 1972.

——. "Die Missionsreden der Apostelgeschichte und Dionys von Halikarnass." *NTS* 39 (1993): 161–77.

——. "TERATEIA. Fiktion und Wunder in der hellenistisch-römischen Geschichtsschreibung und in der Apostelgeschichte." *ZNW* 89 (1998): 66–90.

Pollmann, Karla. "The Transformation of the Epic Genre in Christian Late Antiquity." In *Studia Patristica* Vol. 36, edited by M.F. sWiles amd E.J. Yarnold, 61–75. Leuven: Peeters 2001.

——. "Sex and Salvation in the Vergilian *Cento* of the Fourth Century." In *Romane memento. Vergil in the Fourth Century*, edited by Roger Rees, 79–96. London: Duckworth, 2004.

——. "Jesus Christus und Dionysios. Überlegungen zu dem Euripides-Cento Christis Patiens." *Jahrbuch der Österreichischen Byzantinistik* 47 (1997): 87–106.

Porter, James I. "Hermeneutic Lines and Circles: Aristarchus and Crates on The Exegesis of Homer." In *Homer's Ancient Readers. The Hermeneutics of Greek Epics Earliest Exegetes*, edited by Robert Lamberton and John J. Keaney, 67–114. Princeton, NJ: Princeton University Press, 1992.

Praeder, Susan Marie. "Acts 27:1–28:16: Sea Voyages in Ancient Literature and the Theology of Luke-Acts." *CBQ* 46 (1984): 683–706.

Pucci, John. *The Full-knowing Reader. Allusion and the Power of the Reader in the Western Literary Tradition*. New Haven and London: Yale University Press, 1998.

Rahner, Hugo. *Griechischen Mythen in christlicher Deutung*, Basel: Herder, 1984.

Rajak, Tessa. *Translation & Survival. The Greek Bible of the Ancient Jewish Diaspora*. Oxford: Oxford University Press, 2009.

Ratkowitsch, C. "Vergils Seesturm bei Juvencus und Sedulius." *JAC* 29 (1986): 40–58.

Rawson, Beryl. *Children and Childhood in Roman Italy*. Oxford: Oxford University Press, 2003.

Rees, Roger. *Romane Memento. Vergil in the Fourth Century*. London: Duckworth 2004.

Renehan, Robert. "Classical Greek Quotations in the New Testament." In *The Heritage of the early Church. Essays in Honor of Georges Vasilievich Florovsky*, edited by David Neiman and Margaret Schatkin, 17–46. Orientalia Christiana Analecta 195. Roma: Pont. Institutum Studiorum Orientalium, 1973.

Riley, Gregory J. "Mimesis of Classical Ideals in the Second Christian Century." In *Mimesis and Intertextuality in Antiquity and Christianity*, edited by Dennis R. MacDonald, 91–103. Harrisburg, PA: Trinity Press International, 2001.

Roberts, Michael. *Biblical Epic and Rhetorical Paraphrase in Late Antiquity*, Liverpool: Francis Cairns, 1985.

——. "Vergil and the Gospels: The *Evangeliorum Libri* IV of Juvencus." In *Romane Memento. Vergil in the Fourth Century*, edited by Roger Rees, 47–61. London: Duckworth, 2004.

Rosen, Klaus. *Julian. Kaiser, Gott und Christenhasser*. Stuttgart: J.G. Cotta'sche Buchhandlung, 2006.

Russell, D.A. "De Imitatione." In *Creative Imitation and Latin Literature*, edited by David West & Tony Woodman, 1–16. Cambridge: Cambridge University Press, 1979.

Salzman, Michele Renee. *The Making of a Christian Aristocracy. Social and Religious Change in the Western Roman Empire*. Cambridge, MA: Harvard University Press, 2002.

Sandnes, Karl Olav. *Paul—One of the Prophets? A Contribution to the Apostle's Self-understanding*. WUNT II.43. Tübingen: J.C.B. Mohr, 1991.

——. "Paul and Socrates: The Aim of Paul's Areopagos' Speech." *JSNT* 50 (1993): 13–26.

——. *Belly and Body in the Pauline Epistles*. SNTSMS 120. Cambridge: Cambridge University Press, 2002.

——. "Imitatio Homeri? An Appraisal of Dennis R. MacDonald's 'Mimesis Criticism'." *JBL* 124 (2005): 715–32.

——. "Whence and Whither. A Narrative Perspective on Birth ἄνωθεν (John 3,3–8)." *Bib* 86 (2005): 153–73.

——. "Markus—en allegorisk biografi?," *Dansk Teologisk Tidsskrift* 69 (2006): 275–97.

——. *The Challenge of Homer. School, Pagan Poets and Early Christianity*. LNTS 400. London: T&T Clark, 2009.

——. "Seal and Baptism in Early Christianity." In *Ablution, Initiation, and Baptism in Early Judaism, Graeco-Roman Religion, and Early Christianity*, edited by David Hellholm, Øyvind Norderval and Tor Vegge (Berlin: Walter de Gruyter, 2011) forthcoming.

Scourfield, J.H.D. *Texts and Culture in late Antiquity. Inheritance, Authority, and Change*. Swansea: The Classical Press of Wales, 2007.

Schnapp, Jeffrey T. "Reading Lessons. Augustine, Proba, and the Christian Détournement of Antiquity." *Stanford Literary Review* 9 (1992): 99–123.

Schwindt, Jürgen Paul, "Florilegium," *Brill's New Pauly* 5:470–1.

Shea, Chris. "Imitating Imitation: Vergil, Homer and Acts 10:1–11:18." In *Ancient Fiction. The Matrix of Early Christianity and Jewish Narrative*, edited by Jo-Ann A. Brant, Charles W. Hedrick, Chris Shea, 37–59. SBLSymS 32. Atlanta: Society of Biblical Literature, 2005.

Sheerin, Daniel. "Rhetorical and Hermeneutic Synkrisis in Patristic Typology." In *Nova & Vetera. Patristic Studies in Honor of Thomas Patrick Halton*, edited by John Petruccione, 22–39. Washington D.C.: The Catholic University of America, 1998.

Simons, Robert. "The Magnificat: Cento, Psalm or Imitatio?" *TynBul* 60 (2009): 25–45.

Sivan, Hagith. "Anician Women. The Cento of Proba, and Aristocratic Conversion in the Fourth Century." *VC* 47 (1993): 140–57.

Skarsaune, Oskar. "Judaism and Hellenism in Justin Martyr, Elucidated from his Portrait of Socrates." In *Geschichte—Tradition—Reflexion. Festschrift für Martin Hengel zum 70. Geburtstag Vol. III*, 585–611. Tübingen: J.C.B. Mohr (Paul Siebeck), 1996.

Smith, Stephen H. *A Lion with Wings. A Narrative-Critical Approach to Mark's Gospel.* Sheffield: Sheffield Academic Press, 1996.

Smolak, K. "Beobachtungen zur Darstellungsweise in den Homerzentonen," *Jahrbuch der Österreichischen Byzantik* 28 (1979): 29–49.

Sowers, Brian Patrick. *Eudocia: the Making of a Homeric Christian.* A Dissertation Submitted to the Division of Research and Advanced Studies of the University of Cincinatti in the Department of Classics of the College of Arts and Sciences 2008. www.ohiolink.edu/etd/send-pdf.sgi/sowers.

Speck, Paul. "Sokrates Scholastikos über die beiden Apollinarioi." *Philologus* 141 (1997): 362–69.

Speyer, Wolfgang. "Hierokles I (Sossianus Hierocles)." *RAC* 15: 103–9.

Springer, Carl P.E. "Jerome and the *Cento* of Proba." *StPatr* 27 (1993): 96–105.

Stech, Odil-Hannes. *Das Gewaltsame Geschich der Propheten. Untersuchungen zur Überlieferung des deuteronomistischen Geschichtsbildes im Alten Testament, Spätjudentum und Urchristentum.* WMANT 23. Neukirchen: Neukirchener Verlag 1967.

Stevenson, Jane. *Women Latin Poets. Language, Gender, and Authority, from Antiquity to the Eighteenth century.* Oxford: Oxford University Press, 2005.

Stroumsa, Guy G. "Early Christianity—A Religion of the Book?" In *Homer, the Bible, and Beyond. Literary and Religious Canons in the Ancient World,* edited by Margalit Finkelberg and Guy G. Stroumsa, 153–73. Jerusalem Studies in Religion and Culture 2. Leiden, Boston: Brill, 2003.

——. *The End of Sacrifice. Religious Transformations in Late Antiquity.* Chicago and London: The University of Chicago Press, 2009.

Tannehill, Robert C. "The Story of Israel within the Lukan Narrative." In *Jesus and the Heritage of Israel. Luke's Narrative Claim upon Israel's Legacy,* edited by David P. Moessner, 325–39. Harrisburg, P.A.: Trinity International Press, 1999.

Thraede, Klaus. "Anfänge frühchristlich-lateinischer Bibelepik: Buchgrenzen bei Iuvencus." In *La poesia tardoantica e medievale. I Convegno Internazionale,* edited by Marcello salvadore, 13–23. Alessandria: Edizioni dell' Orso 2001.

——. "Epos." *RAC* 5: 983–1024.

——. "Iuvencus." *RAC* 19: 881–906.

Trout, Dennis E. "Latin Christian Epics of Late Antiquity." In *A Companion to Ancient Epic, Blackwell Companion to the ancient world,* edited by Foley, John Miles, 550–61. Oxford: Blackwell Publishing, 2005.

Tyson, John B. "From History to Rhetoric and Back: Assessing New Trends in Acts Studies." In *Contextualizing Acts. Lukan Narrative and Greco-Roman Discourse,* edited by Todd Penner and Caroline van der Stichele, 23–42. *SBL Symposium* 20. Atlanta: Society of Biblical Literature, 2003.

Usher, M.D. "Prolegomenon to the Homeric Centos." *American Journal of Philology* 118 (1997): 305–21.

——. *Homeric Stitchings. The Homeric Centos of the Empress Eudocia.* Lanham etc.: Rowman & Littlefield Publishers, 1998.

Van der Nat, P.G. "Die Prefatio der Evangelienparaphrase des Iuvencus." In *Romanitas et Christianitas. In Honour of Jan Henrik Waszink,* 249–57. Amsterdam, London: North-Holland Publishing Company, 1973.

——. "Zu den Voraussetzungen der Christlichen Lateinischen Literatur: Die Zeugnisse von Minucius Felix und Laktanz." In *Christianism et Formes Litteraires de l'Antiquite Tardive en Occident,* edited by Alan Cameron and Manfred Fuhrmann, 191–234. Entretiens sur l'Antiquite Classique 23. Geneve: Fondation Hardt 1977.

Van Deun, Peter. "The Poetical Writings of the Empress Eudocia: An Evaluation." In *Early Christian Poetry. A Collection of Essays,* edited by J. den Boeft and A. Hilhorst, 273–82. Supplements *VC* 22. Leiden etc.: Brill, 1993.

Van Unnik, W.C. "A Formulas Describing Prophecy." *NTS* 9 (1962–3): 86–94.

Vardi, Amiel D. "Diiudicatio Locorum: Gellius and the History of a Mode in Ancient Comparative Criticism." *Classical Quarterly* 46 (1996): 492–514.

——. "Canons of Literary Texts at Rome." In *Homer, the Bible and Beyond. Literary and Religious Canons in the Ancient World*, edited by Margalit Finkelberg and Guy G. Stroumsa, 131–52. Jerusalem Studies in Religion and Culture 2. Leiden, Boston: Brill, 2003.

Vegge, Tor. *Paulus und das antike Schulwesen. Schule und Bildung bei Paulus.* BZNW 134. Berlin, New York: Walter de Gruyter, 2006.

Weidemann, Hans-Ulrich Weidemann. "Taufe und Taufeucharistie." In *Ablution, Initiation, and Baptism in Early Judaism, Graeco-Roman Religion, and Early Christianity*, edited by David Hellholm, Øyvind Norderval and Tor Vegge (Berlin: Walter de Gruyter, 2010) forthcoming.

Whitaker, E.C. *Documents of the Baptismal Liturgy. Revised and Expanded by Maxwell E. Johnson*, Collegeville MM: Liturgical Press, 2003.

Whitby, Mary. "The Bible Hellenized. Nonnus' Paraphrase of St. John's Gospel and Eudocia's Homeric Centos." In *Texts and Culture in Late Antiquity. Inheritance, Authority, and Change*, edited by J.H.D. Scourfield, 195–231. Swansea: The Classical Press of Wales, 2007.

Wiesen, David S. "Virgil, Minucius Felix and the Bible." *Hermes* 99 (1971): 70–91.

Wilken, Robert L. "The Homeric Cento in Irenaeus, Adv. Haereses 1, 9, 4." *VC* 21 (1967): 25–33.

——. *The Christians as the Romans Saw Them.* New Haven, CT: Yale University Press, 1984.

Young, Frances M. *Biblical Exegesis and the Formation of Christian Culture.* Peabody, MA: Hendrickson Publishers, 2002.

——. "Classical genres and Christian Disguise; Christian genres in classical guise." In *The Cambridge History of Early Christian Literature*, edited by Frances Young, Lewis Ayres, Andrew Louth, 251–8. Cambridge: Cambridge University Press, 2004.

Zeitlin, Froma I., "Visions and Revisions of Homer." In *Being Greek under Rome. Cultural Identity, the Second Sophistic and the Development of Empire*, edited by Simon Goldhill, 195–266. Cambridge: Cambridge University Press 2001.

REFERENCE INDEX

THE NEW TESTAMENT

Apocrypha and Pseudepigrapha

Early Christian Writings

CLASSICAL WRITINGS

SUBJECT INDEX

MODERN AUTHORS